Jeroen van de Weijer (Ed.)
Representing Phonological Detail
Part I: Segmental Structure and Representations

Phonology and Phonetics

Edited by
Aditi Lahiri

Volume 32

Representing Phonological Detail

Part I: Segmental Structure and Representations

Edited by
Jeroen van de Weijer

DE GRUYTER
MOUTON

ISBN 978-3-11-162036-7
e-ISBN (PDF) 978-3-11-073009-8
e-ISBN (EPUB) 978-3-11-073013-5
ISSN 1861-4191

Library of Congress Control Number: 2022943607

Bibliographic information published by the Deutsche Nationalbibliothek
The Deutsche Nationalbibliothek lists this publication in the Deutsche Nationalbibliografie;
detailed bibliographic data are available on the internet at http://dnb.dnb.de.

© 2024 Walter de Gruyter GmbH, Berlin/Boston
This volume is text- and page-identical with the hardback published in 2023.
Typesetting: Integra Software Services Pvt. Ltd.

www.degruyter.com

Dedicated with fondness to Harry van der Hulst by his teacher, colleagues, students and friends

'Bream from Wonboyn' (2019) by Helga Humbert

Preface

A few years ago a colleague was visiting Shanghai to give a number of talks. He also visited Shanghai International Studies University and gave a presentation on a sign language topic. At that time, it struck me that we both had been PhD students supervised by Harry van der Hulst at Leiden University, and how similarly we had both been affected by Harry's training and philosophy in life and in linguistics. All of his students have been struck by, and I think are now passing on to their own students, a sense of critical wonder about language, a penchant for "logical thinking". It was then that the idea for a celebratory volume was born. We were fortunate to contact a large number of colleagues, including Harry's own teacher in linguistics, who readily promised (and some time later delivered) their articles around the broad theme of "representing phonological detail", also touching upon the interfaces with phonetics, morphology and semantics, i.e. reflecting the broad range of Harry's linguistic interests. We thank all of them here, also as reviewers and critical readers of other articles. A number of external reviewers also kindly contributed their comments. Special thanks to Helga Humbert, who contributed two pieces of artwork, reproduced in the preceding pages.

Part I of this collection deals with segments and representation in general, in phonology and morphology. There is ample attention for vowels, and especially for vowel harmony-related processes. The other chapters touch on consonant representation, first language acquisition, recursion, the phonology–syntax interface and morphological representation. Part II revolves around the themes of syllable structure, stress and sign language. We hope that, together, the two volumes give a good idea of current research strands in phonology and directly related fields, and that they form a fitting tribute to Harry van der Hulst, who has touched so many with his brilliance, expertise and friendship.

Jeroen van de Weijer
Shenzhen, May 2022

Contents

Preface —— IX

Cor van Bree
Umlaut: From Common Germanic to Dutch —— 1

Bert Botma and Maarten Mous
Vowel Copy in Iraqw Verbal Derivation —— 17

Nancy A. Ritter
Hungarian Possessive Allomorphy in the Lexicon —— 33

Markus A. Pöchtrager
The Unbearable Lightness of Being High: Openness as Structure and the Consequences for Prosody —— 71

Keith L. Snider
[+ATR] Dominance in Chumburung —— 91

Ruben van de Vijver and Agnes Benkő
Paradigmatically Conditioned Phonetic Detail in Hungarian Neutral Vowels —— 107

Bert Botma and Colin J. Ewen
Old English Breaking as Vowel Excrescence —— 133

Clemens Poppe and Jeroen van de Weijer
Diachronic Vowel Harmony: From Middle to Modern Korean —— 151

Eugeniusz Cyran
How Much Phonology in 'Laryngeal Phonology'? —— 165

Krisztina Polgárdi
The Representation of Nasal + Stop + Obstruent Clusters in English: Stop Insertion or Stop Deletion? —— 187

Norval Smith
A Perfect Mess in Ancient Greek: The Story of -*ka* —— 201

Claartje Levelt, Eline van den Brink, and Josefine Karlsson
Prompted Self-Repairs in Two-Year-Old Children —— 227

Glyne Piggott
Deriving Variable Phonological Visibility from Word Structure —— 249

Tobias Scheer
Recursion in Phonology: Anatomy of a Misunderstanding —— 265

Aida Talić
Phases and Accent Assignment Domains —— 289

Marcel den Dikken
A Phonosyntactic Representation of Hungarian 'Lowering' —— 307

John A. Goldsmith
Zellig Harris, Phonological Boundaries, and Features —— 327

Ray Jackendoff and Jenny Audring
Blends and Overlaps in Relational Morphology —— 347

Language Index —— 359

Subject Index —— 361

Contents of Part II —— 363

Cor van Bree
Umlaut: From Common Germanic to Dutch

Abstract: This article deals with the Germanic umlaut processes in Common Germanic and Old West-Germanic. Section 1 presents a definition of umlaut and Section 2 gives an overview of different kinds of umlaut processes, including primary i-umlaut and secondary i-umlaut. Their phonological effects are discussed in Sections 3 and 4 attempts to offer an explanation for the various umlaut effects, e.g. why Common Germanic Umlaut precedes the Old West (and East) Germanic Umlaut and why the first Umlaut was limited to short vowels while the second one also applied to long vowels and diphthongs.

Keywords: umlaut, Germanic languages, historical phonology, vowel length, diphthongs

This article[1] deals with the Germanic umlaut processes in Common Germanic[2] (CG)[3] and Old West-Germanic (OWG). Section 1 presents a definition of umlaut and Section 2 gives an overview of different kinds of umlaut processes. For OWG umlaut, a distinction must be made between primary i-umlaut and later secondary i-umlaut. Their phonological effects are discussed in Sections 3 and 4 attempts to offer an explanation for the various umlaut effects. An important question is why the Common Germanic Umlaut precedes the Old West (and East) Germanic Umlaut and not vice versa. And also why the first Umlaut was limited to the short vowels while the second one also applied to long vowels and diphthongs.

---

1 This contribution is a revised version of Chapter 34 of my *Historical Grammar of Dutch* (*Leerboek voor de historische grammatica van het Nederlands*, vol. 1) (van Bree 2016), which also provides extensive discussion of the geographical and morphological aspects of umlaut. I thank both reviewers for their additions and critical remarks.
2 Common Germanic refers to Proto-Germanic after accent shifted (always to the first syllable). Common Germanic already shows rather extensive dialect variation.
3 The following abbreviations are used: CG. = Common Germanic, Du. = Dutch, Eng. = English, Germ. = German, Got. = Gothic, Lat. = Latin, OHG. = Old High German, OE. = Old English, OSa. = Old Saxon, OSL = open syllable lengthening, OWG. = Old West-Germanic, PGm. = Proto-Germanic, PIE. = Proto-Indo-European, StDu. = Standard Dutch, StGerm. = Standard German, Tw. = Twentish.

Cor van Bree, Leiden University

https://doi.org/10.1515/9783110730098-001

1 Definition

The German term 'Umlaut', proposed by Jacob Grimm and sometimes used interchangeably with 'metaphony', refers to a change in a stem vowel usually due to a vowel (e.g. ĭ, ă) but also a *j* (which originally was often an allophone of ĭ) in the next syllable. The change causes assimilation between the stem vowel and the other vowel or *j*, which means they acquire one or more distinctive features in common, e.g. [±high] or [±back]. This is what we refer to as *diachronic* umlaut; see e.g. Fulk (2018) and references cited there for Old Germanic in general and van Loey (1970), van Loon (2014) or van Bree (2016) for Dutch. Synchronically, umlaut can cause a vocalic alternation within a paradigm or between morphologically related forms. Examples are German *tragen* 'to carry'– *er trägt* 'he carries', Du. *recht* 'right' – *richten* 'to direct', *wand* 'wall' – *wenden* 'to turn'. Another example is Du. *sprookje* [o:] 'fairytale'– *spreuk* [ø:] 'proverb', although this might be due to so-called "spontaneous palatalization" (see the next section). Alternations in a paradigm, such as in the German example, are referred to as *synchronic umlaut*. In the form *trägt*, the vowel indicated by <ä> in part indicates the 3rd person singular indicative. In the pair *Mutter–Mütter* 'mother-SG vs. PL', umlaut alone expresses the morphological category of plural. Finally, umlaut can also refer to the reflection in the spelling of synchronic umlaut, like the diacritic in the vowel letters <ä>, <ü>.

In the next section we will present an overview of the umlaut processes that were active in the Germanic languages (see e.g. van Coetsem 1997). Because Old Dutch has not been well preserved we will mainly use examples from Old Saxon, which was a relatively closely related language. These umlaut processes were crucially influenced by consonants: certain consonants or consonant clusters could block or trigger the process. For instance, a-umlaut from PGm. ŭ to CG. ŏ was blocked before a nasal plus consonant, cf. OSa. *gibundan* – *giworpan* (the past participle of the verbs *bindan* 'to bind' and of *werpan* 'to throw', respectively), but the same combination could also act as a trigger, since it could raise PGm. ĕ to ĭ: cf. OSa. *bindan* to *werpan*. I-umlaut of ă to ĕ is blocked, by, among others, a geminate [χ:] (from PGm. *χj): Du. *lachen* 'to laugh'; cf. Got. *hlahjan*; <h> = χ).

2 Overview

In this section we present an overview of the umlaut processes that took place in Germanic, specifically two such processes in Common Germanic and two Old West-Germanic ones (which are also assumed for Old North-Germanic). The first two involve isolated dialect differences, but we assume, following van Coetsem (see also Kylstra 1983, contra I. Fausto Cercignani), that these processes started at the beginning of the Common Germanic period, in which a strong accent had moved to the initial syllable. These first two umlaut processes can be referred to as rl-umlaut, since they consist of raising or lowering, and the latter two processes as fb-umlaut, since they involve fronting or backing. There is an implicational relation: a language with rl-umlaut also has fb-umlaut, but the reverse is not true, so rl-umlaut is more usual (see Buccini 1988, 1995).⁴ For fb-umlaut we can disregard backing, because it is almost completely irrelevant for Dutch. Let us discuss the umlaut processes in turn:

1. Common Germanic i-umlaut of $\breve{e}$ to $\breve{i}$ before i, j (in isolated cases also before $\breve{u}$) in the next syllable: OSa. *birid* 'he bears' – *beran* 'to bear' (PGm. *beran-; Du. *ont-beert* – *ont-beren* 'to lack', with OSL of $\breve{i}$ and $\breve{e}$ to $\bar{e}$). This umlaut also plays a role in the development of $\breve{e}\breve{u}$ to $\breve{i}\breve{u}$: OSa. *kiusid* 'he chooses' – *kiosan* 'to choose' (for *kiosan*, see 2 below; PGm. *keusan-; Du. *kiezen* – *hij kiest* 'to choose–he chooses').⁵ Nasal and consonant (or geminate nasal) could also act as a trigger for the raising of $\breve{e}$ to $\breve{i}$: cf. OSa. *bindan* to *werpan*.⁶

2. Common Germanic a-umlaut, caused by a non-high vowel in the following syllable (especially $\breve{a}$) from $\breve{i}$ to $\breve{e}$ and from $\breve{u}$ to $\breve{o}$: cf. OSa. *wer* 'man' (PGm. *wiraz; Du. *weer-wolf* 'man-wolf' with lengthening before r), OSa. *dohtar* 'daughter' (PGm. *duhtar; Du. *dochter*). A nasal-consonant cluster (or geminate nasal) or j prevent a-umlaut: OE. *nistian* 'to nest' (PGm. *nistjan; Du. *nestelen*, by analogy to *nest*, PGm. *nista-),⁷ OSa. *gibundan* (PGm. *bundan-; Du. *gebonden* 'bound' with a later change from $\breve{u}$ to $\breve{o}$), OSa. *fullian* 'to fill' (Pgm. *fuljan; Du. *vullen* with a later change to [ø]). OSa. *bindan* 'to bind' (PGm. *bendan; Du. *binden*) and OSa. *fillian* 'to skin' (j > i) (PGm. *felljan, cf. OSa. *fel* 'skin'; Du. *villen* 'to skin' – *vel* 'skin') show that $\breve{e}$ becomes $\breve{i}$ in spite of the presence of a in the following syllable. Note that i/j (as well as nasal plus consonant) is the stronger factor, compared to a. A-umlaut also clearly plays a role in the change of $\breve{e}\breve{u}$ to $\breve{e}\breve{o}$ > $\breve{i}\breve{o}$: OSa. *kiosan*, but

---

4 See Goossens (2009) for Old West-Germanic specifically.
5 The ie [i] of *hij kiest*, with *ie* instead of expected *ui* [œi], is analogy with *kiezen*. The behaviour of CG. $\bar{e}\bar{i}$ and the development of so-called $\bar{e}^2$ form a well known problem area in Old Germanic research, which we will therefore not delve into here.
6 Remarkably, $\breve{a}$ was or seemed unaffected by rl-umlaut, maybe because raising of $\breve{a}$ [+back, –low] led to a somewhat centralized variant, around the position of [ə], which was apparently not different enough to cause any change in the spelling.
7 There is no example of PGm. (PIE) *i followed by a nasal-consonant cluster.

cf. *stiurja* 'pay', in which the influence of *j* prevails (*ĕŭ* > *ĭŭ*). Old Saxon and Old High German have *goma* 'man', as expected, but also *guma*, in which the *m* may have prevented umlaut. Note that Proto-Germanic only had a short back vowel *ŭ* (PIE *ŏ* developed to PGm. *ă*), so the CG. *ŏ* created by a-umlaut originally was an allophone of /ŭ/. There was a danger that Common Germanic umlaut would merge the PGm. phonemes /ĭ/ and /ĕ/ into one phoneme with two allophones, but because (among other things) there were a considerable number of exceptions to a-umlaut of *ĭ*, this did not happen.[8]

3. Old West-Germanic primary i-umlaut (by i or j in the next syllable) from *ă* to *ĕ*: OSa. *wendian* 'to turn' – *-wand* (PGm. **wandjan-* – **wand-*; Du. *wenden* – *wand*). This process is blocked by a velar geminate; the velar articulation seems to prevent the process from applying (cf. *lachen*, OSa. *hlahhian*, in the previous section). Umlaut does not apply when the conditioning factor occurs in the third syllable, which explains the difference between OSa. *eđili* 'noble' (factor in the second syllable; Du. *edel*) and *ađali* 'nobility' (no factor in the second syllable; Du. *adel*) (see van Loon 2014: 137). Finally, umlaut does not apply when the conditioning factor is part of the second member of a compound or of a relatively independent suffix: OSa. *(eli)landig* 'in another country = foreign' (cf. Du. *(el)lendig* 'miserable', with *ĕ* probably as a result of influence of the OSa. variant *elilendi* 'exile'), and OSa. *kraftig* 'strong' – *kraft* 'strength' (Du. *krachtig* – *kracht* with ft > χt).[9]

4. The later secondary i-umlaut (by *i* or *j* in the next syllable), which affected all late Old West-Germanic or Old East Dutch vowels including diphthongs:[10] *ŭ* > [ø],[11] *ŏ* > [œ], *ā* > *ē*, *ū* > [y:], *ō* > [ø:] or after development to *ū* > [y:], *ô* (probably

---

8 Different explanations have been proposed for these exceptions, see e.g. van Bree (2016: Ch. 19). Van Coetsem (1997) proposes structural factors were involved, on the assumption that a large number of homophones would have been created. Lloyd (1966) assumes that a-umlaut of *ĭ* did not take place and that for cases in which umlaut appears to apply analogy might have played a role. See also Fulk (2018: § 4.3–4).
9 For discussion of these exceptions, see Pijnenburg et al. (1997: 84) and van Loon (2014: 13). Apart from *ellendig*, also *behendig* 'skilful' (cf. *hand* 'hand') and *inwendig* 'inner' (cf. *wand* 'wall') unexpectedly have an umlaut *ĕ*. Perhaps eastern dialects played a role here.
10 Because a large part of umlaut does not take place in all parts of the Old West-Germanic dialect continuum, we assume that this "secondary" umlaut occurred later than "primary" umlaut, in late Old West-Germanic or early Old East Dutch, Old High German etc. See Iverson and Salmons (1996) for discussion.
11 We stick to the view of Goossens (1989) that i-umlaut of *ŭ* is secondary; traditionally, it is considered as primary.

a light diphthong [oə], later [uə], from CG. ău̯) > [ø:] or [y:], also ă > ä [æ] (to the extent that this vowel had not developed to ĕ by umlaut 3 above). This umlaut process also applies to ĕ vowels that were created by primary i-umlaut, which as a result become even higher, e.g. from [ɛ] to ë [ɛ/ɪ]. The, for the rest, common West-Germanic secondary i-umlaut is largely confined to the eastern half of the Dutch language area. However, the Ingwaeonic (North Sea-Germanic) coastal areas (in the Netherlands and Flanders) do show some relicts, especially in place names. Because the Old Saxon forms do not yet show this umlaut in the spelling, for illustration we will adduce examples from the Eastern Dutch dialect of Twente (near Enschede). So although they are not illustrative, the Old Saxon forms are sometimes mentioned because they show the factors conditioning umlaut. Note that in the western (Standard Dutch) forms additional changes may apply. To rule out effects of later OSL, let us confine ourselves to the originally short vowels in closed syllables. Examples are for ŭ: Tw. *dunne* 'thin' [ø] besides OSa. *thunni*, StDu. *dun* [ø]; for ŏ: Tw. *stökske* [œ], with the old diminutive suffix *-kīn*, cf. *stòk* [ɔ] 'stick', besides StDu. *stokje* – *stok* [ɔ]; for ā: Tw. *kees* 'cheese' [ē] besides OSa. *kāsi*, StDu. *kaas* [a:]; for ū: Tw. *huuske* [y:], with the old suffix *-kīn*, cf. *hoes* [u:] 'house', besides StDu. *huisje* – *huis* [œi] via [y:] from [u:]; for ō: Tw. *greun* 'green' [ø:] besides OSa, *grōni*, StDu. *groen* [u:]; for ău̯: Tw. *deupn* 'to baptize' [ø:] besides OSa. *dōpian* with ō from ô (Got. *dáupjan*), StDu. *dopen*. For ă and ĕ compare Tw. *menneken* diminutive of *man* 'man' (secondary umlaut that applies to ă which had not been changed by primary umlaut) and *heffn* 'to raise' (primary umlaut of ă followed by secondary umlaut, OSa. *haffian*), with the same vowel (merger). (Standard Dutch has *mannetje* from *man* without secondary umlaut and *heffen* only with primary umlaut.) Kempen dialect, another eastern, Brabantian dialect (spoken near Eindhoven) still clearly shows the difference: the umlaut vowel in *heffen* [ɛ] 'to raise' is higher than the vowel in *menneken* [æ].

In the case of ŏ, we are always dealing with ŏ that has taken the place of ŭ by analogy: originally ŏ did not occur before the i-umlaut factor because a-umlaut of ŭ was blocked by *i/j*. Cf. OHG. *loh* – *luhhir*, analogically *loh* – *lohir* > Gm. *Loch* – *Löcher*. In Twentish *stökske*, with the suffix *-kīn*, we would expect umlaut of ŭ (to ø); here the ŭ must therefore also have been replaced by ŏ on analogy of the base. For ŭ, the geographical situation is complicated as a result of spontaneous palatalization, characteristic of the western part of the language area. This resulted in words like *dun* 'thin' with [ø] in the western dialects and the standard language based on these. This seems to be a case of i-umlaut (compare OSa. *thunni*); however, western Dutch also has [ø] in the dialect form *dul* 'mad' (cf. Germ. *toll* without Umlaut) or [ɔ] where umlaut would be expected, as in dialectal *gelok* 'happiness' (cf. Germ. *Glück* with umlaut). (Neither *dol* nor *geluk* in Standard

Dutch reflects the (western) dialect areas.) I-umlaut of ū can only be seen in areas that tend to be quite eastern, due to complicated developments; cf. Tw. *hoes – huuske* 'house – house-DIM'. We can discard i-umlaut of old *ĕ* because this vowel had developed into *ĭ* before *i* or *j* at an earlier stage (see umlaut 1 above).[12]

Both types of umlaut (rl and fb) took place in different time periods, were conditioned in different ways and therefore constitute clearly different phenomena. Still, following Buccini (1988) we can refer to these as one process, in which the phonetic aperture dimension took historical precedence over the front-back dimension.[13] Primary i-umlaut of ă can be regarded as a transition between both types of umlaut: this only involves a short vowel and has a raising as well as a fronting effect. We return to the characteristics of the process in Section 4.

To conclude this section, we saw that we can regard i-umlaut as a case of conditioned palatalization. In the Dutch coastal areas, where this umlaut was only marginally productive, an unconditioned palatalization became operative at a later stage, traditionally referred to as *spontaneous*, probably via an intermediate stage of fronting, and strongly lexically diffuse. There are more differences: while umlaut does not always involve the high vowels ŭ or ū and the long vowels (i.e. in secondary umlaut), spontaneous palatalization involves the reverse: here ŭ is frequently involved although this is limited to the coastal areas, while for ū palatalization extends deeply into the mainland (cf. e.g. de Vaan 2017: Ch. 15).

3 Effects

Morphologically, umlaut led to paradigmatic alternations that have disappeared in Dutch (with some exceptions like *stad* 'city' – *steden* 'cities') but have been preserved in German and have been extended analogically in that language. Geographically, it is especially remarkable that the west of the Dutch language area essentially has only been subject to primary i-umlaut.[14] In this section, however, we will restrict ourselves to the phonological aspects.

---

[12] For ē (ē²), see fn. 4.
[13] However, both types of umlaut behaved differently in different languages: while German for instance has many more words with a-umlaut from *ĭ* to *ĕ* (rl-umlaut) than English (OHG. *zĕbar* 'sacrifice', OE. *tifer*), in the latter language fb-umlaut had a more wide-ranging effect: cf. OHG. *suohhan* (OSa. *sōkjan*), Germ. *suchen* – OE. *sēcan* with derounding, Eng. *to seek*. For English, u-umlaut is also relevant.
[14] See Buccini (1988, 1995); a summary appears in van Bree (2016).

As will be clear at this point, Common Germanic umlaut led to a new phoneme /ŏ/ by way of an allophonic process [u>o] complemented by a number of analogical processes. For front vowels, the phonemic difference between /ĭ/ and /ĕ/ was preserved, due to the exceptions to a-umlaut (cf. fn. 8). On the other hand, the process led to a new distribution because of the allophonic processes [i>ɛ] and [ɛ>i]. Although i-umlaut led to new allophones at the beginning, phonetically a whole new type of sound was created: the front rounded vowel. As for ă, some crowding in the lower front region of articulation arose, which was resolved by either one or two phonemes.

The primary i-umlaut of ă was expressed in the spelling at an early stage (cf. OSa. *betera* 'better', *gesti* pl. vs. *gast* 'guest'). This may indicate that this indeed represents the oldest form of i-umlaut, in which phonologization occurred early on. Phonologization could be the result of analogical processes. When OWG. *gästi* (pl. 'guests'), with *ä* [æ], the umlaut variant of /ă/, is replaced by *gasti-*, conform to the singular, the conditioned variation is disturbed: an ă then also occurs with a following *i*. Examples of this are found in Old Saxon: *fallid* 3rd ps.sg. pres. from *fallan* 'to fall', *handi* pl. of *hand* 'hand', *gastion* dat.pl. of *gast*. Another cause might be the disappearance of umlaut factors as such. There are indications, however, that these continued to have an influence for a long time. We must also take into account the merger of *ä* (primary umlaut) with *ĕ* that already existed: the Old Saxon spellings lead us to think that this merger indeed took place: cf. *geban* 'to give' with an old *ĕ*. So in *gesti* vs. *gast* (or *gasti*) we are dealing with phoneme alternation. Consequently, this *ĕ* could again occur before *i* or *j*, which had not been possible as a result of common Germanic umlaut (see Section 2, umlaut 1). The western dialects and the Standard Dutch have /ă/ in *gast* with old *ă* (pl. *gasten* with analogical ă) vs. /ĕ/ in *werpen* (with old ĕ, OSa. *werpan* 'to throw') and *hel* 'hell' (with ĕ caused by primary umlaut, OSa. *hellia*, Got. *halja*). For the eastern Dutch dialects (see above) we also have to take secondary umlaut into consideration, however: in Old Saxon this umlaut is not yet reflected in the spelling. This type of umlaut operated when primary umlaut was blocked, and creates a new *ä* [æ] (after the merger of older ä with ĕ). This umlaut also affects a higher variant of *ĕ*, indicated here by *ë*, located in between [ɛ] and [I]. So, at least in theory, three vowels are involved apart from *ă*: an open vowel created by secondary i-umlaut of *ă*: *ä* [æ], a higher *ĕ* = the old *ĕ* [ɛ] and an even higher vowel as a result of secondary i-umlaut of *ĕ*: *ë* [ɛ/I], which *ĕ* was created earlier, by primary umlaut of *ă*. To understand this situation it is important to realize that after primary umlaut was active the conditioning factors remained present, so they could still make their influence felt in secondary umlaut. However, this is a rather theoretical situation: three vowels intensely crowded at the front end of the articulation space. This might be too much of a good thing: in practice new *ä* and ĕ usually merge: and at a later stage ë can join too. Dialect differences may remain, however (cf. Twentish and Kempen dialect in the previous section).

Consider the following (summarizing) schema:

stage 1: old /ă/, old /ĕ/
primary i-umlaut (with restrictions) of ă > ä, which merges with ĕ
stage 2: /ă/ sometimes still before i or j, /ĕ/ = old ĕ + ä as a result of primary i-umlaut
secondary i-umlaut of ă (in the remaining cases) and of ĕ
stage 3: /ă/ = ă but no longer before i or j + ä by secondary i-umlaut of ă, /ĕ/ = ĕ without umlaut + ë (higher) as a result of umlaut of ĕ
merger of ä and ĕ to (open) ä
stage 4: /ă/, /ä/, /ë/
merger of ä and ë into one sound: ĕ (mid-open)
stage 5: one phoneme /ĕ/, next to /ă/
(stages 4, 5: conditioning factors disappear or turn into schwa)

Legend: ă = [ɑ], ä = [æ], ĕ = [ɛ], ë = [ɛ/ɪ].

Stage 4 is reflected in the southeastern Kempen dialect (de Bont 1962): *hals* 'neck' with old *ă* vs. dim. *hæls-ken* 'hals-DIM' (secondary umlaut of ă) besides *hæl* 'clear' (old ĕ) vs. *hel* 'hell' (primary umlaut of *ă*, and secondary afterward; cf. Got. *halja*). Consider also the form *kam* 'comb, crest of a hen' with old *ă* vs. the plural form *käm* with secondary umlaut. The examples of secondary umlaut of *ă* mainly occur in the diminutive and plural morphology, but also with certain suffixes, e.g. *brändig* 'burnt' – *brand* 'fire', *vlässen* 'flaxen' – *vlas* 'flax', *stämpel* 'stamp' – *stampen* 'to stamp'.

Stage 4 is also postulated for Old Twentish (Enschede) but around 1938 this was already developing towards stage 5 (Bezoen 1938): *hals, helske* DIM., *hel* 'clear', *helle* 'hell', but compare the conservative Vriezenveen dialect:[15] *hals, hälske* [æ], *helm* 'helmet', *helle*, with merger of ĕ and ë. Western Dutch and Standard Dutch have *hals, halsje* vs. *hel, hel*, so also with two phonemes but with a different distribution: cf. *halsje* which retains the *ă*. Cf. also StDu. *kam. kammen*; *vlas, vlassen*, but *stampen, stempel*. As a result of OSL and other sound laws the distribution in the Kempen dialect is different: ā (PGm. ă), ē (PGm. ă with secondary Umlaut), ē or ei (CG. ĕ), ei (PGm. ă with primary umlaut of *ă* followed by secondary umlaut), cf. *dagen* 'days'; *jeger* 'hunter'; *geve(n)* 'to give', *beweige(n)* 'to move'; *eizel* 'ass' (Lat. *asinus*). Standard Dutch has *dagen, jager, geven, bewegen*,

---

[15] Vriezenveen is a Twentish town north of Almelo.

ezel, respectively, with the same distribution as in closed syllables. (For further details about the dialects, see van Bree 2016: Ch. 45.)[16]

The fact that different vowels start appearing in the spelling indicates that the other cases of secondary umlaut give rise to phonologization. Analogy may again have played an important role here but perhaps for this stage we should also consider the disappearance or weakening of the umlaut factors, as a result of which the umlauted vowels were no longer (clearly) allophonically conditioned.[17] Such processes may have taken a considerable amount of time, however. Merger with existing phonemes played only a minor role, because front vowels were created that had not so far existed: [œ:], [ø:], [y:]. The umlauted *ā* could merge with the *ē* produced by OSL (Cg. *ĕ* or *ĭ*) or with *ê* [ɛə] > ē from PGm. ai: *scheper* 'shepherd' (vs. *schaap* 'sheep', Cg. ā), *schepen* 'ships' (pl. vs. *schip*, Cg. ĭ), *steen* 'stone' (Germ. *stein*, Pgm. ai). These are examples from Standard Dutch, of which *scheper* (note: with secondary umlaut) must have been borrowed from an eastern dialect.

The proposal that umlaut consisted of two phases is therefore based on spelling changes, in which we see that secondary umlaut has a later effect than primary umlaut. The geographical pattern, in which the west only underwent primary umlaut, also indicates that secondary umlaut did not spread across the entire language area. Such a viewpoint explains that umlaut *ë apparently* passed the old *ĕ*, since the development was ă (primary) > ä > ĕ (secondary) > ë.[18] However, the fact that the secondary umlaut vowels entered the spelling relatively late may also have been due in part to the fact that entirely new sounds were created, for which new spelling symbols also had to be devised.

I-umlaut remained active as long as the factors (i/j) were retained. This may explain what could be referred to as *tertiary* umlaut, which is attested in Twentish and in the Kempen dialect (de Bont 1962).[19] In the Kempen dialect, "normal" secondary i-umlaut of ā is ē: *kees* 'cheese' (StDu. *kaas*), or *èè* [æ:] before an immediately adjacent j: *drèèje* 'to turn' (StDu. *draaien*); as a plural or diminutive we

---

16 The development in open syllables in Twentish is complicated because centralising or rising diphthongs came into being, which could later be shortened. For Enschede the sounds are [ɛ:] (ä), [ɛə] (ĕ), [iə] (ë), for Vriezenveen resp. [ɛ:], [jɛ], [iə] (details omitted).
17 In southern Dutch texts influence of French spellings of front rounded vowels may also have played a role.
18 This hypothesis goes back to Moulton (1962). Another solution is offered by Panieri (2012), who assumes a development of *ă* via ə to *ë* in Old High German, which circumvents the more open *ĕ*. An OHG. form such as *hella* 'hell' already shows the disappearance of the umlaut factor. Later both vowels merged anyway, although the courtly poets did not use the two vowels in rhyme (Panieri 2012: 91) in spite of the fact that their spelling had also merged.
19 De Bont distinguishes late Umlaut (= secondary i-umlaut) but also "latest" umlaut. For German, especially Swiss German, see Nübling (2015: 38).

find *drùùj* [drœ:j] 'threads' (StDu. *draden*) and *blùùske* [blœ:skə] 'small bladder' (StDu. *blaasje*). The vowels here must be explained as a result of a (new) i-umlaut of [ɔ:] that developed from earlier *ā*; cf. *droad* and *bloas*, respectively. Does this indeed suggest that the umlauting factors must still have been present? An alternative explanation is that late umlaut of [ɔ:] is a result of analogy with existing umlaut of (short) [ɔ]: [ɔ]:[œ] = [ɔ:]:x; x = [œ:]. This presumes that the language user "knows" there is a correlation between similar phonetically short and long vowels. The Kempen dialect has also examples with umlaut of [ɔ:] which resulted from OSL of ǎ > *ā*: *hij veurt* 3rd ps.sg.pres. vs. *voaren* 'to sail' and *hij druigt* (with a diphthong) from *droagen* 'to carry'. A Swiss German (Alemannic) example is *Pfohl – Phöhle* vs. StGerm. *Pfahl – Phähle* (Du. *paal* 'pole' – *palen* (pl.)).

4 Umlaut as a Process

Umlaut, as described in the preceding sections, can be regarded as a gradual process, and as one process, including rl- as well fb-umlaut. This process developed very gradually over the course of a number of centuries, from Common Germanic into the Middle Ages (spanning almost 1000 years). For a period of time the umlaut factors, which did become weakened, and the changing stem vowels existed side by side. In Common Germanic umlaut, it was not necessarily the case that a new phoneme developed in an individual word immediately: when an ĭ turned into an ĕ, for instance, this may have involved a slightly more open variant of /ĭ/ in the beginning. Maybe because the difference in stress was not yet as strong as later on when the West Germanic Umlaut took place, the Umlaut factors remained unaffected. The result was a situation comparable to vowel harmony with a feature [closed] or [less closed] for the whole word. As far as the back-front dimension is concerned, a transition phase with central vowels may be assumed. (For ǎ and ĕ and variants cf. the preceding section.) Moreover, the consonants between stem vowel and umlauting vowel may have been temporarily slightly palatalized (*mouillé*). Not all vowels were affected at the same time: secondary umlaut involved different isoglosses (which can partly also be interpreted as fall-back lines).[20] This also indicates that the process was geographically gradual, which is closely connected to the existence of a Common Germanic dialect continua (without Gothic) and later an Old West Germanic one. Furthermore conditioning was gradual: i-umlaut was first (in primary umlaut) blocked by χt, but not

---

[20] However cf. Gütter (2011) whose conclusion (on the basis of some place-names) is that in Old High German all velar vowels underwent Umlaut in the first half of the eighth century.

later (in secondary umlaut). Possibly umlaut was also lexically gradual: to the west of the Dender river (East Flanders), for instance, umlaut of *ā* is distributed differently from word to word (alternatively, process reversal might be assumed). (Labov 1994: 453–454 explains the fact that some words did not undergo umlaut as a result of *late stage correction*: when at a late stage the process (*from below*) enters the realm of consciousness, (social) stigma may result, which may in turn cause a small number of forms to be left unaffected.) Finally, phonologization and morphologization (or elimination of the latter) took place gradually and differently for different periods and regions.

What might have been the motivation of umlaut? It seems clear that it must be related to accent shift (which we set as the beginning of the Common Germanic period, see fn. 2), which placed a strong, dynamic accent on the first syllable (cf. van Coetsem 1996; van Coetsem, McCormick, and Hendricks 1981). The strong, centralizing accent made the less prominent syllables less salient in comparison with the accented syllable and therefore prone to weakening. Umlaut could be regarded as a reaction to this. When suffixes or parts of compounds received secondary accent and therefore had relatively more prominence, i-umlaut did not apply at first. However, the weakly accented syllables were not in danger of weakening yet, at least for rl-umlaut. And as we have seen, also for later i-umlaut/fb-umlaut the factors must have been preserved for a while. Still, the hypothesis proposed by van Loey (1944) could still be valid: because the endings contained important morphological information, e.g. about case, number, and tense, the strategy was to encode this information in the stem vowel by anticipatory assimilation. Morphological information, then, does not only concern alternations, such as in *gast – gesti*, but also a case like OSa. *heffian*, in which the conditioning factor for umlaut was present in the whole paradigm but marked a verbal category that was important for inflection, viz. that of the so-called *jan*-verbs (1st class, weak). This all involved not a deletion but the threat of a deletion of morphological information. An argument against this view is that relatively soon the umlaut alternations disappeared as a result of analogical levelling (as shown by the Old Saxon forms in Section 3). An alternative is to consider the process in the light of phonetic motivation, albeit with morphological effects and repercussions. In general, morphology does not play a role in sound changes but afterwards operates through analogical processes.[21] The idea for a phonetic motiva-

---

[21] For Dutch schwa apocope a (negative) phonological conditioning has been assumed: the process does not apply in the regular past tense morphology to prevent the past form from becoming homophonous with the present tense: cf. *hij maakte* ('he made') vs. *hij maakt* ('he makes'). Instances of apocope have occurred, however, after which analogical repair took place (G.R.W. Dibbets, Nijmegen, personal communication).

tion is supported by the fact that the phonetic difference between conditioning factor and stem vowel plays a role: the larger this is, the greater the chance of umlaut (Howell and Salmons 1997). Gradualness of the input is very much consistent with this, resulting in a view of umlaut as a type of strictly phonetically motivated assimilation enhanced by the strong centralized accent that made up a strong accent unit. To rescue the endangered syllable the stem vowel acquired some of its features in anticipation. According to the epenthesis hypothesis (see Fulk 2018: 61), *-ati first turns into *aⁱti, then into *-eti and *-uti first turns into *-uⁱti, and then into *-øti. If assimilation at a distance is deemed objectionable, the intervening consonant can participate in the process: *-ati > *atⁱi > aⁱtⁱi > aⁱti > eti, *uti > *utⁱi > *uⁱtⁱi > *uⁱti >øti. Because the phonetic distance between a-i is larger than for u-i, assimilation takes place sooner in the first case than in the second. A similar development is possible and also attested elsewhere, e.g. in recent palatalization of ă and ŏ before especially n, t, s, st in Amsterdam Dutch: pan 'pan' sounds like [pɑⁱnⁱ] (see van Bree 2012).²²

This does not answer all questions, however. Why does rl-umlaut precede fb-umlaut and not vice versa? Section 3 above even noted an implicational relationship: fb presumes rl. Is a change in aperture less dramatic than a change on the front-back dimension? Indeed it seems that different degrees of aperture seem closer together than front-back positions, which require passing through the whole oral cavity as it were. This corroborates that front vowels merge into each other: ĭ > ĕ, ĕ > ĭ (however, in the posterior part a new back vowel emerges: ŭ > ŏ). I-umlaut does not lead (except for ă) to merger with existing vowels; vowels emerge between [+back] and [-back]: first central and later front rounded. (This creates a rather marked phoneme system: typologically front rounded vowels are less common that their unrounded counterparts. In English and Frisian derounding ensues, as a result of which the developments to existing vowels takes place after all. Whatever the motivation for this unrounding, it makes the vowel less marked again.) Also the question should be raised why rl-umlaut was limited to the short vowels while fb-umlaut also applied to long vowels and diphthongs. Perhaps the latter offer more resistance to change; at any rate, the length difference is relevant to fb-umlaut: the (short) ă, perhaps quickly followed by ŭ, underwent this first.

A final remark: the developments did not extend so far that rl-umlaut resulted in a vowel system of only three vowels: ă before a but not with i/j or nasal–consonant cluster next to ĭ and ŭ. Might this be due to structural factors (cf. fn. 8), the preservation of sufficient distinctions? This question touches upon the issue of

---

22 Umlaut as a compensatory process is also dealt with in Smith (1999).

language change in general. In Ingwaeonic West Germanic, derounding caused a fairly massive merger of phonemes; English and Frisian, however, show that this could be easily compensated for by other sound changes.[23]

5 Conclusion

Section 1 presented a definition of umlaut and Section 2 gave an overview of types of umlaut in Common Germanic and Old West-Germanic. In Common Germanic (ĕ > ĭ, ĭ > ĕ, ŭ >ŏ), *i/j* or *a* are factors conditioning degree of aperture; *i/j* and nasal plus consonant clusters block the influence of *a*. In Old West-Germanic umlaut the only conditioning factor is *i/j* (causing palatalization). This umlaut distinguishes primary umlaut, which affects ă (> ä), and secondary umlaut, which affects all vowels but was mostly restricted to the eastern part of the Dutch language area: ŭ > [ø], ŏ > [œ], ā > ē, ū > [y:], ō > [ø:] or via ū >[y:], ô [oə] via [uə]> [ø] or [y:], and also ă > ä [æ] (to the extent that these had not turned into ĕ as a result of primary umlaut), and ĕ (mostly from ă) > ë (a closer vowel than ĕ). Phonologically (Section 3), Common Germanic umlaut created a new phoneme /ŏ/ and changed the distribution of *ĕ* and *ĭ*. I-umlaut creates a number of new phonemes, viz. the front rounded vowels, while creating crowding in the anterior part of the vowel space: ă, ä, (old) ĕ and ë. In some dialects, *ä* and (old) *ĕ* merge, while in others only one phoneme ĕ remains next to old *ă*. Section 4 summarizes umlaut as a process, with gradualness in different dimensions: in the output, the input, with respect to conditioning factors, geographically and lexically. The question of motivation was raised, which could be addressed in morphological or phonological terms. Umlaut could be regarded as a reaction to the disappearance of morphologically crucial umlaut factors; since these were in fact preserved for a long time, we should consider this as the threat of disappearance. Problematic here is that analogy took place at an early stage, which indicates that these factors were not considered so crucial. We can also think of a phonological motivation because a strong sound group was created with a strong centralizing accent at the beginning. To protect or rescue the less prominent part, the articulation anticipated on the "umlaut factors". Any intervening consonants may have become (temporarily) palatalized as a result. The front rounded vowels created a typo-

---

[23] English has roughly the same number of vowel-phonemes as Dutch, with 13 phonemes to 12, respectively (Collins and Mees 1984); in comparison, Frisian has a remarkably large number, viz. 23 (Cohen et al. 1961). This language has developed new rounded front vowels and diphthongs.

logically marked phoneme system. Frisian and English derounding "normalized" these systems, compensating the loss of phonemes by other changes.

Epilogue

I am pleased to dedicate this contribution to the honouree of this special collection. Harry used to be my student and served as my assistant: he started his career in the historical phonology of Dutch. As early as 1976, he described, together with two fellow students, the history of the Dutch vowel system (van der Hulst, Jansen, and Nijhof 1976). He therefore became aware of umlaut phenomena at an early age, and he has kept up the good work since then (van der Hulst 2018). He will not mind that I have not attempted to follow his theoretical path here, but perhaps this rather traditional contribution will evoke the good memories of that time that we both share.

References

Bezoen, Herman L. 1938. *Klank-en vormleer van het dialect der gemeente Enschede*. Leiden: Brill.

Bont, Anton P. de. 1962. *Dialekt van Kempenland, meer in het bijzonder d'Oerse taol, deel I*. Assen: Van Gorcum.

Bree, Cor van. 2012. Palatalisatie rond Amsterdam. *Nederlandse taalkunde* 17(2). 202–228.

Bree, Cor van. 2016. *Leerboek voor de historische grammatica van het Nederlands*, 2nd edn, 2 vols. Leiden: Leiden University and Online.

Buccini, Anthony F. 1988. Umlaut alternation, variation, and dialect contact: Reconditioning and deconditioning of umlaut in the prehistory of the Dutch dialects. In Thomas J. Walsch (ed.), *Synchronic and Diachronic Approaches to Linguistic Variation and Change. Selected Papers from Georgetown University Round Table on Languages and Linguistics, Georgetown University March 1988*, 63–80. Washington, DC: Georgetown University Press.

Buccini, Anthony F. 1995. Ontstaan en vroegste ontwikkeling van het Nederlandse taallandschap. *Taal en Tongval* 8. 8–66.

Coetsem, Frans van. 1996. *Towards a Typology of Lexical Accent: Stress Accent and Pitch Accent in a Renewed Perspective*. Heidelberg: Carl Winter.

Coetsem, Frans van. 1997. Reconditioning and umlaut in Germanic, and the question of ē2. *NOWELE. North-Western European Language Evolution* 31–32(1). 423–437.

Coetsem, Frans van, Susan M. McCormick & Ronald Hendricks. 1981. Accent typology and sound change. *Lingua* 53. 295–315.

Cohen, Anthonie, Carl L. Ebeling, Klaas Fokkema & André G. F. van Holk. 1961. *Fonologie van het Nederlands en het Fries; Inleiding tot de moderne klankleer*, 2nd edn. The Hague: Martinus Nijhoff.

Collins, Beverley S. & Inger M. Mees. 1984. *The Sounds of English and Dutch*, 2nd edn. Leiden: Brill/Leiden University Press.

Fulk, R. D. 2018. *A Comparative Grammar of the Early Germanic Languages*. (Studies in Germanic Linguistics 3). Amsterdam/Philadelphia: John Benjamins.

Goossens, Jan. 1989. Primaire en secundaire umlaut in het Nederlandse taalgebied. In Arend Quak & Florus van der Rhee (eds.), *Palaeogermanica et onomastica. Festschrift für J.A. Huisman zum 70. Geburtstag*, 61–65. (Amsterdamer Beiträge zur älteren Germanistik 29). Leiden: Brill.

Goossens, Jan. 2009. Dialectgeografische grondslagen van een Nederlandse taalgeschiedenis. *Handelingen van de Koninklijke Commissie voor Toponymie en Dialectologie* 80. 33–258.

Gütter, Adolf. 2011. Frühe Belege für den Umlaut von ahd. /u/, /o/ and /u/. *Beiträge zur Geschichte der deutschen Sprache und Literatur* 133. 1–13.

Howell, Robert B. & Joseph C. Salmons. 1997. Umlautless residues in Germanic. *Journal of Germanic Linguistics* 9(1). 83–111.

Hulst, Harry van der. 2018. *Asymmetries in Vowel Harmony: A Representational Account* (Oxford Linguistics). Oxford: Oxford University Press.

Hulst, Harry van der, Frank Jansen & Jos Nijhof. 1976. Geschiedenis van het Nederlands vokalisme in 104 regels [History of the Dutch vowel system in 104 rules]. Ms, Leiden University.

Iverson, Gregory K. & Joseph C. Salmons. 1996. The primacy of primary umlaut. *Beiträge zur Geschichte der deutschen Sprache und Literatur* 118. 69–86.

Kylstra, A. D. 1983. Zum Alter des "älteren" Umlauts im Germanischen. *Amsterdamer Beiträge zur älteren Germanistik* 19. 1–10.

Labov, William. 1994. *Principles of Linguistic Change*, Volume I: *Internal Factors*. Oxford: Wiley-Blackwell.

Lloyd, Albert L. 1966. Is there an a-umlaut of i in Germanic? *Language* 42(4). 738–745.

Loey, Adolphe van. 1944. Een mogelijke oorzaak van de primaire i-Umlaut. In Henri Draye (ed.), *Feestbundel H. J. Van de Wijer: Den jubilaris aangeboden ter gelegenheid van zijn vijfentwintigjarig hoogleeraarschap aan de RK Universiteit te Leuven 1919–1943*, vol. 2, 121–127. Leuven: Instituut voor Vlaamsche Toponymie.

Loey, Adolphe van. 1970. *Schönfelds historische grammatica van het Nederlands*, 8th edn. Zutphen: Thieme.

Loon, Jozef van. 2014. *Historische fonologie van het Nederlands*, 2nd edn. Leuven and Amersfoort: Universitas.

Moulton, William G. 1962. Zur Geschichte des deutschen Vokalsystems. *Beiträge zur Geschichte der deutschen Sprache und Literatur* 83. 1–35.

Nübling, Damaris. 2015. Zwischen Konservierung, Eliminierung und Funktionalisierung: Der Umlaut in den germanischen Sprachen. In Jürg Fleischer & Horst J. Simon (eds.), *Sprachwandelvergleich*, 15–42. Berlin: Universitätsbibliothek Johann Christian Senckenberg.

Panieri, Luca. 2012. Eine neue phonetische Hypothese zum primären Umlaut von germ. */a/* im Althochdeutschen. *Linguistik Online* 53(12). 85–98.

Pijnenburg, Wil, Karina van Dalen-Oskam, Katrien Depuydt, Tanneke Schoonheim & Joop M. van der Horst. 1997. Vroegmiddelnederlands (circa 1200–1350). In Maarten C. van den Toorn, Wil Pijnenburg, Arjan van Leuvensteijn & Joop M. van der Horst (eds.), *Geschiedenis van de Nederlandse taal*, 69–145. Amsterdam: Amsterdam University Press.

Smith, Regina. 1999. Testing compensatory theories of umlaut. *Leuvense Bijdragen* 88(1–2). 133–151.

Vaan, Michiel A. C. de. 2017. *The Dawn of Dutch: Language Contact in the Western Low Countries before 1200*. (NOWELE Supplement Series 30). Amsterdam/Philadelphia: John Benjamins.

Bert Botma and Maarten Mous
Vowel Copy in Iraqw Verbal Derivation

Abstract: This paper presents a new analysis of a pattern of vowel copy in Iraqw verbal derivation. The main claim is that velar stops, which have previously been analyzed as transparent, are in fact opaque. The resulting pattern is cross-linguistically less marked, since the class of transparent consonants is now restricted to gutturals, i.e. laryngeals, pharyngeals, uvulars, and a series of back fricatives, whose realization is post-velar rather than velar.

Keywords: Vowel copy, transparent consonants, gutturals, velars, rounding, corner vowels, Search and Copy, Iraqw

1 Introduction

Vowel copy (sometimes called vowel echo) is a process in which a vowel undergoes total assimilation to another vowel in an adjacent syllable. In this paper we examine a case of vowel copy in Iraqw, a Cushitic language of Tanzania. The target of the copying process is a vowel which occurs in verbal derivations, where it precedes the last suffix in the word. This vowel is realised as [i(ː)], unless it is preceded by a transparent consonant.[1] In that case, it surfaces as a copy of the preceding vowel, provided that vowel is any of /a i u/. Thus we find forms like [ufaḥaam] 'blow-DUR', where /ḥ/ is transparent, and [baaliim] 'defeat-DUR', where /l/ is opaque (/-m/ is the durative suffix).[2]

The Iraqw facts are analyzed in van der Hulst and Mous (1992), who identify the class of transparent segments as including laryngeals, pharyngeals, uvulars, and velars. The inclusion of velars is typologically highly marked, and presents a serious challenge to an autosegmental analysis of the process. The reason is that velars are normally assumed to have an Oral place node, like vowels. If velars have an Oral place node, then the Oral place nodes of vowels flanking a velar consonant are not adjacent on the place tier. Any interaction between these

---
1 The length of the vowel is determined by the gender of the subject of the verb, and does not concern us here.
2 Vowels in verbal derivations are underlined.

Bert Botma and Maarten Mous, Leiden University Centre for Linguistics, University of Leiden

vowels which does not also involve the intervening velar will therefore violate the No-Crossing Condition, a core principle of Autosegmental Phonology (Goldsmith 1976). This problem does not arise for the other transparent consonants. Following McCarthy (1994), laryngeals, pharyngeals, and uvulars together form the class of gutturals (see also Hayward and Hayward 1989; Rose 1996). On the assumption that these have a Pharyngeal node, any interaction between two vowels flanking a guttural consonant will respect the No-Crossing Condition.[3] The two scenarios are shown in (1ab) (cf. Rose 1996: 77).

(1) a. *V   C   V   b.   V   C   V
        Place Place Place   Place Place Place
         | | | | | |
        Oral   Oral   Oral   Oral | Oral
                                           Phar

In (1a), the Place nodes of both the vowels and the intervening consonant dominate an Oral node. This rules out spreading of the Oral node of the vowel across the consonant. In (1b), the consonant has a Pharyngeal node, which occupies a separate tier. In this configuration assimilation between the vowels is possible, since their Oral nodes are adjacent on the same tier (i.e. the process is 'local').

Our aim in this paper is to show that the Iraqw facts have been misinterpreted in earlier work, and that there is in fact good evidence to treat velars – specifically, velar stops – as being opaque.[4] (For a reanalysis of other cases of velar transparency, see Paradis and Prunet 1994.) Evidence for this comes from an asymmetry that has not been previously observed: after a root-final [k], the vowel in verbal derivations surfaces as [uu] if the preceding vowel is /u/, and as [ii] elsewhere (e.g. [ɬukuum] 'bribe-DUR' vs. [dakiit] 'be placed in a position-MID'). Our explanation for this asymmetry is that velar stops block vowel copy, just like other oral

---

[3] McCarthy (1994) analyses uvulars as having both an Oral and a Pharyngeal node. This captures the observation that uvulars pattern with velars in some respects and with pharyngeals in others. In this paper we make the simplifying assumption that uvulars have a Pharyngeal node only. This seems justified for Iraqw, since we claim that uvulars are transparent to vowel copy but velars are not.
[4] Rose (1996: 77–78) treats vowel copy in Iraqw as a case of transguttural harmony. She is skeptical about the transparency of velars and speculates that velars and uvulars take part in rounding harmony instead. This is not correct, since we find vowel copy of each of /a i u/ across uvulars; see (3).

consonants; instead, the [uu] in forms like [ɬukuum] results from rounding by the root-final [k], which itself derives from underlying /kʷ/.

Our second aim is to provide an analysis of the vowel copy process itself. This issue is not addressed in van der Hulst and Mous (1992), whose focus is on characterising the class of transparent consonants. One interesting property of vowel copy in Iraqw is that the process is conditioned not just by the intervening consonant, but also by the preceding vowel: /a i u/ can be copied, but /e o/ cannot. Another complicating factor concerns the behaviour of labialised consonants, which cause rounding of the following vowel but surface as non-labialised themselves (e.g. [tɬ'aaxuut], the middle form of /tɬ'aaxʷ/ 'buy'). Rounding takes precedence over vowel copy, since /a/ is normally copied across /x/ (cf. [taxaat], the middle form of /tax/, an ideophone with the meaning 'drop of water'). Vowel copy in verbal derivations also displays properties that set it apart from a more general process of vowel copy in the language, which affects vowels that break up consonant clusters (e.g. [biʕⁱni] 'wedge', [duʔᵘma] 'leopard').[5]

The paper is organised as follows. In Section 2 we introduce the relevant data and provide our interpretation of the vowel copy process. Section 3 outlines our theoretical assumptions and presents the analysis. We adopt a model in which segments consist of single-valued elements that are organised in a feature-geometric structure. Our analysis follows in broad lines the approach to vowel harmony in Nevins (2010). In this approach, vowels that are unspecified for the harmonic feature begin a 'Search and Copy' procedure in order to obtain this feature. We show that this approach can be fruitfully applied to the vowel in Iraqw verbal derivations, which lacks underlying place.

2 Iraqw Vowel Copy

We first outline some background regarding Iraqw vowels and consonants, before describing the process of vowel copy. Our data are taken from Mous (1993) and Mous, Qorro, and Kießling (2002).

2.1 Segmental Inventory

Iraqw has a five-vowel system /a i u e o/. Each vowel contrasts for length. There are two diphthongs, /ai au/.

---

[5] We represent these vowels as superscript vowels, which reflects their short duration.

The consonant inventory of Iraqw is given in (2).

(2) Iraqw consonant inventory

p	t		(c)	k	kʷ	q	qʷ	ʕ	ʔ
b	d		(ɟ)	g	gʷ				
t͡sʼ	t͡ɬʼ								
f	s	ɬ	(ʃ)	x	xʷ			ħ	h
m	n		(ɲ)	ŋ	ŋʷ				
w	r	l	j						

A number of comments are in order regarding (2). Palatals are mostly restricted to loans, except /j/. Uvular stops are phonetically affricated and optionally realised as ejectives. Velars and uvulars have labialised counterparts. Labialisation is contrastive, as is shown by near-minimal pairs like /kaah/ 'tell' vs. /kʷaaħ/ 'throw', /faak/ 'finish' vs. /daakʷ/ 'whittle', and similarly for the other velars and uvulars. Evidence from reduplication shows that labialised consonants pattern as single sounds (Downing and Mous 2011). The labial gesture in labialised consonants involves lip compression, while /w/ has lip protrusion (Demolin 2021). This may explain why these sounds pattern differently in vowel copy contexts (see Section 2.2). The back fricatives /x xʷ/ are described as velar in Mous (1993), but our impression is that they are actually post-velar. This would be consistent with their behaviour; we will see below that they pattern with gutturals. Cross-linguistically, this patterning is unsurprising. In his discussion of back consonants, Smith (1988: 215) notes that "it is not uncommon for languages to have fricatives that are articulated further back than the corresponding stops." This is the case in some varieties of Arabic, for example, and also in standard Dutch, where /k/ is velar but /χ/ is uvular.

2.2 Vowel Copy in Verbal Derivation

Vowel copy in Iraqw verbal derivation targets the vowel that predictably occurs before the causative /-s/, the durative /-m/, and the middle /-t/ suffixes, whenever these are final in the word.[6] The data in (3) show that a preceding /a i u/ is copied when the root-final consonant is laryngeal, pharyngeal, or uvular (i.e. a member of the class of gutturals).

---

6 In words with more than one of these suffixes, the vowel precedes the last suffix, e.g. [lak-m-ii-t] 'wait-DUR-MID'.

(3) Vowel copy of /a i u/ across gutturals
 a. naaʔ naaʔaam 'cut hair-DUR'
   waʔalah waʔalahaam 'exchange-DUR'
 b. luuʕ luuʕuum 'hide-DUR'
   kuts'uħ kuts'uħuum 'pinch-DUR'
 c. ts'aaq ts'aqaam 'leak-DUR'
   siiq siiqiit   'cut-MID'
   tɬ'uuq tɬ'uuquum 'kill an animal or a man-DUR'

In the same context /e o/ fail to copy, and the vowel is realised as [ii] instead.[7]

(4) No vowel copy of /e, o/ across gutturals
  gooʔ gooʔiim 'carve-DUR'
  oh ohiim 'seize-DUR'
  leeħ leeħiim 'carry-DUR'

The vowel also surfaces as [ii] when the preceding consonant is labial, coronal, or palatal. Note that this includes /w/.

(5) No vowel copy across non-gutturals
  baal   baaliim 'defeat-DUR'
  hamaatɬ' hamtɬ'iim 'wash-DUR'
  ʕaaj   ʕaajiim 'eat-DUR'
  tutuuw tutuuwiim 'open a new farm-DUR'

The data in (4) and (5) suggest that [ii] is the default realisation of the vowel.
 The situation is more complicated when the preceding consonant is velar.[8] Of the plain velars, /x/ patterns with gutturals, in that the preceding vowel is copied.

(6) Vowel copy across /x/
  tax taxaat 'drip-MID'
  duux duuxuut 'get married-MID'

We suggested above that this patterning may reflect its post-velar realisation.

---

[7] The only exception that we know is [soloʔoot], the middle form of the verb /soloʔ/ 'fall down'.
[8] The velar nasals /ŋ ŋʷ/ do not occur in root-final position of verbs and are therefore absent from vowel copy contexts.

Velar stops display an asymmetry. If the preceding vowel is /a/ or /i/, copying does not take place and the vowel surfaces as [ii] (7a).⁹ As expected, [ii] also occurs if the preceding vowel is /e o/ (7b).

(7) No vowel copy of /i a e o/ across velar stops
    a. dak   dakiit   'be placed in a position-MID'
       siik   sikiim   'slice-DUR'
    b. heek hekiit 'fetch water-DUR'
       doog doogiit 'be increasing it-MID'

But roots with /u/ are different; here the vowel in the verbal derivation is realised as [uu], which might suggest that vowel copy has applied. There are four forms of this type in Mous, Qorro, and Kießling (2002), given in (8). (The derivation of the form [fukuum] is discussed below.)

(8) Apparent vowel copy of /u/ across velar stops
    –   fukuum   'twirl-DUR (firestick)'
    łuuk   łukuum   'bribe-DUR'
    suruuk surkuum   'move aside-DUR'
    tuntuuk tuntukuum 'cover-DUR'

Treating the suffixed forms in (8) as the result of vowel copy is not very appealing, however. Not only is the transparency of velar stops (which would be implied by this account) highly marked, but such an analysis would have the further problem that velar stops are apparently transparent only when preceded by /u/. We therefore propose an alternative interpretation of the forms in (8); rather than vowel copy, we argue that [uu] in the suffixed forms is the result of rounding by the preceding velar stop, which derives from underlying /kʷ/.

According to this analysis, the forms in (8) are part of a more general pattern that is also displayed by the forms in (9), which involve verb roots with a final labialised consonant that is preceded by /a/ or /e/. Note that here, too, we find [uu] in the suffixed forms.

---

9 The same pattern is found in frozen derivations, e.g. /lakiit/ 'wait', /dolakiit/ 'stumble'. The only form which is deviant is /tɬ'akakaat/ 'deny-IMPERF' (with reduplication of the final VC sequence of the root).

(9) Rounding after labialised consonants

tɬ'aaxʷ	tɬ'aax<u>uu</u>t	'buy-MID'
daakʷ	dak<u>uu</u>t	'whittle-MID'
kʷandeekʷ	kʷandak<u>uu</u>m	'do the first hoeing-DUR'
deeqʷ	deeq<u>uu</u>m	'be shaving-DUR'

There are two things worth noting about the rounding of vowels by labialised consonants. The first is that it is limited to this specific environment; rounding does not affect underlying /i/, for example (e.g. [kʷitsiis] 'strike with a small twig', [qʷiriiʕ] 'shine'). This is an important observation for the analysis that we develop in Section 3, because it supports the view that the vowel in verbal derivations is underlyingly placeless.

Second, the suffixed forms in (9) show that labialised stops lose their labialisation when they are adjacent to a rounded vowel. This is due to a general restriction on adjacent rounded segments (labialised consonants and rounded vowels) in the language.[10] Loss of labialisation is fully regular in morphological alternations. It applies, for instance, whenever a rounded vowel in a suffix follows a root-final labialised consonant. Examples include the deadjectival verb /geetɬ'ak-uw/ (10a) and the deverbal compound noun /al-dak-o/ (10b).

(10) Loss of labialisation before rounded vowels
  a. geetɬ'akʷ   'invisible'
     geetɬ'akʷ-ees   'make obscure'
     geetɬ'ak-uw   'become obscure'

  b. al-daakʷ   'explain'
     al-dak-o   'explanation'

---

10 Iraqw has few words which end in a rounded vowel (/u/ or /o/) plus a labialised consonant. The only words of this type have /uŋʷ/ (which occurs productively in denominal verbs ending in /-uum/) or /-oŋʷ/ (which derives from the collective number suffix /-aŋʷ/, with subsequent assimilation of /a/ to /o/). The latter sequence occurs in just three words, viz. /boohooŋʷ/ 'hole', /xoxoŋʷ/ 'broken utensil', and /qotlooŋʷ/ 'corner'. The only other word ending in this sequence is /sandukʷ/ 'boxes', a loanword from Swahili (*sanduku*), and ultimately from Arabic.

Sequences of a rounded vowel and a labialised consonant are also extremely rare inside words. The only examples appear to be the plural form [aakʷakʷiʔi] 'fathers', which in fast speech can be realised as [aakukʷiʔi], the noun [hikʷaa] 'cattle', which is sometimes pronounced [jukʷaa], and the deverbal noun [tuntuukʷee] 'lid-PL'.

There are no sequences of a rounded vowel plus any of /xʷ gʷ qʷ/.

The effect of the restriction is also visible in the forms in (9), where the root-final consonants in the suffixed forms are non-labialised because they are followed by [uu].[11] This suggests, therefore, that these forms result from the interaction of two processes; the vowel in verbal derivations undergoes rounding by the labialised consonant, while the consonant itself loses its labialisation due to the restriction on adjacent rounded segments. In the surface forms, labialisation has therefore shifted from the consonant to the following vowel.

We propose that this analysis is appropriate not only for the suffixed forms in (9) but also for those in (8); that is, we take the underlying form of the verb root in e.g. /tuntuukuum/ to be /tuntuuk^w/, with a final labialised stop. What makes the roots in (8) different from those in (9) is that they contain an *underlying* sequence of a rounded vowel and a labialised stop. We assume that such sequences are also subject to the restriction on adjacent rounded segments. As a result, the labialised stops in these roots surface neither in the base form, nor in the derived middle, causative, and durative forms.

Despite the fact that this analysis is rather abstract, there are good grounds for positing underlyingly labialised stops in the forms in (8). For three of the four verb roots, there is evidence from other alternations which suggests that /k^w/ is underlying. For example, the deverbal noun *tuntuuk^w-ee* 'lid-PL' (one of the few forms which violates the restriction on adjacent rounded segments; see n.10) shows that the root from which it is derived ends in /k^w/, i.e. /tuntuuk^w/, or else the presence of labialisation cannot be explained. The durative form *ɬukuum* has the related nominalisation *ɬukuʔuma* 'bribe'; comparison with *diinkuʔuuma* 'cooperation' (from *dink^{w}a* 'together') suggests that the root is /ɬuuk^w/. The verb *fukuum* 'twirl (a firestick)' would appear to be derived from the noun *fuki* 'block of wood to be used with a twirling stick'. However, verbalisation in *-iim* is unusual, so that it seems better to analyze the noun as being derived from the verb, or from an assumed base *fuk*. We think that there is in fact a more plausible derivation of the durative form *fukuum*. The etymologically related verb *fukukuuʔ* 'make round movements' (with internal reduplication) indicates that there is a verbal base *fukuʔ*. If we apply the durative derivation to this base, we arrive at the form *fukuum*: *fukuʔiim* > *fukuʔuum* > *fukuum* (with vowel copy through glottal stop, which was subsequently lost). The only form for which there is no evidence for /k^w/ from alternations (neither synchronic nor diachronic) is *suruuk*, so that here /k^w/ is motivated exclusively by the [uu] that occurs in the verbal derivation *surkuum*.

---

11 We do not rule out the possibility that [k] in this context is phonetically slightly labialised, but this labialisation is not audible and not distinctive.

As was already noted, we believe that our analysis of the vowel copy data is superior to one in which velar stops are transparent. We also believe that our analysis is superior to one in which an /u/ in a verb root affects the vowel in verbal derivations *via* the velar stop. (This is the reanalysis that Paradis and Prunet (1994) propose for transparent velars in Chinook.) For Iraqw, this would involve the derivation *uk#V → ukʷ#V → ukʷ#u → uk#u*. It seems to us that such an account is problematic, at least as a synchronic analysis of the data. Rounding of /k/ by /u/ directly contravenes the restriction on adjacent rounded segments, and it seems to do little more than create the context in which subsequent rounding of the following vowel can take place. It should in any case be noted that /-ukʷ/ sequences have a special status in Iraqw. They are marginally attested, while other sequences of rounded vowels and (oral) labialised consonants are completely absent, due to the restriction on adjacent rounded segments.

To conclude this section, we consider briefly how vowel copy in verbal derivation differs from another process of vowel copy in Iraqw. Van der Hulst and Mous (1992) observe that clusters of the kind in (11) are subject to an optional process of vowel insertion. The inserted vowel is realised as a short [a] or [ə] (11a), unless it is preceded by a guttural, in which case a preceding /a i u/ is copied (11b).

(11) Insertion and vowel copy of short [ə] or [a]
    a. [xaɬᵃmiit] 'keep quiet all the time'

    b. [biʕⁱni] 'wedge'
       [duʔᵘma] 'leopard'

While this process also involves transparent gutturals, it differs from vowel copy in verbal derivation in several important respects. The inserted vowels in (11) have properties which are associated with 'intrusive' vowels (Hall 2006: 391): their quality is schwa-like or a copy of a nearby vowel, they break up heterorganic clusters, and they are optional, depending on such factors as speech rate. In Hall's account, intrusive vowels are phonologically invisible; they arise through a specific phasing relationship of articulatory gestures, as part of the phonetic implementation.[12]

The properties of the vowel in verbal derivation are fundamentally different. This vowel is invariably present in surface forms, its position is determined by the morphological structure, its length by the gender of the subject of the verb, and its quality by the phonological context. In view of this, we assume that this

---

[12] It is telling that Josephat Maghway (a linguist and native speaker of Iraqw) does not transcribe intrusive vowels in his transcriptions. See e.g. Maghway (1989).

vowel occupies a slot in a morphological template. We further assume that it is deficient: the vowel in verbal derivation lacks phonological content, except for the organising nodes that identify it as vocalic. Given these assumptions, vowel copy can be viewed as the result of this vowel acquiring a place specification. We will work out this idea in Section 3.

3 Theoretical Interpretation

We begin our theoretical interpretation by examining the restrictions that the vowel copy process imposes on the root vowel, outlining our assumptions regarding segmental structure along the way. Recall from (3), (4), and (5) that the corner vowels /a i u/ are copied across an intervening guttural, but /e o/ are not. We attribute this asymmetry to the relative markedness of mid vowels. The presence of mid vowels in a vowel system implies the presence of corner vowels, but not vice versa. In addition, processes of vowel reduction show that mid vowels often 'simplify' to corner vowels in prosodically weak positions.

The markedness of mid vowels can be captured in a theory in which features (or elements) are single-valued, as in Dependency Phonology (e.g. Anderson and Ewen 1987; van der Hulst 1988) and Element Theory (e.g. Harris and Lindsey 1995; Backley 2011). In Element Theory, the five-vowel system of Iraqw can be represented as follows:

(12) Internal structure of Iraqw vowels
    a.   *a* |A| b.   *e* |A,I|
         i |I| *o* |A,U|
         u |U|

In isolation, the elements |A, I, U| are interpreted as /a i u/ (12a), while /e o/ are represented as compounds of |A| with |I| and |U| (12b). Mid vowels are therefore structurally complex; it is this property which makes them formally marked.

The Iraqw facts suggest that place elements are hierarchically organised. We assume that elements representing vocalic place are grouped under a Vowel Place ('V-pl') node. Vowel copy involves spreading of a V-pl node, along with any dependent elements. The V-pl node itself is dominated by an Oral place node, which is in turn dominated by the Place node. This organisation is motivated, among other things, by the observation that vowel copy is a case of 'all or nothing at all': if the root vowel is /e/ or /o/, the vowel in verbal derivation does not copy just one of the vowel's elements, but gets a default specification (the element |I|).

This is shown in (13) for the form [ohiim] 'seize-DUR' (irrelevant structure has been omitted).

(13) No copy of mid vowels (default assignment of |I|)

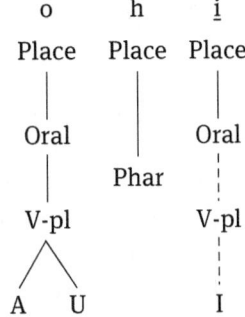

Why should vowel copy be restricted to corner vowels? We suggest that the reason for this is that deficient vowels are unmarked. In Iraqw this is reflected by the fact that they cannot surface with a branching place node.[13]

Our theoretical interpretation of vowel copy is based on the assumption that the vowel in verbal derivations lacks underlying place. (Recall that labialised consonants condition an [uu] in verbal derivations, but do not trigger rounding of underlying vowels.) We assume that the vowel acquires this place from a preceding V-pl node or, if this fails to apply, by default insertion of |I|. Below, we formalise this idea using the approach to vowel harmony in Nevins (2010).

According to Nevins, harmonic vowels are 'needy'. Because they lack the harmonic feature in their underlying form, such vowels initiate a 'Search and Copy' procedure in order to obtain this feature. This procedure is parametrically defined; it may differ, for example, in the domain and in the direction of the search. The procedure may also be subject to additional conditions. For instance, in cases of 'parasitic' harmony, copying of the harmonic feature is possible only if the trigger and target share some other feature value. An example is found in Yawelmani, where rounding harmony applies only if the trigger and target have the same height (see e.g. Archangeli 1984).

Although Nevins' assumptions regarding segmental structure are different from ours, we believe that his approach can be fruitfully applied to the Iraqw

---

[13] This restriction is language-specific. Yamane-Tanaka (2006) observes that Gitksan has vowel copy of /a e o/ across gutturals. However, she notes that these vowels are fully copied across laryngeals but not always across pharyngeals and uvulars, where the mid vowels are optionally realised as [a].

data. Let us assume that the vowel in verbal derivation has an underlying Oral place node, but no dependent V-pl node. Being the last vowel in the word, it must therefore search for a V-pl node to its left. The conditions on the Search and Copy procedure are strict: a V-pl node can be copied only if it is non-branching, and if it is dominated by an Oral place node that is tier-adjacent.[14] (The last condition reflects the fact that vowel copy, unlike vowel harmony, involves a dependency relation between just two vowels.)

The search is successful in the form [daqaam] (14a). Assuming that the Pharyngeal node of the uvular stop is invisible, the vowel in the verbal derivation copies the V-pl node of the vowel to its left, which it 'snatches' through spreading. The search is unsuccessful in [baaliim] (14b). Here the Oral place node of the preceding consonant prevents the search from reaching the V-pl node of the preceding vowel. The search is therefore terminated, and the vowel receives default place.

(14) a. Vowel copy as place 'snatching'   b. Blocking of vowel copy (default place)

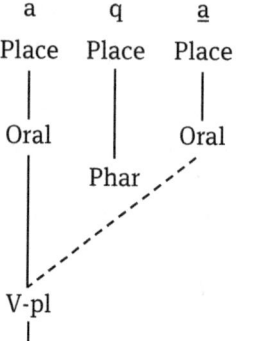 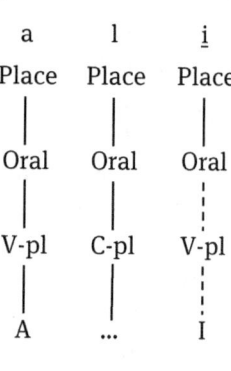

(14a) has the appearance of a standard spreading operation. However, it is important to note that spreading here is instantiated by the feature seeker (the vowel in the verbal derivation), not by the feature bearer (the vowel in the root).

---

14 We assume that the search procedure is relativised to V-pl nodes which occur under an Oral place node. We are agnostic about whether the Pharyngeal node can also dominate a V-pl node.

Support for this target-centric perspective comes from processes in which a needy vowel is also 'greedy'. An example of this is found in vowel harmony in Barra Gaelic.

(15) Barra Gaelic vowel harmony (Nevins 2010: 58)
 a. /tʲimxʲal/ [tʲim<u>i</u>xʲal] 'round about'
    /æmsʲirʲ/ [æm<u>æ</u>sʲirʲ] 'time'
 b. /alpə/ [al<u>a</u>pə] 'Scotland'
    /sʲærv/ [sʲær<u>a</u>v] 'bitter'
    /bulʲkʲ/ [bulʲ<u>i</u>kʲ] 'bellows.GEN.SG'

Nevins' analysis of this pattern (which employs binary-valued features) runs as follows. In Barra Gaelic, [±back] is contrastive for vowels and for all consonants except labials and /n/ (the [−back] consonants in (15) are transcribed as palatalised). Barra Gaelic has a process of vowel epenthesis that breaks up sonorant–obstruent clusters. In (15a), the epenthetic vowel is a copy of the preceding vowel (note that /m/ lacks a backness specification). The copying process in (15b) is more complicated, since the quality of the epenthetic vowel is determined in part by the preceding consonant, which is specified for [±back]. On the assumption that the epenthetic vowel is underlyingly specified for [+vocalic] only, it begins a leftward search to find other vowel features. In a form like [bulʲikʲ], the first specification that the search encounters is the [−back] feature of /lʲ/, which it copies. (This triggers a default rule filling in [−round], since Barra Gaelic bans front rounded vowels.) Because the consonant does not contain any other vowel features, the search continues to the next vowel, which supplies the remaining features, viz. [+high] and [−low]. Nevins concludes from this scenario that the epenthetic vowel is greedy: rather than copy from a single source, it copies the first available feature that it meets, even if this means that its features will be copied from multiple sources.

The search in Iraqw never results in copying from multiple sources. However, the vowel in verbal derivations is greedy to the extent that it copies the first V-pl node that it encounters. In a form like [dak<u>uu</u>t] (from /daakʷ/), it copies the labialisation from the preceding consonant, thereby pre-empting vowel copy, as in (16a). This interpretation is based on the idea that secondary articulations involve a dependent V-pl node (see e.g. Smith 1988; Clements 1991). Given our analysis of root-final velar stops after /u/, exactly the same process applies in a form like [ɬuk<u>uu</u>m] (from /ɬuukʷ/), in (16b). In both forms the V-pl node delinks from the stop, due to the restriction on adjacent labials.

(16) Snatching and delinking of the secondary articulation

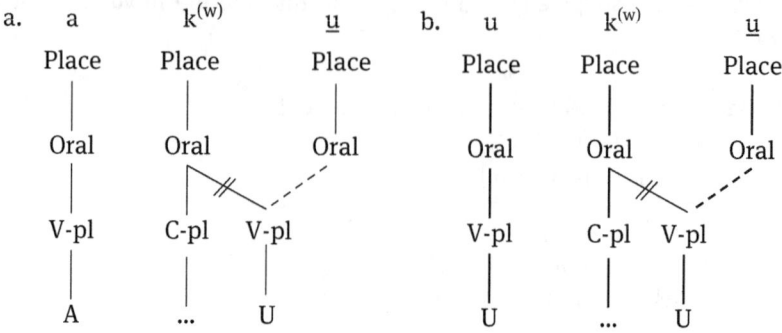

In this analysis, vowel copy and rounding by labialised stops are therefore two manifestations of one and the same process; both are the result of the vowel in the verbal derivation copying the first available V-pl node to its left.

4 Conclusion

The main aim of this paper has been to show that earlier analyses of Iraqw vowel copy have incorrectly included velar consonants in the set of transparent segments. Closer inspection of the data shows that a distinction must be made between velar fricatives and velar stops. Velar fricatives are transparent; like gutturals, they do not block vowel copy of /a i u/. We suspect that the fricatives pattern with gutturals because they are in fact post-velar. Velar stops, on the other hand, are opaque. In the context in which they seem to be transparent (root-finally after /u/), they derive from labialised stops, and it is their labialisation which causes the vowel in the verbal derivation to surface as [uu]. This pattern is obscured by the fact that the stops in question are non-labialised phonetically, as the result of a restriction on adjacent rounded segments. The Iraqw facts receive a straightforward interpretation in a model in which oral and guttural segments have different place nodes, and in which the vowel in the verbal derivation copies the nearest available V-pl node.

References

Anderson, John M. & Colin J. Ewen. 1987. *Principles of Dependency Phonology*. Cambridge: Cambridge University Press.

Archangeli, Diana. 1984. *Underspecification in Yawelmani phonology and morphology*. Cambridge, MA: Massachusetts Institute of Technology PhD dissertation.

Backley, Phillip. 2011. *An Introduction to Element Theory*. Edinburgh: Edinburgh University Press.

Clements, George N. 1991. Place of articulation in consonants and vowels: A unified theory. *Working Papers of the Cornell Phonetics Laboratory* 5. 77–123.

Demolin, Didier. 2021. Iraqw phonetics. Lecture presented at the Samples of linguistic structure course, Leiden University, February 27, 2021.

Downing, Laura & Maarten Mous. 2011. Challenges of Cushitic reduplication for Generalized Template Theory. *Brill's Annual of Afroasiatic Languages and Linguistics* 3. 82–110.

Goldsmith, John. 1976. *Autosegmental phonology*. Cambrdige, MA: Massachusetts Institute of Technology PhD dissertation.

Hall, Nancy. 2006. Cross-linguistic patterns of vowel intrusion. *Phonology* 23(3). 387–429.

Harris, John & Geoff Lindsey. 1995. The elements of phonological representation. In Jacques Durand & Francis Katamba (eds.), *Frontiers of Phonology: Atoms, Structures, Derivations*, 34–79. London: Longman.

Hayward, Katrina & Richard Hayward. 1989. Guttural: Arguments for a new distinctive feature. *Transactions of the Philological Society* 87(2). 179–193.

Hulst, Harry van der. 1988. The geometry of vocalic features. In Harry van der Hulst & Norval Smith (eds.), *Features, Segmental Structure and Harmony Processes (Part II)*, 77–125. Dordrecht: Foris.

Hulst, Harry van der & Maarten Mous. 1992. Transparent consonants. In Reineke Bok-Bennema & Roeland van Hout (eds.), *Linguistics in the Netherlands 1992*, 101–112. Amsterdam: John Benjamins.

Maghway, Josephat B. 1989. Iraqw vocabulary. *Afrikanistische Arbeitspapiere* 18. 91–118.

McCarthy, John J. 1994. The phonetics and phonology of Semitic laryngeals. In Patricia Keating (ed.), *Papers in Laboratory Phonology III: Phonological Structure and Phonetic Form*. 191–233. Cambridge: Cambridge University Press.

Mous, Maarten. 1993. *A Grammar of Iraqw*. Hamburg: Buske.

Mous, Maarten, Martha Qorro & Roland Kießling. 2002. *An Iraqw-English Dictionary* (Cushitic Language Studies 15). Cologne: Rüdiger Köppe.

Nevins, Andrew. 2010. *Locality in Vowel Harmony*. Cambridge, MA: MIT Press.

Paradis, Carole & Jean-François Prunet. 1994. A reanalysis of velar transparency cases. *The Linguistic Review* 11(2). 101–140.

Rose, Sharon. 1996. Variable laryngeals and vowel lowering. *Phonology* 13(1). 73–117.

Smith, Norval. 1988. Consonant place features. In Harry van der Hulst & Norval Smith (eds.), *Features, Segmental Structure and Harmony Processes (Part I)*, 209–236. Dordrecht: Foris.

Yamane-Tanaka, Noriko. 2006. Transguttural harmony in Gitksan: Its variations and typological implications. In Seok Koon Chin & Atsushi Fujimori (eds.), *Proceedings of the 21st NorthWest Linguistics Conference*. 136–152. (UBC Occasional Papers in Linguistics 1).

Nancy A. Ritter
Hungarian Possessive Allomorphy in the Lexicon

Abstract: The third person possessive singular morpheme in Hungarian has been a topic of discussion and debate for decades. Phonological rules have been proposed citing certain contexts where one allomorph or the other (-jV vs. -V) is selected, such as sensitivity to stem-final sounds or the phonological behavior of certain stems. Yet such rules cannot account for other varied contexts where the choice of allomorph either appears arbitrary, as in the case of VC# stems, or may be sensitive to differing derivational suffixes, morphosyntactic categories, or even semantic differences. This paper suggests a way to unify the seemingly different contexts by appealing to cognitive, lexical, declarative schemas á la Jackendoff & Audring (2019). Such cognitive structures are comprised of pieces of linguistic knowledge that include semantics, morphosyntactic structure, and phonological composition and context. Lexical schemas are relationally linked to other words that share the same schematic information. In this way, the parallelism among lexically stored items connects words in the speaker's mind to form a family of lexical items that behave in a certain way, and thus captures generalizations that can be used to explain productive patterns as well as what previously have been considered arbitrary or exceptional, non-productive patterns.

Keywords: Hungarian third person singular possessive suffix, stem-final vowels, stem-final palatals, stem-final sibilants, stem-final consonant clusters, stem-final VC, palatality, Government Phonology, variable element, element/feature checking, licensing, I-tier, OCP, analytic/non-analytic domains, inalienable/alienable possession, morpho-syntax, relational schemas

---

Acknowledgments: I would like to thank the editor of this volume, an anonymous reviewer, and, especially, Péter Siptár for his constructive comments and scrupulous attention to details regarding the data. Lastly, special thanks go to Harry van der Hulst, whose insights and creative approaches to phonological problems have been a great source of influence on this work as well as many others.

Nancy A. Ritter, University of Connecticut

https://doi.org/10.1515/9783110730098-003

1 Introduction

Allomorphic variation of the Hungarian third person possessive suffixal form has been claimed by many to be phonologically unpredictable and arbitrary (Kenesei, Vago, and Fenyvesi 1998; Vago 1980; Rácz 2010; Rácz and Rebrus 2012). Attempting to formulate rules that result in the correct form of the competing allomorphs has proven to be difficult as there are many different contexts to appeal to. Some contexts are phonological and strictly sensitive to stem-final sounds (such as +/- palatal, +/- sibilant, +vocalic), shape of the stem (having a final consonant cluster) or the phonological behavior of certain stems (such as those that trigger lowering of a vowel in certain suffixes, or those that are antiharmonic), while other contexts are sensitive to internal morphological complexity (such as the effect of differing derivational suffixes, such as -ság/ség[1] followed by -V initial variant), morphosyntactic categories (such as adjectives used as nouns), and semantic differences (such as inalienable vs. alienable possession). This paper will focus specifically on the *singular* allomorphs: -jV vs. -V[2] and will attempt to bring together the above seemingly different contexts by appealing to the more cognitive approach of Jackendoff and Audring (2019a, 2019b) wherein declarative schemas in the lexicon relationally link pieces of linguistic structure with each other to uncover deeper generalizations and commonalities with respect to these lexical items and their behavior. With respect to the Hungarian possessive structure, this approach unifies the productive and non-productive patterns found to occur with the allomorphic variants and reduces the notion of arbitrariness that has been associated with the possessive morpheme.

Section 2 presents the various contexts associated with each allomorph of the third singular possessive morpheme, including contexts previously designated as unpredictable or arbitrary. The unproductive as well as unpredictable items are then united under the family resemblance/relational schema approach discussed in Section 3. Productive items, which traditionally would be handled in terms of generative rules, are claimed in this section to be declarative statements that are used for online construction. Section 4 presents conclusions and paths for further research.

---

[1] Words are written orthographically throughout. Those orthographic symbols that differ from their phonetic pronunciation are as follow: <c> = [ts], <cs> = [tš], <dzs> = [dž], <ty> = [c], <gy> = [ɟ], <ny> = [ɲ], <j> = [j], <ly> = [j], <s> = [š], <zs> = [ž], <sz> = [s], <á> = [a/ɑ], <a> = [ɒ], <é> = [e], <e> = [ɛ].
[2] The quality of vowel V will be determined by the harmony system of the language.

2 Presentation and Discussion of Distribution of Allomorphs

For the purposes of this study, a standard dictionary (2 volume *Magyar Angol Nagyszótár* [MAN] 1991) was relied upon to gather the data. In addition, examples extracted from the Hungarian Webcorpus, as noted by other researchers, are also included. Both sources provide data based solely on written sources. There might well be variation found aside from such written data when corpora with more naturalistic spoken data would be included, but such a large-scale study including the latter type of data is beyond the limits of this study.[3] Nonetheless, data of the written type relied upon in the present study are still relevant to a cognitive understanding of the behavior of the third singular possessive allomorphy in Hungarian.

2.1 Categorical Behavior

Researchers agree that the phonological environment of a nominal stem ending in a *vowel* categorically triggers the -jV variant of the possessive across the board. An array of sample examples of morphologically simplex nouns[4] with third person singular -jV are given in (1) below:

(1) *alku-ja* 'bargain', *bú-ja* 'sorrow', *cipő-je* 'shoes', *csacsi-ja* 'young donkey', *csokoládé-ja* 'chocolate', *eskü-je* 'oath', *fésü-je* 'comb', *gábli-ja* 'type of card game', *gyanú-ja* 'suspicion', *habitüé-je* 'habitual visitor', *iniciálé-ja* 'initial (letter)', *kapu-ja* 'gate', *kordé-ja* 'hand cart', *lajbi-ja* 'type of vest', *mackó-ja* 'bear cub', *menü-je* 'menu', *náci-ja* 'Nazi', *nő-je* 'woman', *obligó-ja* 'obligation', *padló-ja* 'flooring', *ráció-ja* 'reason, sense', *resti-je* 'railway restaurant', *sarjú-ja* 'second crop growth', *sí-je* 'ski', *szankció-ja* 'sanction', *tanú-ja* 'witness', *valami-je* 'something', *zászló-ja* 'flag, banner', *zrí-je* 'rumpus'.[5]

---

[3] See Cohn and Renwick (2021) for discussion on the benefits of integrating multiple types of data in understanding phonological behavior.

[4] Many nouns ending in -ó/ő are morphologically complex, where the long mid vowel provides an agentive sense to the root. For example: *nyargal*, verb intransitive, 'to gallop', *nyargaló*, 'a galloper'; *őgyeleg*, verb intransitive, 'to loaf, lounge', *őgyelgő* 'loafer, loiterer'.

[5] Interestingly, certain word-initial sounds (*j/ly-, ny-, ty-, ö-, u-, ü-) have very few of these type of vowel-final endings (not taking into account low vowels -*a* and -*e*).

As might be observed from the above, most vowel-final, non-derivative nouns appear to end in -*u*, -*ú*, -*ü*, -*ű*, -*ó*, -*ő*, -*i*, -*í*,[6] -*é*. The absence of short mid round vowels -*o*, and -*ö* is due to a phonotactic constraint that prohibits these vowels at the end of a word.[7] Siptár and Törkenczy (2000: 146) also note that "word-final -*á* is rare and final -*é* is relatively infrequent." There is also an absence of short -*a* and -*e* before the suffix -jV; however, this is due to an additional condition of the language that nominal root-final short, low vowels (-*a* and -*e*) lengthen before a suffix (typically labelled 'low vowel lengthening', cf. Vago 1980). For example, *ige* 'verb'- *igé-t* 'accusative'/*igé-je* 'poss', *kefe* 'brush' - *kefé-t* 'accusative'/*kefé-je* 'poss', *spárga* 'string'- *spárgá-t* 'accusative'/*spárgá-ja* 'poss', *kasca* 'duck' - *kascá-t* 'accusative'/*kascá-ja* 'poss'. These short 'low' vowels that lengthen, will categorically combine with the -jV allomorph.

The explanation for the exceptionless presence of -jV after vowel-final stems is that it historically originated as a hiatus filler between two vowels, occurring first with stems with final *back* vowels. Siptár and Törkenczy (2000) provide examples of roots with adjacent vowels. Most include a front vowel as one of the two, the context for which an intrusive palatal glide could phonetically fill the gap between the two vowels. What is interesting, however, is that, given that the number of words that end in a vowel in Hungarian is comparatively less frequent than words that end in a consonant or cluster of two consonants, the -jV allomorph has become the more predominant and productive allomorph of the two options.

The next categorical phonological condition with respect to allomorph choice concerns the stem-final consonant when it is either a palatal (-*j/ly*, -*ny*, -*ty*, -*gy*) or a sibilant (-*c*, -*cs*, -*dzs*, -*s*, -*sz*, -*z*, -*zs*). Words with these types of final consonants select the vowel-initial allomorph -V as seen below in (2):

(2) a. words ending in sibilants

nominative	3rd sg. poss	gloss
bu**sz**	busz-a	'bus'
do**boz**	doboz-a	'box'
érzé**s**	érzés-e	'feeling'
gará**zs**	garázs-a	'garage'
csú**cs**	csúcs-a	'point/tip'
bri**dzs**	bridzs-e	'bridge (cards)'
gó**c**	góc-a	'focus'

---

[6] Siptár and Törkenczy (2000: 144, fn. 94) point out that there are only about four monosyllabic nouns that end in long -*í*.
[7] Cf. Siptár and Törkenczy (2000) for discussion of word-final vowel length of high and mid vowels in polysyllabic and monosyllabic words.

b. words ending in palatals

nominative	3rd sg. poss.	gloss
he**ly**	hely-e	'place'
va**j**	vaj-a	'butter'
ará**ny**	arány-a	'proportion'
á**gy**	ágy-a	'bed'

A few exceptions exist, such as: *cesz* → *cesz-je* 'C-flat', *ceszesz* → *ceszesz-je* 'C-double flat', *csíny* → *csíny-je* 'trick',[8] *gúny* → *gúny-ja* 'ridicule', *karnis* → *karnis-ja* 'curtain rod', *kartács* → *kartács-ja* 'tin-case shot' (obsolete), *Kolozs* → *Kolozs-ja* 'Claude', *konkoly* → *konkoly-ja* 'corn-poppy', *kristály* → *kristály-ja* 'crystal', *meszely* → *meszely-je* 'old Hungarian liquid measure (approx. 4/5 of a pint)',[9] *nagy* → *nagy-ja* 'large'. Three additional exceptions occur with words that belong to the class of low vowel lengthening, mentioned above, of words ending in short -*a* or -*e* that lengthen with the addition of a suffix, as with *fa* 'tree' / *fá-ja* 'his tree'. These are: *atya* 'father' / *aty-ja* 'his father', *anya* 'mother' / *any-ja* 'his mother', and *bátya* 'brother' / *báty-ja* 'his brother'. In the case of these three latter exceptions, the final vowel, instead of lengthening, simply deletes (**anyá-ja*).[10] Under a relational theory of schemas, discussed in Section 3, these three exceptions would pattern similarly by way of analogy because they share the same semantic/phonological grouping. The other dozen or so exceptions pale in number compared to the large number of words ending in either a sibilant or palatal that do follow the generalization. These few exceptional words would have to be marked as such in the lexicon.

It is not remarkable that initial [j] of the -jV allomorph should not appear after sibilants nor palatals as initial [j] of other morphemes, such as the verbal imperative or subjunctive -j, does not surface in its glide form after sibilants or palatals, but rather obstruentizes by means of progressive assimilation with the stem final sibilant (cf. Ritter 2000 for further explanation). Example (3) below exhibits the obstruentization pattern of the glide in the varied phonological contexts:

---

[8] Péter Siptár (personal communication) has noted that of some of these exceptions, alternate more frequently occurring forms exist, which follow the phonological conditions set out in (2): cf. *csíny-e*, *karnis-a*, *kartács-a*, *Kolozs-a*, *konkoly-a*, *kristály-a*.
[9] This word has an alternate spelling, i.e., *messzely*. Under the entry for this spelling, the vowel-initial suffix is required.
[10] The third singular possessive form *anyá-ja* does exist for the homonym *anya* meaning '(screw) nut'.

(3) behavior of verbal suffixes with initial /j/
   a. When following a verbal root ending in a sibilant, the imperative /j/ suffix fully assimilates to the preceding sibilant:
   'read, 2nd sg. imperative'   olvas + j   [-ʃʃ]
   'be careful, 2nd sg. imperative'   vigyáz + j   [-zz]
   'play, 2nd sg. imperative'   játsz + j   [-ts:]

   b. When following verbal roots ending in /st/ with the addition of the imperative /j/, final /t/ deletes and the word behaves similarly to words ending in sibilants in which the palatal glide then fully assimilates to the sibilant /s/:
   'postpone, 2nd sg. imperative'   halaszt + j   [-ss]
   'miss, 2nd sg. imperative'   mulaszt + j   [-ss]
   'stick, 2nd sg. imperative'   ragaszt + j   [-ss]

   c. Also, when following a verbal root ending in /t/, the imperative palatal glide obstruentizes, in that it becomes a sibilant itself:
   'love, 2nd sg. imperative'   szeret + j   [-ʃʃ]
   'show, 2nd sg. imperative'   mutat + j   [-ʃʃ]
   'tie, 2nd sg. imperative'   köt + j   [-ʃʃ]
   'heat, 2nd. sg. imperative'   fü:t[11] + j   [-tʃ:]
   'gather, 2nd sg. imperative'   gyü:jt + j   [-tʃ]
   'keep, 2nd sg. imperative'   tart + j   [-tʃ]

   d. When following 3rd singular indicative/imperative definite roots ending in palatals, the glide assimilates to the final palatal:
   'leave, 3rd sg. definite'   hagy + ja   [-ɟ:a]
   'throw, 3rd sg. definite'   hány + ja   [-ɲ:a]

Rácz (2010) correlates the similar behavior found in the nominal and verbal paradigms with respect to avoiding stems ending in sibilant/palatal consonants followed by a -j suffix. He further notes (2010: 11) "that while the verbal paradigm opts for assimilation to avoid the illicit clusters, the nominal possessive paradigms erases (or excludes) the glide altogether." His focus then turns to why the different

---

11 There are some exceptions to generalizations regarding VVt and VCC (e.g., the imperative forms of *lát* 'see', *bocsát* 'let', *megbocsát* 'forgive', *elbocsát* 'dismiss', and *fest* 'paint', curiously enough, end in a geminate voiceless palatal fricative). Such exceptions have been claimed to arise from phonological structural differences in these words (cf. Ritter and Vago 1999).

categories choose different methods to repair such illicit consonant sequences,[12] though does not explore why the grouping itself is frowned upon in the language, other than to appeal to articulatory difficulty in pronouncing a palatal or sibilant/glide sequence (2010: 23). In exploring this grouping further, it is interesting to point out that the opposite order of root-initial palatal consonant followed by a front vowel is quite minimally restricted.[13] For example, for palatal glide *j-* initial roots plus front vowel, most words begin with #*je-*, as in *jegec* 'crystal', *jegenye* 'poplar', *jegy* 'ticket', *jel* 'sign', *Jenő* 'Eugene', *Jeremiás* 'Jeremiah', *jezsuita* 'Jesuit', and their respective derivatives. There are fewer words with initial #*jé-*: *jég* 'ice', *jéger* 'Jaeger pants', *jérce* 'pullet', *jésít* 'palatalize', and *Jézus* 'Jesus'. Only one word was found with initial #*ji-* and that was *jiddis* 'Yiddish'.[14] As for initial palatal stops, *ty-* and *gy-*, again most morphologically simplex words have *-e* as the preferred following palatal vowel: *gyenge* 'weak', *gyep* 'lawn', *gyerek* 'child', *gyermek* 'child', and *gyertya* 'candle'. There are fewer words with initial #*gyé-*: *gyékény* 'bulrush', *gyémánt* 'diamond', and *gyér* 'thin'. Only two words were found with #*gy-* followed by high front *-i* or *-í*: *gyík* 'lizard' and *gyilkol* 'murder'. There were no words that were found beginning with the voiceless palatal stop #*ty-* followed by a front vowel. For the palatal nasal, there are several words beginning with #*nye-*, such as: *nyegle* 'overbearing', *nyekereg* 'creak', *nyel* 'to swallow', *nyelv* 'tongue', *nyenyere* 'hurdy gurdy', *nyer* 'win', *nyereg* 'saddle', *nyeremény* 'prize', *nyeretlen* 'maiden race', *nyers* 'raw', *nyes* 'trim', *nyest* 'beech-marten', *nyeszlett* 'puny' and their respective derivatives. Only two words were found with initial #*nyé-* : *nyél* 'handle' (although this vowel shortens in other forms of the word: *nyelet* 'accusative', *nyele* 'possessive'), and *nyérc*, a variant of *nerc* 'mink'. Several words were found with initial #*nyi(:)-*: *nyifog* 'to yelp', *nyihog* 'to neigh', *nyikkan* 'to squeak', *nyíl* 'arrow', *nyílik* 'to open', *nyilatkozik* 'to declare', *nyilvánít* 'to evidence', *nyír* 'to cut' or 'birch tree', *nyirkos* 'moist', *nyirok* 'lymph', *nyivákol* 'to yowl' and respective derivatives, compounds, etc.

---

12 See Rácz (2010) for an explanation which appeals to analogy among the different paradigmatic categories.
13 Grimes (2010) notes that stronger co-occurrence restrictions can be found between a vowel and following consonant than between CV sequences; yet, several have been uncovered during this project.
14 The palatal glide seems to disprefer higher front vowels following it. In a Government Phonology (GP) approach using elements and the concept of headedness, the palatal glide, represented as an empty-headed expression with a palatal I element in dependent position of that expression, would disprefer contexts in which a vocalic expression with an I element head immediately follows it. The lower front vowel [ɛ], however, is less offensive as its segmental representation has an A head with I dependent. (See Ritter 1995, 1999 for intra-segmental elemental expressions).

Sibilants, on the other hand, do not yield the same co-occurrence behavior with following front vowels. For instance, there are many examples of words beginning with the voiceless alveolar affricate and fricative: #ce-, #cé, #ci(:)-, #sze-, szé-, and szi(:)- . The voiced fricative -z begins to show some constraint before the front vowels -é and -i(:). Only three words were found with #zé-: zénó 'Zeno', zéró 'zero', and zérus 'cipher' and close to a dozen with #zi-: ziccer 'billiard stroke', zigóta 'zygote', zihál 'to pant', zilált 'disorderly', ziliz 'marshmallow', zimankó 'raw weather', zimáz 'zymase', zivatar 'thunderstorm', zizeg 'rustle', and respective derivatives. The palatal sibilants also exhibit some odd co-occurrence restrictions. Both the voiced and voiceless palatal sibilants evidence a limitation in words *only* with following front vowel -é: csép 'flail', csér 'tern', csésze 'cup', cséve 'spool', cséza 'light carriage', séf 'chef', sékel 'shekel', séma 'pattern', sémi 'Semitic', sérelem 'grief, injury', sért 'to injure', sérv 'hernia', séta 'stroll', zsémbel 'to grumble', zsén 'embarrassment', and zséter 'milkpail'. There are no words with initial voiced palatal affricate #dzsé- and very few with following -e and -i(:): dzsem 'jam', dzsembori 'jamboree', dzsentri 'gentry', dzsessz 'jazz', dzsida 'lance', dzsigg 'jig', dzsinn 'genie', dzsip 'jeep'.[15]

To recap, it seems that word-initial *oral palatal* consonants prefer not to have a following front vowel; however, if they do, there is a gradient preference in that -e is preferred, less so -é, and least so i(:). Only the voiceless palatal stop ty- completely disallows a following front vowel.[16] With sibilants, the voiceless alveolar ones (c, sz) show no specific limitation on front vowels in general, while the voiced alveolar fricative (z) shows least preference for following -é vowel. For palatal sibilants, all varieties (cs, s, zs), except for the voiced affricate, show least preference for -é, while the voiced affricate variety exhibits a gradient preference with -e, then -i(:), and no examples of -é.

The above restricted behavior of palatals, especially, seems to suggest that the language disprefers local combinations of palatal segments despite whether they are -C]C- combinations or #CV combinations. Further exploration of such co-occurrence restrictions in contexts such as word-final -VC# combinations or

---

[15] Keating (1988) and Keating and Lahiri (1993) have proposed that palatal stops are phonetically doubly articulated complex segments similar to affricates. Keating (1988: 87) characterized palatals as being "articulated like 'consonantal' front vowels." So it is interesting that palatal stop ty-, palatal affricate dzs-, and slightly less so with palatal stop gy-, all show very limited co-occurrence with a following front, palatal vowel.

[16] The only regularly occurring word beginning with ty- is tyúk 'hen' and its derivatives. Péter Siptár has pointed out that the interjection tyű exists with palatal vowel following initial ty-. However, Ameka (1992: 105) has pointed out that interjections tend to be peripheral to a language's phonological system and may consist of "sounds and sound sequences that are not found in other parts of the language".

final syllable $CV# of polysyllabic words has not been addressed due to space limitations of this paper. Palatality could be claimed to be a linguistic cue that has come to be one of the important features of the Hungarian language (in addition to initial syllable stress, rhythm patterns, and vowel harmony) and that operates as a marker of cultural identity among the speakers of Hungarian signaling group membership. It seems to be a crucial element in the cognitive structure of the language. As a marker having a cognitive focus, such function could lead to encoding palatality in the grammar. It is then understandable that the grammar would impose a well-formedness constraint on its usage. One brief explanation proposed here as to why the language disfavors sequences of palatals may appeal to the language wanting to strike a balance of such palatality, first on a local segmental level within the root as well as at a higher tier of palatal (I) interactions between palatality of the stem, as determined by either the final C or final V, and palatality of the affix. This idea will be returned to in Section 2.2 below.

The final categorical behavior with respect to the choice of possessive allomorph is conditioned by the presence of a stem-final consonant cluster. Clusters, including geminates, that end in a non-sibilant/non-palatal consonant categorically occur with the -jV allomorph, as seen in (4a). Interestingly, Rebrus and Rácz (2010) point out that the preference for -CC stems selecting -jV 'is stronger for stems ending in a dental stop.' They found an 84% occurrence of stems ending in -CT# occurring with -jV from the Hungarian Webcorpus.[17]

Clusters, the final member of which is a sibilant or palatal, however, follow the same generalization as discussed in (2) above, namely, occurring with the vowel-initial variant -V. Examples of such clusters are given in (4b).

There is a third sub-group of the -CC context, and that group contains words where the final member of the cluster is -*v*, as can be seen in (4c). It is interesting to note that only sonorants can appear as the preceding consonant of this cluster type, with the exception of **-dv**.[18] In both cluster types, /v/ occurs in post-consonantal coda context (V**Cv** #), a position that typically favors obstruentization (cf. Ritter 2000). Moreover, according to Siptár and Törkenczy (2000: 129), only one instance of intervocalic -vj- exists: *szov**j**et* 'Soviet'. Here /v/ is the only member of the coda, which is a weaker position, and should behave more as a sonorant when preceding an onset, in accordance with syllable contact laws. Perhaps this dual behavior of /v/ as sonorant as well as obstruent may play a role in it being less likely to sequentially precede /j/, another sonorant, which can also obstruentize

---

[17] Kiefer (1985) also points out the frequency of consonant clusters ending in -*t*/-*d* but also includes -*ng* and -*nk*.
[18] The language has very few final clusters where both members are obstruents, e.g., *copf* 'braid'.

in similar post-consonantal contexts as noted in (3) above (see Ritter 2000 for discussion of such behavior). Another interesting fact with respect to the sequence -vj- can be seen in monosyllables of the form CVC where final C = /v/. The majority of these words select the vowel-initial -V allomorph of the possessive: *év* 'year'/*év-e*, *ív* 'arch'/*ív-e*, *öv*[19] 'belt'/*öv-e*, *rév* 'ferry'/*rév-e*, *sav*[20] 'acid'/*sav-a*, *szív* 'heart'/*szív-e*. There are only two exceptions found that occur with the -jV allomorph: *sáv* 'stripe'/*sáv-ja* and *táv* 'distance'/*táv-ja*.[21] Again, this could be due to a constraint in the language that disfavors -vj- sequences for sonority reasons. But note that most words that end in /v/, albeit in -C or -CC context (see 4c below) contain front vowels. As will be discussed in Section 2.2 on variation in consonant-final stems, front vowel stems typically occur with the vowel-initial allomorph of the possessive.

Lastly, there are also words that end with a -CC cluster that fall into another closed class of nouns referred to as 'lowering stems'. These are stems that take a low vowel -*a* or -*e* with the accusative (-*t*) or plural (-*k*), where regularly a mid-vowel (*o, e, ö*) would be used, e.g., *bók* 'compliment'/*bók-ot* 'accusative' vs. *fog* 'tooth'/*fog-at* 'accusative' (cf. Siptár and Törkenczy 2000: 41 for a list of the most frequent examples).

(4) Words ending in -CC
    a. Where final C is *non*-sibilant/*non*-palatal

nominative	3rd sg. poss	gloss
cse**pp**	csepp-je	'drop'
kolo**mp**	kolomp-ja	'cow bell'
szö**rp**	szörp-je	'syrup'
co**mb**	comb-ja	'thigh'
sze**rb**	szerb-je	'Serbian'
blö**ff**	blöff-je	'hoax'
co**pf**	copf-ja	'braid'
go**lf**	golf-ja	'golf'
omle**tt**	omlett-je	'omelet'
verdi**kt**	verdikt-je	'verdict'
rece**pt**	recept-je	'recipe'
sza**ft**	szaft-ja	'juice, gravy'
adve**nt**	advent-je	'Advent'

---

19 This word belongs to the category of 'lowering stems'.
20 This also falls under the category of a 'lowering stem'.
21 The similarity in rhymal resemblance -*áv*, could fall under a schema that the learner recognizes.

aszfa**lt**	aszfalt-ja	'asphalt'
fü**rt**	fürt-je	'lock of hair'
smara**gd**	smaragd-ja	'emerald'
offszá**jd**	offszájd-ja	'off-side'
cse**nd**	csend-je	'silence'
bá**rd**	bárd-ja	'hatchet'
ca**kk**	cakk-ja	'scalloped work'
arabe**szk**	arabeszk-je	'arabesque'
bara**ck**	barack-ja	'peach'
ba**nk**	bank-ja	'bank'
pa**rk**	park-ja	'park'
cafra**ng**	cafrang-ja	'fringe, tassle'
dramatu**rg**	dramaturg-ja	'drama critic'
karte**ll**	kartell-je	'cartel'
fi**lm**	film-je	'film'
konsze**rn**	konszern-je	'concern'

b. Where final C is sibilant or palatal

bo**rz**	borz-a	'badger'
bo**rs**	bors-a	'pepper'
index[**ks**]	index-e	'school record'
ka**rc**	karc-a	'scratch'
pé**nz**	pénz-e	'money'
tá**rs**	társ-a	'companion'
gyümö**lcs**	gyümölcs-e	'fruit'
ko**rty**	korty-a	'a swallow of liquid'
hö**lgy**	hölgy-e	'lady'
me**ggy**	meggy-e	'sour cherry'
faja**nsz**	fajansz-a	'delft-ware'
ár**ny**[22]	árny-a	'shade'
kö**nny**[23]	könny-e	'tear'
fé**rj**	férj-e	'husband'
ga**lly**[24]	gally-a	'twig'

---

22 This word also falls under the subcategory of lowering stem: *árny/árny-at* 'accusative'.
23 Lowering stem: *könny-et* 'accusative'.
24 Lowering stem: *gally-at* 'accusative'.

c. Where final C = /v/

eny**v**	enyv-e	'glue'
köny**v**[25]	könyv-e	'book'
öly**v**[26]	ölyv-e	'hawk'
el**v**	elv-e	'policy'
nyel**v**	nyelv-e	'tongue, language'
ellensze**nv**	ellenszenv-e	'antipathy'
ha**mv**[27]	hamv-a	'snuff'
ér**v**	érv-e	'argument'
kese**rv**	keserv-e	'complaint'
sé**rv**	sérv-e	'hernia'
te**rv**	terv-e	'plan'
sza**rv**[28]	szarv-a	'horn'
ke**dv**	kedv-e	'mood'
ne**dv**	nedv-e	'moisture'
ü**dv**	üdv-e	'salvation'

d. Where stem selects low linking vowel with accusative/plural[29]

á**ll**	áll-a	'chin'
vá**ll**	váll-a	'shoulder'
szaká**ll**[30]	szakáll-a	'beard'
fa**rk**	fark-a	'tail'
u**jj**	ujj-a	'finger'
ta**lp**	talp-a	'sole'
to**ll**	toll-a	'feather, pen'

---

25 Lowering stem: *könyv-et* 'accusative'.
26 Lowering stem: *ölyv-et* 'accusative'.
27 This is also a lowering stem: *hamv-at* 'accusative'.
28 Lowering stem: *szarv-at* 'accusative'.
29 Two lowering stem exceptions have been found that select for the -jV allomorph: *föld* 'earth'/ *föld-et* 'accusative'/*föld-je* 'poss.' and *hold* 'moon'/*hold-at* 'accusative'/*hold-ja* 'poss.'.
30 In a relational schema approach, the learner recognizes that nominal lowering stems with the rhyme -*áll* are linked to the vowel-initial possessive allomorph.

There are some exceptions to these generalized patterns as seen in (5):

(5) Exceptions
    a. Where final C is *non*-sibilant/*non*-palatal

kelt	kelt-e	'date of a letter'	cf. keze**lt**-je 'patient'
térd	térd-e	*'knee'	cf. ka**rd**-ja 'sword'
test	test-e	*'body'	cf. e**st**-je 'evening'
mell	mell-e	*'chest'	cf. karame**ll**-je 'caramel'
orr	orr-a	*'nose'	cf. biza**rr**-ja 'bizarre'
pörk	pörk-e	'scab, crust'	cf. pa**rk**-ja 'park'
se**lyp**	selyp-e	'lisper'	
dö**lyf**	dölyf-e	'arrogance'	
hüve**lyk**	hüvelyk-e[31]	*'thumb, inch'	cf. se**jk**-je 'sheikh'
ci**kk**	cikk-e	'news article'	cf. ca**kk**-ja 'scallop'
se**gg**	segg-e	*'buttocks'	
dzsi**gg**	dzsigg-e	'jig'	cf. bri**gg**-je 'brig'
griff	griff-e	'griffon'	cf. szki**ff**-je 'skiff'
smize**tt**	smizett-e	'lowboy'	
te**tt**	tett-e	'action'	cf. bale**tt**-je 'ballet'

    b. Where final C is sibilant/palatal

kre**cc**	krecc-je	'dross'	cf. he**cc**-e 'prank'
mufu**rc**	mufurc-ja	'lout'	cf. ko**rc**-a 'hem'
fran**c**	franc-ja	'syphillis'	cf. lán**c**-a 'chain'
vindfix[**ks**]	vindfi[ks]-je	'weatherstrip'	cf. kódex[**ks**]-e 'codex'

These exceptions can be marked as such in the lexicon. However, it is interesting to note that several of the non-sibilant/non-palatal nouns that select for the vowel-initial variant are semantically related by being part of a class of body parts (see glosses marked with an asterisk). As relational schemas also include semantic information, the learner may realize that nouns ending in final -CC related to body parts generally select for the vowel-initial variant.[32]

In the next section, the seemingly non-categorical context of (C)**VC** is explored with respect to choice of allomorph.

---

31 The form *hüvelyk-je* also exists.
32 If schemas were related by semantics alone, then several of the lowering stems referring to body parts (already designated as selecting the vowel-initial variant) would also be included in this set of relational items, such as *áll* 'chin', *váll* 'shoulder', *ujj* 'finger', *talp* 'sole'. This is understandable as body parts are prototypical inalienable nouns which would need to select the vowel-initial variant that denotes an inherent relation.

2.2 Allomorph Variability with Consonant-Final (-VC) Roots

While researchers have agreed upon the categorical behavior of allomorph choice, as discussed in 2.1 above, they have also declared the distribution following -VC roots to be absent of generalizations and arbitrary (cf. Rebrus and Rácz 2010; Rácz 2010; Rácz and Rebrus 2012; Rebrus, Szigetvári, and Törkenczy 2017). Kiefer (1985) attempts to build subcategories of rules that are sensitive to (a) loan words, (b) certain productive derivational suffixes of both the old layer of the language and newer forms, (c) analogical pressure, (d) homonymy, and (e) alienable vs. inalienable types of possession.[33] Ritter (2002) noted a statistical tendency toward certain generalizations, such as roots that contain a final back vowel select for the -jV variant (following Papp 1975), while roots that end in a front vowel select for the vowel-initial variant. As expected, final consonants that belong to the palatal/sibilant set select for the vowel-initial variant and are thus not included. Also not included are the closed set of nouns that shorten the long vowel of the root when a vowel-initial suffix is added, e.g. *nyúl* 'hare', but *nyul-at* 'accusative'/*nyul-a* 'poss.' (cf. Ritter 1995: 10 for a list of such examples). Other closed classes of nouns are not included, such as stems exhibiting a vowel/zero alternation (*bokor* 'bush'/*bokr-a* 'poss.'); stems that undergo metathesis (*teher* 'burden'/*terhe* 'poss.'); stems ending in high and mid rounded vowels, which either shorten, delete or change the root vowel and add [v] before a vowel-initial suffix (*kő* 'stone'/*köv-e* 'poss.', *szó* 'word'/*szav-a* 'poss.', *falu* 'village'/*falv-a* 'poss.'). These closed classes behave in a categorical manner with respect to selecting the vowel-initial allomorph of the possessive. In a system of relational schemas, the learner would recognize the phonological contexts of these related items.

Examples of -VC that are external to these closed classes are given in (6–7) below.

---

[33] Semantic differences will arise with use of the different possessive allomorphs. The closer, more intrinsic, inalienable meaning is associated with the historical -V allomorph, and may be associated with prototypical type inalienable nouns, such as body parts and kinship terms. The alienable meaning, denoting the noun as part of a collection owned by an Agent, is associated with the more productive -jV variant. Den Dikken (2015) analyzes the inalienable relation as a predicate-specifier structure, while claiming that the alienable relation involves a predicate-complement structure. As an example, the noun *talp* 'sole' (a lowering stem: *talp-at* 'sole. accusative') plus the -V allomorph: *talp-a* would be used to denote the inherent, part of a whole, meaning, such as the sole of a shoe or a foot. However, in order to denote an alienable possession of the sole for use by a cobbler, the -jV variant would be used: *talp-ja*. (See Elekfi 2000; Ortmann and Gerland 2014; Farkas and Alberti 2016 for further discussion on this topic).

(6) Back vowel roots with -jV allomorph
   a. Examples of monosyllables (*a - g*, non-exhaustive)

ár	'flood'	bot	'stick'	csúf	'laughing stock'
bab	'bean'	bróm	'bromine'	dák	'Dacian'
báb	'doll'	búb	'crown of the head'	dán	'Dane'
bak	'buck'	búg	'crease'	dob	'drum'
bal	'left side'	búr	'Boer'	dóm	'cathedral'
bál	'ball/dance'	cáp	'tragus'	dór	'Dorian'
bán	'ban'	col	'inch'	drót	'wire'
bar	'bar'	csáb	'attraction'	dúr	'major key'
bár	'night club'	csap	'faucet'	fan	'pubis'
bók	'compliment'	csáp	'tentacle'	flór	'lisle thread'
bón	'voucher'	csat	'clasp'	gal	'gal'
bór	'boron'	csók	'kiss'	gát	'dam'

   b. Examples of polysyllables (*a - b*, non-exhaustive)

abrak	'fodder'	agyag	'clay'
acat	'thistle'	alak	'form'
acetát	'acetate'	alap	'base'
adag	'dosage'	albán	'Albanian'
Adám	'Adam	alkohol	'alcohol'
aerográf	'aerograph'	alkóv	'alcove'
aeroplán	'airplane'	állat	'animal'
aerosztát	'aerostat'	aluminát	'aluminate'
afgán	'Afghan'	amidol	'amidol'
agát	'agate'	angol	'Englishman'
aggregát	'aggregate'	anód	'anode'
agrár	'agrarian, adj.'	anorák	'anorak'
apát	'abbot'	autokláv	'boiler'
aposztróf	'ibid'	aval	'ibid'
apród	'pageboy'	avar	'forest floor'
arab	'Arab'	azúr	'azure'
arak	'arrack'	azsúr	'hem stitch'
árkád	'arcade'	bádog	'sheet iron'
arzenál	'arsenal'	balkon	'balcony'
asztag	'stack'	banán	'banana'
aszteroid	'ibid'	barát	'friend'
atom	'ibid'	barbár	'Barbarian'
augur	'ibid'	blokád	'blocade'
autogram	'autograph'	bozót	'thicket'

(7) Front vowel roots with -V allomorph
   a. Monosyllables (*b - sz*, non-exhaustive)

bér	'wage'	év	'year'	ín[34]	'tendon'	nyűg	'shackle'
bőr	'skin'	fék	'brake'	ív	'arch'	öl[35]	'lap'
bűn	'crime'	fém	'metal'	kép	'picture'	őr	'guard'
cím	'address'	föl[36]	'skimmings'	kém	'spy'	öv[37]	'belt'
cég	'firm'	fül[38]	'ear'	köb	'cube'	per	'lawsuit'
csel	'trick'	gép	'machine'	kör	'circle'	pér	'grayling'
csök	'pizzle'	göb	'knot'	lék	'leak'	rév	'ferry'
csőr	'beak'	gyök	'root'	lép	'spleen'	rím	'rhyme'
dög	'carcass'	heg	'scar'	lét	'existence'	rög	'soil'
eb	'dog'	hír	'news'	nem	'sex'	seb	'wound'
ék	'wedge'	hit	'faith'	nép	'people'	sör	'beer'
él	'edge'					szív	'heart'

   b. Examples of polysyllables (*a – f*, non-exhaustive)

adalék[39]	'data'	cilinder	'top hat'
adapter	'ibid'	cinóber	'cinnabar'
ágyék	'groin'	cvikker	'pince-nez'
ajándék	'gift'	csődör	'stallion'
bélyeg	'stamp'	csömör	'nausea'
beteg	'invalid'	csütörtök	'Thursday'
billér	'balancer'	december	'ibid'
bitumen	'ibid'	detektív	'ibid'
bokszer	'brass knuckles'	dózer	'bulldozer'
börtön	'prison'	drukker	'fan'
cekker	'shopping bag'	dzsóker	'joker-card'
címer	'coat of arms'	dzsömper	'jumper'
ében	'ebony'	ereszték	'joint'
éger	'alder'	észter	'ester'
egyed	'individual'	étel	'food'
egyén	'person'	falanszter	'phalanstery'

---

[34] Lowering stem as well as anti-harmonic stem selecting a back vowel, rather than expected front vowel: *ín* / *in-ak* 'plural' / *in-a* 'poss.'.
[35] Lowering stem: *öl-ek* 'plural'.
[36] Lowering stem: *föl-et* 'accusative'.
[37] Lowering stem: *öv-et* 'accusative'.
[38] Lowering stem: *fül-et* 'accusative'.
[39] The words *adalék*, *ágyék*, *ajándék* all select for back-vowel stems.

éjjel	'night'	farmer	'ibid'
ekartőr	'valve'	féder	'spring'
ékezet	'written accent'	fegyver	'weapon'
eledel	'food'	felleg	'cloud'
ember	'person'	fennek	'fennec'
emlék	'souvenir'	fergeteg	'storm'
ének	'song'	fészer	'shed'
enzim[40]	'enzyme'	fiáker	'horse carriage'

The question arises as to why the glide-initial allomorph -jV would be sensitive to the quality of the final harmonic vowel of the root. The final *harmonic* vowel of the root is claimed here to be the head of the domain of the root.[41] The harmonic vowel is not always the absolute, final vowel of the root as can be seen in examples, such as *afrik-ja* 'seaweed-poss.', *acél-ja* 'steel-poss.', *aszpik-ja* 'aspic-poss.', where the final vowel is transparent to the harmony effect seen on the suffix vowel that is triggered by the true harmonic head. The theoretical claim here is that the vocalic head of the root enters into a feature checking relationship with the initial consonantal position of the suffix. This implies two things in a representational account: firstly, that in the lexical representation of the possessive affix, there is always an onset position[42] and secondly, that the features are checked on a feature tier that is not sensitive to syllabic position. Whether the segmental expression in the onset position of the affix is realized or not is determined by whether the sole dependent element within the expression in that position is licensed. Following van der Hulst (2018), the present proposal enlists the concept of a 'variable' element to refer to an element that is unlicensed in the lexical representation. While van der Hulst posits a variable element to be in a vocalic nucleic position, which, in order to be realized, depends upon an invariably licensed element in an adjacent nucleic position,[43] the present proposal extends the concept of variability of an element to reside within the consonantal onset position of the possessive suffix that alternates between -j and

---

40 Alternative variant is *enzim-je*.
41 In Government Phonology, phonological licensing of segments within a root begins with the vocalic head of the root. Harris (1998: 336) defines phonological licensing as " . . . relations that hold within the prosodic hierarchy, ranging from the skeletal tier through the successively higher domains of the syllabic constituent, the foot and the prosodic word . . . ". The unlicensed nucleic head of the root domain would be licensed at some higher level of projection.
42 Since the consonant-initial affix (-jV) is synchronically the productive form, it is hypothesized here to be the underlying form in the cognitive mental representation of this affix.
43 All nuclei are projected to a level in which they are visible to each other, and thus local at that level.

0. This onset position contains a segmental expression with a variable palatal element (I) in dependent position of the empty-headed segmental expression: (_. (I)).⁴⁴,⁴⁵ The variable element requires feature checking for licensing, but not, however, in the traditional sense of feature attracting. Rather, feature checking in this context, between palatal elements of differing segmental types of different morphemes, disfavors feature attraction. Such checking instead promotes a disharmony between such palatal elements, and works as a cue to signaling morpheme segmentation.

In traditional Government Phonology, two mechanisms were introduced: *proper government*, which sanctioned the *absence* of elemental content in a nucleus that was properly governed by an adjacent nucleus on the nucleic tier and allowed for vowel/zero alternations, and *licensing*, which sanctioned the *presence* of elemental content in a segment, as used in cases of harmony. Van der Hulst (2020: 246–247) discusses this two-way response with respect to variability, as follows:

> I will assume that there are two types of licensing; licensing which permits the presence of a variable element, and thus harmony, and licensing which silences a variable element. For the latter, which is the reverse of *licensing* content, I will use the term *silencing*. If we employ the variable notation for both situations (i.e. harmony and vowel/zero alternation) this would mean that this notation itself is neutral with respect to what enforces the variable element to be present or absent. Rather, this would follow from specifying the nature of the licensing relationship.

In the case of disharmony with respect to the possessive suffix, it is proposed here that the lexical representation of the onset position of the possessive suffix contains a variable (I) element, which must be checked, due to its unlicensed status, by the preceding harmonic vowel head. 'Checking' here would be similar to the operation of proper government. If the harmonic head vowel of the root is front containing an invariable, licensed I element and precedes the possessive suffix with a variable (I) element in its onset, the two I elements will see each other on the I-tier, resulting in a clash. This type of OCP violation will force (or allow)

---

44 The segmental expression is represented within parentheses with the head on the left side and the dependent on the right, divided by the diacritic period. The internal parentheses around the palatal (I) element signal that it is unlicensed.

45 While the segmental representation of /j/ consists of an (I) element in the dependent position of the segmental expression, the high front vowel /i/, containing the same sole palatal element in its expression, has a reverse order with the element I as head of its segmental expression. This difference in head vs. dependent position may account for why the I headed segment *i(:)* only occurs in invariant suffixes, such as terminative suffix *-ig* 'up to' and not in alternating ones, while empty-headed /j/ with (I) in the dependent position can participate in alternation of *j* and 0.

the variable element to remain unlicensed, and thus phonetically unrealized. In other terms, the fully licensed I element of the vowel would properly govern the adjacent variable (I) element on the I-tier, silencing the latter's phonetic realization. On the surface, this yields the appearance of roots with harmonic front vowels selecting for the vowel-initial allomorph of the possessive. Example (8) illustrates this process with (a) a monosyllabic front vowel root and (b) a polysyllabic front vowel root:

(8) Analysis of front vowel roots with vowel-initial allomorph
    a. Monosyllabic front vowel root
        (I.)   *(_.(I))   I- tier (clash)
        [O N   O N]   [O   N]
        [c (I.) m 0⁴⁶] [(_.(I)) (A.I)]⁴⁷
        cím 'address' + *e*

    b. Polysyllabic front vowel root
        (I.)   *(_.(I)) (clash)
        [O N   O N O   N   O N] [O   N]
        [b (I.AU) r 0 t (I.AU) n 0] [(_.(I)) (A.I)]
        börtön 'prison' + *e*

If the head vowel of the root does not contain the palatal element I, in essence a true back vowel, then when feature checking occurs at the I-tier, there is no invariable I element projected to that tier which could license the silence of the variable (I) element. Consequently, the variable element must surface in that onset position and will become phonetically realized.

(9) Analysis of back vowel roots with glide-initial allomorph
    a. Monosyllabic back vowel root
                        (_.(I))   I-tier (no clash)
        [O N   O N] [O   N]
        [d (U.A) m 0] [(_.(I)) (A._)]
        dóm 'cathedral' + *ja*

---

46 In Government Phonology surface final-consonants are underlyingly represented as onsets with a following empty nucleus.

47 The elements A, I, and U can be combined in various head/dependent relations to yield the vowel inventory of the language. The element I in the expression (A.I) arises as a result of syntagmatic local spreading of the I element on the nucleic level. For a discussion of elemental spreading and its interaction with paradigmatic intrasegmental licensing constraints see Ritter (1999).

b. Polysyllabic back vowel root

```
                              (_.(I))      (no clash)
[O  N      O   N      O   N]  [O      N ]
[b  (A._)  r   (A._)  t   o]  [(_.(I)) (A._)]
barát 'friend' + ja
```

The feature checking on the I-tier prevents against an overabundance of palatality in the word and is claimed to be the mechanism responsible for the difference in *j*- realization. The palatal features/elements that enter into this checking relation are not claimed to be local at any segmental level, but rather belong to separate domains. There is a prosodic feature associated with the head of the root domain [. . . V . . .] that checks the prosodic feature of the edge of the analytic suffix domain [(_.(I)) V] to ensure against a clash. Evidence that the possessive suffix is in its own domain comes from differences in behavior of root final -*t* and suffix -*j* sequences. With the possessive suffix, a word such as [bot][ja] 'his stick' is perceived as having a stronger, clear, distinctive boundary between the root-final -*t* and suffix-initial -*j*, as opposed to the weaker boundary that exists between -*t* and -*j* as shown in the assimilation processes in (3) above. In the latter cases or where coronal oral or nasal stops combine with the imperative or 1st plural or 3rd singular verbal suffix -*j*, the palatal glide co-articulates with the stop to produce existing independent palatal consonants of the language, e.g., *lát + ja* [lac:a] 'see. 3rd sg. definite', *ad + juk* [aɟ:uk] 'give. 1st pl. definite', *men + jen* [mɛɲ:ɛn] 'go. sg. imperative', *tol + juk* [toj:uk] 'push. 1st pl. definite'. The behavior in these latter cases suggests that the root plus verbal suffix undergo a process that acts upon the entire string, similar to a synthetic, non-analytic domain.[48] Such phonetic differences in behavior of suffixes beginning with -*j* reflect effects of differing boundary domain types in the lexical representation. Such a qualitative boundary effect will block the phonetic effect of palatalization across the analytic [A] [B] nominal domain yet allow it to cross the seemingly non-analytic [A B] verbal domain where the phonology is blind to the morphological boundaries.[49] The

---

[48] One might propose that the independent palatal oral and nasal stops themselves are derived by the same co-articulation rule, thus reducing the number of phonemes in the language's inventory. These three segments would have a 'free ride' in their realization as segments in the language. In such case, then the rule would first apply within the root and then to the entire derived environment.

[49] Siptár and Törkenczy (2000: 5) also claim that analytic morphological domain boundaries are opaque to such phonotactic constraints.

blocking of palatalization across an analytic domain creates a qualitative distinction between these two domain types. The stronger analytic boundary preventing similar palatalization from occurring across an analytic nominal domain also prevents adjacency of palatal elements from these separate morphophonological domains on the I-tier by forcing the variable, unlicensed element of the suffix to remain phonetically inaudible.[50] Such a view that relies on a computational parsing system of domains can offer a new perspective on understanding the seemingly arbitrary realization of the possessive suffix.

For the closed classes of nouns of the older layer of the language, as discussed previously, which categorically select for the vowel-initial possessive allomorph, these noun types are not considered part of the phonological grammar in the present approach as they represent diachronic events that are outside of the computational system and are thus not learnable in the same way (cf. Kaye 2014: 262). As such these noun types are lexically represented within a non-analytic domain, where each type would fall under a schema that captures that type's family resemblance (cf. Section 3).

Despite the above phonological explanation for the computation of allomorph selection, there are many examples, outside of the closed classes, that appear to defy these processes. A list of such examples is given in (10) and (11).

(10) Back vowel roots with exceptional vowel-initial allomorph
    a. Monosyllabic roots (all inclusive)

bog	'knot'	kár	'damage'	tor	'feast'
bor	'wine'	kor	'age'	zug	'nook'
dal	'song'	lak	'cottage'		
far	'backside'	nyom	'trail'		
fok	'step'	ok	'reason'		
hon	'fatherland'	por	'dust'		
hón	'armpit'	sor	'row'		
húg[51]	'younger sister'	szag	'smell'		
jog	'claim'	szám	'number'		
kar	'faculty (university)'	tan	'doctrine'		

---

50 The cognitive construct of an analytic boundary in the mind of the speaker is crucial in order to distinguish a morphologically complex word containing a front vowel root and possessive vowel suffix from nouns that end in the low vowels -*a* or -*e*. For example, the simple nominal root [*medve*] 'bear' vs. the complex word [[*nedv*] *e*] 'moist.possessive'.
51 A kinship term that prefers the inalienable possessive form -V.

b. Polysyllabic roots (non-exhaustive)

ablak[52]	'window'	bocskor	'sandal'
agyar	'tusk'	bútor	'furniture'
alabástrom	'alabaster'	búvár[53]	'diver'
album	'album'	csarnak	'ship rope'
állag	'stock'	csarnok	'hall'
állapot	'state of affairs'	császár[54]	'emperor'
angyal	'angel'	csomor	'wart'
áram	'current'	dallam	'melody'
asztal	'table'	faktor	'factor'
balzsam	'balsam'	faktótum	'handyman'
fátum	'fate'	kosbor	'orchid'
folyam	'river'	naptávol	'aphelion'
futam	'vocal run'	oltár	'altar'
gádor	'cellar entrance'	oszlop	'pillar'
hajnal	'dawn'	osztag	'squad'
határ	'boundary'	ótvar	'eczema'
homlok	'forehead'	paplan	'quilt'
idom	'form'	polgár	'citizen'
jávor	'maple tree'	roham	'attack'
kántor	'cantor'	rovar	'insect'

---

[52] The possession of this noun is primarily one of a part-whole relation within an inherent structure, such as a house, and thus takes the -V inalienable possessive allomorph as the unmarked case. The possessive form *ablak-ja* would denote a more distant, animate possessor, such as *someone's* window. A declarative schema that can capture such semantic relational differences in possession can explain the seemingly exceptional behavior of this and other nouns.

[53] Péter Siptár notes that the form *búvár-a* is used in the specialized meaning of 'someone deeply involved in studying a subject, e.g., *a történelem búvára* "the diver" of history, someone who studies history very deeply.' The possessive form *búvár-ja* would be the diving company's diver. A difference perhaps due to inalienable vs. alienable possession.

[54] According to Farkas & Alberti (2016), 'rulers of nations can be considered to be encoded in language as inalienable parts of their nations.' Thus selection of the inalienable possessive variant -V based on semantics overrides the phonological generalization.

(11) Front vowel roots with exceptional glide-initial allomorph
   a. Monosyllabic roots (all inclusive)

bég	'Turkish governor'	din	'dyne'
brit	'Britisher'	dzsem	'jam'
*cél[55]	'target'	dzsip	'jeep'
cet	'whale'	dzsinn	'genie'
csép	'flail'	flip	'flip'
*csík	'strip'	fríg	'Phrygian'
*csín	'neatness'	géb	'goby'
csőd	'bankruptcy'	gél	'fruit jelly'
csüd	'instep'	gén	'gene'
csűr	'barn'	gém	'heron'
pléd	'rug type'	sín	'rail'
prém	'fur'	*síp	'whistle'
prím	'prime number'	*sír	'grave'
rét	'meadow'	spin	'spin'
rőf	'yard measure'	szlem	'slam in cards'
séf	'chef'	stíl	'style'
stég	'landing stage'	sül	'porcupine'
gím	'hind of deer'	*kín	'pain'
gir	'symmetry axis'	kög	'disc flower'
gőg	'arrogance'	kőr	'hearts'
gyep	'lawn'	krém	'cream'
*gyík	'lizard'	len	'flax'
*híd[56]	'bridge'	méd	'Mede'
hím	'male animal'	mén	'stallion'
*ír	'balm'	pék	'baker'
ír	'Irishman'	píp	'pip'
kén	'sulphur'	*pír	'blush'
sün	'hedgehog'	trén	'baggage train'
svéd	'Swede'	űr	'void'

---

55 * denotes anti-harmonic front vowel roots that select back vowel suffixes. These vowels act as if they are back and thus follow the rule of back vowel roots selecting the -jV allomorph.

56 Though *híd* is anti-harmonic, it is also a lowering root: *híd-at* 'bridge. accusative', which would normally select for the -V allomorph. The more marked characteristic of being anti-harmonic takes precedence here.

szér	'frame'	zűr	'mix-up'
szír	'Syrian'	*zsír	'fat/grease'
szvit	'music suite'		
tét	'wager'		

b. Polysyllabic roots (non-exhaustive)

*acél[57]	'steel'	deficit	'deficit'
*afrik	'seaweed'	delén	'delaine'
*adrenalin	'adrenaline'	ebéd	'lunch'
allűr	'behavior'	ecet	'vinegar'
belég	'voucher'	előd	'predecessor'
bifsztek	'steak'	erőd	'fortress'
citrin	'citrine'	etil	'ethyl'
cölöp	'stake'	fenilén	'phenylene'
csembők	'glomerule'	fenyér	'health'
decibel	'decibel'	fibrin	'fibrin'
*fluorid	'fluoride'	karusszel	'carousel'
*gallér	'collar'	klarinét	'clarinet'
gobelin	'tapestry'	koncér	'whitefish'
gravűr	'engraving'	kosztüm	'suit'
hematit	'hematite'	köcsög	'pitcher'
hermelin	'ermine'	menyét	'weasel'
hidrogén	'hydrogen'	motel	'motel'
hörcsög	'hamster'	parfüm	'perfume'
*Judit	'Judith'		
*kabin	'cabin'		

From a cursory glance, it appears that the exceptions are quite numerous. However, it will be shown in the following section that various words are derived by productive and non-productive morphemes or what were once historically morphemes where the visibility of the internal structure has been lost. Such phonological shapes can be identified by the learner and associated with one of the specific allomorphs. Moreover, the semantics of certain words that are encoded as inalienable in the language effects the choice of allomorph as well. The concept of inalienable nouns is also recognized by speakers in determining

---

[57] Here, in the polysyllabic group, the * denotes roots where the head vowel is not the final vowel of the stem as the final vowel is transparent to harmony. The preceding back vowel is the head of the root as it selects for back harmonic vowel suffixes and would thus follow the rule of back vowel headed roots selecting the -jV allomorph.

the choice of variant and can thus override phonological generalizations. Such pieces of information can be bundled into cognitive declarative schemas that the learner constructs.

3 Family Resemblance/Relational Schema Approach

To sum up the facts presented in Section 2 regarding which allomorph is selected by which nouns, we have observed a number of categorical phonological contexts requiring one allomorph over the other, such as nouns ending in a vowel, nouns ending in a sibilant or palatal consonant and nouns ending in two consonants. Also noted were certain closed classes of nouns that selected for the vowel-initial variant. A theoretical analysis of the phonological generalization regarding final-vowel quality of ... CVC nouns and choice of possessive variant was presented, noting the existence of exceptions. Semantics was then also noted as playing a role in allomorph selection, especially where certain nouns have an inherent inalienable relation to a possessor and thus occur in the unmarked case with the vowel-initial variant.[58] In the next section, the effect of morpho-syntactic nominal affixes in the selection of possessive variant, especially with respect to such -VC exceptions, will be addressed.

3.1 The Addition of Morpho-syntactic Information

Morpho-syntactic categorical structures have also been found to display preferences for one variant over the other. As Kiefer (1985: 104) has pointed out there are a number of noun-forming derivational suffixes that also determine the choice of suffix variant. He notes that the *j*-initial variant does not appear after the suffix *-ság/-ség* nor does it occur after the suffix *-dék*, except in a few instances (e.g., *szálladék* 'sublimate'/*szálladék-ja* 'poss.', *szerdék* 'booty (obs.)'/*szerdék-je*). Furthermore, according to Kiefer, the suffix *-hatnék/hetnék* always requires the *j*-initial variant of the suffix. There is also the derivational affix *–(a)ték* that selects

---

[58] Such occurrence is in keeping with generalizations made regarding conceptual distance between a noun and its possessor being related to markedness of structural shape, i.e., inalienable possession tends to be of a simpler, unmarked, morphological form, which in Hungarian would be the vowel-initial variant. (Cf. Seiler 1983; Chappell and McGregor 1996; Haspelmath 2008).

for the -V allomorph, as in the following possessive forms: *érték-e* 'value' < *ér* 'be worth (sg)', *hagyaték-a* 'legacy' < *hagy* 'to leave/allow', *fogyaték-a* 'deficiency' < *fogy* 'to decrease', *lépték-e* 'scale' < *lép* 'to step', *mérték-e* 'measurement' < *mér* 'to measure', et alia.

Ritter (2002) noted additional morphemes which consistently occur with one of the possessive suffix variants and not the other. For example, words ending in *-tróp, -szkóp, -sztát, -plán, -gram, -tron*, are always followed by the *j*-initial suffix variant (e.g., *anemoszkóp* 'anemoscope', *baroszkóp* 'baroscope', *endoszkóp* 'endoscope', *filantróp* 'philanthropist', *heliotróp* 'heliotrope', *mizantróp* 'misanthrope', *heliosztát* 'heliostat', *hidroplán* 'sea-plane', *monoplán* 'monoplane', *kardiogram* 'cardiogram', *mikrotron* 'microtron', *ciklotron* 'cyclotron', *elektron* 'electron', et alia). Another back-vowel morpheme that consistently occurs with the *j*-initial suffix variant is *-gráf* (e.g., *ciklográf* 'cyclograph', *anemográf* 'anemograph', *asztrográf* 'astrograph', *autográf* 'autograph', *diagráf* 'diagraph', *diktográf* 'dictograph', *heliográf* 'heliograph', et alia).[59] Since the final vowel of these morphemes is back, they also may be following the generalization discussed above regarding back vowels and the *j*-initial suffix variant. A tendency has also been noticed with regard to deverbalized nouns formed by the suffix *-at/et*. The majority of these nouns co-occur with the vowel-initial variant of the possessive, despite the quality of the final vowel of the stem (e.g., *élet* 'life' < *él* 'to live', *emelet* 'upper story' < *emel* 'to lift', *adat* 'facts' < *ad* 'to give', *gondolat* 'thought' < *gondol* 'to think', *felelet* 'answer' < *felel* 'to answer', *akarat* 'wish' < *akar* 'to want', *áradat* 'deluge' < *árad* 'to flood', *ékezet* 'accent (in writing)' < *ékez* 'to mark with an accent', *kapcsolat* 'connection' < *kapcsol* 'to connect', *mondat* 'sentence' < *mond* 'to say', *méret* 'measurement, size' < *mér* 'to measure', etc.). Similarly, the derivational suffix *-d*, which typically forms fractions from numerals, regularly is followed by the vowel-initial variant of the possessive despite the quality of the stem-final vowel (e.g., *ötöd* 'fifth', *heted* 'seventh', *kilenced* 'ninth', *harmad* 'third', *nyolcvanad* 'ninetieth', *század* 'century', *hányad* 'share, portion', et alia). The suffix *-dik*, which also attaches to numerals, but creates ordinal numbers, similarly takes only the vowel-initial suffix variant of the possessive (i.e., *harmadik* 'third', *negyedik* 'fourth', *hatodik* 'sixth', *hányadik* 'which, how many-eth', and so forth). Although this morpheme contains what appears to be a front vowel, this vowel is transparent (cf. *harmadik-at* 'acc.') and plays no role in the harmonic selection of the front/back quality of the following suffix vowel. Moreover, as can be seen from the preceding example, the morpheme *-dik* converts the root mor-

---

[59] While these may look like possible compound words, there are no independent words with these phonological shapes.

pheme into a lowering stem (cf. *hat* 'six'/*hat-ot* 'accusative' vs. *hatodik* 'sixth'/ *hatodik-at* 'accusative'). These data yield further evidence to support the fact that lowering stems occur with the vowel-initial variant of the possessive suffix.

Another suffix noticed to occur only with the vowel-initial suffix is *-nok/- nök* despite the fact that *-nok* has a back vowel. This can be seen in possessive examples such as, *hírnök-e* 'herald' < *hír* 'news', *írnok-a* 'clerk' < *ír* 'write', *gondnok-a* 'guardian' < *gond* 'care/worry', *döntnök-e* 'judge' < *dönt* 'overturn', *dalnok-a* 'singer' < *dal* 'song', *hivatalnok-a* 'state official' < *hivatal* 'office', *parancsnok-a* 'commander' < *parancs* 'order', etc. Similarly, the noun-ending *-nár*, which appears on a number of bound root nouns and has an agentive sense, is always followed by the -V variant despite that it has a back vowel, e.g., *bodnár-a* 'cooper', *bognár-a* 'wainwright', and *kasznár-a* 'bailiff'. Another morpheme-like entity is *-(i)um*, which, despite having a final back vowel, typically occurs with the vowel-initial allomorph (*abszolútum-a* 'absolute', *agglomerátum-a* 'agglomerate', *atribútum-a* 'attribute', *baktérium-a* 'microbe', *fixum-a* 'fixed salary', *gimnázium-a* 'high school', *kollégium-a* 'college', *publikum-a* 'audience', among many more).[60] Similarly, the morpheme shapes *-tor, -or, -ior* select the -V variant despite having a final back vowel (*adminisztrátor-a* 'administrator', *akcelerátor-a* 'accelerator', *dekorátor-a* 'decorator', *generátor-a* 'generator', *ekvátor-a* 'equator', *kollektor-a* 'collector', *professzor-a* 'professor', *szektor-a* 'sector', among many others).[61] Ritter (2002) noted that 87% of words ending in *-tor* are followed by the vowel-initial variant. Kiefer (1985: 103) claims that " . . . nouns ending in *-tor, -ter, -er, -um* which were *borrowed earlier* [emphasis added], in general, take *-a/-e*." With respect to words ending in *-ter* and *-er*, Ritter (2002) found that 80% of the total of such words are followed by the vowel-initial variant.[62] This is not such a surprising pattern since the final vowel of such words is front *e*, which accordingly should occur with the vowel-initial variant of the suffix, following the phonological generalization cited above.

---

[60] Nine exceptions were found where the noun ending in *-(i)um* selects the -jV allomorph: *aggregátum-ja* 'aggregate', *oposszum-ja* 'opossum', *ammónium-ja* 'ammonium', *duodenum-ja* 'duodenum', *faktum-ja* 'fact', *bárium-ja* 'barium', *auditórium-ja* 'auditorium', *kvantum-ja* 'quantum', *lórum-ja* 'type of card game'.

[61] Eight exceptions were found where the noun ending in *-tor* selects the -jV allomorph instead. These are *akkumulátor-ja* 'storage battery', *duplikátor-ja* 'duplicator', *aszpirátor-ja* 'aspirator', *gátor-ja* 'lattice', *monitor-ja* 'monitor', *pásztor-ja* 'shepherd', *imposztor-ja* 'imposter', *viviszektor-ja* 'vivisector'.

[62] Considering that *-er* is the second most frequent VC sequence across all words, according to Grimes (2010), with a token frequency of 5,199,034, 80% of such words occurring with the vowel-initial variant is quite a large set.

Kiefer further claims that newer borrowed words with these endings will either opt for the more productive *-ja/-je* ending or will take the *-a/-e* ending due to analogical pressure from established word patterns. This idea of analogical patterning throughout the nominal system in Hungarian with respect to possessive allomorph selection is very much operative and can be captured by schematic cognitive structures as will be seen below. An example of such patterning can be seen with the derivational suffix *-al* that selects for the -V allomorph, as in *fonal*[63]*-a* 'yarn' < *fon* 'to spin', *huzal-a* 'cable' < *húz* 'to pull', *vonal-a* 'line' < *von* 'to draw/pull', *hozatal-a* 'delivery' < *hoz* 'to bring', *behozatal-a* 'imported goods' < *behoz* 'to bring in'. By analogy, other nouns ending in *-al*, which don't have a clear, independent base root follow the same pattern of selecting the vowel-initial variant of the possessive: *asztal-a* 'table', *hajnal-a* 'dawn', *nappal-a* 'daytime', *angyal-a* 'angel', *oldal*[64]*-a* 'side', *viadal-a*, 'fight'.[65] Similarly, the noun-forming morpheme *-am*, though containing a back vowel, selects the vowel-initial variant, as in *állam-a* 'state' < *áll* 'to stand', *dallam-a* 'melody' < *dal* 'song', *folyam-a* 'river' < *folyik* 'to flow', *futam-a* 'vocal run' < *fut* 'to run', *hozam-a* 'revenue' < *hoz* 'to bring', *huzam-a* 'in a single stretch' < *húz* 'to draw/pull', *roham-a* 'assault' < *ró* 'to cut', *tartam-a* 'duration' < *tart* 'sustain'. By analogy, the monomorpheme *balzsam-a* 'balsam' also takes the -V allomorph, as does the morphologically complex *párhuzam-a* 'parallel'.[66]

(12) Morpho-syntactic affix selection of the possessive:

-V variant	-jV variant
-ság/ség	-hatnék/hetnék
-dék	-gráf
-(a)ték	-gram
-at/et	-szkóp
-al	-sztát
-am	-tróp

---

[63] *fonal* is also a lowering stem: *fonal-at* 'accus.'.
[64] This is a lowering stem noun: *oldal-ak* 'side.plural'.
[65] Four exceptions were found to select for the -jV variant: *Antal-ja* 'Anthony', *aval-ja* 'aval', *fagyal-ja* 'privet (kind of shrub)', *pacal-ja* 'tripe'. These are exceptions to the analogy with the morpho-syntactic pattern; however, they do follow the phonological generalization of root with final back vowel selecting for the -jV variant.
[66] Two words were found with *-am* ending that select for the -jV variant: *program-ja* 'program' and *volfram-ja* 'wolfram'. Since *-am* is part of the morpho-phonological shape *-gram*, which selects for the -jV variant, it may be that speakers construe this *-am* of *program* to follow the behavior of *-gram* by analogy, though there is no semantic correlation with *-gram* in that word. Typically nouns ending in *-ám* select the -jV variant.

-d   -tron
-dik   -plán
-nok/nök
-nár
-(á)tor, (t)or/(t)er
-(i)um

3.2 Relational Schemas

Schemas are cognitive structures in the lexicon that an individual creates in order to organize elements of knowledge acquired through experience in understanding the composition and behavior of words. Such word schemas are comprised of pieces of linguistic knowledge, such as semantics, morpho-syntactic structure, phonological composition/context. These pieces of information can be relationally linked to other words that share that same information. In this way, parallelism among stored items in the lexicon capture certain generalizations that can be identified and can be used to explain what previously have been considered exceptional and/or non-productive patterns. There is no notion of derivation in declarative schema theory, nor any concept of there being an input, some procedure, and then an output, as there is in rule-based theory. Jackendoff and Audring (2019a: 395) note that there are many 'composite items' in language that cannot be constructed by applying general rules. They include, as an example, words that may have an identifiable affix, yet the base roots of such words are not independent morphemes from which to derive such complex words, as seen with bound roots or cranberry morphemes. An example of identifiable affixes with bound roots in the case of Hungarian would fall under the $-(i)um$ type affix, where, for example, *impérium* 'empire' looks like a complex word composed of a root and affix -$(i)um$, due to the fact that this affix occurs so often in the language. However, the base *impér* is not an independent root in the language. Based on the relational schematic approach of Jackendoff and Audring (2019a, 2019b), there would be a schema encoding information for the entire word (13a) as well as a schema for the affix that would be shared by all similar *-ium* items:

(13) *impérium* 'empire'
    a. Semantics: $EMPIRE_1$ b. [N -ium] schema
        Morphsyntax: $[_N - aff_2]_1$ Semantics: $[ENTITY]_y$
        Phonology: /imper ium_2/$_1$ Morphosyntax: $[_N - aff_2]_y$
                                                       Phonology: / . . . $(i)um_2$/$_y$

The co-index 1 in (13a) links the three levels of the word together. The co-index 2 links the morpho-syntactic affix to its phonological structure.[67] The category of the bound root is blank as its category status cannot be determined due to its absence of distribution in the phrasal syntax. The fact that the affix has no semantics of its own designated in its schema in (13b) hinges on the fact that its base has no semantics of its own and therefore it is impossible to say to what sense of the meaning of 'empire' the affix contributes. The schema for the affix would then be linked to all word schemas that share that piece of information, as in *adverbium* 'adverb', *afélium* 'aphelium', *affixum* 'affix', *akvárium* 'aquarium', *stipendium* 'scholarship', *szilencium* 'suspension', *terrénum* 'domain', among many others.

Since Hungarian is an agglutinative language, one affix schema can be related to another affix schema. As was discussed in Section 3.1 above, the affix *–(i)um* typically co-occurs with the vowel-initial variant of the possessive suffix. The relational schemas would be as follows:

(14) Schema for the possessive vowel-initial allomorph
      [N -V] schema
      Semantics: [INALIENABLE POSSESSION $[X]_x]_z$
      Morphosyntax: $[_N - aff_2]_x\, aff_3]_z$
      Phonology: $/ \ldots (i)um_2/_x\, a_3]_z$

The schema in (14) denotes that the vowel-initial variant of the possessive, which is also associated with the property of inalienable possession, combines with all words with the affix *–(i)um*.

Similarly, looking at words ending in *-szkóp* that are typically followed by the *-jV* allomorph, first we would have a schema for a word with this affix, such as *baroszkóp* 'baroscope' (15a), then we would have a schema for the affix *-szkóp* itself (15b) and finally a schema for the possessive *-jV* variant (15c).

(15) *baroszkóp* 'baroscope'
      a. Semantics: $BAROSCOPE_6$ b. [N -szkóp] schema
         Morphosyntax: $[_N - aff_5]_6$ Semantics: $[INSTRUMENT]_a$
         Phonology: $/baro\ szkóp_5/_6$ Morphosyntax: $[_N - aff_5\,]_a$
                                              Phonology: $/ \ldots szkóp_5/_a$

---

[67] Jackendoff and Audring (2019a, 2019b) discuss various ways of co-indexing and use of variables. The formalization is not taken up as a matter of concern in this article. What is crucial is that instances are directly related to each other and linked in some conventional way through co-indexation.

c. [N -jV] schema
   Semantics: [ALIENABLE POSSESSION [X]$_b$]$_c$
   Morphosyntax: [$_N$ – aff$_5$]$_b$ aff$_7$]$_c$
   Phonology: / ... szkóp$_5$/$_b$ jV$_7$]$_c$

The schema in (15b) relates words, such as *baroszkóp* to all other *-szkóp* nouns regardless of the independence of the base root. The schema in (15c) then states that there are nouns ending with the affix *-szkóp*, denoting properties of some kind of instrument, that will co-occur with the -jV variant, which also denotes alienable possession.

Such an approach that links morpho-syntactic structures to phonological shapes can capture generalizations among words that would normally be considered exceptional with respect to categorically productive natural rules or would fall under non-productive, closed classes. Given that the morphosyntactic structure does not necessarily have to contain clear, identifiable word bases that correlate with specific semantic properties, words, nonetheless, are still assumed to have structure allowing schematic relations to include phonological shapes that look like affixes but have no semantic content of their own, primarily due to their base having no independent, free form. For example, there are many words in Hungarian with the ending *-it* that go against the phonological generalization, discussed in Section 2.2, of a final front-vowel selecting for the *j*-less allomorph (*adamit-ja* 'adamite', *affidavit-ja* 'affidavit', *albit-ja* 'albite', *brit-je* 'British person', *cisztolit-ja* 'cystolith', *csalit-ja* 'shrubbery', *deficit-je* 'deficit', *dinamit-ja* 'dynamite', *explicit-je* 'explicit', *favorit-ja* 'favorite', *gambit-ja* 'gambit', *gránit-ja* 'granite', *invit-je* 'invitation', *Judit-ja* 'Judith', *kárpit-ja* 'curtain', *keramit-ja* 'glazed tile', *licit-je* 'auction', *Margit-ja* 'Margaret', *megalit-ja* 'megalith', *profit-ja* 'profit', *vizit-je* 'visit', *szvit-je* 'musical suite', *tranzit-ja* 'transit', among others).[68] While Kiefer (1985: 103, 109) pointed out that recent loan words typically select for the -jV allomorph, an approach that takes family resemblance into account can more accurately and specifically account for such a sweeping generalization. In the case of final *-it*, the suffix can denote an array of items, such as minerals, fossils, chemical compounds, and explosives. By analogy, however, other words with such phonological ending also follow the pattern of selecting for the -jV variant. Schematic relations can then be constructed in the learner's mind linking the morpho-phonological structure *-it* of the noun with the -jV possessive allomorph.

---

[68] Only three exceptions were found where *-it* selects for the vowel-initial variant. These are *felzit-e* 'felsite', *hit-e* 'belief', *porfirit-e* 'porphyrite'.

(16) *dinamit* 'dynamite'
    a. Semantics: DYNAMITE$_{10}$ b. [N -it] schema
        Morphosyntax: [$_N$ – aff$_{11}$]$_{10}$ Semantics: [PROPERTY]$_f$
        Phonology: /dinam it$_{11}$/$_{10}$ Morphosyntax: [$_N$ – aff$_{11}$]$_f$
                                                                            Phonology: /... it $_{11}$/$_f$

    c. [N -jV] schema
        Semantics: [ALIENABLE POSSESSION [X]$_h$]$_c$
        Morphosyntax: [$_N$ – aff$_{11}$]$_h$ aff$_7$]$_c$
        Phonology: / ... it $_{11}$/$_h$ jV$_7$]$_c$

The coindex h in (16c) denotes a relational link with any word that has the same pattern of structure, i.e., any word ending in *-it*.

Other morpho-phonological structures have also been found to occur with the -jV variant, contra the generalization regarding final front-vowels occurring with the -V variant. Some of these are *-ér*, *-id*, *-in*, *-il*, *-üC*, *-űC* (*Albin-ja* 'Albin', *allűr-je* 'behavior', *amid-ja* 'amide', *bibliofil-je* 'bibliophile', *bordűr-je* 'fringe', *brazil-ja* 'Brazilian', *aneurin-ja* 'aneurin', *aszpirin-je* 'aspirin', *attitűd-je* 'attitude', *automobil-ja* 'automobile', *babér-ja* 'laurel', *beduin-ja* 'beduin', *Benjámin-ja* 'Benjamin', *chagrin-ja* 'chagrin', *csüd-je* 'in-step', *csűr-je* 'barn', *fenyér-je* 'health', *furnér-ja* 'veneer', *gallér-ja* 'collar', *gavallér-ja* 'cavalier', *gin-je* 'gin', *glukozid-ja* 'glucoside', *gravűr-je* 'engraving' *hibrid-je* 'hybrid', *kabin-ja* 'cabin', *klotűr-je* 'closure', *kommün-je* 'commune', *koncér-ja* 'whitefish', *kosztüm-je* 'suit', *sül-je* 'porcupine', *sün-je* 'hedgehog', *szér-je* 'frame', *űr-je* 'void', *valkür-je* 'Valkyrie', *zselatin-ja* 'gelatin', *zűr-je* 'mix-up', *zsanér-ja* 'hinge', et alia).[69] While there are a few nouns ending with *-ér* that do follow the phonological rule of final front-vowel selecting the vowel-initial possessive variant, these would fall under a *productive* type schema, which would contain a *generative* function in addition to the relational function discussed above. Jackendoff and Audring (2019a: 399) consider productive and non-productive schemas to be similar, aside from the fact that the former also allows for on-line construction of items. They note that there is no principled distinction between these two sorts of schemas, aside from a diacritic on their variables expressing their degree of openness. "All schemas – productive or unproductive – have a **relational** function, in which they link to existing lexical items stored in the lexicon and capture generalizations among them." The combinatorial procedure of unification combines pieces of information from different

---

69 Very few exceptions have been found where these morpho-phonological pieces of information occur with the vowel-initial variant of the possessive. They are *szil-e* 'elm tree', *rüh-e* 'itch', *ük-e* 'great-great-grandparent', *szűk-e* 'shortage', *nikkelin-e* 'copper nickel'.

declarative templates. For instance, the phonological explanatory representation presented in (8) in Section 2.2 could simply be stated as a positive constraint in which the vowel-initial variant of the possessive occurs after -VC# of a noun, where V is a front vowel. This is captured in the schema below:

(17) Productive schema for vowel-initial allomorph
Semantics: [INALIENABLE POSSESSION ([NOUN]$_x$)]$_y$
Morphosyntax: [N$_x$, Poss$_{1*}$]$_y$
Phonology: [/ ... V$_{(+Frnt)}$C/$_x$ V$_{1*}$] /$_y$

The morpho-syntax of this possessive variant and its phonology are linked by the co-index 1. The asterisk denotes its open productive nature under the specific context. This coindex can form a relational link with any word that has the same pattern of structure. The co-index for the noun (x) also forms a relational link with any word that has the same stated pattern of structure. Therefore, given the schema for the noun *bér* 'wage', a new schema for *bér-e* (18b) will be created directly from the two schemas, (18a) and (17), that motivate it.

(18) a. *bér* 'wage'
    Semantics: WAGE$_{10}$
    Morphosyntax: N$_{10}$
    Phonology: /ber/

b. *bére* 'wage.poss.'
    Semantics: [POSSESSION (WAGE)$_{10}$]$_y$
    Morphosyntax: [N$_{10}$ Poss$_{1*}$]$_y$
    Phonology: /**ber**$_{10}$ e$_{1*}$/$_y$

For those non-productive, exceptional nouns ending in -*ér* that occur with the -jV allomorph, their schema structures will be different in that – *ér* will be mentally construed as an affix with which the -jV variant will co-occur.[70]

(19) a. *gallér* 'collar'
    Semantics: [COLLAR$_{12}$]$_z$
    Morphosyntax: [$_N$ – aff$_{13}$]$_z$
    Phonology: /gal er$_{13}$/$_z$

b. [N -ér] schema
    Semantics: [PROPERTY]$_g$
    Morphosyntax: [$_N$ – aff$_{13}$]$_g$
    Phonology: / ... er$_{13}$/$_g$

c. [N -jV] general schema
    Semantics: [ALIENABLE POSSESSION [X]$_h$]$_c$
    Morphosyntax: [$_N$ – aff$_{13}$]$_h$ aff$_7$]$_c$
    Phonology: / ... er $_{13}$/$_h$ jV$_7$]$_c$

---

[70] This is plausible as there are no monosyllables with -*ér* followed by the -jV variant.

d. *gallérja* 'collar.poss.' schema
   Semantics: [ALIENABLE POSSESSION [gallér]$_{12}$]$_c$
   Morphosyntax: [$_N$ – aff$_{13}$]$_{12}$ aff$_7$]$_c$
   Phonology: /gal er $_{13}$/$_{12}$ jV$_7$]$_c$

This schema approach that incorporates a productive aspect as well as a relational one and that appeals to the idea of morpho-phonological family resemblance, challenges previous claims that "the phonological shape of the stem underdetermines the allomorph selection" (Rebrus, Szigetvári, and Törkenczy 2017; Rácz and Rebrus 2012).

While Jackendoff and Audring (2019a, 2019b) focus heavily on the link between morpho-syntax and phonology, a third piece of information of a schema, namely, the semantic component can also be recognized by the learner to co-occur with one of the possessive allomorphs versus the other. At the end of Section 2.2, it was pointed out that many of the final -CC nouns that exceptionally occurred with the vowel-initial allomorph belonged to the semantically related domain referring to the body and its parts: *áll-a* 'chin', *váll-a* 'shoulder', *szakáll-a* 'beard', *fark-a* 'tail', *ujj-a* 'finger', *talp-a* 'sole', *toll-a* 'feather', *térd-e* 'knee', *test-e* 'body', *mell-e* 'chest', *orr-a* 'nose', *hüvelyk-e* 'thumb, inch', *segg-e* 'buttocks', *szív-e* 'heart', *bél-e* 'bowels',[71] *nyelv-e* 'tongue'.[72] Many of these nouns, but not all, also fall under the category of lowering stems, which categorically select for the vowel-initial allomorph. Moreover, several -VC nouns within the same semantic domain that contain a final back-vowel behave exceptionally in that they select for the -V variant: *fog-a* 'tooth', *nyak-a* 'neck', *hát-a* 'back', *homlok-a* 'forehead', *garat-a* 'pharynx'.[73] Given that the vowel-initial variant of the possessive can denote inalienable possession, the use of this variant in the unmarked case indicating an inherent relation between such nouns and their host is logical despite whether it lines up with the phonological rules of the language. However, a schematic approach is able to capture this cognitive understanding simply because the semantics is incorporated into the mental codification of words. A possible schema for *fog-a* 'tooth.poss.' would be created from the shared parts of the schema for *fog* and the schema for the -V allomorph of inalienable possession.

---

[71] Belongs to shortening stems: *bél* → *bele* in possessive, similar to words such as *madár* 'bird' → *madara* in possessive.
[72] Exceptions include *csont-ja* 'bone.poss.'.
[73] The noun *kar* 'arm', however, follows the phonological pattern selecting for the -jV variant. This may be due to the fact that there is another *kar* noun in the language meaning 'staff, body, profession' that already occurs with the vowel-initial variant.

(20) a. *fog* 'tooth'
　　　　Semantics:　　　[TOOTH (BODY PART)$_\alpha$]$_m$
　　　　Morphosyntax:　N$_m$
　　　　Phonology:　　　/fog/$_m$

　　b. [N -V] schema
　　　　Semantics:　　　[INALIENABLE POSSESSION [X (BODY PART)$_\alpha$]$_x$]$_z$
　　　　Morphosyntax:　[$_N$ N $_\alpha$]$_x$ aff$_3$]$_z$
　　　　Phonology:　　　/ … $_\alpha$ /$_x$ a$_3$]$_z$

　　c. *fog-a* 'tooth.poss.' schema
　　　　Semantics:　　　[INALIENABLE POSSESSION [fog $_\alpha$] $_m$]$_z$
　　　　Morphosyntax:　[fog $_\alpha$] $_m$ aff$_3$]$_z$
　　　　Phonology:　　　/fog $_\alpha$ /$_m$ a$_3$]$_z$

The idea of rules operating at different levels or cycles does not come into play in this approach. Rather, information or experience that the learner has gleaned is organized in these types of schematic templates in the learner's mind as a way to respond to the complex data that the learner is confronted with. The learner perceives morphological, semantic, and phonological cognitive patterns and encodes relationships among words that fall into certain patterns.[74] This includes idiosyncratic closed classes of nouns that behave in certain patterns. Lack of space does not permit further exposition of this approach with respect to the various closed classes noted in Section 2.2.

4 Conclusions

The third person possessive singular morpheme in Hungarian has been a topic of discussion and debate for decades. Phonological rules have been proposed citing certain contexts where one allomorph or the other is selected. Kiefer (1985) has noted an array of other factors that contribute to the selection of allomorph, such as type of morphological affix in a complex word, the existence of homonymy, and whether a stem is of an older layer of the language or a more recent borrowing. The question of what constitutes a recent borrowing, such as in which time

---

[74] See Jackendoff and Audring (2019a: 400) for further explication regarding learnability of schemas.

frame the word entered,[75] and how a learner acquiring the language would know that a word is a recent borrowing has not been addressed.

A learner, building up their lexicon, relies on the instances of pieces of information they come across during their experience. In choosing a possessive allomorph, phonology clearly plays a role for certain noun sets, such as closed classes of nouns, nouns ending in sibilant or palatal consonants, nouns ending in vowels, nouns ending in geminate consonants. However, morphosyntactic information has shown to play a role as has semantics. The totality of this information that the learner has about a certain noun allows the learner to select the appropriate allomorph. Nouns ending in -VC that are non-sibilant/non-palatal have been especially labelled as arbitrary with respect to allomorph selection. Rácz and Rebrus (2012) have explained the arbitrariness of such nouns' selection as analogical pressure exerted by the verbal definite paradigm. The approach of relational schemas taken up in this paper also incorporates the notion of analogy but instead of deferring to independent terms belonging to a different category with an affix that has a different function, the pieces of knowledge acquired for a certain noun are linked to the same pieces of information found in other nouns that have similar morpho-phonological entities or semantics. The approach of relational schemas uses the conventional notation of co-indexing to indicate the relational links made by a speaker. Relational links have been shown to occur across the semantics as well as morphosyntax. Moreover, pieces of information that may seem like bases but have no independent meaning nor category can also be relationally linked and have been shown to connect words in the mind of the speaker to form a family of lexical items that together behave in a certain way, an association which might not have been connected under other approaches. In this way, the exceptional/arbitrary behavior of nouns with respect to allomorph selection can be better understood and may well reduce the burden of having to memorize a large amount of exceptional items that seem totally arbitrary.

---

75 Nádasdy (1989: 195), in his discussion of borrowed consonant lengthening, considers 'recent' borrowings into the language to be words that have been borrowed 'since about 1750.' Zaicz (1982: 56) claims that elements of Old Hungarian, occurring after the settlement, date to the end of the 16th century. Are borrowings subsequent to that date then considered 'recent' or 'foreign'? Kertész (2003: 64), in her discussion of loanword vowel harmony, considers 'recent' 'to refer to elements that have become part of the vocabulary in the last 50–100 years'. While Csapó (1971: 27) in discussing English sporting terminology in Hungarian, points to terms as early as 1895. This points out that there is no consensus with respect to a firm definition of which words fall under 'recent' or would be marked as [+foreign].

References

Ameka, Felix. 1992. Interjections: The universal yet neglected part of speech. *Journal of Pragmatics* 18(2-3). 101-118.
Chappell, Hilary & William McGregor. 1996. Prolegomena to a theory of inalienability. In H. Chappell & W. McGregor (eds.), *The Grammar of Inalienability: A Typological Perspective on Body Part Terms and the Part-Whole Relation*, 3-30. Berlin: Mouton de Gruyter.
Cohn, Abigail C. & Margaret E. Renwick. 2021. Embracing multidimensionality in phonological analysis. *The Linguistic Review* 38(1). 101-139.
Csapó, József. 1971. English sporting terminology in Hungarian: A study of the processes of assimilation and rejection. *Hungarian Studies in English* 5. 5-50.
Den Dikken, Marcel. 2015. On the morphosyntax of (in)alienably possessed noun phrases. In Katalin É. Kiss, Balázs Surányi & Éva Dékány (eds.), *Approaches to Hungarian: Papers from the 2013 Piliscsaba Conference*, vol. 14, 121-145.
Elekfi, László. 2000. Semantic differences of suffixal alternates in Hungary. *Acta Linguistica Hungarica* 47(1). 144-177.
Farkas, Judit & Gábor Alberti. 2016. The relationship between (in) alienable possession and the (three potential) forms of possessed nouns in Hungarian. *Linguistica* 56(1). 111-125.
Grimes, Stephen M. 2010. *Quantitative investigations in Hungarian phonotactics and syllable structure*. Bloomington: Indiana University PhD dissertation.
Harris, John. 1998. Licensing inheritance: An integrated theory of neutralisation. *Phonology* 14(3). 315-370.
Haspelmath, Martin. 2008. Syntactic universals and usage frequency: 3. Alienable vs. inalienable possessive constructions. Lecture. Leipzig Spring School on Linguistic Diversity, Leipzig.
Hulst, Harry van der. 2018. *Asymmetries in Vowel Harmony: A Representational Account*. Oxford: Oxford University Press.
Hulst, Harry van der. 2020. *Principles of Radical CV Phonology: A Theory of Segmental and Syllable Structure*. Edinburgh: Edinburgh University Press.
Jackendoff, Ray & Jenny Audring. 2019a. Relational morphology in the parallel architecture. In Jenny Audring & Francesca Masini (eds.), *The Oxford Handbook of Morphological Theory*, 390-408. Oxford: Oxford University Press.
Jackendoff, Ray & Jenny Audring. 2019b. *The Texture of the Lexicon: Relational Morphology and the Parallel Architecture*. Oxford: Oxford University Press.
Kaye, Jonathan. 2014. The ins and outs of phonology. In Sabrina Bendjaballah, Noam Faust, Mohamed Lahrouchi & Nicola Lampitelli (eds.), *The Form of Structure, the Structure of Form*, 255-269. Amsterdam/Philadelphia: John Benjamins.
Keating, Patricia A. 1988. Palatals as complex segments: X-ray evidence. *UCLA Working Papers in Phonetics* 69. 77-91.
Keating Patricia A. & Aditi Lahiri. 1993. Fronted velars, palatized velars, and palatals. *Phonetica* 50(2). 73-101.
Kenesei, István, Robert M. Vago & Anna Fenyvesi. 1998. *Hungarian*, 1st edn. London: Routledge.
Kertész, Zsuzsa. 2003. Vowel harmony and the stratified lexicon of Hungarian. *The Odd Yearbook* 7. 62-77.
Kiefer, Ferenc. 1985. The possessive in Hungarian: A problem for natural morphology. *Acta Linguistica Academiae Scientiarum Hungaricae* 35(1/2). 85-116.

Nádasdy, Adám. 1989. Consonant length in recent borrowings into Hungarian. *Acta Linguistica Hungarica* 39. 1–4.
Ortmann, Albert & Doris Gerland. 2014. She loves you, -ja-ja-ja: Objective conjugation and pragmatic possession in Hungarian. In Doris Gerland, Christian Horn, Anja Latrouite & Albert Ortmann (eds.), *Meaning and Grammar of Nouns and Verbs*, 269–314. Düsseldorf: Düsseldorf University Press.
Papp, Ferenc. 1975. *A magyar főnév paradigmatikus rendszere* [The paradigmatic system of the Hungarian noun]. Budapest: Akadémiai Kiadó.
Rácz, Péter. 2010. *Hungarian phonology and morphology: Discord in the possessive allomorphy of Hungarian*. Budapest: Eötvös Loránd University Master's Thesis.
Rácz, Péter & Péter Rebrus. 2012. Variation in the possessive allomorphy of Hungarian. In Ferenc Kiefer, Mária Ladányi & Péter Siptár (eds.), *Current Issues in Morphological Theory: (Ir)regularity, Analogy and Frequency. Selected Papers from the 14th International Morphology Meeting, Budapest, 13–16 May 2010*, vol. 322, 51. Amsterdam/Philadelphia: John Benjamins.
Rebrus, Péter & Péter Rácz. 2010. Complexity and distinctiveness in the possessive allomorphy of Hungarian. In *Old World Conference in Phonology*, vol. 7.
Rebrus, Péter, Péter Szigetvári & Miklós Törkenczy. 2017. Asymmetric variation. In Geoff Lindsey and Andrew Nevins (eds.), *Sonic Signatures*, vol. 14, 163–187. Amsterdam/Philadelphia: John Benjamins.
Ritter, Nancy A. 1995. *The role of universal grammar in phonology: A Government Phonology approach to Hungarian*. New York: New York University PhD dissertation.
Ritter, Nancy A. 1999. The effect of intrasegmental licensing conditions on elemental spreading. In S. J. Hannahs and Mike Davenport (eds.), *Issues in Phonological Structure*, 53–72. Amsterdam: John Benjamins.
Ritter, Nancy A. 2000. Hungarian voicing assimilation revisited in head-driven phonology. In Gábor Alberti and István Kenesei (eds.), *Approaches to Hungarian*, vol. 7, 23–50. Szeged: JATE Press.
Ritter, Nancy A. 2002. The Hungarian personal possessive suffix revisited. In István Kenesei and Péter Siptár (eds.), *Approaches to Hungarian*, vol. 8, 283–309. Budapest: Akademiai Kiado.
Ritter, Nancy A. & Robert M. Vago. 1999. Subsyllabic constituency in Hungarian: Implications for moraic phonology and government phonology. In John Rennison and Klaus Kühnhammer (eds.), *Phonologica 1996: Syllables!!?. Papers from the Eighth International Phonology Meeting*, 219–245. Leiden: Holland Academic Graphics.
Seiler, Hansjakob. 1983. *Possession as an Operational Dimension of Language*. Tübingen: Narr Verlag.
Siptár, Péter & Miklós Törkenczy. 2000. *The Phonology of Hungarian*. Oxford: Oxford University Press.
Vago, Robert M. 1980. *The Sound Pattern of Hungarian*. Washington, DC: Georgetown University School of Language.
Zaicz, Gábor. 1982. Word-structure and etymology (on the ancient layer of words of unknown origin in the Hungarian language). *Acta Linguistica Academiae Scientiarum Hungaricae* 32. 53–70.

Markus A. Pöchtrager
The Unbearable Lightness of Being High: Openness as Structure and the Consequences for Prosody

Abstract: GP 2.0, a further development of Government Phonology (GP), assumes that certain properties which have so far been assumed to be melodic are better understood as structural. This includes the element **A**, responsible (amongst other things) for the representation of aperture in vowels. This paper argues that such a reinterpretation of aperture also sheds light on the prosodic properties of vowels, in particular what counts as metrically heavy or light.

Keywords: Government Phonology, vowels, vowel height, aperture, melodic structure, metrical strength

1 Introduction

High vowels (plus schwa, if present) display various signs of weakness, often linked to prosodic weakness: Those vowels are typical outcomes of reduction in languages like Brazilian Portuguese (Cristófaro Alves da Silva 1992) or Eastern Catalan (Wheeler 2005). They are found in unstressed position in English and count as metrically weaker, thus their occurrence in final position allows for preantepenultimate stress (i.e. unexpectedly far to the left) in words like *árbitrary*, *álligator*, or *présidency* (Burzio 1994: 15–17 et passim). They can undergo devoicing in Japanese (Fujimoto 2015) and are uneasy with secondary stress in Finnish (Anttila 2008; Karvonen 2010). This enumeration could be continued.

"Weakness" is a term difficult to define exactly, as is "prosody" (or "prosodic weakness"). Most of the examples given above are clearly linked to prosody in that they interact with stress or otherwise depend on the syntagmatic dimension of a phonological form (following the definition of prosody in Lehiste (1970)). The vowels show weakness in a Vennemannian sense (Hyman 1975: 165), i.e. by being closer to zero on a path of reduction, but also in their inability to bear certain attributes (stress, accent, voicing).

Markus A. Pöchtrager, Universität Wien, e-mail: markus.poechtrager@univie.ac.at

https://doi.org/10.1515/9783110730098-004

In this contribution, which focuses on English (Received Pronunciation, RP) but whose results go beyond it, I will explore how this weakness can be derived from a structural approach to the representation of vowels. In doing this, I build on and expand the arguments on the English vowel system made in Pöchtrager (2021a).

The approach is "structural" in that it assumes that a certain property (here: aperture), while commonly understood as a melodic property on a par with rounding, backness etc., had better be reinterpreted on a par with other structural properties, such as length. As such, the paper builds and elaborates on work on the internal structure of vowels within Government Phonology (GP) 2.0 as presented in Pöchtrager (2018, 2020, 2021a, 2021b). The more general question, whether a given phonological property is to be taken as melodic or structural, has a long history, both within GP (e.g. Jensen's (1994) replacement of the stop element by a structural configuration) as well as outside (e.g. the reinterpretation of the feature [long] as structural, or of contour tones as sequences of level tones instead of indivisible units in Autosegmental Phonology (Goldsmith 1976)).

The paper is organised as follows: Section 2 discusses the special status of the element **A**, along with reasons for why it should be reinterpreted as a structural configuration, and the implications of that for the representation of (English) vowels. Section 3 looks at English stress and its relationship to the vowel inventory. Section 4 attempts to derive that relationship from a structural approach to vowel quality, while Section 5 also brings in quantity. Section 6 looks at the general implications of the proposal.

2 The Special Status of A

Phonological models employing privative melodic primes (I will use the GP designation "elements") usually contain the classic trio **A**, **I**, **U** (with typographic variation in their appearance on paper, such as being set in boldface or between straight lines).[1] That **A** is different from the other two is often acknowledged, though sometimes more implicitly than explicitly. In Particle Phonology (Schane 1984; Broadbent 1999) it is the only particle that can occur multiple times in a complex expression. Within Dependency Phonology, Anderson and Ewen (1987: 215) note

---

1 Following Broadbent (1991, 1999), Cyran (1997), Goh (1997) etc., I take **A** to correspond to [–high] in vowels and to represent coronality in consonants. Within GP alternative proposals have been made for coronals. Backley (2011) argues that, depending on the language, **I** or **A** represent coronality. Those arguments are addressed in Pöchtrager (2013).

that **A** combines more freely with the elements **I** and **U** than do those two with each other, as reflected in the typology of vowel systems (front rounded vowels rarer than mid vowels). In Government Phonology, special provision is made for **A** in several places, such that segments containing it are better governors than those without (Kaye 2000) or that **A** prefers not to be a head within a phonological expression (Cobb 1997) etc.; this is a rather mixed bag of traits with no unifying property from a formal point of view.

Finding the *key* property that would set **A** apart from the other elements is non-trivial, and in any case does not follow from a theory that takes **A**, **I**, **U** as basic elements of equal status. GP 2.0 (Pöchtrager 2006; Kaye and Pöchtrager 2013; Živanovič and Pöchtrager 2010) is characterised by an appreciation of such asymmetries between phonological objects and finds that many properties which had been assumed to be melodic are actually better understood as structural. This also applies to the (former) element **A**, where one unifying property is its interaction with structure, discussed in more detail in Pöchtrager (2006, 2010, 2012, 2013, 2020, 2021a, 2021b, in preparation). More precisely, **A**, especially (but not only) in consonants, interacts with (constituent) structure in that it allows for bigger structures than otherwise possible. This special property of coronals was noticed at least as early as Fudge (1969), who provided a syllabic position ("termination") reserved for coronals. Selkirk's (1982) restrictions of certain coda positions in the English syllable to coronals continue that tradition; as do the notion of appendix (Hall 2002; Vaux and Wolfe 2009) and, within GP, the onset-specifier approach by Botma, Ewen and van der Torre (2008). All these concepts are meant to shed light on why, for example, the upper size limit of English monosyllabic words is VVC (*seek*, *late*) or VCC (*sink*, *left*), unless both consonants are coronals: *fiend* (*fiemp, *fienk), *count* (*coump, *counk), *feast* (*feasp, *feask) etc. are all VVCC. The long vowel [ɑː] (**A** by itself) allows for similar excesses, as in (Southern British) *draft* or *task*, where one coronal consonant is sufficient. The patterns are more complex than can be illustrated in this short demonstration, and the reader is referred to the aforementioned references for further details.

Providing a special syllabic position to house coronals is no answer to *why* they enjoy this special status. GP 2.0. tries to build this special property into the theory by reinterpreting objects that were thought to contain **A** as structurally *bigger*. This seems counter-intuitive at first glance, since if more of something can be fitted into a syllable (two consonants where we only expect one, say), we might assume that this "something" is smaller. Instead, GP 2.0 proposes the following: **A** is replaced by a certain structural configuration (i.e. more than a single skeletal slot), but part of that structure is "unused" and available. Those unused positions can be claimed by adjacent segments or can themselves house independent segments. For example, the long vowel in *fiend* can only come about because the vowel is free to "borrow" room from the final cluster, whose two members are coronal. In total, this gives rise to sequences that are bigger than normally allowed. This particular conception also parallels other structural reinterpretations in the theory (e.g. of the element **H** (Pöchtrager 2006)).

How are these structures organised then? Skeletal positions in GP 2.0 come in two flavours, heads and non-heads. The earliest incarnations of the theory (Pöchtrager 2006, 2010; Kaye and Pöchtrager 2013) distinguished between two heads: a nuclear head xN and an onset head xO for vowels and consonants, respectively. Each head could project upwards maximally twice, i.e. xN–N′–N″ and xO–O′–O″.[2] In addition, (limited) head adjunction was allowed (i.e. a head could be split up into two instances of itself) in order to replace the old **A**-element and, at the same time, to provide the extra space coronals and some non-high vowels seem to come with (as suggested above).

In Pöchtrager (2018, 2020, 2021a, 2021b) this model was refined and the number of heads was doubled, resulting in two types of nuclear head (xn and xN) and two types of onset head (xo and xO), with xn on top of xN, and xo on top of xO, if both are present (examples in a moment). Here we will not go into the internal structure of xo and xO (Pöchtrager 2021b, in preparation, for a discussion of onset heads), but limit ourselves to the bipartite structure of nuclei.

Before we look at some representative structures, we need to take up the issue of length and English vowels. Following the argumentation in Pöchtrager (2006), two different types of length are to be distinguished. A pair like *bit*/*beat* illustrates lexical length, where a lexically short vowel contrasts with a lexically long one. This type cooccurs with the tense/lax distinction, a set of terms I will avoid. Instead, I will refer to vowels belonging to the tense set as T-type, those belonging to the lax set as L-type.[3] Lexical length differs from the second type,

---

2 This is clearly inspired by X-bar theory. In Pöchtrager (2006: ch. 3) nuclei could project even further, thus including adjacent consonants and creating higher-level units. An alternative to such unrestricted projection of nuclei is having other ("functional") heads that unite the projections of various heads. This alternative is currently being explored (Pöchtrager in preparation), as it holds the promise of uniform projections and highlighting the properties and behaviour of individual heads, similar to the prosodic constituents of Prosodic Phonology (Nespor and Vogel 1986). We cannot go into this here, and will only be able to look at snippets of structure to the extent that they are relevant for our purposes.

3 For a similar strategy for Dutch cf. van Oostendorp (2000). The terms tense/lax have a troubled history. Their names suggests articulatory correlates in muscle tension, empirical support for which is lacking, however. For further discussion and details cf. Pöchtrager (2020: 54–57) and references contained therein. Note furthermore that a tense "vowel" like [eɪ] as in *face* contains a quality ([ɪ]) that by itself would be treated as "lax" (as in *fit*). T-type/L-type are intended as neutral (yet mnemonic) terms.

phonological length. Phonological length is highly sensitive to the phonological context, unlike lexical length, which (in most cases) must be treated as lexically given; hence the names. The vowels in pairs like *bit*/*bid* or *beat*/*bead* differ in phonological length, in correlation with the right-hand context: Longer before tautosyllabic lenis consonant (*bid*, *bead*) and finally (*bee*), shorter before tautosyllabic fortis consonant (*bit*, *beat*). While GP 2.0 has its origins in the detailed analysis of those two types of length (Pöchtrager 2006, 2015), we will only need to concern ourselves with lexical length here.[4]

With these preliminaries out of the way, we can turn to actual representations. (1) shows the vowel portions of *peak*, *pick*, *bake*, and *peck* along with the final consonants in abbreviated form.[5]

(1) a. *peak*   b. *pick*   c. *bake* (Northern)   d. *peck*

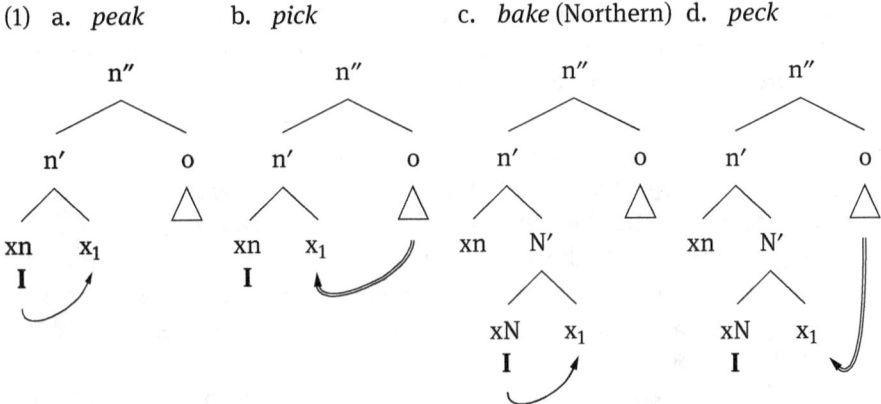

---

4 Suffice it to say that the longer vowel in *bid* (as opposed to *bit*) comes about by the vowel m-commanding (i.e. claiming as its own, see below) a position inside the final consonant: Lenis consonants like *d* come with an unused position (unlike fortis consonants) that a preceding vowel can "borrow" for additional length. For details cf. Pöchtrager (2006).

A reviewer inquires why "lexical/phonological" is not simply referred to as "phonological/phonetic". That latter dichotomy usually presupposes that the domain of phonology is delineated by (all and only) a contrast in meaning; the remainder is phonetic/allophonic. This structuralist assumption was rejected in (Classic) Generative Phonology (Chomsky 1964), as it is in Government Phonology (Kaye 1989; Harris 1999). From a parsing point of view, the phonological length of a vowel is much more important than the nature of the following consonant (Clayards 2018; Penney, Cox, and Szakay 2021), and we must also bear in mind that phonological theory is to account for *any* phonological system. While the representations required to encode English phonological length often seem predictable (and thus non-contrastive), exactly the same representations are not predictable in other languages (such as Estonian, Pöchtrager 2006) and must thus form part of phonological theory anyway, in order to express lexical distinctions that cannot be argued away.

5 Note that (1c) gives a Northern pronunciation with [eː] instead of [eɪ]; the latter would have its melody I in x_1, cf. Pöchtrager (2020) for details.

Contrasting *peak/pick* (1a–b) we see that they share the same basic structure (Polgárdi 2012; Pöchtrager 2020) but differ in the fate of the nuclear complement x_1. In a T-type nucleus (1a) that position is melodically commanded (m-commanded for short) by its head xn, i.e. the complement receives the same interpretation as its head, which in this case is annotated with the element **I**. Together, they yield a long, front high vowel. In an L-type nucleus (1b) x_1 is *not* m-commanded by the nuclear head xn. Instead, x_1 is silenced via p-licensing emanating from a following onset.[6] This captures, amongst other things, the fact that (stressed) L-type nuclei require a following consonant (Anderson (2004) calls the L-type "transitive"), or that a coda consonant (replacing and taking up the same position as x_1) as in *pi__n__k* will also guarantee an L-type nucleus (as there is no second position that would be needed for a T-type nucleus).

Moving on to (1c–d) we see how the introduction of a second head, xN, allows us to represent openness without **A**. That is, the mid vowels are set apart structurally from the high vowels, not melodically. Again, the relationship of x_1 to its neighbours (m-command from a preceding nuclear head vs. p-licensing from a following consonant) encodes T-type/L-type. Note that xN could also project twice (not given in (1)) to yield L-type [æ] (*bat, bad*) and its T-type counterpart [ɛː]; the latter lacking in RP but occurring in North-American pronunciations of *mad* etc. (Kaye 2012).

The projections of xN allow us to capture what old **A**, a melodic property, used to express, while at the same time incorporating the idea that **A** be replaced by structure. I hasten to add that xN goes beyond a simple replacement of old **A**, as we shall see in Sections 4–6.

After this whirlwind introduction to some aspects of the internal structure of vowels (which really only scratched the surface) we are ready to look at prosody and metrical weight.

3 The Link to Prosody

In English, truly unstressed positions (a term to be clarified in a moment) allow schwa (*bitt__er__, sof__a__*) as well as the high vowels [ɪ/iː] (*attic, pony*), [ʊ/uː] (*margin-*

---

[6] The Empty Category Principle (ECP) is central in all versions of GP (Kaye, Lowenstamm, and Vergnaud 1990; Charette 1991), but a translation of its various subclauses into GP 2.0, whose theory of constituent structure is much more elaborate, is still underway. P-licensing as a relation (not as a state of a position) was used in Pöchtrager (2006) as a relatively local relationship that would silence a position as part of a bigger constituent, i.e. in traditional parlance it would silence part of a consonant/vowel.

ally, in variation with [ə]: *album, issue*), and [ɨ] (*ros__e__s*; not for all speakers). Note that lexical length of the high vowels seems to play no role. To single out this group, Burzio (1994: 17) introduces the notion of weak syllables, which he defines as containing "consonantal (sonorant) nuclei [and the] high vowels *i, u*".[7] Such weak syllables are restricted to the periphery of the word, and behave as extraprosodic for foot-structure. This explains why we can find words with pre-antepenultimate stress (*áccuracy, présidency*): The final vowel is weak and the preceding syllables form a ternary foot (Burzio 1994: 16, ex. 2a).[8] Similarly, *álligàtor* has two feet and main stress lands on the first foot, which is only possible because the second (and final) foot ends in a weak syllable, and so that entire foot counts as weak and does not qualify for main stress (Burzio 1994: 16, ex. 3e).[9]

Note that for Burzio the shape of the set of vowels allowed in a weak syllable (*i, u*, schwa/syllabic rhotic) does not follow from anything else, but is simply stipulated. In GP 2.0, on the other hand, these are exactly the vowels that are small in size, so it seems imperative that that link between (i) the internal organisation of vowels and (ii) prosodic structure and stress be explored.[10]

However, in order to appreciate this point, we first need to talk about how many degrees (and what kinds) of stress are needed for English, and that is by no means a settled issue. This takes us back to the term "truly unstressed" at the beginning of this section. That the final syllable in *rubber* is unstressed will probably find unanimous assent (hence "truly unstressed"). But what about *rabbi*? Is its final syllable unstressed or does it bear secondary stress? Several recent papers by Szigetvári (2016, 2017, 2020) dedicate themselves to exactly that question. While his arguments for which vowels can bear stress are quite elegant, Szigetvári is more interested in description and not so much concerned with the internal composition of vowels in terms of phonological building blocks. The question of why that link exists or how vowel quality is related to prosody remains largely unaddressed. I will briefly sum up the gist of Szigetvári's account and we shall see that

---

7 Some cases of schwa are subsumed under his "consonantal nuclei". "Syllabic consonants" are treated as [ɨ] plus consonant in GP 2.0, cf. also footnote 14.
8 In other accounts final -*y* is treated as extrametrical (e.g. Liberman and Prince 1977: 293), which Burzio argues against extensively.
9 Burzio assumes that only final syllables can be weak, and therefore only final feet can be weak. Also, for Burzio *álligàtor* ends in a syllabic rhotic, but in the variety under consideration here this corresponds to schwa, which patterns as weak.
10 In other/earlier versions of GP those vowels would be characterised by containing at most one element, cf. e.g. Backley (2011: 50ff) for discussion. Restricting the number of elements will not delimit the set adequately, as this would also allow for [ɑː]. Requiring the vowels in weak position to be unheaded would (correctly) eliminate that vowel, but also (incorrectly) exclude the unstressed vowel in *issue* etc.

many properties can actually be made to follow from GP 2.0. Szigetvári's transcriptions, which deviate somewhat from common practice (for reasons discussed in the aforementioned papers), will be set in boldface in the remainder of this text.

Szigetvári distinguishes between stress and accent. Accent (for him) is concerned with the organisation of rhythm and is therefore to some extent movable, as in *thirtéen* vs. *thírteen mén*. Every word or a lexical category has to have one accent. That characterisation shows that what Szigetvári calls accent corresponds to what other people call stress. Szigetvári's notion of stress, on the other hand, is an inherent, immutable property of a vowel. The status of a vowel as stressed or unstressed does not change and is independent of and unaffected by that of neighbouring vowels. Longer strings of only stressed vowels are perfectly fine, just as longer strings of round vowels are. The two notions of accent and stress are linked by a one-way implicational relationship: Accent requires (and thus guarantees) stress, but stress does not guarantee accent.

Since I find the nomenclature somewhat infelicitous, I will use the term "stress" for Szigetvári's "accent" in this article, while his distinction "stressed/unstressed" will be referred to as "strong/weak" (as hyponyms of "strength"). In fact, very similar arguments on the nature of stress (in the sense in which it is used in this article) are made in Ladefoged and Johnson (2011), who also argue that unstressed vowels must be divided into "unreduced/reduced" (which essentially parallels strong/weak), though, unlike Szigetvári, they neither explicitly discuss the vowel qualities involved nor the clues that allow for the identification of (un)reduced vowels.[11] In any case, in the terminology used here, the implication at the end of the previous paragraph will translate as in (2).

(2) Implication A: Stress implies a strong vowel.
     (Contraposition: weak vowels do not bear stress.)

While (2) establishes a relationship between stress and strength,[12] it still leaves unaddressed which vowels count as strong to begin with. Szigetvári assumes 6 basic vowel qualities, **i e a o u ə**. Those six vowels by themselves underlie the short vowel system, and at the same time form the basis for the rest of the inventory: For example, the long vowel in *fee* is analysed as a sequence of short vowel and glide, **ij**; and the same is true for the **əw** in *foe*. The word *fear* has a long monophthongal **iː** (i.e. short vowel plus length diacritic) etc. The chart in (3) gives the entire inven-

---

[11] As we shall see soon, whether a vowel is strong/weak does not always transpire from its quality, which is why Ladefoged & Johnson's term "(un)reduced" also strikes me as unfortunate.
[12] We ignore stress under focus, which can also occur on what would otherwise be an unstressed vowel: "I said SoPHIE, not soFA". (Thanks to a reviewer for this example.)

tory along with the IPA symbols usually employed in the transcription of English. (4) repeats (3) and aligns the symbols with the names of the standard lexical sets used in Wells (1982: 127ff) for reference. Note that Szigetvári treats [ʌ/ə] as the same vowel ə, following Fabricius (2007), and that he does not list [ɨ].

(3) i.   ii.
   a. i   [ɪ]   ij   [iː]   iː   [ɪə]
      ə   [ʌ/ə]   əw   [əʊ]   əː   [ɜː]
      u   [ʊ]   uw   [uː]   uː   [ʊə]
   b. e   [e]   ej   [eɪ]   eː   [ɛː/ɛə]
      a   [æ]   aj   [aɪ]   aw   [aʊ]   aː   [ɑː]
      o   [ɒ]   oj   [ɔɪ]   oː   [ɔː]

(4) i.   ii.
   a. i   KIT   ij   FLEECE   iː   NEAR
      ə   STRUT/commA   əw   GOAT   əː   NURSE
      u   FOOT   uw   GOOSE   uː   CURE
   b. e   DRESS   ej   FACE   eː   SQUARE
      a   TRAP   aj   PRICE   aw   MOUTH   aː   START
      o   LOT   oj   CHOICE   oː   FORCE

The chart in (3) is divided into four sectors (ai, aii, bi, bii) with different shading. Both divisions are visual aids for the discussion of strength. There are two implicational relationships linking a particular vowel to strength. Firstly, all the vowels in (3ii), shaded in grey, are followed by the length mark ː. The majority of cases covered by those vowels derive from forms with historical *r*, but not exclusively, e.g. *father*, *palm*. They correspond to Wells's (1982: 175ff) part-system D, and all of them count as strong. Length (Szigetvári's length mark, that is) implies strength.

(5) Implication B: Vowels bearing (Szigetvári's) length mark are strong.

Secondly, the vowels **e a o** are always strong, irrespective of whether there is a glide following them or not. This covers all of (3b), again shaded in grey.

(6) Implication C: The vowels **e a o** are strong.

Sector (3bii) is involved in both implications (and hence darker shaded); the vowels making up that area are strong both on account of the length mark (5) and of their quality (6).

The vowels we have seen so far are all strong. The last remaining sector, (3ai), contains **i ə u** (by themselves or with following glides). Those vowels can be either strong *or* weak, and again, this is independent of whether there is a glide following.

The discussion so far shows two things. Firstly, there are no particular vowel qualities that are only weak (the vowels in (3ai) could be either weak or strong), but there are certain vowel qualities that are always strong (everything but (3ai)). Secondly, while for the majority of cases strength can be determined by quantity or quality (being an **e**, say, guarantees being strong), this does not hold for the set in (3ai). If appearances do not reveal the strength of the vowel, we will have to rely on behaviour to determine it.

Some examples will illustrate all this before we move any further. The vowel **e** in *face* is strong by its very nature; the fact that it is followed by a glide (giving **ej**) has no relevance for strength. This is the only (strong) vowel of the word and it bears stress. The same vowel **e** occurs in *látex* as both the first vowel (**ej**) and the second (**e**). Since both vowels are strong either one is a candidate for stress, and in this word stress happens to be on the penult. Recall that stress requires a strong vowel, but being strong does not imply stress (implication A). Accordingly, the position of stress, though sometimes predictable from other factors (syllable structure, morphological structure, word-class etc.), will have to be lexically marked at least to some extent: Szigetvári gives the example of *átoll* and *antíque* where both vowels in each word are strong, and yet stress falls in different positions in the two in isolation. This is interpreted as a difference in stress levels by other authors, e.g. by Hayes (1995) and Giegerich (1992): *átòll* (primary–secondary) vs. *àntíque* (secondary–primary). Each word has two (adjacent) stresses for those two authors, but the two stresses differ in degree. For Szigetvári, on the other hand, each word has one stress only (initial in *átoll*, final in *antíque*), but both words have exclusively strong vowels. The vowels that would by counted as truly unstressed for Hayes and Giegerich are the ones Szigetvári refers to as weak: weak schwa (**ə**) and the weak high vowels (**i u**), exactly the same set we have seen before with Burzio.

Let us then finally address the idea that **i ə u** may be either strong or weak. This can be illustrated with the initial vowels in *úgly* (strong and stressed) vs. *agrée* (weak and therefore automatically unstressed). This difference is even reflected in transcriptions of quality, with [ʌ] for the first vowel in *ugly* but [ə] for *agree*. For Szigetvári, this is simply strong vs. weak **ə**, respectively. In the same fashion, *manatee* and *vanity* both end in **ij**, which is strong in the first word and weak in the second. So while there might be some phonetic cue for the strength of **ə** ([ʌ] when strong, [ə] when weak), this is not true of the other vowels that can be strong or weak (3ai). In order to determine then whether, say, an [ɪ] (**i**) is strong or weak (it could be either), we will have to look at behaviour. That behaviour is sometimes superior to the acoustic signal in locating stress is of course an argument also made by Hayes (1995: ch. 2) in establishing stress as a phonologically relevant property to begin with.

One such test would be "tappability" of d/t when it precedes a strong or weak vowel, respectively. (Varieties other than British English are obviously better suited for that task.) Both *áutism*/*náutilus* have a strong first vowel (**oː**, strong by quality and length mark), both times followed by **i**. However, the **i** is strong in *áutism* and weak in *náutilus*, as evidenced by differences in tapping, which is blocked before a strong vowel but not before a weak vowel. The same difference can be seen in *mánatee*/*vánity* (strong vs. weak final **ij**). (Some speakers have the same contrast for final [əʊ] **əw** in *veto*/*Vito*.) Syncope can serve as a further test: The final **ij** in *family* is weak, hence syncope of the preceding vowel is possible, unlike in *jubilee* with its final strong **ij**. Further tests offered by Szigetvári are the location of excrescent consonants (*prin*[t]*ce* vs. *princess*) and certain aspects of the distribution of glides (*val*[j]*ue* but *absol*[*j]*ute*).

While Szigetvári brings together a number of interesting observations where he links several phonological phenomena to strength, strength itself is not derived from any higher principles. Certain vowels are strong by stipulation, others either strong or weak. Similarly, a link between strength and stress is established, but why that link should exist remains unclear. That is, none of the implications A, B, C in (2, 5–6) follow from anything else. This is exactly where GP 2.0 comes in, because I will argue in the next section that that model can make better sense of (2, 5–6). We will start with the last implication.

4 GP 2.0 and Strength

Szigetvári does not break down his vowels into smaller phonological units, and it is therefore impossible to determine a common factor underlying strength. We can establish that strength is guaranteed by either a length mark (5) or a certain degree of openness (6), but it is still unclear how those two are connected. From the point of view of GP 2.0, it is reassuring to see that Szigetvári's notion of strength can be read off the bipartite structure of nuclei, and at the same time we can also explain why strength is an inherent property of a vowel as he assumes.

There are two key ingredients. Firstly, all *weak* vowels can be expressed by structures that require only one nuclear head. Let us look at why. A crucial assumption of the theory is that openness is expressed by structural complexity (Section 2). We saw in (3ai) that only **i ə u** can be weak, and all of these require just one head. That is, being weak implies having only one nuclear head. Crucially, the converse does not hold: Not all vowels with only one head are guaranteed to be weak, which is the reason why **i ə u** can be either, i.e. both weak and strong. This raises a further question, though: If both the strong and the weak versions of **i ə u** require one head only, then how are they distinguished? The answer is simple: Our system provides two heads, xn and xN. The projection of *either* one will provide enough room to express **i ə u**. It is the *kind* of head that distinguishes weak from strong. More precisely: Strong vowels always involve a projection of the higher head xn. Vowels lacking that head are then by definition weak. Strong **i** involves a projection of xn, while weak **i** involves a projection of xN. The strong and weak versions of each vowel are contrasted in (7).[13]

(7) a. Strong **i u ə** (strong ə = [ʌ])

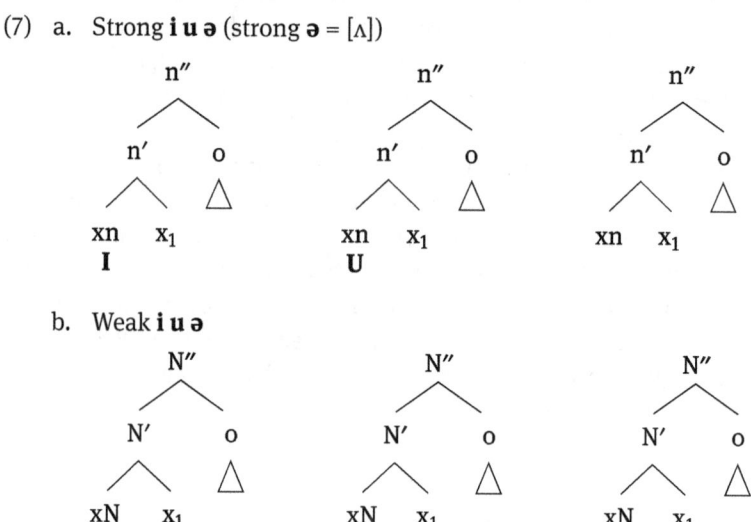

b. Weak **i u ə**

Annotation by elements (**I**, **U** or nothing) gives us the three different qualities; x_1 will be used for length (Section 5), and the specifier serves as the position where a final consonant can be embedded (Pöchtrager 2006: ch. 3).

The (epenthetic) vowel [ɨ] in *roses* or *badges* (as opposed to schwa in *Rosa's* or *badgers*) is not mentioned in Szigetvári's papers, and presumably he (like many speakers) does not distinguish that vowel from [ɪ], i.e. his (weak) **i**. Both vowels

---

13 Translation of the trees in (7) into articulatory terms (high, mid etc.) is possible if *empty* positions are counted: **i u** have the same amount of structure as **ə**, but in **ə** more positions are empty, which thus counts as mid, not high (Pöchtrager 2018, 2020, 2021a for discussion).

are expressible in principle in GP 2.0: Weak [ɪ] contains **I** and has the structure given in (7b), while (central) [ɨ] has no elements and one level of projection less than schwa, i.e. only up to N′.[14]

It might then seem that we have simply replaced one dichotomy (strong/weak) by another (containing xn/not containing xn). But in fact, equating xn with being strong allows us to make an interesting (and correct) prediction: A vowel that is bigger (in the sense of having more structure) than **i ə u** will by necessity contain both heads, xn *and* xN. That is, any vowel bigger than **i ə u** is guaranteed to be strong, which is exactly what implication C in (6) is meant to capture. Declaring xn the "strong" head automatically derives (6), that **e a o** are strong. Note furthermore that a structurally big vowel will automatically be strong, but being strong does not require a big vowel; it only requires the right head. The trees in (8) illustrate this.

(8) a. [æ/ɛː]   b. [ɪ/iː]   c. [ɪ/iː]
    (inherently) strong   strong   weak

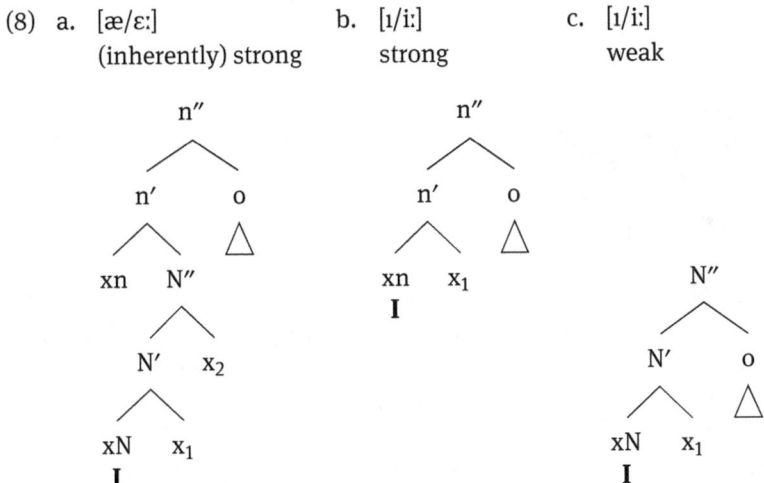

It is important to note that the bipartite structure of nuclei fulfils two roles simultaneously: For one thing, it allows us to reinterpret the old element **A** as a structural configuration. In addition, by declaring xn the strong head, we understand why the vowels of English divide up in the way we saw in (3), with the bigger vowels counting as strong. Strong/weak are not simply labels that are attached to random (sets of) vowels, but follow from the architecture of the theory.

Two further issues need to be addressed. Firstly, the trees in (8) make clear that while we can declare xn the strong head, there is nothing comparable to say

---

14 I take "syllabic consonants" to be a sequence of [ɨ] plus consonant phonologically.

about **A**. That is, there is no unique head that would count as *the* replacement of **A**. (7) shows the difference between a strong **i** and a weak one, by exploiting the two different heads, but clearly we would not want to say of either one that it contained (the replacement of old) **A**. Neither xn nor xN as such replaces old **A**; it is the amount of structure in a vowel that allows for the replacement of that element.

Secondly, there is the issue of length, or rather Szigetvári's length mark. We will take up that point in the next section.

5 Length

Implication B in (5) stated that vowels where Szigetvári assumes a length mark count as strong. The chart in (9) repeats and collapses (3ii) and (4ii).

(9) a.
iː	[ɪə]	NEAR
əː	[ɜː]	NURSE
uː	[ʊə]	CURE

b.
eː	[ɛː/ɛə]	SQUARE
aː	[ɑː]	START
oː	[ɔː]	FORCE

The vowels in (9b) are strong by implications B (5) and C (6) at the same time (quality and length mark). Given their (relatively open) quality they will automatically involve both xn *and* xN and, by that token, count as strong. This leaves us with (9a), whose GP 2.0 representations are given in (10).

(10) a. [ɪə] as in *beard*   b. [ʊə] as in *gourd*   c. [ɜː] as in *bird*

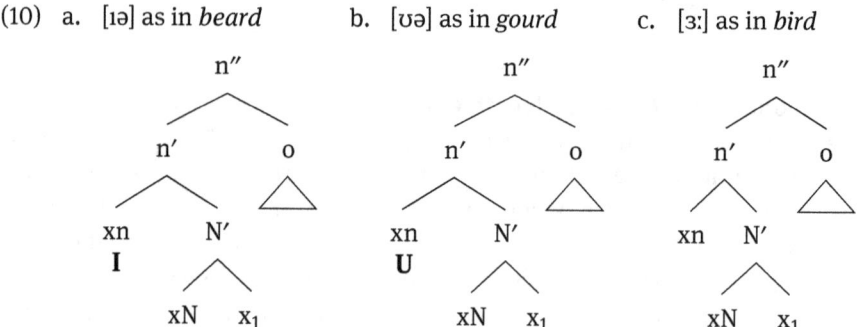

The so-called centering diphthongs [ɪə] and [ʊə] (*near, cure*) contain two heads again, and the higher head xn is annotated with the elements **I** or **U**. N′, the complement of xn, contains two empty positions (xN and x_1), and this is exactly the same number of empty positions underlying schwa, cf. (7). The position x_1 is neither m-commanded (by xn nor xN), nor is it p-licensed, and accordingly the entire substructure N' gets spelled out as schwa. In other words, [ɪə] and [ʊə] are basically high vowels with a schwa embedded inside.[15] Finally, the vowel [ɜː] as in *nurse* (9a) has about the same degree of aperture as the vowels in *square* or *force* (9b) and differs from schwa. Schwa can still be expressed with one single head, but [ɜː] does not make the cut and requires a second head.

The gist of all this is the following: All the vowels where Szigetvári puts a length mark require a second head for one reason or another within GP 2.0. We therefore also derive implication 2 (5), that all these vowels count as strong. Where the two accounts differ is that Szigetvári takes length as the crucial factor, while GP 2.0 focuses on quality here; but with that quality comes a second head.

One last issue remains with vowels that employ only one head. (11) repeats strong and weak **i** from (7).

(11) Strong (left) and weak (right) **i** again

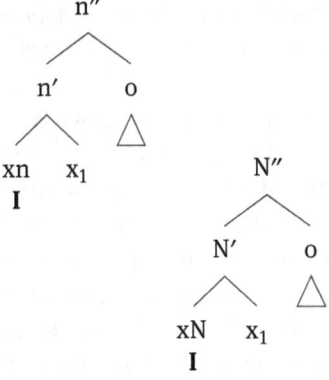

In both cases, x_1 could be m-commanded by the head (xn or xN, respectively) or not, that is, both the strong and the weak version could display lexical length. This is borne out, giving us four logical possibilities: strong T-type (*tea*, *manatee*), weak T-type (*vanity*), strong L-type (*autism*), and weak L-type (*nautilus*).

---

15 Note also that in (10a), unlike in (1c–d), **I** sits in the higher head xn. The vowels in (9b), i.e. [ɛː/ɛə]/[ɑː]/[ɔː], are more open and thus involve more (empty) structure, viz. a projection of xN up to N″. This, together with the location of melody (xn or xN), is relevant in whether (part of) the lower projection is spelled out as [ə], cf. Pöchtrager (2020: 65ff, 2021a) for more extensive discussion.

That same position x_1 could also be replaced by a coda (in the GP sense of Kaye 1990), which is possible no matter if the vowel is strong or weak. This is exactly what we expect given that (11) have exactly the same structure and only differ in what head they are a projection of. The noun *addict* has a weak [ɪ] followed by the coda-onset cluster [kt]; the weakness of the vowel is shown by tapping being possible. In *edict* tapping is blocked, i.e. the vowel must be strong, and yet it is followed by the same cluster [kt]. The same applies to the vowel in *Pict*, which is stressed (thus strong).

6 Stress and xn and Further Clues for Weakness

If xn is what makes an English vowel strong, two further questions emerge: (i) What about the link to stress and (ii) is this a peculiarity of English only?

As for the first question, this was implication A in (2): stress requires a strong vowel. We now know that being strong means containing xn, but that does not mean we could *equate* xn with stress, of course, since words like *latex* etc. contain two strong vowels but only one stress. At best we can say that xn functions as a landing site for stress, in the same way that stressed positions function as landing sites for intonational tunes.[16]

As for the second question, having a designated head that gives "strength" is by no means unique to English. Pöchtrager (2018) argues that unstressed positions in Brazilian Portuguese and Eastern Catalan impose a cap on the size of vowels permitted. But closer inspection reveals that prosodically weak positions do not indiscriminately restrict their vowels by size, but rather bar specific heads (that is, xn) and their projections from prosodically unfavourable positions.

This can even be extended to the realm of consonants. The replacement of **A** required the splitting up of nuclei into two distinct heads. The same is true for consonants (onset heads) in order to represent coronality (cf. Section 2). Many varieties of English target coronal plosives (the biggest objects in the system, Pöchtrager 2016, 2021b) in weak position by tapping or glottaling, which can again be interpreted as the removal of structure, and in particular of the higher (and stronger?) head xo, the counterpart of xn. This might be a further indication that the higher heads count as stronger. Further research will have to show to what extent this assumption can be substantiated.

---

16 Within GP 2.0, a position being a landing site usually means that the position can be embedded by a higher (stress?) head, but I will leave that open for further research.

References

Anderson, John. 2004. Contrast in phonology, structural analogy, and the interfaces. *Studia Linguistica* 58(3). 269–287.
Anderson, John & Colin J. Ewen. 1987. *Principles of Dependency Phonology*. Cambridge: Cambridge University Press.
Anttila, Arto. 2008. Word Stress in Finnish. Unpublished ms.
Backley, Phillip. 2011. *An Introduction to Element Theory*. Edinburgh: Edinburgh University Press.
Botma, Bert, Colin J. Ewen & Erik Jan van der Torre. 2008. The syllabic affiliation of postvocalic liquids: An onset-specifier approach. *Lingua* 118. 1250–1270.
Broadbent, Judith M. 1991. Linking and intrusive r in English. *UCL Working Papers in Linguistics* 3. 281–301.
Broadbent, Judith M. 1999. A new approach to the representation of coronal segments. In S. J. Hannahs & Mike Davenport (eds.), *Issues in Phonological Structure: Papers from an International Workshop*, 1–25. Amsterdam/Philadelphia: John Benjamins.
Burzio, Luigi. 1994. *Principles of English Stress*. Cambridge: Cambridge University Press.
Charette, Monik. 1991. *Conditions on Phonological Government*. Cambridge: Cambridge University Press.
Chomsky, Noam. 1964. *Current Issues in Linguistic Theory*. London/The Hague/Paris: Mouton.
Clayards, Meghan. 2018. Individual talker and token covariation in the production of multiple cues to stop voicing. *Phonetica* 75. 1–23.
Cobb, Margaret. 1997. *Conditions on nuclear expressions in phonology*. London: University of London/School of Oriental and African Studies dissertation.
Cristófaro Alves da Silva, Thaïs. 1992. *Nuclear phenomena in Brazilian Portuguese*. London: University of London/School of Oriental and African Studies dissertation.
Cyran, Eugeniusz. 1997. *Resonance Elements in Phonology: A Study in Munster Irish*. Lublin: Wydawnictwo Folium.
Fabricius, Anne. 2007. Variation and change in the trap and strut vowels of RP: A real time comparison of five acoustic data sets. *Journal of the International Phonetic Association* 37(3). 293–320.
Fudge, Erik C. 1969. Syllables. *Journal of Linguistics* 5. 253–286.
Fujimoto, Masako. 2015. Vowel devoicing. In Haruo Kubozono (ed.), *Handbook of Japanese Phonetics and Phonology*, 167–214. Berlin: Mouton de Gruyter.
Giegerich, Heinz J. 1992. *English Phonology: An Introduction*. Cambridge/New York/Melbourne: Cambridge University Press.
Goh, Yeng-Seng. 1997. *The Segmental Phonology of Beijing Mandarin*. Taipei: Crane Publishing.
Goldsmith, John. 1976. *Autosegmental Phonology*. Bloomington: Indiana University Linguistics Club.
Hall, Tracy Alan. 2002. Against extrasyllabic consonants in German and English. *Phonology* 19. 33–75.
Harris, John. 1999. Release the captive coda: The foot as a domain of phonetic interpretation. *UCL Working Papers in Linguistics* 11. 165–194.
Hayes, Bruce. 1995. *Metrical Stress Theory: Principles and Case Studies*. Chicago/London: University of Chicago Press.
Hyman, Larry M. 1975. *Phonology: Theory and Analysis*. New York: Holt, Rinehart and Winston.

Jensen, Sean. 1994. Is ʔ an element? Towards a non-segmental phonology. *SOAS Working Papers in Linguistics & Phonetics* 4. 71–78.

Karvonen, Daniel. 2010. A moraic mismatch in Finnish: The status of coda consonants. Paper presented at the Old World Conference in Phonology 7 (OCP), Nice, France, 28 January 2010.

Kaye, Jonathan. 1989. *Phonology: A Cognitive View*. Hillsdale, NJ: Lawrence Erlbaum.

Kaye, Jonathan. 1990. 'Coda' licensing. *Phonology* 7(2). 301–330.

Kaye, Jonathan. 2000. A user's guide to government phonology (GP). Unpublished Ms.

Kaye, Jonathan. 2012. Canadian raising, eh? In Eugeniusz Cyran, Henryk Kardela & Bogdan Szymanek (eds.), *Sound, Structure and Sense: Studies in Memory of Edmund Gussmann*, 321–352. Lublin: Wydawnictwo KUL.

Kaye, Jonathan, Jean Lowenstamm & Jean-Roger Vergnaud. 1990. Constituent structure and government in phonology. *Phonology* 7(2). 193–231.

Kaye, Jonathan & Markus A. Pöchtrager. 2013. GP 2.0. *SOAS Working Papers in Linguistics & Phonetics* 16. 51–64.

Ladefoged, Peter & Keith Johnson. 2011. *A Course in Phonetics*, 6th edn. Boston: Wadsworth.

Lehiste, Ilse. 1970. *Suprasegmentals*. Cambridge, MA/London: MIT Press.

Liberman, Mark & Alan Prince. 1977. On stress and linguistic rhythm. *Linguistic Inquiry* 8(2). 249–336.

Nespor, Marina & Irene Vogel. 1986. *Prosodic Phonology*. Dordrecht: Foris.

Oostendorp, Marc van. 2000. *Phonological Projection: A Theory of Feature Content and Prosodic Structure*. Berlin/Boston: Mouton de Gruyter.

Penney, Joshua, Felicity Cox & Anita Szakay. 2021. Effects of glottalisation, preceding vowel duration, and coda closure duration on the perception of coda stop voicing. *Phonetica* 78(1). 29–63. DOI: https://doi.org/10.1159/000508752.

Pöchtrager, Markus A. 2006. *The structure of length*. Vienna: University of Vienna dissertation.

Pöchtrager, Markus A. 2010. The structure of A. Paper presented at the 33rd GLOW Colloquium, Wrocław, 13–16 April.

Pöchtrager, Markus A. 2012. Deconstructing A. Paper presented at the MFM Fringe Meeting on Segmental Architecture, University of Manchester, 23 May.

Pöchtrager, Markus A. 2013. On A. Paper presented at the Workshop on Melodic Representation, University College London, 12 March.

Pöchtrager, Markus A. 2015. Beyond the segment. In Eric Raimy & Charles E. Cairns (eds.), *The Segment*, 44–64. Hoboken, NJ: Wiley.

Pöchtrager, Markus A. 2016. It's all about size. In Péter Szigetvári (ed.), *70 Snippets to Mark Ádám Nádasdy's 70th Birthday*. http://seas3.elte.hu/nadasdy70/pochtrager.html (last accessed June 2022).

Pöchtrager, Markus A. 2018. Sawing off the branch you are sitting on. *Acta Linguistica Academica* 65(1). 47–68.

Pöchtrager, Markus A. 2020. Tense? (Re)lax! A new formalisation for a controversial contrast. *Acta Linguistica Academica* 67(1). 53–71.

Pöchtrager, Markus A. 2021a. English vowel structure and stress in GP 2.0. In Sabrina Bendjaballah, Ali Tifrit & Laurence Voeltzel (eds.), *Perspectives on Element Theory*, 157–183. Berlin: Mouton de Gruyter. DOI: https://doi.org/10.1515/9783110691948.

Pöchtrager, Markus A. 2021b. Towards a non-arbitrary account of affricates and affrication. *Glossa* 6(1): 61. 1–31. DOI: https://doi.org/10.5334/gjgl.1116.

Pöchtrager, Markus A. In preparation. Sonorants, obstruents, and A. Ms.

Polgárdi, Krisztina. 2012. The distribution of vowels in English and trochaic proper government. In Bert Botma & Roland Noske (eds.) *Phonological Explorations: Empirical, Theoretical and Diachronic Issues*, 111–134. Berlin/New York: Mouton de Gruyter.

Schane, Sanford A. 1984. The fundamentals of particle phonology. *Phonology Yearbook* 1. 129–155.

Selkirk, Elisabeth. 1982. The syllable. In Harry van der Hulst & Norval Smith (eds.), *The Structure of Phonological Representations*, volume 2, 337–383. Dordrecht/Cinnaminson: Foris.

Szigetvári, Péter. 2016. No diphthong, no problem. In Jolanta Szpyra-Kozłowska & Eugeniusz Cyran (eds.), *Phonology, Its Faces and Interfaces*, 123–141. Frankfurt: Peter Lang.

Szigetvári, Péter. 2017. English stress is binary and lexical. In Geoff Lindsey & Andrew Nevins (eds.), *Sonic Signatures: Studies Dedicated to John Harris*, 264–275. Amsterdam/Philadelphia: Benjamins.

Szigetvári, Péter. 2020. Posttonic stress in English. In Krzysztof Jaskuła (ed.), *Phonetic Explorations*, 163–189. Lublin: Wydawnictwo KUL.

Vaux, Bert & Andrew Wolfe. 2009. The appendix. In Eric Raimy & Charles E. Cairns (eds.), *Contemporary Views on Architecture and Representations in Phonology*, 101–143. Cambridge, MA: MIT Press.

Wells, John C. 1982. *Accents of English 1: An Introduction*. Cambridge: Cambridge University Press.

Wheeler, Max W. 2005. *The Phonology of Catalan*. Oxford/New York: Oxford University Press.

Živanovič, Sašo & Markus A. Pöchtrager. 2010. GP 2.0 and Putonghua, too. *Acta Linguistica Hungarica* 57(4). 357–380.

Keith L. Snider
[+ATR] Dominance in Chumburung

Abstract: A topic of recurrent interest in phonological theories, particularly within theories of feature representation (e.g., Van der Hulst 2018), is feature value assymetries. This paper looks at ATR vowel harmony in Chumburung [ncu], a Guang language spoken in Ghana, and examines several ways in which the system manifests dominance of [+ATR] over [–ATR]. These include: aggressive spreading of [+ATR] to roots within complex and compound stems and across word boundaries, greater frequency of [–ATR] lexemes over +ATR lexemes, [–ATR] being the default feature value, [+ATR] spreading allophonically (/a/ has a [+ATR] allophone derived through [+ATR] spreading), and [+ATR] being the feature value that surfaces when vowels coalesce.

Keywords: vowel harmony, ATR, feature value assymetry, default feature, vowel coalescence, Guang

1 Introduction

The present work[1] describes the asymmetric nature of [ATR] (Advanced Tongue Root) harmony in Chumburung [ncu], a Guang language spoken in Ghana, and demonstrates that in this language, [+ATR] is dominant (i.e., [–ATR] vowels assimilate to [+ATR] vowels in different environments). Several tendencies of vowel systems in which [+ATR] is dominant emerge from studies such as Casali (2003, 2008, 2018) and van der Hulst (2018), and these appear in (1).

---

1 I first wish to acknowledge my indebtedness to Harry van der Hulst. Harry was my co-promotor in my doctoral program at Leiden (1990), and he became a good friend. His generous help and insight into my Chumburung data at the time was invaluable, and it continues to inspire me. I am further indebted to Isaac Demuyakor, a middle-aged native speaker of Chumburung, for providing the data for this paper and for allowing me to associate his name with this study. Finally, I am grateful to Rod Casali, Steve Parker, and Jim Roberts for valuable comments on previous drafts, and to Larry Hyman for his excellent reviewer's suggestions. Thank you everyone for your help, and I take full responsibility for any remaining deficiencies.

Keith L. Snider, SIL International

https://doi.org/10.1515/9783110730098-005

(1) Traits of [+ATR] dominance
   a) [+ATR] spreads "aggressively," that is, it spreads to roots, as opposed to only harmonizing affixes (van der Hulst 2018: 294).
   b) [−ATR] roots tend to be more numerous than [+ATR] roots.
   c) [−ATR] tends to be the default feature value.
   d) [+ATR] is the feature value that tends to surface allophonically, beyond the limits of structure preservation (van der Hulst 2018: 294).
   e) [+ATR] tends to surface in vowel coalescence environments.

Based on a survey of some 110 African languages, Casali (2003) concludes that: a) [+ATR] is dominant in the overwhelming majority of languages in which [+ATR] is contrastive in high vowels, but b) that [−ATR] is dominant for the majority of languages in which [ATR] is not contrastive in high vowels. Following van der Hulst (2018: 253), I refer to this conclusion as "Casali's Correlation." Casali (2008) labels the first type of languages, those that are mainly [+ATR] dominant, as "2IU" languages because there are two sets of IU vowels, viz. *i/u* and *ɪ/ʊ*. Similarly, he labels the second type of languages, those that are mainly [−ATR] dominant, as 1IU languages because they have only one set of IU vowels, typically *i/u*. In this paper, I demonstrate that with two sets of high vowels, *i/u* and *ɪ/ʊ*, Chumburung is a 2IU language that manifests all the traits in (1) that are tendencies in languages with [+ATR] dominance.[2]

Snider (1990) describes Chumburung as having nine vowel phonemes, four of which are [+ATR], and five of which are [−ATR]. In addition, /a/ has a [+ATR] allophone [ə] (discussed in Section 6) that occurs in complementary distribution with [a] and which only occurs before [+ATR] vowels. The Chumburung vowel inventory is set out in (2).

(2) Chumburung vowel inventory

		[−bk]	[+bk, −rd]	[+rd]
[+high]	[+ATR]	i		u
	[−ATR]	ɪ		ʊ
[−high, −low]	[+ATR]	e	[ə]	o
	[−ATR]	ɛ		ɔ
[+low]	[−ATR]		a	

---

2 [+ATR], of course, is not the only dominant feature value for vowels in Chumburung; [+round] and [−high] are also dominant. Drawing heavily on van der Hulst and Smith (1985) and van der Hulst (1988), Snider (1989) posits the unary features u, a, and A to respectively represent [+round], [−high], and [+ATR].

Roots in Chumburung can only be monosyllabic or disyllabic, and they are either [−ATR] or [+ATR], as shown in (3).

(3) [ATR] patterning in noun roots[3]

[−ATR]		[+ATR]	
wʊ́rí	'skin'	bùnì	'butterfly'
bɔ̀tí	'sack'	dʒèrì	'termite'
dápʊ̀	'hawk'	tírê	'younger brother'
sìnsá	'language'	wòrí?	'pestle'

Historically at least, there has been a tendency for scholars to regard [ATR] harmony in many African languages as root-controlled; i.e., [+ATR] is not dominant, but rather [+ATR] and [−ATR] are symmetric, and affixes simply harmonize with the [ATR] value of the roots to which they are adjacent. See for example Aoki (1968) and Clements (1981) with reference to Akan [aka], and Bakovic (2001) with reference to Eastern Nilotic. However, more recent studies demonstrate that spreading of [+ATR] from suffixes to roots is attested in several languages including Kinande [nnb] (Archangeli and Pulleyblank 2002; Hyman 2002) and Gunu [yas] (Boyd 2015). While superficially, [ATR] harmony in Chumburung might also appear to be root-controlled, it is not root-controlled.

The paper is organized as follows. Section 2 presents data that superficially support the notion that [ATR] harmony in Chumburung is root-controlled. However Section 3 reveals that [ATR] harmony is not root-controlled by demonstrating that [+ATR] spreads aggressively to roots, i.e., it spreads to roots within complex and compound stems and also to roots across word boundaries. Section 4 demonstrates that [−ATR] lexemes are significantly more numerous than [+ATR] lexemes, Section 5 demonstrates that [−ATR] is the default feature value, Section 6 demonstrates that [+ATR] surfaces allophonically, and Section 7 demonstrates that [+ATR] is the feature value that surfaces when vowels coalesce.

2 Superficial Root-Controlled Harmony

Chumburung has a noun class system in which nouns are assigned to various classes. Although the nouns of some classes do not take prefixes (e.g., dùŋ 'heart'), the nouns of most classes take prefixes that indicate the classes to which

---

[3] Surface tone is marked on all examples in this paper. For descriptions of Chumburung tone, see Chapter 5 of Snider (2018) and Chapter 4 of Snider (2020).

the nouns are assigned (Snider 1988, 1990). In each case, the [ATR] values of the prefix vowels are consistently harmonic with the [ATR] values of the vowels of the stems to which they are assigned. In this section, we look at the behaviour of two of these prefixes: *I*- and *O*-. Since noun class prefixes in the language never occur in neutral (i.e., non-harmonizing) environments, it is impossible to ascertain from these data alone whether noun class prefixes are underlyingly [+ATR] or [−ATR].

In (4), [ATR] harmony may be seen between stems whose singular forms take no segmental singular prefix and whose plural forms take the plural *I*- noun class prefix. Throughout this paper, vowels that harmonize to [+ATR] are underlined to make the data clearer.

(4) [ATR] harmony between stems and plural *I*- noun class prefix

	Singular	Plural	Gloss
a) [+ATR]	kísî	<u>í</u>-kísî	'fetish'
	fé	<u>í</u>-fé	'rope'
	wú	<u>ì</u>-wú	'thorn'
	d͡ʒòonò	<u>í</u>-d͡ʒóonô	'dog'
	d͡ʒɜ̌ndè?	<u>ì</u>-d͡ʒɜ̌ndè?	'onion'
b) [−ATR]	síkâŋ	ì-síkâŋ	'knife'
	kɛ́?	ì-kɛ́?	'edge'
	púní	ì-púní	'door'
	bɔ́	í-bɔ́	'hole'
	k͡pá	ì-k͡pá	'path'

These data demonstrate a clear correspondence between the [ATR] value of the stem vowel and the [ATR] value of the *I*- prefix immediately to its left. This alone does not demonstrate that [+ATR] is spreading leftward in this environment as one could equally argue that it is [−ATR] that is spreading since the prefix is consistently realized with the [ATR] specification of the stem.

Like their *I*- class counterparts in (4), the singular *O*- class prefix vowels in (5) harmonize with the [ATR] values of the stems to which they are affixed.

(5) [ATR] harmony between stems and plural *O*- noun class prefix

	Singular	Gloss
a) [+ATR]	<u>ó</u>-wúrê	'chief'
	<u>ò</u>-jú	'thief'
	<u>ó</u>-k͡pé	'witch'
	<u>ò</u>-lùŋ	'eagle'

b) [−ATR] ɔ-tʃíʔ   'woman'
          ɔ-kúfɔ́   'bride'
          ɔ́-fɔ́   'guest'
          ɔ̀-ɲárí   'man'

As noted above, it is impossible to ascertain from the examples in (4) and (5) whether these affixes are underlyingly [+ATR] or [−ATR] since they are consistently realized with the [ATR] value of the roots to which they are adjacent. However, given that in these next sections of the paper, [+ATR] spreading is demonstrated to occur, and [−ATR] spreading is demonstrated not to occur, I assume that all harmonizing affixes in the language are underlyingly [−ATR] and only assimilate to [+ATR] when they undergo spreading from [+ATR] roots.

3 [+ATR] Spreads Aggressively

Despite the widespread harmonization between the [ATR] values of affixes and those of adjacent roots, as described above, there is nevertheless considerable evidence that [ATR] harmony in Chumburung is not symmetric, and that [+ATR] is the dominant, spreading value. This evidence comes in the form of environments in which [+ATR] spreads to roots that are otherwise realized [−ATR] in neutral environments such as isolation. In this section we first examine spreading of [+ATR] to roots within complex and compound stems, then spreading of [+ATR] to roots across word boundaries.

3.1 [+ATR] Spreads to Roots within Stems

The asymmetric nature of [ATR] harmony in Chumburung may be seen by comparing the behaviours of two derivational suffixes, [+ATR] -*dʒi* 'diminutive' and [−ATR] -*pʊ́* 'agent'.[4] In the case of the former, [+ATR] spreads from suffix to root, while in the case of the latter [−ATR] does not spread from suffix to root. Although the [ATR] values of most affixes harmonize with the [ATR] values of the roots to

---

[4] While other suffixes exist in the language, these two are the most productive suffixes of which I am aware that affix directly to roots.

which they are adjacent (see Section 2), these two suffixes are non-harmonizing and consistently retain their [ATR] values in all environments.[5]

In (6), [+ATR] spreads leftward to the root from the diminutive suffix -d͡ʒí, which is a grammaticalization of the noun kí-d͡ʒí 'seed'.[6]

(6) Spreading of [+ATR] from suffix to root within complex stems[7]
   kà[bi̖i̖-d͡ʒí]   'hill'   cf. kì[bíʔ]   'mountain'
   kà[bù̖ŋ-d͡ʒí]   'brook'   cf. [bòŋ]   'river'
   kì[nàná̖-d͡ʒí]   'descendent' cf. [nàná]   'grandparent'

It is clear from (6) that: a) [ATR] harmony in Chumburung is not root-controlled since the [ATR] values of the roots alternate in these examples while the [+ATR] value of -d͡ʒí remains constant, and b) it is [+ATR] that is spreading from the suffix to the roots, since the roots are realized [+ATR] only when they precede -d͡ʒí.[8]

Next, compare the examples in (6) above, where [+ATR] spreads from a suffix to roots, with the examples in (7), where a [−ATR] suffix has no effect on the [ATR] quality of preceding roots.

(7) Failure of [−ATR] to spread from suffix to root within complex stems
   ó[ŋú-pʊ̂]   'see-er'   cf. ŋù   'see'
   ò[fé-pʊ́]   'sell-er'   cf. fè   'sell'
   ó[bó-pʊ̂]   'hatch-er' cf. bò   'hatch'

-pʊ 'agent' is the only [−ATR] suffix not to harmonize with respect to [+ATR] in Chumburung. In this respect, it contrasts with the definite article -ɔ́, which does harmonize with respect to [+ATR] (e.g., lɔ̀ŋ/lɔ̀ŋ-ɔ́ 'compound/the compound' and kìlíŋ/ kìlíŋ-o̖ 'song/the song').

---

5 Interestingly, the same [−ATR] -pʊ́ 'agent' suffix does harmonize in Nawuri [naw], a Guang language closely related to Chumburung (e.g., ɔ-lɔ-pʊ 'sick person' vs. o-sum-pu̖ 'messenger' (Casali 1995: 29)). The tones for these Nawuri words were not included in Casali (1995).
6 Evidence that -d͡ʒí is part of the stem and not affixed to the stem may be seen in that the noun class to which the now complex stem belongs (e.g., ká-, in the case of kà[bi̖i̖-d͡ʒí] 'hill') is different from that of the corresponding simple stem (e.g., kí-, in the case of kì[bíʔ] 'mountain'). In Chumburung, the prefix of the noun indicates the noun class to which the stem (as opposed to the root) is assigned.
7 The brackets in (6) through (8) enclose stems.
8 The question arises whether [+ATR] spreading from suffix to root spreads to more than just the first syllable. As discussed in Section 3.2, unbounded, gradient, postlexical leftward spreading of [+ATR] occurs in Chumburung. At this point however, the domain of [+ATR] spreading from suffixes to roots remains a question for further investigation.

The asymmetric nature of [ATR] harmony may also be seen in the alternations of [ATR] values when compound stems are created.⁹ In each of the compound stems in (8), the assimilation is always unidirectional (viz. [−ATR] → [+ATR]).

(8) [+ATR] spreading within compound stems
kí[ɲápú̱-⁺t͡ʃú]	'milk'	cf. kí-ɲápô̱	'breast'	ɲ̀-t͡ʃú	'water'
kì[nə̱ə̱-ɲî]	'cow'	cf. náa-tí	'bovine'	ɲí	'mother'
[pìrá⁺kó-t͡ʃi̱i-sɛ́]	'sow'	cf. pìrá⁺kó	'pig'	ɔ̀-tí̂?	'woman'
[kérí-bû̱ŋ]	'armpit'	cf. kérí	'side'	kìsáríɪ-bùn-rɔ̀	'wrist'
				cf. kìsárí̂?	'hand'

In (8), [+ATR] spreads from right-to-left in the first two examples, and left-to-right in the second two. The examples in (6) through (8) clearly demonstrate that: a) the behaviours of [+ATR] and [−ATR] are not symmetric, and b) [+ATR] is the value that is spreading.

3.2 [+ATR] Spreads to Roots across Word Boundaries

[+ATR] spreads both leftward and rightward across word boundaries in Chumburung, although the spreading behaviors are not symmetric: whereas leftward spreading is unbounded, rightward spreading affects only the first vowel of the following word. This is in keeping with Hyman's (2008) observation for Bantu languages that anticipatory phonology is favored over preservative phonology.

In Chumburung, postlexical leftward spreading of [+ATR] occurs both optionally and gradiently. The spreading is unbounded, but the effect diminishes the further left it spreads and the lower the vowel. The effect is therefore most easily heard auditorily on the last vowel of the first word, and even on that vowel, the assimilation is sometimes incomplete (leading to a vowel that is auditorily intermediate in quality), especially with lower vowels. In the examples of postlexical leftward spreading in (9), only the last vowel of the first word (i.e., the environment where the spreading result is most evident) is shown to undergo [+ATR] spreading. However, to help distinguish those vowels potentially affected by leftward [+ATR] spreading in (9), from those unaffected by rightward [+ATR] spreading in (10), a small circle is placed beneath all vowels potentially affected

---

9 How the phonological behaviour of compounds might differ from that of derived nouns is not clear at this point and is part of an ongoing study of the tone system.

by leftward [+ATR] spreading. The first example in (9) also demonstrates leftward [+round] spreading.

(9) Leftward spreading of [+ATR] to roots across word boundaries[10]

kípíní bùnì	→ kípínú bùnì	'mortar's butterfly'	cf. kípíní	'mortar'
kíɲápô kítʃíní	→ kíɲápú *kítʃíní	'breast's vein'	cf. kíɲápô	'breast'
ɔ́fáasɛ́ kérí	→ ɔ́fáasé kérí	'leopard's side'	cf. ɔ́fáasɛ́	'leopard'
kòwɔ́ bùnì	→ kòwó búnì	'snake's butterfly'	cf. kòwɔ́	'snake'
áká kúdú	→ áká kúdú	'ten wives'	cf. áká	'wives'

These data in (9) leave no doubt as to which feature is spreading postlexically. In each example, the final vowel of the first word is consistently [−ATR] in isolation and is only [+ATR] when it precedes a [+ATR] vowel across a word boundary. It is also the case that [−ATR] does not spread leftward in the same environment (e.g., bùnì kɛ́ʔ → [bùnì kɛ́ʔ] *[bùnì kɛ́ʔ] 'butterfly's edge'). This may be further seen in the examples in (10) below.

Like its leftward counterpart, the rightward spreading of [+ATR] across word boundaries occurs optionally and gradiently, although its effects extend only to the first syllable. Also, as may be seen by comparing (10)a-b with (10)c-e, only high vowels are affected. In (10)c-e, [+ATR] does not spread rightward due to the [−high] status of the target vowels. As in (9) above, [+round] also spreads leftward in these examples where applicable.

(10) Rightward spreading of [+ATR] to roots across word boundaries

a. bùnì kítʃâŋ	→ bùnì kítʃâŋ	'butterfly's room'	cf. kítʃâŋ	'room'
b. bùnì kòkɔ́	→ bùnù kùkɔ́	'butterfly's debt'	cf. kòkɔ́	'debt'
c. bùnì kɛ́ʔ	→ bùnì kɛ́ʔ	'butterfly's edge'	cf. kɛ́ʔ	'edge'
d. bùnì lɔ́	→ bùnù lɔ́	'butterfly's sore'	cf. lɔ́	'sore'
e. bùnì dápʊ́	→ bùnì dápʊ́	'butterfly's hawk'	cf. dápʊ́	'hawk'

For further discussion of leftward and rightward spreading of [+ATR] across word boundaries in Chumburung, see Snider (1985, 1989).

---

[10] While some of the glosses in these examples and elsewhere might suggest these data to be less than natural (e.g., 'mortar's butterfly'), given the productivity of this construction and the personification prevalent in Chumburung folk stories, most Chumburung speakers, including the language consultant who provided these data, have little trouble imagining relevant scenarios for these possessive phrases.

4 [−ATR] Roots Outnumber [+ATR] Roots

A second trait often associated with [+ATR] dominance is asymmetry between the relative frequencies of [−ATR] and [+ATR] roots, with [−ATR] roots typically outnumbering [+ATR] roots. For example, in his descriptions of [+ATR] dominance in Nawuri [naw] and Diola-Fogny [dyo], respectively, Casali (2002, 2018) notes that [−ATR] roots significantly outnumber [+ATR] roots in both languages.[11]

Lexemes in my Chumburung database with [−ATR] only vowels significantly outnumber those with [+ATR] only vowels. As shown in (11), nouns whose vowels are all [−ATR] outnumber their [+ATR] counterparts by a factor of 1.67, with a similar figure of 1.71 for verbs.[12]

(11) Distribution of [ATR] in lexemes

	Nouns		Verbs	
[−ATR]	557	62.7%	347	63.1%
[+ATR]	332	37.3%	203	36.9%
Total	889	100.0%	550	100.0%

Since the counts were all taken from single word utterances in my Chumburung word list database, as opposed to from a corpus of texts, no single lexeme was counted multiple times. Undoubtedly however, some repetition of roots is present due to the inclusion of lexemes with compound and complex stems (cf. ɔ̀-t͡ʃíʔ 'woman' and kìrì-t͡ʃíʔ 'fiancée'). The preponderance of lexemes with [−ATR] only vowels, compared with [+ATR] only vowels in Chumburung, is very much in keeping with Casali's observation that [−ATR] roots tend to outnumber [+ATR] roots in languages in which [+ATR] is dominant.

5 [−ATR] Is the Default Feature Value

Both van der Hulst (2018: 295) and Casali (2018: 201) observe that in environments where [+ATR] is restricted or blocked, [−ATR] is realized as the default vowel in languages in which [+ATR] is dominant. In Chumburung, [+ATR] is restricted

---

[11] Casali (2018) discusses the connection between lexical frequency and dominance in terms of expectations about markedness. In particular, he affirms the traditional expectations that dominant feature values should also be marked (see also De Lacy 2006; Rice 2007).
[12] These numerical counts are very different from chance: for nouns, $\chi^2(1) = 56.9$, $p < .0001$; for verbs, $\chi^2(1) = 37.7$, $p < .0001$.

from independent pronouns as a class, and these are consistently realized [−ATR] in isolation. These are set out in (12).

(12) Independent pronouns

	Singular	Plural
1st person	mú	à-ní
2nd person	fú	mì-ní
3rd person	mù	bà-mú

The fact that independent pronouns consistently surface in isolation as [−ATR] suggests that [−ATR] is the default specification for [ATR] in Chumburung.

6 [+ATR] Surfaces Allophonically

Despite the lack of a phoneme /ə/, [ə] surfaces as an allophone of /a/ in the different [+ATR] leftward spreading environments discussed in Section 3. For example, due to the leftward spreading of [+ATR] in complex stems (cf. Section 3.1), /a/ is realized as [ə] when followed by a [+ATR] vowel (e.g., /kìnàná-d͡ʒí/ → [kìnə̀nə́-d͡ʒí] 'descendent'). [ə] also surfaces in prefixes whose vowels are /a/ when they are affixed to stems that begin with [+ATR] vowels (e.g., kùbé / ə̀-kùbé 'coconut/s). However, when those same prefixes are affixed to stems that begin with [−ATR] vowels, the prefix vowel is [a] (e.g., lɔ̀ŋkɔ́ / à-lɔ̀ŋkɔ́ 'hare sg/pl'). The fact that [ə] surfaces only as an allophone of /a/ due to [+ATR] spreading is strong support for the claim that [+ATR] is dominant in Chumburung.

7 [+ATR] Is Preserved in Vowel Hiatus Resolution Processes

One manifestation of [+ATR] dominance found in some languages is preservation of [+ATR] rather than [−ATR] in vowel hiatus resolution processes.

In Chumburung, when two vowels are brought into adjacency across word boundaries within phrases, the first vowel is deleted and the second vowel surfaces. If the second vowel is [−high], it surfaces intact, regardless of either vowel's [ATR] specification, as is the case in data sets (15) through (18).[13] Compare, for

---

[13] Here and in data sets (13) through (18), the resultant vowel in each example is underlined.

example, /kəkindʒí ókpé/ → [kəkindʒ ókpé] 'fish's witch' with /kəkindʒí ɔ́fɔ́/ → [kəkindʒ ɔ́fɔ́] 'fish's guest'. If however, the second vowel is [+high], as is the case in data sets (13) and (14), the resultant vowel is realized [+ATR] if either input vowel is [+ATR] (e.g., /kəkindʒí ɪkpá/ → [kəkindʒ i̯kpá] 'fish's paths' and /kwàkú ɪkpá/ → [kwək^w i̯kpá] 'Kwaku's paths'). It is also the case that if the first vowel is [–high], the second vowel (i.e., the resultant vowel) is also realized [–high] (e.g., /kpáŋŋá ídʒó/ → [kpáŋŋ edʒó] 'horse's yams' and /kpáŋŋá ɪkpá/ → [kpáŋŋ e̯kpá] 'horse's paths). Finally, if the first input vowel is [+round], glide formation occurs if the consonant that precedes the first vowel is oral, and if the second vowel is [–round] (e.g., /ɔ́fɔ́ áfɔ́/ → [ɔ́f^w áfɔ́] 'guest's guests'). However, if the consonant that precedes the first vowel is [+nasal], glide formation does not take place (e.g., /dʒòonò áfɔ́/ → [dʒòon áfɔ́] 'dog's guests). Glide formation also does not take place if the second vowel is [+round] (e.g. /ɔlʊ́pʊ́ ɔ́fɔ́/ → [ɔlʊ́p ɔ́fɔ́] 'weaver's guest').

Although vowel hiatus resolution in Chumburung is described in previous publications (e.g., Snider 1985, 1989; and Hansford 1988), none of these publications actually presents a complete set of systematic data to support the respective claims; I therefore take the liberty in data sets (13) through (18) immediately below to make just such a presentation in the hope that other scholars will find these data useful.

In Chumburung, the noun-noun possessive construction employed in these data sets is extremely productive, and it permits one to place into adjacency almost any noun with any other noun. While any of the nine vowels in the language can occur on the right edges of words, only ɔ~o, ɪ~i, and a~ə, the vowels of prefixes, can occur on their left edges.[14] These following data sets therefore present each possible combination of vowels.

(13) Coalescence of V+i

	1st word	2nd word		Surface Form	Gloss
i+i → i	kəkindʒí	ídʒó	→	[kəkindʒ ídʒó]	'fish's yams'
ɪ+i → i	náatí	ídʒó	→	[náat ídʒó]	'cow's yams'
u+i → i	kwəkú	ídʒó	→	[kwək^w ídʒó]	'Kwaku's yams'
ʊ+i → i	ɔlʊ́pʊ́	ídʒó	→	[ɔlʊ́p^w ídʒó]	'weaver's yams'
e+i → e	ókpé	ídʒó	→	[ókp edʒó]	'witch's yams'
ɛ+i → e	nànátʃísɛ́	ídʒó	→	[nànátʃís edʒó]	'grandmother's yams'

---

14 Although the examples of coalescence provided in these examples are of noun phrases, vowel coalescence in verb phrases behaves identically, and it involves the same two surface vowel inventories for the input vowels.

o+i → e	d͡ʒòonò	íd͡ʒó	→	[d͡ʒòon éd͡ʒó]	'dog's yams'
ɔ+i → e	ɔ́fɔ́	íd͡ʒó	→	[ɔ́fʷ éd͡ʒó]	'guest's yams'
a+i → e	k͡páŋŋá	íd͡ʒó	→	[k͡páŋŋ éd͡ʒó]	'horse's yams'

(14) Coalescence of V+ɪ

	1st word	2nd word		Surface Form	Gloss
i+ɪ → i	kəkìnd͡ʒí	ìk͡pá	→	[kəkìnd͡ʒ í⁺k͡pá]	'fish's paths'
ɪ+ɪ → ɪ	náatí	ìk͡pá	→	[náat í⁺k͡pá]	'cow's paths'
u+ɪ → i	kwəkú	ìk͡pá	→	[kwək͡ʷ í⁺k͡pá]	'Kwaku's paths'
ʊ+ɪ → ɪ	ɔ̀lʊ́pʊ́	ìk͡pá	→	[ɔ̀lʊ́pʷ í⁺k͡pá]	'weaver's paths'
e+ɪ → e	ók͡pé	ìk͡pá	→	[ók͡p é⁺k͡pá]	'witch's paths'
ɛ+ɪ → ɛ	nànát͡ʃísɛ́	ìk͡pá	→	[nànát͡ʃ ís ɛ⁺k͡pá]	'grandmother's paths'
o+ɪ → e	d͡ʒòonò	ìk͡pá	→	[d͡ʒòon ek͡pá]	'dog's paths'
ɔ+ɪ → ɛ	ɔ́fɔ́	ìk͡pá	→	[ɔ́fʷ ɛ⁺k͡pá]	'guest's paths'
a+ɪ → ɛ	k͡páŋŋá	ìk͡pá	→	[k͡páŋŋ ɛ⁺k͡pá]	'horse's paths'

(15) Coalescence of V+o

	1st word	2nd word		Surface Form	Gloss
i+o → o	kəkìnd͡ʒí	ók͡pé	→	[kəkìnd͡ʒ ók͡pé]	'fish's witch'
ɪ+o → o	náatí	ók͡pé	→	[náat ók͡pé]	'cow's witch'
u+o → o	kwəkú	ók͡pé	→	[kwək ók͡pé]	'Kwaku's witch'
ʊ+o → o	ɔ̀lʊ́pʊ́	ók͡pé	→	[ɔ̀lʊ́p ók͡pé]	'weaver's witch'
e+o → o	ók͡pé	ók͡pé	→	[ók͡p ók͡pé]	'witch's witch'
ɛ+o → o	nànát͡ʃísɛ́	ók͡pé	→	[nànát͡ʃ ís ók͡pé]	'grandmother's witch'
o+o → o	d͡ʒòonò	ók͡pé	→	[d͡ʒòon ók͡pé]	'dog's witch'
ɔ+o → o	ɔ́fɔ́	ók͡pé	→	[ɔ́f ók͡pé]	'guest's witch'
a+o → o	k͡páŋŋá	ók͡pé	→	[k͡páŋŋ ók͡pé]	'horse's witch'

(16) Coalescence of V+ɔ

	1st word	2nd word		Surface Form	Gloss
i+ɔ → ɔ	kəkìnd͡ʒí	ɔ́fɔ́	→	[kəkìnd͡ʒ ɔ́fɔ́]	'fish's guest'
ɪ+ɔ → ɔ	náatí	ɔ́fɔ́	→	[náat ɔ́fɔ́]	'cow's guest'
u+ɔ → ɔ	kwəkú	ɔ́fɔ́	→	[kwək ɔ́fɔ́]	'Kwaku's guest'
ʊ+ɔ → ɔ	ɔ̀lʊ́pʊ́	ɔ́fɔ́	→	[ɔ̀lʊ́p ɔ́fɔ́]	'weaver's guest'
e+ɔ → ɔ	ók͡pé	ɔ́fɔ́	→	[ók͡p ɔ́fɔ́]	'witch's guest'
ɛ+ɔ → ɔ	nànát͡ʃísɛ́	ɔ́fɔ́	→	[nànát͡ʃ ís ɔ́fɔ́]	'grandmother's guest'
o+ɔ → ɔ	d͡ʒòonò	ɔ́fɔ́	→	[d͡ʒòon ɔ́fɔ́]	'dog's guest'

| ɔ+ɔ → ɔ | ófɔ́ | ófɔ́ | → | [ɔ́f ɔ́fɔ́] | 'guest's guest' |
| a+ɔ → ɔ | k͡páŋŋá | ófɔ́ | → | [k͡páŋŋ ɔ́fɔ́] | 'horse's guest' |

(17) Coalescence of V+ə

	1st word	2nd word		Surface Form	Gloss
i+ə → ə	kəkìnd͡ʒí	ə́k͡pé	→	[kəkìnd͡ʒ ə́k͡pé]	'fish's witches'
ɪ+ə → ə	náatí	ə́k͡pé	→	[náat ə́k͡pé]	'cow's witches'
u+ə → ə	kwəkú	ə́k͡pé	→	[kwəkʷ ə́k͡pé]	'Kwaku's witches'
ʊ+ə → ə	ɔ́lʊ́pʊ́	ə́k͡pé	→	[ɔ́lʊ́pʷ ə́k͡pé]	'weaver's witches'
e+ə → ə	ók͡pé	ə́k͡pé	→	[ók͡p ə́k͡pé]	'witch's witches'
ɛ+ə → ə	nànát͡ʃísɛ́	ə́k͡pé	→	[nànát͡ʃís ə́k͡pé]	'grandmother's witches'
o+ə → ə	d͡ʒòonò	ə́k͡pé	→	[d͡ʒòon ə́k͡pé]	'dog's witches'
ɔ+ə → ə	ófɔ́	ə́k͡pé	→	[ófʷ ə́k͡pé]	'guest's witches'
a+ə → ə	k͡páŋŋá	ə́k͡pé	→	[k͡páŋŋ ə́k͡pé]	'horse's witches'

(18) Coalescence of V+a

	1st word	2nd word		Surface Form	Gloss
i+a → a	kəkìnd͡ʒí	áfɔ́	→	[kəkìnd͡ʒ áfɔ́]	'fish's guests'
ɪ+a → a	náatí	áfɔ́	→	[náat áfɔ́]	'cow's guests'
u+a → a	kwəkú	áfɔ́	→	[kwəkʷ áfɔ́]	'Kwaku's guests'
ʊ+a → a	ɔ́lʊ́pʊ́	áfɔ́	→	[ɔ́lʊ́pʷ áfɔ́]	'weaver's guests'
e+a → a	ók͡pé	áfɔ́	→	[ók͡p áfɔ́]	'witch's guests'
ɛ+a → a	nànát͡ʃísɛ́	áfɔ́	→	[nànát͡ʃís áfɔ́]	'grandmother's guests'
o+a → a	d͡ʒòonò	áfɔ́	→	[d͡ʒòon áfɔ́]	'dog's guests'
ɔ+a → a	ófɔ́	áfɔ́	→	[ófʷ áfɔ́]	'guest's guests'
a+a → a	k͡páŋŋá	áfɔ́	→	[k͡páŋŋ áfɔ́]	'horse's guests'

From these data, it is clear that when the second vowel is [+high], as is the case for the examples in (13) and (14), if either or both vowels are [+ATR], it is always the [+ATR] value that surfaces when vowels coalesce. This is due to the "antagonism" that commonly exists between [-high] vowels (especially [+low] vowels) and the feature [+ATR] in languages with 2IU systems (cf. Archangeli and Pulleyblank 1994; Casali 2016). The surfacing of [+ATR] when either of the coalescing vowels is [+high] is a strong indicator of [+ATR] dominance.

To conclude, [+ATR] is seen as dominant in Chumburung by: a) [+ATR] spreading aggressively, b) [-ATR] roots being more numerous than [+ATR] roots, c) [-ATR] being the default feature value, d) [+ATR] being the feature value that surfaces allophonically, and e) [+ATR] surfacing phonetically in vowel coalescence environments.

References

Aoki, Haruo. 1968. Toward a typology of vowel harmony. *International Journal of American Linguistics* 34. 142–145.

Archangeli, Diana & Douglas Pulleyblank. 1994. *Grounded Phonology*. (Current Studies in Linguistics 25). Cambridge, MA: MIT Press.

Archangeli, Diana & Douglas Pulleyblank. 2002. Kinande vowel harmony: Domains, grounded conditions and one-sided alignment. *Phonology* 19. 139–188.

Bakovic, Eric. 2001. Vowel harmony and cyclicity in Eastern Nilotic. *Proceedings of the Berkeley Linguistic Society* 27. 1–12.

Boyd, Virginia. 2015. *The phonological systems of the Mbam languages of Cameroon with a focus on vowels and vowel harmony*. Leiden: Leiden University Doctoral dissertation. http://hdl.handle.net/1887/36063.

Casali, Roderic F. 1995. *Nawuri Phonology*. (Language Monographs 3). Legon: Institute of African Studies, University of Ghana.

Casali, Roderic F. 2002. Nawuri ATR harmony in typological perspective. *Journal of West African Languages* 29(1). 3–43.

Casali, Roderic F. 2003. [ATR] value asymmetries and underlying vowel inventory structure in Niger-Congo and Nilo-Saharan. *Linguistic Typology* 7. 307–382.

Casali, Roderic F. 2008. ATR harmony in African languages. *Language and Linguistics Compass* 2. 496–549. http://onlinelibrary.wiley.com/doi/10.1111/j.1749-818X.2008.00064.x/abstract.

Casali, Roderic F. 2016. Some inventory-related asymmetries in the patterning of tongue root harmony systems. *Studies in African Linguistics* 45. 95–140.

Casali, Roderic F. 2018. Markedness and dominance in the ATR harmony system of Diola-Fogny. *Journal of African Languages and Linguistics* 39(2). 201–239.

Clements, George N. 1981. Akan vowel harmony: A nonlinear analysis. *Harvard Studies in Phonology* 2. 108–177.

De Lacy, Paul. 2006. *Markedness: Reduction and Preservation in Phonology*. Cambridge: Cambridge University Press.

Hansford, Keir. 1988. *A phonology and grammar of Chumburung*. Ms., Preliminary version of 1991 doctoral dissertation, School of Oriental and African Studies, London.

Hulst, Harry van der. 1988. The geometry of vocalic features. In Harry van der Hulst and Norval Smith (eds.), *Features, Segmental Structure and Harmony Processes, Part II*, 77–125. Dordrecht: Foris Publications.

Hulst, Harry van der. 2018. *Asymmetries in Vowel Harmony*. Oxford: Oxford University Press.

Hulst, Harry van der and Norval Smith. 1985. Vowel features and umlaut in Djingili, Nyangumarda and Warlpiri. *Phonology Yearbook* 2. 277–303.

Hyman, Larry M. 2002. Is there a right-to-left bias in vowel harmony? Paper presented at the Ninth International Phonology Meeting, Vienna. November 1, 2002. http://linguistics.berkeley.edu/~hyman/Hyman_Vienna_VH_paper_forma.pdf.

Hyman, Larry M. 2008. Directional asymmetries in the morphology and phonology of words, with special reference to Bantu. *Linguistics* 46(2). 309–350.

Rice, Keren. 2007. Markedness in phonology. In Paul de Lacy (ed.), *Cambridge Handbook of Phonology*, 79–98. Cambridge: Cambridge University Press.

Snider, Keith L. 1985. Vowel coalescence across word boundaries in Chumburung. *Journal of West African Languages* 15(1). 3–13.
Snider, Keith L. 1988. The noun class system of proto-Guang and its implications for internal classification. *Journal of African Languages and Linguistics* 10(2). 137–163.
Snider, Keith L. 1989. Vowel coalescence in Chumburung: An autosegmental analysis. *Lingua* 78. 217–232.
Snider, Keith L. 1990. *Studies in Guang phonology*. Leiden: Leiden University Doctoral dissertation.
Snider, Keith L. 2018. *Tone Analysis for Field Linguists*. Dallas: SIL International.
Snider, Keith L. 2020. *The Geometry and Features of Tone*, 2nd edn. Dallas: SIL International.

Ruben van de Vijver and Agnes Benkő
Paradigmatically Conditioned Phonetic Detail in Hungarian Neutral Vowels

Abstract: In Hungarian palatal vowel harmony in words in which the last vowel is [+back] take suffixes with back vowels and words with final front vowels almost always take suffixes with [−back] vowels. A limited number of monosyllabic words in which the vowel is one of these front vowels [iː], [i], [eː] or [e] are followed by suffixes that take back vowels. Some have argued that neutral vowels are phonetically more retracted in words which take suffixes with back vowels than in in words that take suffixes with front vowels. Others have denied such a difference. We conducted a production experiment in which we investigated the properties of neutral vowels in monosyllabic words in order to shed light on question as to the presence of paradigmatically conditioned phonetic detail in Hungarian. This is important, because the presence of paradigmatically conditioned phonetic detail in Hungarian, shows that such effects go beyond those established as a consequence of incomplete neutralization.

On the basis of our findings it is necessary to address the question of the representation of paradigmatically conditioned phonetic detail. We discuss several proposals that have been advanced, but all of them have drawbacks. We propose a usage-based view.

Keywords: neutral vowels, Hungarian, paradigmatically conditioned phonetic detail, representations, incomplete neutralization

---

Acknowledgements: We thank the audiences of the 18th International Morphology Meeting in Budapest and CoST 2018, Düsseldorf for their questions and comments. We have benefitted from discussions with Marios Andreou and Peter Sutton, and three anonymous reviewers for this chapter.
   This research is part of project D05 of SFB 991 *The structure of representations in language, cognition, and science* which is funded by the DFG.

Ruben van de Vijver, Heinrich-Heine-Universität, Universitätsstraße 1, 40225 Düsseldorf, e-mail: ruben.vijver@hhu.de
Agnes Benkő, Eötvös Lóránd University, Budapest, Hungary, e-mail: bagnes@infornax.hu

1 Introduction

More and more systematic phonetic effects are found in morphophonology.[1] Not only is the realization of segments affected by their morphological affiliation (Ben Hedia and Plag 2017; Plag, Homann, and Kunter 2015; Plag, Kunter, and Lappe 2007), but paradigm uniformity effects also cause phonetic details in one word form in the paradigm to reflect the phonetics of other word forms. Even though the Dutch words *bed* [bɛt] 'bed' and *pet* [pɛt] 'cap' appear to end in the same consonant, the vowel in [bɛt] is slightly longer than the one in [pɛt], reflecting longer length of the vowel before [d] in the paradigmatically related plural *bedden* [bɛdə] (Warner, Good, et al. 2003; Warner, Jongman, et al. 2004; Warner, Good, et al. 2006). The cases of phonetically conditioned paradigmatic uniformity discussed so far in the literature almost all deal with cues for voicing of adjacent obstruents, but there are also a few cases discussed of phonetically conditioned paradigmatic uniformity that affect segments that are not adjacent. For example, Braver (2019) discusses incomplete lengthening in Japanese.

Another case of phonetically conditioned paradigmatic uniformity that affects segments that are not adjacent is found in Hungarian vowel harmony and will be the empirical focus of this chapter. In Hungarian the vowel backness of the suffix is determined by the last vowel in the stem. If the last vowel is back, suffix vowels are also back, and when it is front, suffix vowels are almost always front. We say almost always, because there is a handful of monosyllabic words that have a front, unrounded vowel that take suffixes with back vowels. (Benuš and Gafos 2007; Szeredi 2016) present data to show that neutral vowels are more retracted phonetically in words that take suffixes with back vowels than in words that take suffixes with front vowels. But others have disputed these facts (Blaho and Szeredi 2013; Markó et al. 2019). We will present new evidence to support earlier findings that this effect exists (Benuš and Gafos 2007; Szeredi 2016). We will focus on the uninflected words in a paradigm, since these provide crucial evidence that phonetic detail is a result of the influence of inflected words on uninflected words in a paradigm.

---

[1] The first author owes a special debt to Harry: When I was working on my MA-thesis under the supervision of Harry, I asked him whether the conclusions of my thesis had any cognitive relevance. Yes, he said, these representations represent what we know about language. I think that was the moment I realized I was not just trying to learn about language, but to learn about what we know about language. What I did not realize was that this thought would be guiding all my further research. Whatever I have learned between then and now, I would never have learned it if it weren't for Harry's encouragement, his generosity in sharing ideas and his willingness to listen to any crazy idea of mine. Dank je Harry!

There are about 60 monosyllabic words with front vowels that take suffixes with back vowels. As one cannot predict which monosyllabic words with front vowels take suffixes with back vowels, this knowledge has to be stored in the mental lexicon. If there is any phonetic retraction of these front vowels in the uninflected monosyllabic words other members of their paradigm take suffixes with back vowels then this retraction is the consequence of the word being in a paradigm with suffixes with back vowels. As a result, the phonetic detail present in uninflected forms also has to be stored in the mental lexicon. The extant proposals for such representations need to be extended, because they focus on the representation of phonetic details among phonologically contrasting segments (Kirby 2010; van Oostendorp 2008; Yu 2011), or assume a baseline realization (Braver 2019). We will propose that this phonetic detail is the consequence of whole word storage (Lõo, Järvikivi, and Baayen 2018; Lõo et al. 2018; Manker 2020) and the coarticulatory influence of words in a paradigm (van de Vijver and Baer-Henney 2019).

1.1 Paradigm Uniformity Effects

In addition to phonological uniformity effects (Albright 2010; Hall 2005; Harris 1989; Steriade 2008), there are also paradigm uniformity effects that affect the phonetics of word forms. An example of this comes from Dutch, as was briefly mentioned above. Voiced and voiceless obstruents contrast everywhere except word-finally (Booij 1995). The singular *bed* [bɛt] 'bed' which has the plural *bedden* [bɛdə], seems to end in the same obstruent as *pet* [pɛt] 'cap', which has the plural [pɛtə]. Careful study showed that the loss of contrast is not complete (Ernestus and Baayen 2006, 2007a, 2007b; Warner, Good, et al. 2006). The vowel in [bɛt] is slightly, but systematically, longer than the vowel in [pɛt]. The difference in length of the vowel in [bɛt] and [pɛt] is strongly reminiscent of the length of vowels before fully voiced and fully voiceless stops; vowels before fully voiced obstruents are longer than before fully voiceless obstruents (Chen 1970). The longer vowel in [bɛt] makes this word form more similar to the word form in the plural. The paradigmatically conditioned phonetic detail in the vowel length in [bɛt] can therefore be understood as an instance of paradigm uniformity. In this case, too, it is the form with most contrastive information – the plural which contains the information about the voicing of the stem-final obstruent – that is the basis for other word forms to emulate. Similar effects have been attested in many languages (Braver 2011, 2014; Charles-Luce and Dinnsen 1987; Dinnsen 1985; Dmitrieva, Jongman, and Sereno 2010; Ernestus and Baayen 2006, 2007a, 2007b; Kleber, John, and Harrington 2010; Kleber 2011; Port and Crawford 1989; Port,

Mitleb, and O'Dell 1981; Röttger, Winter, and Grawunder 2011; Röttger, Winter, Grawunder, et al. 2014; Slowiaczek and Dinnsen 1985; Warner, Good, et al. 2006).

In the cases reviewed above the phonetic detail could be used to recover a contrast among consonants that would otherwise be lost. There is, however, evidence, to which we will add in this paper, that paradigmatically conditioned phonetic details are also found within different tokens of one segment (or a natural class of segments) depending on morphophonological properties of the paradigm. This is the case in Hungarian to which we will now turn.

1.2 Paradigmatically Conditioned Phonetic Effects in Hungarian

Paradigmatically conditioned phonetic details have also been reported for vowel harmony in Hungarian (Benuš and Gafos 2007; Szeredi 2016) but Blaho and Szeredi (2013) fail to find evidence for the existence of such details. There is a regular rapport between the backness of the final vowel in a stem in Hungarian and the backness of the vowels in suffixes (Törkenczy 2011, 2021). For example, the word *ló* [loː] 'horse' has a back vowel in the stem and its dative form is [loːvnɔk] with a back vowel in the dative suffix; the word *tűz* [yːz] 'fire' has a front vowel in the stem and its dative form is [yːznɛk] with a front vowel in the dative suffix. These facts are illustrated in Table 1.

Table 1: Hungarian monosyllabic words illustrating the relation between the vowel in the uninflected, monosyllabic word (nominative) and the vowel in a suffix of an inflected member of its paradigm (dative).

	Nominative		Dative		Gloss
iː, i	víz	[viːz]	víz-nek	[viːznɛk]	water
yː, y	tűz	[tyːz]	tüz-et	[tyːznɛk]	fire
uː, u	kút	[kuːt]	kút-nak	[kuːtnɔk]	well
øː, ø	kő	[køː]	köv-nek	[køːvnɛk]	stone
oː, o	ló	[loː]	lóv-nak	[loːvnɔk]	horse
eː, ɛ	kéz	[keːz]	kéz-nek	[keːznɛk]	hand
aː, ɔ	nyár	[ɲaːr]	nyár-nak	[ɲɔːrnɔk]	summer

This regular phonological connection between the vowels in the stem and the vowels in the suffix is disrupted by front, unrounded vowels [iː, i, eː, e], which are commonly known as neutral vowels Törkenczy (2011, 2021). In a small set of monosyllabic words in which the vowel is neutral, the vowel in a following suffixes is back rather than front. For example, the word *híd* [hiːd] 'bridge' takes the accusative [hidɔt] with a back vowel (Benuš and Gafos 2007; Blaho and Szeredi 2013; Hayes and Londe 2006; Szeredi 2016; Törkenczy 2011, 2021).[2] In Table 2 an example is given of one word with a neutral vowel that combines with a suffix with a front vowel and one word with a neutral vowel that combines with a suffix with a back vowel.

Table 2: Neutral vowels combine with front and back suffixes.

Nominative		Dative		Gloss
víz	[viːz]	víznek	[viːznɛk]	water
híd	[hiːd]	hídnak	[hiːdnɔk]	bridge

As the pronunciation of a vowel is affected by a preceding vowel even across intervening consonants (Öhman 1966), this effect may generalize to a regressive coarticulation of vowels. This would affect the articulation of neutral vowels depending on the vowel in the suffix. This possibility was investigated by Benuš and Gafos (2007) who performed an articulatory study in which they measured the position of the tongue in neutral vowels in words that take either suffixes with back vowels or suffixes with front vowels. They conducted an Electromagnetic midsaggital articulometry (EMMA) in which small receivers are attached to the the articulators in order to track the movements and position of the tongue. In addition, Benuš and Gafos performed an ultrasound study.

Three speakers of Budapest Hungarian participated in the study, and they read aloud 44 polysyllabic target words (7 pairs with [iː], 8 pairs with [i] and 7 pairs with [eː]) and 16 monosyllabic target words (5 pairs with [iː], 1 pair with [i] and 2 pairs with [eː]) in a carrier sentence. Benuš and Gafos found that in polysyllabic words the tongue positions for neutral vowels surrounded by back vowels are slightly, but statistically significantly retracted. In monosyllabic words the same effect is found: The receivers indicate that the tongue is further back in words with neutral vowels that take suffixes with back vowels than in words with neutral vowels that take suffixes with front vowels.

Benuš and Gafos conclude that neutral vowels are further back if they are surrounded by back vowels. This can be explained as a consequence of coarticulation. It is noteworthy, though, that neutral vowels in monosyllabic uninflected

---

[2] The stem vowel shortens in open syllables, for details see Törkenczy (2011, 2021). This effect is irrelevant for our concerns.

words are also further back when their inflected forms take suffixes with back vowels. This effect is more difficult to analyze as coarticulation, since the vowel that would cause such coarticulation is not present in the target word.

This interesting work sparked research to validate its findings, especially since the behavior of neutral vowels had previously been analyzed as completely lexical and categorical (Blaho and Szeredi 2013). They criticized Benuš and Gafos methodologically, since their conclusions are based on data of only three speakers.

Blaho and Szeredi (2013) addressed the methodological issue of having too few participants and questioned whether the articulatory retraction is large enough to have any acoustic consequences, something Benuš and Gafos doubted. Blaho and Szeredi did an acoustic analysis of neutral vowels in antiharmonic stems pronounced by 12 native speakers of different dialect areas in Hungary; Budapest Hungarian and Párkány Hungarian, a town in the north of Hungary at the Slovakian border.

They asked native speakers to produce words with harmonic and words with antiharmonic vowels in a carrier sentence, and analyzed the formants of the target vowels at their mid point. They found that the quality of the vowel in the suffix does not correlate with the phonetic realization of the transperent vowel. In other words the F2 value of the vowel in *his* [his] 'believe 3sg', which is harmonic is the same as the F2 value of the vowel in *nyit* [ɲit] 'open 3sg.', which is antiharmonic. They conclude that, even if there is articulatory fronting of neutral vowels (Benuš and Gafos 2007), the amount of fronting has no acoustic effects.

Szeredi (2016) addresses the contradiction between the findings of Benuš and Gafos and Blaho and Szeredi. He investigated the antiharmonic and neutral vowels [iː] and [i]. He did not measure the properties of [ɛ], since there are only a handful of pertinent stems. He acoustically analyzed the neutral vowels of 48 stems in 3 conditions as produced in a reading experiment by 16 participants. Szeredi measured the mid points of the target vowels. The effects in all conditions were very similar, but one condition will be directly comparable to our work, and so we report this condition first.

In one condition the stems were uninflected, but embedded in a carrier sentence. In this condition he found that antiharmonic [i] has an F2 that is on average 20 Hz lower than harmonic [i]. This difference is not significant, however. The difference between the F2 of antiharmonic and harmonic [iː] is 11.4 Hz; a small difference that is not significant. It is interesting that the size of the effect was larger in [i] than in [iː]. This chimes with results reported by Mády, Bombien, and Reichel (2008); Mády and Reichel (2007) on variation among the realization of Hungarian vowels. Their measurements were based on vowels that were included in words embedded in carrier sentences, as were the measurements of Szeredi. They found that there was a greater amount of variation with realizations of [i] than among tokens of [iː] or [eː]. This greater range for [i] may have been exploited by the speakers, and is reflected by a greater difference among F2 values in the different contexts in the results of Szeredi.

In the other two conditions – words in isolation and in inflected words – the effects were similar. neutral vowels in words that take suffixes with back vowels have a lower F2 – are more retracted – than those in words that take suffixes with front vowels.

Szeredi (2016) ran a rating study with inflected nonsense words to investigate whether Hungarian native speakers use small phonetic differences in the degree of retraction of neutral vowels to predict the type of suffix. He manipulated vowels to create tokens of each type of neutral vowel and made sure that within each vowel type tokens differed with respect to F2. One group of tokens within each vowel type had an F2 that was 250 Hz lower than a second group of the same type. He based the formant values of the vowels on the results of a classification study of vowels that he had run separately. It turns out that nonsense words with artificially retracted vowels do not prompt more choices of suffixes with back vowels than suffixes with front vowels. He concludes that even though native speakers appear to systematically produce more retracted neutral vowels if they occur in words that take suffixes with back vowels, they do not use vowel retraction to choose a suffix type.

However, the literature offers an alternative to a generalization of the effect to novel items. Ernestus and Baayen (2003) investigated whether Dutch native speakers extend the voicing neutralization found in words to nonsense words. They asked native speakers to inflect nonsense words. They found the inflection of nonsense words depended on their segmental make up. If the segmental make up of the nonsense word resembled the segmental make up of many existing words that all had a voicing neutralization, the nonsense words were more likely to exhibit a voicing neutralization. We may therefore expect that if the nonsense words have a segmental make up that resembles existing words, the existing words will be used as analogues to the inflection of the resembling nonsense words.

These studies leave us with contradictory results. Even though Benuš and Gafos found a small, but systematic articulatory retraction effect for neutral vowels in the context of back vowels, and szeredi found an acoustic effect of tongue retraction, Blaho and Szeredi failed to find an acoustic correlate of such retraction. One goal of this study, then, is to increase our confidence in the existence or the non-existence of acoustic correlates of the retraction of neutral vowels in monosyllabic words that take suffixes back vowels in the rest of their paradigms. This will assist us in assessing the theoretical status of the retraction. A secondary goal is to assess whether any difference in retraction of neutral vowels in existing words is generalized to novel words.

1.3 Theoretical Accounts of Paradigmatically Conditioned Phonetic Effects

The discovery of paradigmatically conditioned phonetic detail in cases of incomplete neutralization prompted Port and Leary (2005) to announce the demise of phonological theory. They argued that paradigmatically conditioned phonetic detail cannot be analyzed with the available categorical phonological tools. A fundamental tenet of phonological theory, according to Port and Leary (2005), is that categories are categorical and not continuous. The incomplete neutralization facts show that there is a systematic, but continuous contrast between word-final obstruents. The consistency of the effect makes an account in phonological theory necessary, but the categorical nature of phonology precludes such an account.

Van Oostendorp (2008) took issue with this proposition and showed that it is very well possible to provide an analysis of incomplete neutralization using the categorical tools of formal phonology. The starting point of van Oostendorp's analysis is a basic assumption within the framework of Optimality Theory (Prince and Smolensky 2004): The underlying form must be contained in the surface form, and nothing from the underlying representation can be destroyed. The underlying form of an incompletely neutralized word-final obstruent is specified by the feature [VOICE]. This feature stands in an abstract, structural relation to the segment in the surface form to which it belongs. There is also another relation, the pronunciation relation, which holds between the segment in the surface form and its underlying features. This relation mediates the pronunciation of the structure. However, in languages with final devoicing the pronunciation relation between the word-final segment and the underlying feature [VOICE] violates a constraint against pronouncing the feature [VOICE] in a word final obstruent. Since there is no pronunciation relation between the segment and the feature [VOICE] the feature is not pronounced, but since the underlying feature cannot be destroyed, it remains there and this unpronounced feature is interpreted by the phonetic module.

van Oostendorp's proposal works in the technical formal sense; it distinguishes between truly voiceless final obstruents and devoiced final obstruents. But it is contradictory and therefore unsatisfactory: The feature [VOICE] is phonologically present, but not pronounced, since that would violate a constraint against pronouncing voiced codas. This phonologically unpronounced feature at some point is interpreted by the phonetic module; in other words, it is pronounced. The exact mechanism of how the phonetic module interprets this unpronounced feature (and how this knowledge is acquired) has been left for phoneticians to flesh out.

It remains to be seen whether this analysis can be extended to other cases of morphologically conditioned phonetic detail. For example, in the Hungarian cases a stem vowel with the feature [−BACK] is phonetically more back if it is surrounded by other vowels that are [+BACK]. Even if an argument can be made that the feature [−BACK] is not pronounced, it is not clear how this would result in making the vowel phonetically more back.

A recent proposal to deal with the effects of incomplete neutralization in phonological theory is proposed in Braver (2019). He proposes the Weighted Paradigm Uniformity Theory. The theory builds on the assumption that words in paradigms tend to adjust to one another, and that grammatical constraints can be weighted. Segments have a canonical realization, and are penalized for deviations from the canon. However, the deviation can still be the best compromise for the realization of a segment. This is the case when the realization of the base–the base is the member of the paradigm to which other members are made uniform–differs from the canonical realization of the target segment. The realization of the target segment will then be adjusted by a certain amount.[3]

Applying this theory to the Hungarian neutral vowels is not straightforward, though. It is not clear what is meant by canonical. Is the pronunciation of any 'true' back vowel canonical, and if so, what formant values are to be considered canonical? Vowels are notoriously variable (Mády and Reichel 2007; Mády, Bombien, and Reichel 2008) and even if it is possible to calculate the mean formant values for a vowel, it is not clear whether native speakers treat this value as canonical (Boersma 2006).

There also exist theories that propose to include phonetic detail in phonological representations, but these deal with phonetic detail in phonological contrasts, not with morphophonologically conditioned phonetic details. Flemming (2001, 2013) proposed to include phonetic detail in order to represent differences in contrastiveness. The phonetic cues to the feature [VOICE] are less salient at the end of a word in comparison to the beginning of a word. Flemming (2001, 2013) represents this by using phonetic dimensions of a feature that are different in different positions. Extensions of this approach have been proposed by Kirby (2010) and Yu (2011).

Finally, there are exemplar-based theories (Ambridge 2020; Bybee and Beckner 2010; Frisch 2017; Goldinger 1998) that can account for the presence of phonetic details in morphophonology. In these theories all words a listener encounters are stored veridically, both with respects to their phonetic properties and their

---

3 It will be adjusted by the squared difference between the canonical pronunciation of the segment and its actual pronunciation multiplied by the weight of the pertinent constraint. This way of calculating the realization of the pronunciation of a segment is rather arbitrary, and does not take into account measures that we know affect the realization of segments, such as family size (Ben Hedia and Plag 2017; Lõo et al. 2018; Tomaschek et al. 2019).

meaning. Stored exemplars in memory are organized on the basis of similarities in phonetic properties and meaning. Since words in a paradigm are similar in their phonetic make up and their meaning, they affect each other's processing and pronunciation. These theories not only are able to explain morphophonologically determined phonetic detail, such effects are a consequence of such theories.

A recent instantiation of an exemplar theory is formulated by Manker (2020). His investigation of the question what detail is stored in memory shows that predictable coarticulatory effects undergo a certain level of abstraction in memory, whereas unpredictable coarticulatory effects are more faithfully stored (Manker 2020). We argue that this is also the case in Hungarian: the vowel harmony found in a paradigm with non-neutral vowels is predictable and therefore stored (and represented) abstractly, whereas the vowel harmony of neutral vowels is unpredictable and lexicalized. This will cause the coarticulation of words in paradigms with neutral vowels to be stored faithfully and show up as a phonetic effect.

Our Experiment

We conducted an experiment to test the hypothesis of Manker (2020). We focus on the phonetic properties of neutral vowels in monosyllabic, uninflected words. If there is paradigmatically conditioned phonetic detail then we expect to find that neutral vowels in monosyllabic words that take suffixes with back vowels are more retracted – they have a lower F2 – than neutral vowels in words that take front suffixes. It will turn out that we do indeed find such an effect. We will use both words and nonsense words in order to assess whether the retraction is generalized to new items.

2 Method

We wanted to investigate the hypothesis that the degree of retractedness of neutral vowels varies with their choice of suffix vowels; neutral vowels in monosyllables that take suffixes with back vowels are more retracted than neutral vowels that take suffixes with front vowels.

To test the hypothesis of Manker (2020) we used a production experiment in which we asked our participants to *silently* read a sentence in which a word or a nonce was inflected Röttger, Winter, Grawunder, et al. (2014). This gave the participant the information about the frontness or the backness of the vowel in the suffix. The participants were then asked to read *aloud* the uninflected variant of the word which appeared in a gap in the next sentence. We recorded the sentences pronounced by the participants and we used the recording to analyze the formants (see Section 3.)

We used 30 existing monosyllabic stems with a neutral vowel that take front suffixes (15 nouns and 15 verbs) and 30 existing monosyllabic stems with a neutral vowel that take back suffixes (15 nouns and 15 verbs). In addition, for each monosyllabic stem we created a corresponding nonsense word, which differed from the existing word only in the onset. The nouns were inflected with the dative suffix (the [nɔk], [nɛk] allomorphs) and the verbs were inflected with the third person plural allomorphs (also [nɔk] and [nɛk]).

Examples of sentences with words (in bold) are given below: All sentences are given in the Appendix.

ɔtɛstɛn ɔt͡ʃiːknɔk piroʃaːkɛl vaːlnia. hɔɔt͡ʃiːk nem siːnɛzøːdik ɛl, ɔtɛst nɛm eːrveːɲeʃ.

The **band** on the test should turn red. If the **band** is not colored, the test is not valid.

pɛciɛk **hisnɛk** ɔføldøɲkiːvyliɛk leːtɛzeːʃeːbɛn. ɔz ɛmbɛrɛk tøpːʃeːge pɛrsɛnɛm **his** ɔz ijeʃmibɛn.

Peti and his friends **believe** in the existence of aliens. The majority of people do not **believe** in such things.

We tested twenty-one monolingual native speakers of Hungarian, fourteen of them women, at the phonetics lab at the Heinrich-Heine-Universität in Düsseldorf. They were paid 10 Euros for their participation.

3 Results

We used Praat (Boersma and Weenink 2018) to measure the formants of the target vowels. First we isolated the vowels in the words and we measured the formants at their midpoint. We looked for 5 formants in a range up to 5500 Hz for women and in a range up to 5000 Hz for men with a time step of 0.01 seconds.

In order to assess the location in the vowel space of the vowels produced in our experiment we plotted the F1 and F2 values in Figure 1. We did this because Mády and Reichel (2007); Mády, Bombien, and Reichel (2008) found that the length distinction in Hungarian vowels is gradually being replaced by quality distinction. They reported that the quality of [i] shows a great deal of variabilty, such that it overlaps with the quality of both [iː] and [eː]. In addition, Szeredi

(2016) reports that in a classification study Hungarian listeners are better able to distinguish between tokens of [i] that differ in F2, than between tokens of [iː].

In agreement with the findings of Mády and Reichel (2007); Mády, Bombien, and Reichel (2008) the distribution in vowel space of the vowels produced in our experiment shows that the difference between [iː] and [i] is a difference in quality.[4] Short [i] is lower and more retracted than [iː]. Moreover, the distribution of [i] is located in between [iː] and [eː]. This is illustrated in Figure 1.

Inspection of the distribution of the formant values showed that the values were not distributed normally, but rather had a logarithmic distribution. We therefore transformed the formant values logarithmically for our analysis. We performed a linear mixed effects regression analysis on our data. We analyzed the results for [iː], [i] and [eː] separately, because these vowels differ inherently in height and backness of the tongue (Mády and Reichel 2007; Mády, Bombien, and Reichel 2008) (see also Figure 1). We did not analyze the items with an [ɛ] as there were no words with such a vowel that take back suffixes.

We begin with the results of our linear mixed effects model that we calculated with the lme4 package in R (Rlme4, Bates et al. 2015) for [iː]. Upon inspection of our data for [iː] we noticed that five items were obviously mispronounced. They had F1 values larger than 1000 Hz or F2 values smaller than 750 Hz. We excluded these items, which accounted for 0.5% of the total amount of [iː] tokens.

Speakers were given random intercepts, but not the items or the suffixes, since there is a small closed set of existing words with neutral vowels, and there are two fixed suffixes. Fixed factors were Suffix (-[nɛk] (front vowel), -[nɔk] (back vowel)) and Word (Nonsense word, Word). The log(F2) formant values were used to assess any differences between the fixed factors.

It turns out that [iː] in words has a slightly more front F2 value than in nonces, and there is no significant effect for the factor suffix (see Table 3).

Table 3: Linear mixed effects model for the vowel [iː].

	Est	Std. Er	df	t value	Pr(>|t|)
(Intercept)	7.79	0.02	22.04	361.06	0.00
nek	−0.01	0.01	1090.02	−1.40	0.16
word	0.02	0.01	1090.07	2.10	0.04

We continue with the mixed effects model analysis of the vowel [i]. Visual inspection of the data for [i] revealed that there were five tokens with an F1 higher than

---

[4] We also found the quantity difference. As this is not crucial we do not dwell on it.

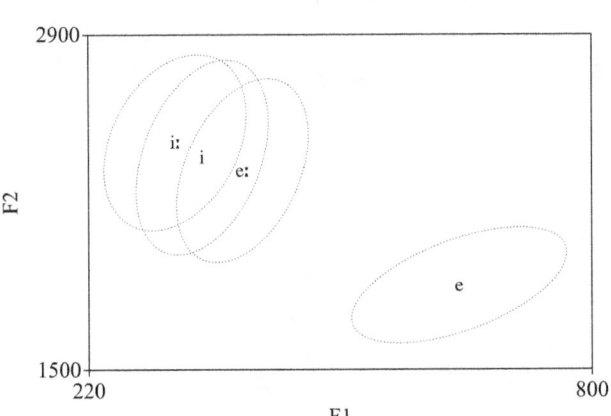

Figure 1: Formants with concentration ellipses. One ellipse covers 39.3% of the data (Boersma and Weenink 2018). Long [iː] is slightly higher and more front than short [i], which, in turn is more high and more front than [eː]. The range of [i] overlaps with both [iː] and [eː] See (Mády and Reichel 2007 and Mády, Bombien, and Reichel 2008 for similar findings.).

600 Hz. We excluded these items. As for the analysis of [iː], we gave speakers random intercepts and used Suffix and Word as fixed factors. The analysis shows that the neutral vowels [i] in monosyllabic words which take suffixes with front vowels when inflected have a higher F2 value than neutral vowels in monosyllabic words which take suffixes with back vowels when inflected. The vowels in words are lower than the vowels in nonces (see Table 4.)

Table 4: Linear mixed effects model for the vowel [i].

	Est	Std. Er	df	t value	Pr(>|t|)
(Intercept)	7.76	0.02	36.87	337.05	0.00
nek	0.04	0.02	455.44	2.10	0.04
word	−0.04	0.02	455.97	−2.16	0.03

The effect of the type of suffix on the retraction of [i] is illustrated in Figure 2, in which the F2 values and the F1 values of tokens with [i] are depicted. The blue line is for monosyllables that take suffixes with back vowels and the red line is for monosyllables that take suffixes with front vowels. The blue line is lower than the red line, which shows that neutral vowels in monosyllabic words that take suffixes with back vowels are more back than neutral vowels in words that take suffixes with front vowels.

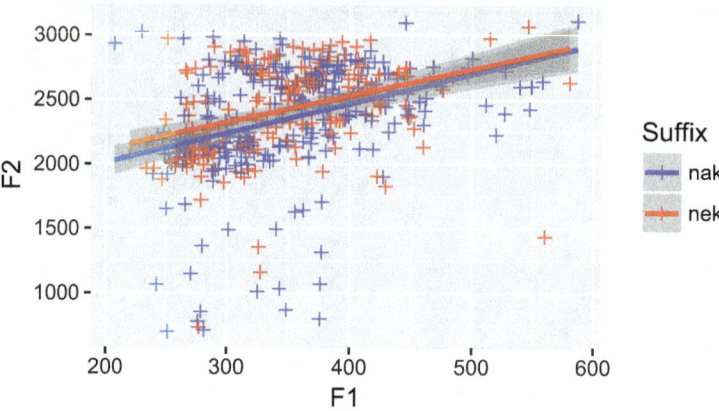

Figure 2: The vowel i is more retracted in monosyllabic words that take suffixes with back vowels (blue) than in monosyllabic words that take suffixes with front vowels (red).

Figure 3 illustrates the word effect. In uninflected words [i] is more retracted than in nonsense words when it occurs with back suffixes when they are inflected.

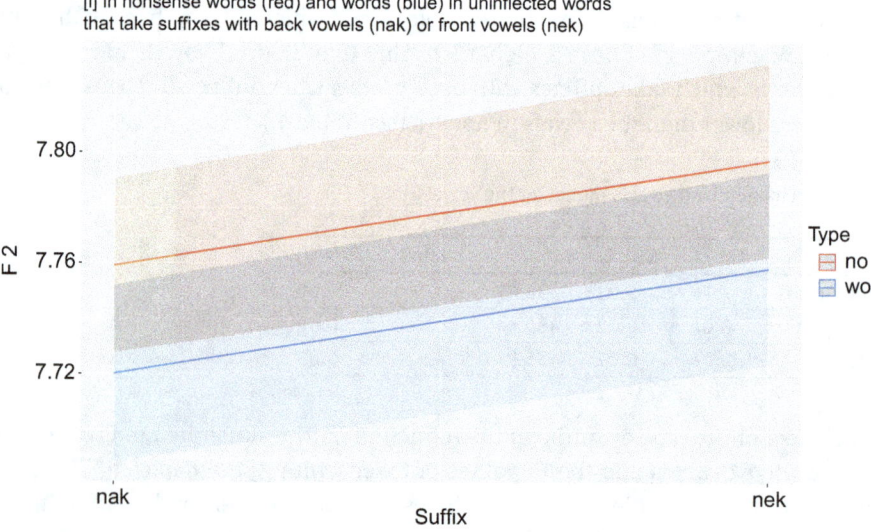

Figure 3: [i] is more retracted in words (wo) and nonces (no) if these take suffixes with back vowels.

The same analysis as for the other vowels was carried out for [eː]. It turns out that the F2 values of [eː] vowels are the same, irrespective of kind of vowel in the suffixes of the inflected variants of the words, and also irrespective of whether the item is a word or not (see Table 5.)

Table 5: Linear mixed effects model for the vowel [eː].

	Est	Std. Er	df	t value	Pr(t)
(Intercept)	7.73	0.03	50.85	261.83	0.00
nek	−0.00	0.02	437.04	−0.20	0.85
word	0.03	0.02	437.05	1.63	0.10

4 Discussion

We conducted our experiment in order to shed light on the question whether the lexicalized vowel harmony of non-neutral vowels results in measurable paradigmatically conditioned phonetic details in Hungarian neutral vowels. In our production experiment Hungarian native speakers silently read a sentence with an inflected word or nonsense word with a neutral vowel, followed by reading out loud of a sentence with its uninflected variant. The formants of these vowels were measured and compared. We found a consistent effect of retraction for the vowel [i] and a generalization of this effect to nonsense words for this vowel.

Benuš and Gafos (2007) did find very small articulatory effects for two of their three speakers and they surmised that these small effects would have no acoustic consequences; Blaho and Szeredi (2013) found that there is a tendency for neutral vowels to be more front if they occur in words that are inflected with suffixes with front vowels, than if they occur in words that are inflected with suffixes that take back vowels. The tendency was, however, not statistically significant; Szeredi (2016) found small differences between antiharmonic and harmonic neutral vowels. Antiharmonic vowels are slightly more back than harmonic vowels, but it is only in suffixed words that this difference was statistically significant.

We found significant retraction for the vowel [i], but not for [iː] or [eː]. In view of previous results on the nature of Hungarian vowels this result is not unexpected. We ascribe the fact that we only found the effect in [i] and not in [iː] or [eː] to the inherent variation of [i], which has been attested independently (Mády and Reichel 2007; Mády, Bombien, and Reichel 2008). Moreover Szeredi (2016) found that Hungarian are able to distinguish tokens of [i] on the basis of phonetic differences in F2, but not [iː] or [eː]. Figure 1 illustrates that the space for [i] overlaps with both [iː] and [eː]. This makes it harder to pronounce an unambiguous token of [i], which may make the [i] more susceptible to coarticulatory effects. The effort to keep [i] distinct from [iː] and [eː] may be too great, and it may be better to instead invest articulatory effort into keeping [iː] and [eː] distinct. Our data is furthermore in full agreement with the data presented by Szeredi (2016: 86). These data also show that the greatest effect in monosyllabic words that were presented in carrier sentences – as in our experiment – is found for [i], and the effect for [iː] is much smaller.

The effect we found for nonsense words, see Figure 3, can be explained by analogy (Ernestus and Baayen 2003). Our nonsense words were based on existing words; we only changed the onset. Native speakers based their inflections of nonsense words on existing words. Therefore, if a nonsense word resembles a word that takes a suffix with a back vowel, the nonsense word also takes a suffix with a back vowel and the vowel of the nonsense word is therefore slightly retracted. It may be argued that there are many words that are similar to the nonsense word that take harmonic suffixes. However, a small number of salient examples, that go against the statistical grain so to speak, exert an influence that is larger than expected on the basis of their statistical prevalence (Olejarczuk, Kapatsinski, and Baayen 2018). The fact that nonsense words are overall pronounced with higher F2 is a consequence of hypo-articulation (Lindblom 1990).

Our results fit in with the previous findings in that the effect is infinitesimal. In combination with previous research (Benuš and Gafos 2007; Szeredi 2016), a picture emerges that shows that the effect is systematic. Even if the tendency does not always reach significance it is (almost) always in the same direction: Antiharmonic neutral vowels are more retracted than harmonic neutral vowels, even in uninflected words in which there is no other [+BACK] vowel that could serve as a coarticulatory target.

Neutral vowels in Hungarian show paradigmatically conditioned phonetic detail. This adds to existing work in which phonetics encroaches upon phonology Flemming (2001, 2013); Kirby (2010); Yu (2011) and morphology (Ben Hedia and Plag 2017; Plag, Kunter, and Lappe 2007; Plag, Homann, and Kunter 2015), in ways that go beyond much research documenting the phonetic effects of incomplete neutralization and flapping (Braver 2011, 2014; Charles-Luce and Dinnsen 1987; Dinnsen 1985; Dmitrieva, Jongman, and Sereno 2010; Ernestus and Baayen 2006, 2007a, 2007b; Port and Crawford 1989; Port, Mitleb, and O'Dell 1981; Röttger, Winter, and Grawunder 2011; Röttger, Winter, Grawunder, et al. 2014; Slowiaczek and Dinnsen 1985; Warner, Good, et al. 2006).

5 Conclusion

Neutral vowels in Hungarian show paradigm uniformity effects that cannot be reduced to a neutralized contrast, as our data have shown. This shows that the effect is general and that the categorical and continuous cases should be analyzed in the same way. Our finding provide a further support for assuming that systematic phonetic effects are found in morphophonology, as predicted by exemplar-theory.

Competing Interests

The authors have no competing interests to declare.

Appendix: Hungarian Sentences

Minden népnek vannak érdekes szokásai. Néhány . . . azonban nagyon szokatlan hagyományokkal rendelkezik.
Sok hírnek nincsen valóságalapja. Ez a . . . is nagyon gyanús.
Ennek a helynek különleges hangulata van. A történelem során ez a . . . fontos szerepet játszott.
Nézd, Petiék cinganak a játszótéren. Mit csinál Peti? . . .
Laci nem igazán örült a dísznek. Feltette a polcra, és a . . . ott porosodott hetekig.
Petiék gyakran finganak. Mit csinál Peti? . . . Gyümölcsök inganak az ágakon, az egyik gyümölcs azonban alig . . . .
Nézd, Petiék gábnak a játszótéren. Mit csinál Peti? . . .
Hiába futott 10 km-t, a célba érés után arcán nyoma sem volt a pírnak. A . . . néhány perc alatt eltűnt az arcáról.
A gyerekek az óvodában egész délelőtt fantáziaállatokat rajzoltak.
Zsuzsi kétszarvú állatát bilmnek nevezte el. Az állat neve . . .
A gyerekek az óvodában egész délelőtt fantáziaállatokat rajzoltak.
Zsuzsi kétszarvú állatát físnek nevezte el. Az állat neve . . .
Nézd, Petiék cürnek a játszótéren. Mit csinál Peti? . . .
A gyerekek az óvodában egész délelőtt fantáziaállatokat rajzoltak.
Zsuzsi kétszarvú állatát bejnek nevezte el. Az állat neve . . .
Nézd, Petiék vúnnak a játszótéren. Mit csinál Peti? . . .
Nézd, Petiék vengenek a játszótéren. Mit csinál Peti? . . .

Nézd, Petiék diltanak a játszótéren. Mit csinál Peti? ...
Laci nem igazán örült a sípnak. Feltette a polcra, és a ... ott porosodott hetekig.
Nézd, Petiék mestenek a játszótéren. Mit csinál Peti? ...
Petiék gyakran félnek. Mit csinál Peti? ...
Petiék intenek a sofőrnek, hogy álljon meg. Ha senki nem ... a sofőrnek, nem fog megállni.
Petiék gyakran vívnak. Mit csinál Peti? ...
A gyerekek az óvodában egész délelőtt fantáziaállatokat rajzoltak.
Zsuzsi kétszarvú állatát zérnek nevezte el. Az állat neve ...
Nézd, Petiék gednek a játszótéren. Mit csinál Peti? ...
A gyerekek az óvodában egész délelőtt fantáziaállatokat rajzoltak.
Zsuzsi kétszarvú állatát mácnak nevezte el. Az állat neve ...
A gyerekek az óvodában egész délelőtt fantáziaállatokat rajzoltak. Zsuzsi kétszarvú állatát raznak nevezte el. Az állat neve ...
Nézd, Petiék bernek a játszótéren. Mit csinál Peti? ...
A gyerekek az óvodában egész délelőtt fantáziaállatokat rajzoltak.
Zsuzsi kétszarvú állatát fépnek nevezte el. Az állat neve ...
Ennek a térnek különleges hangulata van. A történelem során ez a ... fontos szerepet játszott.
Nézd, Petiék lortanak a játszótéren. Mit csinál Peti? ...
Nézd, Petiék bisznek a játszótéren. Mit csinál Peti? ...
Nézd, Petiék vitnak a játszótéren. Mit csinál Peti? ...
Laci nem igazán örült az ingnek. Feltette a polcra, és a ... ott porosodott hetekig.
Néhány sírnak senki sem viseli gondját. Az a ... például teljesen elhanyagolt.
A gyerekek az óvodában egész délelőtt fantáziaállatokat rajzoltak.
Zsuzsi kétszarvú állatát vingnek nevezte el. Az állat neve ...
A gyerekek az óvodában egész délelött fantáziaállatokat rajzoltak. Zsuzsi kétszarvú állatát vírnak nevezte el. Az állat neve ...
Nézd, Petiék fórnak a játszótéren. Mit csinál Peti? ...
Nézd, Petiék vütnek a játszótéren. Mit csinál Peti? ...
Nem tesz jót a sebnek, ha koszos lesz. ügyelj rá, hogy a ... mindig tiszta maradjon.
Nézd, Petiék minganak a játszótéren. Mit csinál Peti? ...
A szülők semmit sem tiltanak ok nélkül. Ha anyu valamit ..., annak oka van.
Nézd, Petiék dítanak a játszótéren. Mit csinál Peti? ...
A gyerekek az óvodában egész délelőtt fantáziaállatokat rajzoltak. Zsuzsi kétszarvú állatát fúdnak nevezte el. Az állat neve ...

A gyerekek az óvodában egész délelőtt fantáziaállatokat rajzoltak. Zsuzsi kétszarvú állatát zsíknak nevezte el. Az állat neve . . .
Petiék gyakran sírnak. Mit csinál Peti? . . .
A gyerekek az óvodában egész délelőtt fantáziaállatokat rajzoltak. Zsuzsi kétszarvú állatát kótnak nevezte el. Az állat neve . . .
A gyerekek az óvodában egész délelőtt fantáziaállatokat rajzoltak. Zsuzsi kétszarvú állatát píjnak nevezte el. Az állat neve . . .
Az évnek ebben a szakaszában általában hideg van, de persze minden . . . más.
A gyerekek az óvodában egész délelőtt fantáziaállatokat rajzoltak. Zsuzsi kétszarvú állatát cavnak nevezte el. Az állat neve . . .
Ha két síknak létezik egy közös pontja, akkor a két . . . metszi egymást.
Petiék állandóan kérnek valamit. Amikor Peti valamit . . . , mindig ideges leszek.
Nézd, Petiék gisznek a játszótéren. Mit csinál Peti? . . .
A gyerekek az óvodában egész délelőtt fantáziaállatokat rajzoltak. Zsuzsi kétszarvú állatát űfnek nevezte el. Az állat neve . . .
Nézd, Petiék sélnek a játszótéren. Mit csinál Peti? . . .
Nézd, Petiék tőfnek a játszótéren. Mit csinál Peti? . . .
Laci nem igazán örült a szíjnak. Feltette a polcra, és a . . . ott porosodott hetekig.
A célnak mindig a szemed előtt kell lebegnie. Jegyezd meg, a . . . a legfontosabb.
Ennek a hídnak nem tetszik a színe. Ha pirosra festenénk, ez a . . . sokkal szebb lenne.
Ekkora kínnak nem szabadna senkit sem kitenni. Ekkora . . . képes bárkit tönkretenni.
Petiék állandóan szednek valamit. Amikor Peti valamit . . . , mindig ideges leszek.
A gyerekek az óvodában egész délelőtt fantáziaállatokat rajzoltak. Zsuzsi kétszarvú állatát sűznek nevezte el. Az állat neve . . .
A fahasábok a kandallóban égnek. Az egyik fahasáb azonban valamiért nem . . . rendesen.
Ezzel a gyakorlatsorral a zsírnak nincs esélye. Néhány hét alatt a hasi . . . teljesen eltűnik.
A gyerekek az óvodában egész délelőtt fantáziaállatokat rajzoltak. Zsuzsi kétszarvú állatát míknak nevezte el. Az állat neve . . .
Petiék nagyon türelmesek, sosem szítanak vitákat. Kati viszont állandóan vitát . . . .
A gyerekek az óvodában egész délelőtt fantáziaállatokat rajzoltak. Zsuzsi kétszarvú állatát híknak nevezte el. Az állat neve . . .

Nézd, Petiék séznek a játszótéren. Mit csinál Peti? . . .
Nézd, Petiék rűmnek a játszótéren. Mit csinál Peti? . . .
Ennek a filmnek már a címe sem tetszik. Lehet, hogy jobb lenne egy másik. . . .
A teszten a csíknak pirossá kell válnia. Ha a . . . nem színeződik el, a teszt nem érvényes.
Nézd, Petiék nernek a játszótéren. Mit csinál Peti? . . .
Nézd, Petiék fagnak a játszótéren. Mit csinál Peti? . . .
Nézd, Petiék zírnak a játszótéren. Mit csinál Peti? . . .
Nézd, Petiék tírnak a játszótéren. Mit csinál Peti? . . .
Petiék gyakran írnak. Mit csinál Peti? . . .
A gyerekek az óvodában egész délelőtt fantáziaállatokat rajzoltak. Zsuzsi kétszarvú állatát húfnak nevezte el. Az állat neve . . .
A gyerekek az óvodában egész délelőtt fantáziaállatokat rajzoltak. Zsuzsi kétszarvú állatát jévnek nevezte el. Az állat neve . . .
A gyerekek az óvodában egész délelőtt fantáziaállatokat rajzoltak. Zsuzsi kétszarvú állatát gyüfnek nevezte el. Az állat neve . . .
A gyerekek az óvodában egész délelőtt fantáziaállatokat rajzoltak. Zsuzsi kétszarvú állatát rűnnek nevezte el. Az állat neve . . .
Nézd, Petiék lírnak a játszótéren. Mit csinál Peti? . . .
A gyerekek az óvodában egész délelőtt fantáziaállatokat rajzoltak. Zsuzsi kétszarvú állatát dújnak nevezte el. Az állat neve . . .
A gyerekek az óvodában egész délelőtt fantáziaállatokat rajzoltak. Zsuzsi kétszarvú állatát rölnek nevezte el. Az állat neve . . .
Petiék gyakran festenek. Mit csinál Peti? . . .
A gyerekek az óvodában egész délelőtt fantáziaállatokat rajzoltak. Zsuzsi kétszarvú állatát fívnek nevezte el. Az állat neve . . .
Nézd, Petiék búdnak a játszótéren. Mit csinál Peti? . . .
A gyerekek az óvodában egész délelőtt fantáziaállatokat rajzoltak. Zsuzsi kétszarvú állatát vílnak nevezte el. Az állat neve . . .
Nézd, Petiék gáknak a játszótéren. Mit csinál Peti? . . .
Nagyon örülnek a bajnoki címnek, a . . . megszerzését a hétvégén meg is ünneplik.
A telefonok ma egész nap csengenek. Az egyik még most is . . . .
A gyerekek az óvodában egész délelőtt fantáziaállatokat rajzoltak. Zsuzsi kétszarvú állatát hínnek nevezte el. Az állat neve . . .
A gyerekek az óvodában egész délelőtt fantáziaállatokat rajzoltak. Zsuzsi kétszarvú állatát méjnak nevezte el. Az állat neve . . .
Petiék állandóan visznek valamit. Amikor Peti valamit . . . , mindig ideges leszek.

Ennek a széknek nem tetszik a színe. Ha pirosra festenénk, ez a ... sokkal szebb lenne.
A gyerekek az óvodában egész délelőtt fantáziaállatokat rajzoltak. Zsuzsi kétszarvú állatát kírnak nevezte el. Az állat neve ...
Nézd, Petiék bidnak a játszótéren. Mit csinál Peti? ...
A gyerekek az óvodában egész délelőtt fantáziaállatokat rajzoltak. Zsuzsi kétszarvú állatát zővnek nevezte el. Az állat neve ...
Egy izomnak vagy ínnak a meghúzódása komoly fájdalommal járhat. Az izom vagy ... pihentetése ebben az esetben elengedhetetlen.
Petiék gyakran hívnak engem. Amikor Peti engem ..., mindig elszaladok.
Nézd, Petiék lirtanak a játszótéren. Mit csinál Peti? ...
A gyerekek az óvodában egész délelőtt fantáziaállatokat rajzoltak. Zsuzsi kétszarvú állatát pebnek nevezte el. Az állat neve ...
A gyerekek az óvodában egész délelőtt fantáziaállatokat rajzoltak. Zsuzsi kétszarvú állatát rélnak nevezte el. Az állat neve ...
A héjnak nevezett külső réteg nagyon kemény. Ez a ... megvéd a komolyabb sérülésektől.
Nézd, Petiék mírnak a játszótéren. Mit csinál Peti? ...
Petiék gyakran néznek engem. Amikor Peti engem ..., mindig elszaladok.
Nézd, Petiék tívnak a játszótéren. Mit csinál Peti? ...
Nézd, Petiék tinganak a játszótéren. Mit csinál Peti? ...
A gyerekek az óvodában egész délelőtt fantáziaállatokat rajzoltak. Zsuzsi kétszarvú állatát zípnak nevezte el. Az állat neve ...
Első látásra víznek tűnt, aztán kiderült, hogy alkohol. A ... semleges illatú.
A gyerekek az óvodában egész délelőtt fantáziaállatokat rajzoltak. Zsuzsi kétszarvú állatát zejnek nevezte el. Az állat neve ...
Nézd, Petiék pérnek a játszótéren. Mit csinál Peti? ...
A csónakok békésen ringanak a kikötőben. Egy csónak pedig a távolban ....
Petiék gyakran szidnak engem. Amikor Peti engem ..., mindig elszaladok.
Petiék állandóan szívnak valamit. Amikor Peti valamit ..., mindig ideges leszek.
Nézd, Petiék vognak a játszótéren. Mit csinál Peti? ...
A gyerekek az óvodában egész délelőtt fantáziaállatokat rajzoltak. Zsuzsi kétszarvú állatát vímnek nevezte el. Az állat neve ...
Nézd, Petiék lintenek a játszótéren. Mit csinál Peti? ...
Nézd, Petiék pégnek a játszótéren. Mit csinál Peti? ...
A zsíros ételek árthatnak a szívnek. A ... egészséges működéséhez kevesebb zsírra van szükség.
Petiék nem mernek szembenézni a nehézségekkel. Kati azonban bátor, és szembe ... nézni a nehézségekkel.

Petiék állandóan vesznek valamit. Amikor Peti valamit . . . , mindig ideges leszek.

Petiék holnap csótányokat irtanak az épületben. Senki nem lehet az épületben, amikor Peti csótányt . . . .

Laci nem igazán örült a nyílnak. Feltette a polcra, és a . . . ott porosodott hetekig.

Petiék állandóan mérnek valamit. Amikor Peti valamit . . . , mindig ideges leszek.

A bankban új számlát nyitnak nekem. Kata is eljött velem, de ő nem . . . új számlát.

Petiék minden nap korán kelnek. Zsuzsi azonban sosem . . . korán. Nézd, Petiék bűrnek a játszótéren. Mit csinál Peti? . . .

Katiék nem bírnak a kutyájukkal. Aki nem . . . a kutyájával, vigye kutyaiskolába.

Ennek a színnek egyik árnyalata sem tetszik. Melyik másik . . . lenne megfelelő?

Nézd, Petiék mörnek a játszótéren. Mit csinál Peti? . . .

A gyerekek az óvodában egész délelőtt fantáziaállatokat rajzoltak. Zsuzsi kétszarvú állatát gídnak nevezte el. Az állat neve . . .

A gyerekek arról beszélgettek, hogy milyen hangja van egy gyíknak. Kati szerint a . . . nem tud hangot kiadni.

Petiék gyakran vernek engem. Amikor Peti engem . . . , mindig elszaladok.

A gyerekek az óvodában egész délelőtt fantáziaállatokat rajzoltak. Zsuzsi kétszarvú állatát zírnak nevezte el. Az állat neve . . .

Petiék a farmon egész nap birkákat nyírnak. Nagyon óvatosnak kell lenni, amikor valaki birkát . . . .

Laci nem igazán örült a díjnak. Feltette a polcra, és a . . . ott porosodott hetekig.

A gyerekek az óvodában egész délelőtt fantáziaállatokat rajzoltak. Zsuzsi kétszarvú állatát ríjnak nevezte el. Az állat neve . . .

Nézd, Petiék gyívnak a játszótéren. Mit csinál Peti? . . .

A gyerekek az óvodában egész délelőtt fantáziaállatokat rajzoltak. Zsuzsi kétszarvú állatát réknek nevezte el. Az állat neve . . .

Nézd, Petiék pelnek a játszótéren. Mit csinál Peti? . . .

Furcsa íze van a tejnek. Inkább kiöntőm és . . . helyett iszom valami mást.

Nézd, Petiék zérnek a játszótéren. Mit csinál Peti? . . .

A gyerekek az óvodában egész délelőtt fantáziaállatokat rajzoltak. Zsuzsi kétszarvú állatát szófnak nevezte el. Az állat neve . . .

Nézd, Petiék durtanak a játszótéren. Mit csinál Peti? . . .

A gyerekek az óvodában egész délelőtt fantáziaállatokat rajzoltak. Zsuzsi kétszarvú állatát fínnak nevezte el. Az állat neve . . .
Nézd, Petiék resznek a játszótéren. Mit csinál Peti? . . .
A gyerekek az óvodában egész délelőtt fantáziaállatokat rajzoltak. Zsuzsi kétszarvú állatát kúznak nevezte el. Az állat neve . . .
Nézd, Petiék gívnak a játszótéren. Mit csinál Peti? . . .
Petiék hisznek a földönkívüliek létezésében. Az emberek többsége persze nem . . . az ilyesmiben.
A gyerekek az óvodában egész délelőtt fantáziaállatokat rajzoltak. Zsuzsi kétszarvú állatát fírnek nevezte el. Az állat neve . . .
A gyerekek az óvodában egész délelőtt fantáziaállatokat rajzoltak. Zsuzsi kétszarvú állatát rínnak nevezte el. Az állat neve . . .
A gyerekek az óvodában egész délelőtt fantáziaállatokat rajzoltak. Zsuzsi kétszarvú állatát díznek nevezte el. Az állat neve . . .

References

Albright, Adam. 2010. Inflectional paradigms have bases too: Arguments from Yiddish. *Natural Language & Linguistic* Theory 28(3). 475–537.
Ambridge, Ben. 2020. Against stored abstractions: A radical exemplar model of language acquisition. *First Language* 40(5–6). 509–559.
Bates, D., Mächler, M., Bolker, B., and Walker, S. 2015. lme4: Linear mixed-effects models using eigen and s4. *r package version* 1.1–8, http://CRAN.Rproject.org/package=lme4.
Ben Hedia, Sonia and Ingo Plag. 2017. Gemination and degemination in English prefixation: Phonetic evidence for morphological organization. *Journal of Phonetics* 62. 34–49.
Benuš, Stefan and Adamantios Gafos. 2007. Articulatory characteristics of Hungarian transparent vowels. *Journal of Phonetics* 35(3). 271–300.
Blaho, Sylvia and Dániel Szeredi. 2013. Hungarian neutral vowels: A micro-comparison. *Nordlyd* 40(1). 20–40.
Boersma, Paul. 2006. Prototypicality judgments as inverted perception. In Gisbert Fanselow, Caroline Féry, Ralf Vogel, and Matthias Schlesewsky (eds.), *Gradience in Grammar. Generative Perspectives* (167–184). Oxford University Press.
Boersma, Paul and David Weenink. 2018. *Praat: Doing Phonetics by Computer (version 6.0.39)* [computer program]. Tech. rep. Universiteit van Amster-dam. http://www.praat.org/.
Booij, Geert. 1995. *The Phonology of Dutch.* Oxford: Clarendon Press.
Braver, Aaron. 2011. Incomplete neutralization in American English flap-ping: A production study. *University of Pennsylvania Working Papers in Linguistics* 17(1). 5.
Braver, Aaron. 2014. Imperceptible incomplete neutralization: Production, non-identifiability, and non-discriminability in American English flap-ping. *Lingua* 152. 24–44.
Braver, Aaron. 2019. Modelling incomplete neutralisation with weighted phonetic constraints. *Phonology* 36(1). 1–36.

Bybee, Joan L. and Clay Beckner. 2010. Usage-based theory. In *The Oxford Handbook of Linguistic Analysis*.
Charles-Luce, Jan and Daniel A. Dinnsen. 1987. A reanalysis of Catalan de-voicing. *Journal of Phonetics* 15(2). 187–190.
Chen, Matthew. 1970. Vowel length variation as a function of the voicing of the consonant environment. *Phonetica* 22(3). 129–159.
Dinnsen, Daniel A. 1985. A re-examination of phonological neutralization. *Journal of Linguistics* 21(2). 265–279. http://www.jstor.org/stable/4175789.
Dmitrieva, Olga, Allard Jongman, and Joan Sereno. 2010. Phonological neutralization by native and non-native speakers: The case of Russian final devoicing. *Journal of Phonetics* 38(3). 483–492. http://dx.doi.org/10.1016/j.wocn.2010.06.001.
Ernestus, Mirjam and R. Harald Baayen. 2003. Predicting the unpredictable: Interpreting neutralized segments in Dutch. *Language* 79. 5–38.
Ernestus, Mirjam and R. Harald Baayen. 2006. The functionality of incomplete neutralization in Dutch: The case of past-tense formation. *Laboratory Phonology* 8. 27–49.
Ernestus, Mirjam and R. Harald Baayen. 2007a. Intraparadigmatic effects on the perception of voice. *Amsterdam Studies in the Theory and History of Linguistic Science Series* 4 286. 153–174.
Ernestus, Mirjam and R. Harald Baayen. 2007b. Paradigmatic effects in auditory word recognition: The case of alternating voice in Dutch. *Language and Cognitive Processes* 22(1). 1–24.
Flemming, Edward S. 2001. Scalar and categorical phenomena in a unified model of phonetics and phonology. *Phonology* 18(1). 7–44. http://www.jstor.org/stable/4420187.
Flemming, Edward S. 2013. *Auditory Representations in Phonology*. Routledge.
Frisch, Stefan A. 2017. Exemplar theories in phonology. In *The Routledge Handbook of Phonological Theory*, 553–568. Routledge.
Goldinger, Stephen D. 1998. Echoes of echoes? An episodic theory of lexical access. *Psychological Review* 105(2). 251.
Hall, Tracy A. 2005. Paradigm uniformity effects in German phonology. *Journal of Germanic Linguistics* 17(4). 225–264.
Harris, John. 1989. Towards a lexical analysis of sound change in progress. *Journal of Linguistics* 25(1). 35–56.
Hayes, Bruce and Zsuzsa C. Londe. 2006. Stochastic phonological knowledge: The case of Hungarian vowel harmony. *Phonology* 23(1). 59–104.
Kirby, James P. 2010. *Cue selection and category restructuring in sound change*. Chicago: University of Chicago PhD thesis.
Kleber, Felicitas. 2011. *Incomplete neutralization and maintenance of phonological contrasts in varieties of Standard German*. Munich: Ludwig-Maximilians-Universität München PhD thesis.
Kleber, Felicitas, Tina John, and Jonathan Harrington. 2010. The implications for speech perception of incomplete neutralization of final devoicing in German. *Journal of Phonetics* 38. 185–196.
Lindblom, Björn. 1990. Explaining phonetic variation: A sketch of the h&h theory. In *Speech Production and Speech Modelling*. 403–439.
Lõo, Kaidi, Juhani Järvikivi, and R. Harald Baayen. 2018. Whole-word frequency and inflectional paradigm size facilitate Estonian case-inflected noun processing. *Cognition* 175. 20–25. http://dx.doi.org/https://doi.org/10.1016/j.cognition.2018.02.002. http://www.sciencedirect.com/science/article/pii/S0010027718300325.

Lõo, Kaidi, Juhani Järvikivi, Fabian Tomaschek, Benjamin V. Tucker, and R. Harald Baayen. 2018. Production of estonian case-inflected nouns shows whole-word frequency and paradigmatic effects. *Morphology* 28(1). 71–97.

Mády, Katalin, Lasse Bombien, and Uwe D. Reichel. 2008. Is Hungarian losing the vowel quantity distinction? In *Proc. 8th international seminar on speech production.* Strasbourg.

Mády, Katalin and Uwe D. Reichel. 2007. Quantity distinction in the Hungarian vowel system – just theory or also reality? In Jürgen Trouvain and William Barry (eds.), *Proceedings of the 16th international congress of phonetic sciences,* 1053–1056.

Manker, Jonathan. 2020. The perceptual filtering of predictable coarticulation in exemplar memory. *Laboratory Phonology: Journal of the Association for Laboratory Phonology* 11(1). http://dx.doi.org/10.5334/labphon. 240.

Markó, Alexandra, Márton Bartók, Tamás Gábor Csapó, Tekla Etelka Grázi, and Andrea Deme. 2019. Articulatory analysis of transparent vowel /i:/ in harmonic and antiharmonic Hungarian stems: Is there a difference? In *Interspeech 2019.*

Öhman, Sven. 1966. Coarticulation in VCV utterances: Spectrographic measurements. *The Journal of the Acoustical Society of America* 39(1). 151–168.

Olejarczuk, Paul, Vsevolod Kapatsinski, and R. Harald Baayen. 2018. Distributional learning is error-driven: The role of surprise in the acquisition of phonetic categories. *Linguistics Vanguard* 4(s2).

Plag, Ingo, Julia Homann, and Gero Kunter. 2015. Homophony and morphology: The acoustics of word-final S in English. *Journal of Linguistics.* 1–36.

Plag, Ingo, Gero Kunter, and Sabine Lappe. 2007. Testing hypotheses about compound stress assignment in English: A corpus-based investigation. *Corpus Linguistics and Linguistic Theory* 3(2). 199–232. http://dx.doi.org/10.1515/CLLT.2007.012.

Port, Robert and Penny Crawford. 1989. Incomplete neutralization and pragmatics in German. *Journal of Phonetics* 17(4). 257–282.

Port, Robert and Adam Leary. 2005. Against formal phonology. *Language* 81(4). 927–964.

Port, Robert, F. Mitleb, and M. O'Dell. 1981. Neutralization of obstruent voicing in German is incomplete. *The Journal of the Acoustical Society of America* 70(S1). S13.

Prince, A. and Paul Smolensky. 2004. Optimality Theory: Constraint Interaction in Generative Grammar. (Ms. Rutgers University, New Brunswick and University of Colorado at Boulder [Technical Report No. 2, Rutgers University Center for Cognitive Science]. Malden MA/Oxford UK/Victoria Australia: Blackwell.

Röttger, Timo, Bodo Winter, and Sven Grawunder. 2011. The robustness of incomplete neutralization in German. In *Proceedings of the 17th International Congress on Phonetic Sciences,* 1722–1725. Hong Kong.

Röttger, Timo, Bodo Winter, Sven Grawunder, James Kirby, and Martine Grice. 2014. Assessing incomplete neutralization of final devoicing in German. *Journal of Phonetics* 43. 11–25.

Slowiaczek, Louisa M. and Daniel A. Dinnsen. 1985. On the neutralizing status of Polish word-final devoicing. *Journal of Phonetics* 13(3). 325–341.

Steriade, Donca. 2008. A pseudo-cyclic effect in Romanian morphophonology. In Asaf Bachrach and Andrew Nevins (eds.), *Inflectional Identity,* 313–360. Oxford University Press.

Szeredi, Dániel. 2016. *Exceptionality in vowel harmony.* New York University PhD thesis.

Tomaschek, Fabian, Ingo Plag, Mirjam Ernestus, and R. Harald Baayen. 2019. Phonetic effects of morphology and context: Modeling the duration of word-final s in English with

naıv̈ e discriminative learning. *Journal of Linguistics.* 1–39. http://dx.doi.org/10.1017/
S0022226719000203.
Törkenczy, Miklós. 2011. Hungarian vowel harmony. In Marc van Oostendorp, Colin J. Ewen, Keren Rice, and Elizabeth V. Hume (eds.), *The Blackwell Companion to Phonology,* vol. 5, chap. 123, 2963–2989. John Wiley & Sons.
Törkenczy, Miklós. 2021. Hungarian vowel harmony. In Mark Aronoff (ed.), *Oxford Bibliographies in Linguistics.* Oxford University Press.
Van de Vijver, Ruben and Dinah Baer-Henney. 2019. Paradigms in the mental lexicon: Evidence from German. *Frontiers in Communication* 3. 65. http://dx.doi.org/10.3389/fcomm.2018.00065. https://www.frontiersin.org/article/10.3389/fcomm.2018.00065.
Van Oostendorp, Marc. 2008. Incomplete devoicing in formal phonology. *Lingua* 118(9). 1362–1374.
Warner, Natasha, Erin Good, Allard Jongman, and Joan Sereno. 2003. Orthography and underlying form in incomplete neutralization. *Acoustical Society of America Journal* 114(4). 2396–2396.
Warner, Natasha, Erin Good, Allard Jongman, and Joan Sereno. 2006. Orthographic vs. morphological incomplete neutralization effects. *Journal of Phonetics* 34(2). 285–293.
Warner, Natasha, Allard Jongman, Joan Sereno, and Rachèl Kemps. 2004. Incomplete neutralization and other sub-phonemic durational differences in production and perception: Evidence from Dutch. *Journal of Phonetics* 32(2). 251–276.
Yu, Alan. 2011. Contrast reduction. In Jason Riggle John Goldsmith and Alan Yu (eds.), *The Handbook of Phonological Theory,* 291–318. Chichester: Wiley On line Library.

Bert Botma and Colin J. Ewen
Old English Breaking as Vowel Excrescence

Abstract: We argue that Old English Breaking, a diphthongisation process which affected front vowels, involved vowel excrescence. The key to our proposal is that the consonantal targets of breaking (traditionally, /l r x/) were articulated with a retracted tongue root. This implies that the fricative trigger was radico-uvular /χ/ rather than dorso-velar /x/. We interpret the breaking process itself as the result of a specific gestural timing relationship between the tongue root gesture of the consonant and the dorsal gesture of the preceding front vowel.

Keywords: diphthongisation, tongue root retraction, Articulatory Phonology, gestural conflict, vowel excrescence, breaking, Old English

1 Old English Breaking: Background

Old English (OE) Breaking was a sound change which took place "very early in the prehistoric OE period" (Hogg 1992: 84), perhaps around the fourth and fifth centuries, "but probably taking until about the ninth century" (Lass 1994: 48). Many aspects of the process are controversial, and there is considerable disagreement in the literature, both about the nature of the change itself and about the environment which triggered it. Davenport (2005: 64) offers an account which represents a commonly accepted interpretation:

> OEB [Breaking] was a diphthongisation process affecting both the long and short front vowels of OE (that is, long and short /i e æ/) when these were followed by either (i) a cluster initiated by a liquid /l r/ or (ii) the velar fricative /x/ (with or without a following consonant). In these environments a back vowel was epenthesised between the front vowel and the triggering consonant(s).

Hogg (1992: 66) notes that there is not a great deal of dialectal variation in the way in which breaking applies. (The notable exception are Anglian dialects, where we do not find diphthongisation in the breaking environments but retraction.) However, "there is considerable variation according to phonological environment. An adequate rule of thumb . . . is that the likelihood of breaking decreases in relation to increasing height and length of front vowel".

Bert Botma and Colin J. Ewen, Leiden University Centre for Linguistics, University of Leiden

https://doi.org/10.1515/9783110730098-007

(1) gives some representative data (from Davenport 2005: 64, 73; Goth. = Gothic, OHG = Old High German, OS = Old Saxon).

(1) a. /rC/ OE heorte — OS herta 'heart'
weorþan — OHG werden 'become-INF'
sweord — OS swerd 'sword'
bearn — OHG barn 'child'
earm — Goth. arms 'arm'
hiorde ~ heorde — OHG hirti 'shepherd'
steorra — OHG sterno 'star'
b. /lC/ OE eolh — OHG elaho 'elk'
meolcan — OHG melkan 'milk-INF'
seolh — Goth. selhs 'seal'
eald — OHG alt 'old'
healdan — OS haldan 'hold-INF'
eall — OHG all 'all'
c. /x(C)/ OE feohtan — OHG fehtan 'fight-INF'
eoh — Goth. ehu 'horse'
eahta — OHG ahta 'eight'
seah — OHG sah 'see-3SG.PRT'
leoht — OHG lihti 'light'
miox ~ meox — Goth. mihst 'excrement'
tiohhan — Goth. tihhojan 'consider-INF'

Like other clusters, geminate /r/, /l/ and /x/ trigger breaking, as shown by the forms *steorra*, *eall* and *tiohhan* in (1). Notice that /w/ is also claimed to be a trigger in the process (Hogg 1992: 85; Lass 1994: 48). We do not consider this here, and indeed put aside a range of philological matters, such as scribal variation, issues concerning orthographic representation, e.g. the lack of an *æa* spelling and the variation between *io* and *eo*, etc., the controversial status of the syllabic nuclei characterised by most scholars as 'short diphthongs',[1] the relationship between the diphthongs arising from Breaking and the original Germanic diphthongs, etc. For discussion of issues such as these, see for example Lass and Anderson (1975), Dresher (1985), Howell (1991), Lass (1994), and references there. Our focus in this paper is much more limited. We examine the nature of the diphthongisation process (in Section 2) and the articulatory phonetic properties which the trigger-

---

1 See on this the discussion of what is referred to as the 'digraph' controversy in Lass and Anderson (1975: 75ff).

ing consonants have in common (in Section 3). Section 4 presents an analysis of our observations in terms of an approach to phonological representation based on the kinds of gestures proposed in Articulatory Phonology. We should state at the outset that it is, of course, hard to find direct evidence for any of the claims we make about the phonetic realisation of Old English segments. Nevertheless, we believe that we can gain some fruitful insights into the mechanics of OE Breaking by comparing this process to similar phenomena in languages that are spoken today.

2 The Nature of the Diphthongisation Process

Although there is general agreement that OE Breaking involves diphthongisation, the exact quality of the second element of the diphthong is a matter of some debate. The 'traditional' approach assumes that this element was, at least initially, some kind of back vowel. Thus Smith (2007: 92) (see also Smith 2002) observes that "Breaking (or 'Fracture') is the term generally used by Anglicists to describe a process of diphthongisation whereby, between a front vowel and certain single consonants or consonant clusters, a back glide vowel developed, at first as [u] . . . This back vowel combined with the original front vowel to form a diphthong." Similarly, Lass and Anderson (1975: 74) characterise the process as involving epenthesis of a "protective" back "glide vowel", [u], or perhaps [ʊ] (see also Campbell 1959: 54; Lass 1994: 51).

These approaches seem to be in agreement that OE Breaking 'proper' involved the first step in the summary in (2), taken from Davenport (2005: 65):

(2) OE   Diphthong
     Breaking   Height Harmony
     /i/   →   [iu]   →   [eo]
     /e/   →   [eu]   →   [eo]
     /æ/   →   [æu]   →   [æɑ]

However, there is disagreement on the subsequent step. For some authors (e.g. Lass and Anderson 1975: 90–91; Gussenhoven and van de Weijer 1990: 317; Davenport 2005: 65), this involves the operation of a rule of Diphthong Height Harmony, as shown in (2), whereby the second element of the diphthong becomes identical in height to the first element (notice further that in the case of the high vowel, the diphthong resulting from breaking is held to have fallen together with the mid vowel, so that both yield [eo]). Other writers argue that [u] "subsequently lowered and centred to [ə]" (Smith 2007: 92), thus giving the centring diphthongs [iə], [eə] and [æə] (or perhaps just [eə] and [æə]).

Our own interpretation of the diphthongisation process, which we develop below, is that the quality of the second part of the diphthong was different depending on whether the following consonant was /l/, /r/ or /x/, but that these vowels were likely not perceived as distinct by listeners. We will refer to the second element of the diphthongs that resulted from OE Breaking as 'excrescent' (for this term, see e.g. Levin 1987; Gick and Wilson 2006). The characteristic property of excrescent vowels is that they lack an independent vocalic gesture, but arise as the result of a conflict between the articulatory gestures of surrounding segments – in the case of OE Breaking, between the gestures of the front vowel and the following consonant.

3 Phonetic Insights into the Breaking Environment

The status and representation of /l r x/ as a natural phonetic and/or phonological class have constituted a recurrent issue of debate in discussions of OE Breaking. The assumption that the diphthongisation involved the introduction of some kind of back vowel depends crucially on the claim that the breaking triggers are the source of this backness (given the assumption that a natural class shares some phonetic property or combination of properties). Thus Lass (1994: 49) observes that "[the breaking contexts] naturally prompt insertion of a 'transition' [in our terms, 'excrescent'] vowel of back quality as an assimilatory response to the front-to-back movement".

One commonly held traditional view is that /x/ is uncontroversially back in Old English, and that preconsonantal /l r/ are 'backed' or 'dark', i.e. velarised, uvularised, or pharyngealised (cf. Quirk and Wrenn 1955: 145; Hogg 1992: 84; Lass 1994: 49–50). On the view that velarisation of /l r/ is involved, "all the breaking and retraction environments then share some approximation or contact between the tongue back and the velum" (Lass 1994: 50). Some writers go further, claiming that the primary articulation of OE /r/ was uvular, rather than it merely having a secondary ('backed') articulation in preconsonantal position (e.g. Lass and Anderson 1975: 85–86; Smith 2007: 100). Notice that if we assume that backness was the feature triggering breaking, some other property must also be involved: OE /k/ is also back, as are [ŋ] and [ɣ], but they do not trigger breaking.

However, as we have already observed, word-final singleton /l r/, as opposed to singleton /x/, do not trigger breaking, as shown in (3) (from Davenport 2005: 66):

(3) *Breaking and non-breaking contexts*
   a. feoh   'cattle'
      feohtan   'fight-INF'
   b. wer   'man'
      weorþan   'become-INF'
   c. wæl   'slaughter'
      weald   'forest'

Accounts which assume that all the triggers for breaking involve backness therefore require the ancillary assumption that backed realisations of /l r/ first developed before consonants and were later extended to word-final contexts. We discuss this point further in Section 3.1, in connection with the weakening of /l r/ in postvocalic position.

3.1 /l/ and /r/ as Breaking Triggers

As we have seen, the traditional interpretation of /l r/ as triggers for OE Breaking is either that they had a secondary 'back' articulation (i.e. they were velarised, uvularised, or pharyngealised) in coda position, or, in the case of /r/, that its primary articulation was uvular. However, much phonetic and phonological work suggests that postvocalic liquids are characterised by properties which do not necessarily involve raising of the back of the tongue, thus casting doubt on an analysis which characterises OE Breaking as backness assimilation. We can distinguish two such properties. Firstly, in many languages postvocalic liquids are typically more 'vocalic' than their counterparts in onset position. For example, many dialects of Modern Standard Dutch have postvocalic realisations of /l/ which do not involve the alveolar closure found in onset position, while loss of postvocalic /r/ in non-rhotic dialects of English is preceded by 'weakening', in which the articulation of the rhotic becomes progressively less consonantal, i.e. more approximant-like (see e.g. McMahon 1996). It is in such varieties, i.e. those with approximant-like realisations of /l r/, that we find breaking effects. With regard to Dutch, Koopmans-van Beinum (1969: 247) observes that vowels preceding a syllable-final /r/ are lengthened and have a diphthongised quality, with the formant values of the latter portion of the vowel approximating those of schwa, e.g. *mier* [miəɹ] 'ant'. Collins and Mees (1999: 200) note further that "word-final /r/ may be replaced by a close [ə] off-glide", as in [mïə̯], while "many speakers realise /l/ as a strongly pharyngealised vocoid without any alveolar contact, i.e. an unrounded back vowel of a [ɣ] type", as in *koel* [kuɣ] 'cool' (1999: 197).

Both Howell (1991) and Denton (2001) argue that /l r/ acted as triggers for OE Breaking not because of any velarisation or any other 'backness' property, but because they were vowel-like approximants of the kind found in Modern Dutch. The fact that these realisations were apparently restricted to word-internal contexts at the time when breaking occurred is phonetically not implausible. Diachronic evidence suggests that the gradual weakening process which eventually led to non-rhotic varieties also began in word-internal environments, and only later affected word-final /r/ (see e.g. McMahon 1996; Minkova 2014).

Phonetic research has revealed a second property of /l r/, viz. that their articulation in many varieties of English involves pharyngeal constriction (see e.g. Lindau 1985; Sproat and Fujimura 1993; Catford 2001; Gick, Kang, and Whalen 2002). This gesture is most prominent in syllable-final position. Following Uldall (1958), Catford (2001: 172) calls this /r/ 'molar'. Molar realisations of /r/ "have, as common features, a 'bunched' tongue, with the tip and blade somewhat retracted into the body of the tongue, and lateral contacts between the dorsal surface of the tongue and the premolar and/or molar teeth. There may be considerable sulcalisation in the velar–uvular area and always some retraction of the tongue root backwards into the pharynx". Similar claims have been made for Dutch, with evidence from ultrasound tongue imaging showing that both /l/ and /r/ have pharyngealised allophones in coda position (Scobbie, Sebregts, and Stuart-Smith 2006).

Along with Howell and Denton, we assume that the trigger for the diphthongisation of a front vowel preceding a liquid in OE Breaking was not the purported backness of the liquid, but its vocalicness, with the quality of the inserted vowel being determined by what we assume to be the pharyngealised quality of the postvocalic liquid – or, in other words, by the involvement of the tongue root as active articulator; we refer to such articulations as 'radical' below. We presume that, as in, for example, Modern Dutch, the quality of an excrescent vowel before /r/ was not phonetically *identical* to that of an excrescent vowel before /l/, because of the different configurations for the two liquids; nevertheless, it seems likely that these vowels were not perceived as being distinct.

3.2 /x/ as a Breaking Trigger

The phonetic likelihood of /x/ triggering breaking is at first sight less clear. Although, as we have seen, Lass (1994: 49) claims that the natural response to a sequence of a front vowel and a velar consonant is the insertion of a transitional vowel of back quality, this is perhaps not the phonetically most likely strategy. A more typical response to a sequence of a front vowel and a velar fricative is fronting of the fricative, as shown for German in (4), which illustrates "the distribution of postvocalic, syllable-final [ç] vs. [x]" (Hall 1989: 2).

(4) German
    siech [ziːç] 'sickly'   Buch [buːx] 'book'
    ich [ɪç] 'I'   Spruch [ʃpʀʊx] 'saying'
    reich [ʀaeç] 'rich'   Koch [kɔx] 'cook'
    Pech [pɛç] 'bad luck'   Bach [bax] 'brook'

Wiese (1996: 210–213) notes that there is further variation between [x] and uvular [χ], with the uvular being found after low vowels (e.g. *Bach* [baχ]) and the velar after [uː oː] (e.g. *hoch* [hoːx] 'high'), with both variants occurring after [ʊ ɔ] (e.g. *Loch* [lɔx ~ lɔχ]) 'hole'. He treats all three fricatives ([ç x χ]) as having a specification for the articulator [dorsal], i.e. they are all produced with the body of the tongue.

Some accounts of OE Breaking have also recognised the fact that sequences of vowels and dorsal fricatives typically display coarticulation. Denton (2001: 161), for example, notes that postvocalic *h* at the relevant stage of Old English "is most commonly thought to have had the quality of [x], which may have been further fronted to [ç] after front vowels", as in the German examples in (4). It is unclear, however, why [ç] following a front vowel should trigger insertion of a back element.

We are not aware of any reported cases of transitions from front vowels to velar /x/ in the phonetic literature, i.e. cases that might lend support to the analysis of OE Breaking as involving assimilation to a back target. This is not surprising, given that both front vowels and velar fricatives are articulated with the tongue body; it is the fact that they share an articulator that leads to the assimilation of the fricative to the vowel in German. There is, then, no need to assume a transition when two segments share the same 'value' for an articulator; just as, say, the nasal in Modern English *bunch* has a palato-alveolar (rather than alveolar) realisation because it shares an articulator ([coronal]) with the following affricate, so a vowel and a following dorsal consonant share phonetic 'place'. Observations such as these cast further doubt on the traditional analysis of OE Breaking before /x/ as involving insertion of a back vowel as a result of assimilation to a dorsal fricative.

This leads us to the hypothesis that the fricative in Old English was like its Modern Standard Dutch counterpart in having an overwhelmingly *uvular* realisation, i.e. [χ]. The assumption that the fricative was uvular rather than velar is in itself not very surprising. There are a number of languages in which back fricatives are more retracted than the corresponding stops; in addition to Standard Dutch, this includes, for example, some varieties of Arabic (Smith 1988) and Iraqw (Botma and Mous, this volume).

Given our hypothesis, we might expect to find evidence of excrescence or retraction of vowels before /χ/ in Dutch. However, an informal production experiment with 18 speakers of Standard Dutch (Dreschler et al. 2008) showed that while front vowels were generally retracted before /l/ and /r/, no such effect occurred before /χ/ – insofar as this could be reliably measured at all, since the vowels before fricatives were phonetically much shorter than those before liquids. We conclude from the lack of vowel retraction (or indeed diphthongisation) that Dutch uvular /χ/ is realised with the tongue body as main articulator, i.e. that it is dorsal, like /x/.

However, this is not the only possible realisation of [χ]. Catford (1977: 160) observes that the production of what he calls 'dorso-uvulars' involves the "dorsal *or* radical surface of the tongue against the extreme end of the soft palate, including the uvula" [our emphasis] (cf. also Abercrombie 1967: 51). Recent phonetic work has shown further that uvulars are produced with tongue root retraction. Based on ultrasound data, Howson and Kochetov (2020: 2849) observe that the uvular rhotic /ʀ/ in Sorbian "has a constriction target located in the uvular-pharyngeal area produced with the tongue body and a constriction in the lower pharynx produced with the tongue root." Their data show that /ʀ/ differs from velar stops like /g/ in that the latter are highly susceptible to coarticulatory effects from neighbouring vowels. The uvular rhotic, on the other hand, shows very little coarticulation, its tongue root gesture being especially robust. Howson and Kochetov conclude from this that velars and uvulars have distinct gestural representations: velars have a tongue body gesture only, while uvulars have both a tongue body gesture and a tongue root gesture.

There is a substantial amount of evidence that uvulars trigger both retraction and excrescence effects. Al-Ani (1970) observes that uvulars lower the F2 of a following /i/ or /a/ in Arabic. Ladefoged and Maddieson (1996) observe the same for K'ekchi. Sequences of a front vowel and a uvular also trigger vowel excrescence. This is the case in Nootka, for example, where we find forms like [sɪᵊqmɪs] 'pus' (from /sɪqmɪs/). According to Gick and Wilson (2006), the excrescent schwa results from a gestural conflict between the dorsal articulation of the vowel and the radical articulation of the consonant; if both are 'faithfully' executed, the result is a transitional schwa-like vowel. A similar process is found in Nivkh, where /e/ diphthongised to [eę] or [ea] before a uvular, with the initial part of the diphthong having been reanalysed as palatalisation of the preceding consonant (Botma and Shiraishi 2014).

The data considered above support our hypothesis that the back fricative in Old English was radico-uvular, i.e. a uvular fricative that is produced with the tongue root as active articulator. We do not take a position on the exact involvement of the tongue root; this may have involved a backing and raising gesture towards the uvula along the lines observed by Catford, or retraction of the tongue root backwards into the pharyngeal cavity with simultaneous backing and raising of the tongue body, similar to what Howson and Kochetov observe for Sorbian.[2] In either case, there would have been a gestural conflict between the tongue root gesture of the fricative and the tongue body gesture of the preceding vowel. In Section 4 we will see that such articulatory conflicts receive a straightforward interpretation in the framework of Articulatory Phonology.

4 A Gestural Approach to Old English Breaking

Our analysis employs a simplified version of the Articulatory Phonology framework in Browman and Goldstein (1986, 1989, 1992). Articulatory Phonology assumes that the primitives of phonological representation are articulatory gestures. The grammar regulates how these gestures are timed with respect to each other. We believe that this framework is particularly suitable for modelling articulation-based sound changes of the type displayed by OE Breaking.

We focus here on the gestures involved in articulations made with the tongue, viz. the tongue tip, tongue dorsum, and tongue root gestures. (These correspond to what are called 'active articulators' in traditional phonetic descriptions.) We distinguish the relevant 'articulator sets' in (5), from Browman and Goldstein (1989) (notice that tongue root is introduced there, but not discussed).

(5) *articulator*   *constriction location*
    tongue tip (TT)   dental
                           alveolar
                           postalveolar
                           palatal

    tongue dorsum (TD)   **palatal**
                           velar
                           uvular

    tongue root (TR)   **uvular**
                           pharyngeal

---

[2] Howson and Kochetov note that Sorbian speakers typically realise /ʀ/ as a uvular approximant or fricative in initial position, e.g. *rad* [ʁat]~[χat] 'gladly'. In final position /ʀ/ is vocalised, e.g. *žer* [ʒeɐ] 'caries'; the ultrasound data show that here, too, the tongue root gesture is maintained.

We assume, with Browman and Goldstein (1989: 224), that "a number of articulations made with the tongue cannot be clearly categorised as being made with either TT or TB",[3] citing palatals and palato-alveolars, among others. We would add that this applies equally to uvulars, whose production, as we have seen, may involve both the tongue dorsum and the tongue root as active articulator.

On the assumption that the uvular fricative in Old English was a consonant whose production involved a tongue root (TR) gesture (either as a primary articulation, or in addition to a TD gesture), a sequence such as [iχ] might have the schematic gestural representation in (6). (The labels 'wide' and 'narrow' refer to the degree of constriction of the sounds concerned.)

(6) *Gestural sequencing*

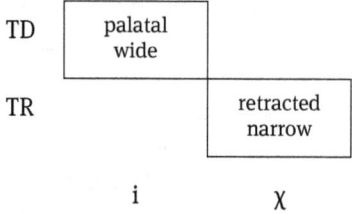

Here the two gestures, tongue dorsum and tongue root, are sequentially ordered, such that the offset of the dorsal gesture coincides with the onset of the tongue root gesture. However, if the two gestures are temporally overlapped, we get something like (7).[4]

(7) *Gestural overlap: excrescence before /χ/*

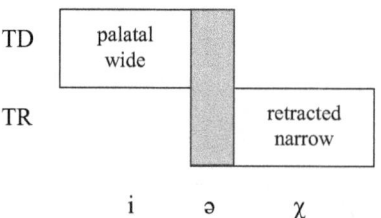

---

3 Browman and Goldstein use 'tongue body' (TB), rather than tongue dorsum.
4 We do not make any claims about the duration of the 'segments' involved; the diagrams are purely for illustration.

The period of overlap here is essentially a retracted front vowel; something whose percept might well be a schwa, or some other relatively neutral central or back vowel. The excrescent vowel is therefore the automatic result of the phasing relationship of the dorsal gesture of the vowel and the radical gesture of the following consonant. We assume that an excrescent vowel emerged regardless of the type of vowel (all vowels involve a dorsal gesture), but that it was salient only when the vowel was front, when the articulatory 'distance' between the vowel and the breaking trigger is greatest.

Importantly, this account of breaking as schwa excrescence before the fricative is equally applicable to the other two consonants involved, /l r/, which, we have argued, also involve tongue root retraction.

(8) *Gestural overlap: excrescence before /l r/*

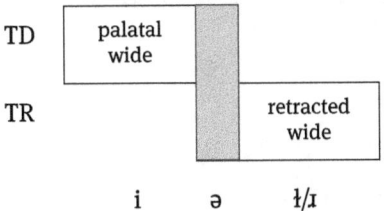

The only difference in the Articulatory Phonology model is the specification for the degree of constriction of the tongue root gesture, an issue which we do not consider here.

It is interesting to compare our proposal with Gick and Wilson's (2006) account of sequences of a high vowel + liquid, as in an English word like *heel*. Gick and Wilson observe that one realisation of this word is *hee[ə]l*, with an excrescent schwa, as the result of a phasing relationship similar to that which we suggest underlies OE Breaking. However, Gick and Wilson are agnostic about whether the retracted articulations that they discuss are dorsal or radical (they refer to such articulations as involving the 'tongue dorsum/root'). We suggest that schwa excrescence in Old English arose as a result of the timing relationship between two distinct articulators, viz. the tongue dorsum and the tongue root. Cross-linguistic support for this comes from the Sorbian data discussed above, which provide evidence for a tongue root gesture which is *independent* from the tongue dorsum gesture.

Our account also allows a natural interpretation of the situation in Anglian dialects of Old English. Here we do not find diphthongisation in breaking contexts, but retraction of the vowel, at least of /æ/ preceding /l/, and in Northumbrian, /r/ (called 'combinative breaking' by Hogg 1992: 92), as illustrated in (9):

(9) OE 'laxing'/'retracting' dialects
West Saxon   Anglian
healf   half   'half'
sweord   sword   'sword'
wearp   uarp   'he threw'

Gick and Wilson (2006: 651–652) identify a number of similar cases in other languages, observing that these languages prefer "to compromise the achievement of articulatory targets. That is, rather than let the TR go to its fully advanced position for /i/, these languages reduce or eliminate that vowel gesture without advanced TR". In the cases that they consider, this results in "a laxed or lowered vowel".

In our analysis, where we assume distinct tongue body and tongue root gestures, this process would involve gestural overlap, such that the vowel has a retracted tongue root *throughout* its production. This is shown in (10) for the vowel + liquid sequence in Anglian *half*.

(10) *Gestural overlap: 'laxing'*

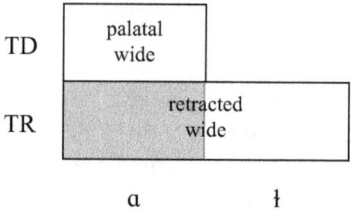

We assume that retraction also involved 'gestural reduction' (for this notion, see e.g. Browman and Goldstein 1986) of the palatal gesture of the vowel.

Our analysis also predicts that radico-uvular fricatives will behave differently with respect to preceding front vowels than dorso-velar fricatives, which, in terms of the gestural model adopted here, share a tongue dorsum gesture with vowels. In our analysis, gestural representations of the kind in (11) are therefore impossible.

(11) *(Impossible) monogestural VC sequence*

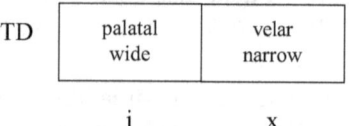

The reason for this, we argue, is that there cannot be more than one constriction location within a single tongue dorsum sequence. When the vowel and the following fricative involve a single dorsal gesture we find familiar situations such as that already discussed for German, in which a front vowel must be followed by an *ich*-laut (front/palatal), and a back vowel by an *ach*-laut (back/velar); in such cases the fricative is dorsal, and shares its place with the preceding vowel (i.e. both front/palatal and back/velar are dorsal articulations).

Consider in this respect the process sometimes referred to as Middle English (ME) Breaking (Jones 1989: 141ff; Kwon 2012), in which, as in OE Breaking, vowels followed by a dorsal fricative diphthongise:

(12) *Middle English Breaking* (from Jones 1989: 141ff; Kwon 2012: 36–37)
    a. ploh   plouʒ   'plough'
        douhter douʒter 'daughter'

    b. rūh   rough   'rough'
        laghter laughter 'laughter'

    c. ehhte   eighte   'eight'
        fehtan feight   'fight'

Unlike in OE Breaking, in ME Breaking we find excrescence of front vowel after front vowel, and back vowel after back vowel, suggesting that the fricative in question is indeed dorsal, and that the sequence of vowel and fricative is obligatorily 'homorganic', e.g. [eɪçtə] and [laʊxtər] (or perhaps [laʊχtər], with a dorsal uvular). Only a sequence of dorsal vowel and radical fricative will allow schwa excrescence of the type found in OE Breaking.

5 Discussion

Liquid + consonant clusters, in Old English and in general, are unstable. Many processes lead either to vowel excrescence or to vocalisation of the liquid, with breaking and laxing as possible subsequent steps. OE Breaking is one of many processes which illustrates these effects. In addition, the facts of OE Breaking suggest that postvocalic dorsal fricatives are also unstable. We have attributed this to their sharing a gestural specification with the preceding vowel, as a result of which they have comparatively little perceptual salience.

Our account suggests, then, that one way in which velar fricatives can ensure their continued survival is to become perceptually more prominent by 'acquiring' a tongue root gesture.⁵ In some feature-based approaches, the acoustic salience of /χ/ is expressed by characterising it as 'strident', as opposed to /x/ (cf. e.g. Harris and Lindsey 1995: 70; Carr and Montreuil 2013: 54). Consider in this respect the development of the postvocalic velar fricatives in Middle English in (12) above, which were lost after some back vowels (12a) but became labiodental after others (12b) (note that Harris and Lindsey and Carr and Montreuil also characterise /f/ as strident). Much the same observations can be made about postvocalic palatal fricatives, which also have comparatively little perceptual salience; notice, for example, the eventual loss of the fricatives in the Middle English forms in (12c). Palatal fricatives and affricates may become more prominent by shifting their place to palato-alveolar, as in English *church*, or they may shift their place to alveolar, as in French *cent* 'hundred'. Both in the case of a dorsal fricative becoming (radico-) uvular, and that of a palatal fricative becoming palato-alveolar, the fricative acquires a gestural specification that is *independent* from that of the preceding or following vowel. In both cases, two articulatory gestures are involved, and hence there is potential for temporal mismatching. We suggest that the environment for OE Breaking arose in part from such a change.

What happened to the vowel + fricative sequences in the wake of OE Breaking? In Anglian dialects, the effects of breaking were undone by a process called 'Anglian Smoothing' (see e.g. Hogg 1992: 142–152; Dresher 1993; Howell and Wicka 2007), whereby the diphthongs reverted to the original monophthongs, perhaps when followed by "palatal allophones of the velar phonemes /x, k, ɣ/, that is [ç, c, ʝ]", although this is by no means certain (Hogg 1992: 143). In other dialects, too, the diphthongs appear to have undergone subsequent monophthongisation. The traditional account of this development is that the diphthongs were created in the same context in which they were subsequently lost, but this is clearly unattractive, since such a development would lack any phonetic motivation. We suggest instead that the changes which affected the vowels resulted from changes in the gestural specification of the fricative. The fricative was radico-uvular when OE Breaking was active, with the tongue root gesture of the fricative being sufficiently prominent to effect diphthongisation. The subsequent 'smoothing' of the preceding vowels suggests that the fricative later became dorso-uvular, presumably through a change in the relative prominence of its tongue body and tongue root gestures.⁶ Further reduction of the tongue root gesture would then have

---

5 Consider the realisation of /χ/ in Standard Dutch, in which "the rasping phenomenon comes down to a strong degree of uvular tension, caused by a strong air turbulence, resulting in considerable perceptual prominence" (Smakman 2006: 233).
6 We would expect such a change to have involved a period during which there was phonetic variation between different 'back' realisations of the fricative. This kind of variation is also ob-

resulted in the 'monogestural' dorsal fricatives that we find in Middle English, which later disappeared from the language.

6 Conclusion

We have argued that /l r x/, which behave as a natural class in OE Breaking, are likely to have been articulated with a retracted tongue root. This implies that the fricative was radico-uvular /χ/ rather than dorso-velar /x/. The tongue root articulation of the breaking triggers created a gestural conflict with the dorsal articulation of the preceding vowel. The result of this was an excrescent vowel, which arose as an automatic consequence of the transition from a dorsal to a radical articulation.

References

Abercrombie, David. 1967. *Elements of General Phonetics*. Edinburgh: Edinburgh University Press.
Al-Ani, Salman. 1970. *Arabic Phonology: An Acoustical and Physiological Investigation*. The Hague: Mouton.
Altairi, Hamed, Jason Browne, Catherine Watson & Bryan Gick. 2017. Tongue retraction in Arabic: An ultrasound study. In Karen Jesney, Charlie O'Hara, Caitlin Smith & Rachel Walker (eds.), *Supplemental Proceedings of the 2016 Annual Meeting on Phonology*. http://dx.doi.org/10.3765/amp.v4i0.3995.
Botma, Bert & Hidetoshi Shiraishi. 2014. Nivkh palatalisation: Articulatory causes and perceptual effects. *Phonology* 31(2). 181–207.
Browman, Catherine P. & Louis Goldstein. 1986. Towards an articulatory phonology. *Phonology Yearbook* 3. 219–252.
Browman, Catherine P. & Louis Goldstein. 1989. Articulatory gestures as phonological units. *Phonology* 6(2). 201–251.
Browman, Catherine P. & Louis Goldstein. 1992. Articulatory phonology: An overview. *Phonetica* 49(3–4). 155–180.
Campbell, Alistair. 1959. *Old English Grammar*. Oxford: Clarendon Press.
Carr, Philip & Jean-Pierre Montreuil. 2013. *Phonology*, 2nd edn. Basingstoke: Palgrave Macmillan.
Catford, J. C. 1977. *Fundamental Problems in Phonetics*. Edinburgh: Edinburgh University Press.
Catford, J. C. 2001. On Rs, rhotacism and paleophony. *Journal of the International Phonetic Association* 31(2). 171–185.

---

served by Altairi et al. (2017), who, in a phonetic study of tongue root retraction in Arabic, find that four of their eight speakers produce uvular fricatives as velars.

Collins, Beverley & Inger M. Mees. 1999. *The Phonetics of English and Dutch*, 4th edn. Leiden: Brill.

Davenport, Mike. 2005. Old English Breaking and syllable structure. In Philip Carr, Jacques Durand & Colin J. Ewen (eds.), *Headhood, Elements, Specification and Contrastivity: A Phonological Festschrift for John Anderson*, 63–76. Amsterdam: John Benjamins.

Denton, Jeanette Marshall. 2001. Phonetic insights into the articulation of early West Germanic /r/. In Hans van de Velde & Roeland van Hout (eds.), *R-atics: Sociolinguistic, Phonetic and Phonological Characteristics of /r/*, 159–172. Brussels: Etudes & Travaux.

Dreschler, Gea, Kathrin Linke, Thijs Porck & Annemarie Post. 2008. Heulp! Yet another approach to Old English breaking. Ms, University of Leiden.

Dresher, B. Elan. 1985. *Old English and the Theory of Phonology*. New York/London: Garland.

Dresher, B. Elan. 1993. The chronology and status of Anglian smoothing. In Sharon Hargus & Ellen M. Kaisse (eds.), *Studies in Lexical Phonology*, 325–341. San Diego: Academic Press.

Gick, Bryan, A. Min Kang & Doug H. Whalen. 2002. MRI evidence for commonality in the post-oral articulations of English vowels and liquids. *Journal of Phonetics* 30(3). 357–371.

Gick, Bryan & Ian Wilson. 2006. Excrescent schwa and vowel laxing: Cross-linguistic responses to conflicting articulatory targets. In Louis Goldstein, Douglas Whalen & Catherine T. Best (eds.), *Papers in Laboratory Phonology 8: Varieties of Phonological Competence*, 635–659. Berlin/New York: Mouton de Gruyter.

Gussenhoven, Carlos & Jeroen van de Weijer. 1990. On V-place spreading vs. feature spreading in English historical phonology. *The Linguistic Review* 7(4). 311–332.

Hall, Tracy Alan. 1989. Lexical phonology and the distribution of German [ç] and [x]. *Phonology* 6(1). 1–17.

Harris, John & Geoff Lindsey. 1995. The elements of phonological representation. In Jacques Durand & Francis Katamba (eds.), *Frontiers of Phonology: Atoms, Structures, Derivations*, 34–79. London/New York: Longman.

Hogg, Richard M. 1992. *A Grammar of Old English*. Vol. 1: *Phonology*. Oxford: Blackwell.

Howell, Robert B. 1991. *Old English Breaking and Its Germanic Analogues*. Tübingen: Niemeyer.

Howell, Robert B. & Katerina Somers Wicka. 2007. A phonetic account of Anglian smoothing. *Folia Linguistica Historica* 28(1–2). 187–214.

Howson, Phil & Alexei Kochetov. 2020. Lowered F2 observed in uvular rhotics involves a tongue root gesture: Evidence from Upper Sorbian. *Journal of the Acoustical Society of America* 147(4). 2845–2857.

Jones, Charles. 1989. *A History of English Phonology*. London: Longman.

Koopmans-van Beinum, Florien J. 1969. Nog meer fonetische zekerheden. *De Nieuwe Taalgids* 62. 245–250.

Kwon, Young-Kook. 2012. Labialization and loss of Middle English /x/. *English Language and Linguistics* 18(1). 35–54.

Ladefoged, Peter & Ian Maddieson. 1996. *The Sounds of the World's Languages*. Oxford: Blackwell.

Lass, Roger. 1994. *Old English: A Historical Linguistic Companion*. Cambridge: Cambridge University Press.

Lass, Roger & John M. Anderson. 1975. *Old English Phonology*. Cambridge: Cambridge University Press.

Levin, Juliette. 1987. Between epenthetic and excrescent vowels. *Proceedings of the West Coast Conference on Formal Linguistics* 6. 187–201.

Lindau, Mona. 1985. The story of r. In Victoria A. Fromkin (ed.), *Phonetic Linguistics*, 157–168. Orlando: Academic Press.

McMahon, April. 1996. On the use of the past to explain the present: The history of /r/ in English and Scots. In Derek Britton (ed.), *English Historical Linguistics 1994*, 73–89. Amsterdam/Philadelphia: John Benjamins.

Minkova, Donka. 2014. *A Historical Phonology of English*. Edinburgh: Edinburgh University Press.

Quirk, Randolph & C. L. Wrenn. 1955. *An Old English Grammar*. London: Methuen.

Scobbie, Jim, Koen Sebregts & Jane Stuart-Smith. 2006. From subtle to gross variation: An ultrasound tongue imaging study of Dutch and Scottish English /r/. Paper presented at the 14th Manchester Phonology Meeting, 25–27 May.

Smakman, Dick. 2006. *Standard Dutch in the Netherlands: A sociolinguistic and phonetic description*. Radboud Universiteit Nijmegen PhD dissertation. Utrecht: LOT Publications.

Smith, Jeremy J. 2002. The origins of Old English Breaking. In Yoko Iyeiri & Margaret Connolly (eds.), *'And gladly wolde he lerne and gladly teche': Essays on Medieval English Presented to Professor Matsuji Tajima on His Sixtieth Birthday*, 39–50. Tokyo: Kaibunsha.

Smith, Jeremy J. 2007. *Sound Change and the History of English*. Oxford: Oxford University Press.

Smith, Norval. 1988. Consonant place features. In Harry van der Hulst & Norval Smith (eds.), *Features, Segmental Structure and Harmony Processes (Part I)*, 209–236. Dordrecht: Foris.

Sproat, Richard & Osamu Fujimura. 1993. Allophonic variation in English /l/ and its implications for phonetic implementation. *Journal of Phonetics* 21(3). 291–311.

Uldall, Elizabeth. 1958. American 'molar' R and 'flapped' T. *Revista do Laboratório de Fonética Experimental da Faculdade de Letras da Universidade de Coimbra* 4. 103–106.

Wiese, Richard. 1996. *The Phonology of German*. Oxford: Oxford University Press.

Clemens Poppe and Jeroen van de Weijer

Diachronic Vowel Harmony: From Middle to Modern Korean

Abstract: Middle Korean had an active vowel harmony system, the remnants of which can still be observed in certain constructions in modern varieties of Korean. In this article, we consider the consequences of vowel harmony for the representations of vowels in Middle Korean and Modern Seoul Korean from an RCVP perspective. We pay particular attention to the status of the element |A| as a head or dependent, and whether the fourth element |∀| is necessary in an analysis of the vowel systems of the two varieties.

Keywords: Vowel harmony, diachrony, Korean, RCVP, head–dependency

1 Introduction

There are two ways in which historical developments in language should be captured by phonological theories, such as theories of segmental features. First, it should be possible to represent segmental systems at different stages of a language adequately, and it should be possible to represent changes in such systems using the theory's features or elements, preferably in a simple way. Secondly but closely connected to the first objective, it should be possible to represent rules or constraints in a language at different stages, and account for, or at least express, changes in such rules, again preferably in a simple way.

In this chapter we try to establish how changes in the vowel system of Korean could be captured in Radical CV Phonology (RCVP) (van der Hulst 2020), to see if this slightly unusual system (with multiple central vowels) can adequately be expressed in RCVP, especially in connection with the vowel harmony rule which was active in Middle Korean, but of which only vestiges are left in the modern language (Modern Seoul Korean; henceforth MSK). Both vowel and harmony systems are discussed briefly in earlier work by van der Hulst (e.g. 1988, 2018), but here we wish to delve a little deeper and also assess whether current RCVP can adequately capture these systems or whether modifications are needed.

Clemens Poppe and Jeroen van de Weijer, Waseda University, Shenzhen University

https://doi.org/10.1515/9783110730098-008

This paper is organised as follows: in Section 2 we start with the representation of the Middle Korean vowel system and the possible analysis of vowel harmony. Section 3 deals with the modern language and seeks an account for the development of the vowel inventory and harmony rule. In doing so, we will focus on two particular aspects of RCVP: the use of the fourth element ∀, and the distinction between primary and secondary elements. In the final section we discuss the implications of the analysis for the RCVP theory.

2 Vowel Harmony in Middle Korean

2.1 Analysis Based on Primary |A| or [low]

Vowel harmony in Middle Korean (MiK) is discussed by van der Hulst (2018: § 10.2.1). The MiK vowel system as interpreted by van der Hulst (2018: 402–404) is given in (1), where the arrows indicate harmonic relations:

(1)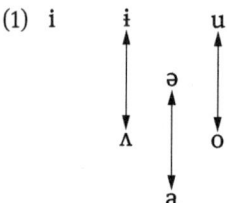

Traditionally, the seven vowels have been grouped into three 'bright' vowels /ʌ a o/, three 'dark' vowels /ɨ ə u/, and one neutral vowel /i/. Examples of vowel harmony (adapted from J.-K. Kim 2000; glosses added) are given in (2) below, with glosses of the grammatical suffixes and particles added by the authors. The examples in (2a) show the alternations between /ʌ/ and /ɨ/, between /a/ and /ə/, and between /u/ and /o/. Those in (2b) show that [i] is a transparent vowel that can follow both bright and dark vowels in stems, and those in (2c) show that some stems with /i/ take /ʌ/ while others take /ɨ/ (2c).[1]

---

1 Ko (2012: 179) cites examples from Park (1994) of stems that take either type of suffix, e.g. *kilh-ʌl* ~ *kilh-ɨl* 'road-accusative', *pih-ʌmjə* ~ *pih-ɨmjə* 'sow/scatter/sprinkle-and/while' (glosses added).

(2) a. nalah-ʌl   'country-accusative'   nimkɨm-ɨl   'king-accusative'
       pʌlʌm-aj   'mind-locative'   tɨlɨh-əj   'field-locative'
       al-om   'know-nominalizer'   təl-um   'reduce-nominalizer'

    b. kʌli-om   'hide-nominalizer'   kɨli-um   'paint-nominalizer'
       kotʰi-om   'repair-nominalizer'   pskəti-um   'fall-nominalizer'
       hanapi-lʌl   'grandfather-accusative' məli-lɨl   'head-accusative'

    c. nic-ʌni   'forget-since'   pskini-nʌn 'meal-topic'
       nil-ɨsi   'rise-honorific'   pisk-ɨn   'titled-adnominal'

Under the interpretation in (1), vowel harmony is a type of height harmony that involves the phonetic feature [low]: apart from the neutral vowel /i/, there are three low vowels /ʌ a o/ and three non-low vowels /ɨ ə u/. Other types of analyses are possible, however, e.g. based on the phonetic distinction between ATR and RTR. Secondly, the location of /ʌ/ is controversial; there is no consensus on the phonetic and phonological features this vowel had. Both of these factors have caused considerable discussion and have led to a number of competing analyses of vowel harmony in MiK (see Ko 2012 for an overview).[2]

To account for alternations like those in (2), van der Hulst (2018) compares an analysis based on primary |A| (the feature [low]) with an analysis based on secondary |A| ([RTR]). The RCVP representations of the analysis based on primary |A| are given in (3), where we added the element |I| to the vowel /i/, which although lacking in van der Hulst (2018) is necessary as the vowel /ə/ is already analyzed as an empty vowel. Since van der Hulst seems to have overlooked this point, we would here like to present an objective comparison between the two types of analyses within the RCVP model.[3]

The representations in (3) are based on the following mappings between phonetic properties and phonological elements. To start with, the non-high vowels

---

[2] As discussed by Ko (2012: 174), the MiK vowel /ʌ/ has changed into a range of different vowels in Modern Korean: /ɨ/, /a/, /o/ and incidentally into /ə/. Jeju Korean is the only dialect in which the vowel was retained; in this dialect it is realized as /ɔ/. The representation of /ʌ/ in (3) is reasonable considering these historical changes, but this also holds for the RTR-based analysis (see again Ko 2012: 174).

[3] An analysis based on underspecified |I| could in theory be saved by adding elements to /ə/, for instance |∀| and secondary |A|. In such an analysis, harmony would involve a combination of the addition of A (the usual type of harmony) as well as 'promotion' of |A|: the element is acquired in the alternations between /ɨ u/ and /ʌ o/, respectively, and gains primary status in the alternation between /ə/ (∀, A) and /a/ (A). On this account, however, it is not clear why |∀| gets deleted when secondary |A| is promoted to primary |A|. We thank a reviewer for pointing this out to us.

/ʌ o a/ all contain the element |A|. In terms of phonetic features, this primary |A| can be thought of as corresponding to [low]. The element |∀|, the aperture counterpart of |A|, appears in both high and mid vowels, which means it corresponds to [non-low]. This element can be thought to be also part of the vowels /u/ and /o/, but as it is not contrastive in those vowels, it is omitted for those vowels in (3). The order in which the elements are given reflects the presumed universal ranking of the elements for vowels – A > U > I/∀, which is derived from the element geometry of RCVP.

(3) i   ɨ   u   ə   ʌ   o   a
                        A   A   A
                U   U
     I
         ∀   ∀

Before we look at how we can deal with the neutral status of /i/, let us consider phonological processes in Middle Korean and later stages of the language which point to an active element I. Ko (2012: 184–185), referring to J. Kim (2000), gives examples of three types of palatalization (4a) and vowel umlaut resulting in off-glide diphthong creation (4b), processes which already took place in the sixteenth and fifteenth century, respectively.

(4) a. t-palatalization: tipʰ   → cipʰ   'straw'
       k-palatalization: kil   → cil   'road'
       h-palatalization: him   → sim   'strength'

    b. vowel umlaut: kjecip → kjejcip 'woman'
                          kuljeki → kujljeki 'wild goose'
                          cjepi   → cjejpi   'swallow'

It is difficult to imagine formalizing palatalization before front vowels without an element I. If /i/ contains |I|, there must be another reason why /i/ does not take part in any alternations and mixes freely with vowels from either harmonic set (i.e. /ə ɨ u/ vs. /a ʌ o/). Here we suggest a very simple solution: a co-occurrence constraint which bans the combination of |I| with |A|.

(5) I → ¬ A

Van der Hulst (2018, 2020) discusses different kinds of co-occurrence constraints, and points out that "[e]very phonological theory must employ constraints in order to define the set of contrastive segments" (van der Hulst 2020: 348).

Next, we can consider the underspecification of /ə/ in the analysis based on primary |A| or [low]. If the position of this vowel in the vowel triangle was indeed close to schwa, one could say that leaving it underspecified for any element is phonetically motivated. Moreover, the alternation with the vowel /a/, which has the element |A|, seems natural. A drawback of the analysis, however, is that /ɨ/ and /ʌ/ rather than /ə/ were used as the default epenthetic vowels in Middle Korean. Good examples of the default nature of these vowels comes from suffix allomorphy, examples of which are given in (6) (adapted from Lee and Ramsey 2011: 216 as in Poppe 2020). As shown in (6); when the stem ends in a consonant, the ending -(ʌ/ɨ)myə 'and also' starts with either /ʌ/ or /ɨ/, depending on the nature of the vowels in the stem, but when the stem ends in a consonant, the vowel is absent.

(6) a. mol-ʌmyə   'do not know-and also'
    b. mit-ɨmyə   'believe-and also'
    c. hʌli-myə   'break through-and also'

The fact that many different suffixes show this kind of allomorphy suggests that not /ə/, but /ɨ/ and /ʌ/ have minimal specifications. In fact, these vowels are often referred to as 'minimal vowels' in studies of the Middle Korean and earlier stages of the Korean language (Ito 2013; Lee and Ramsey 2011; Martin 1992; Whitman 1985, 1994). In the next section, we will therefore develop an analysis in which /ɨ/ and /ʌ/ have minimal specifications.

2.2 Analysis Based on Secondary |A| or [RTR]

The analysis based on primary |A| or [low] is not the only one that van der Hulst (2018) considers; he also discusses the alternative analysis based on secondary |A| in (7) (2018: 404), which embodies the RCVP version of [RTR] harmony.[4]

---

[4] A reviewer remarks that the use of secondary elements is reminiscent of the distinction between the head and complement tier introduced by Backley and Takahashi (1998). While the two approaches have in common that the same element may be used twice within the same representation – an option which is not available in most element-based approaches – a crucial difference is that in RCVP, the distinction between primary and secondary elements does not replace the head-dependent distinction but rather is an extra option. The idea of using the same element twice within a single segment was already proposed in van der Hulst (1988). See van der Hulst (2018, 2020) for detailed discussions of and motivations for the distinction between primary and secondary elements.

(7) i   ɨ   u   ə   ʌ   o   a
               A   A
               U   U
          ∀   ∀
                    A   A   A

Although this analysis is not adopted by van der Hulst (2018), an analysis based on an RTR-based distinction may be preferable from a historical viewpoint. Notice that as in the analysis above in (3), the vowel /i/ in (7) is completely underspecified. As this type of analysis has the same problems as those discussed in the previous section, we would like to argue in favor of yet another analysis, in which /ʌ/ and /ɨ/ – rather than /i/ – are the default vowels. An analysis along these lines was actually proposed for MiK by van der Hulst (1988), and more recently by Poppe (2020). Building on these works, we propose the RCVP analysis in (8), where |I|, |U| and |A| stand for [coronal], [rounded], and [low], respectively, and secondary |A| stands for [RTR].

(8) i   ɨ   u   ə   ʌ   o   a
               A   A
               U   U
     I
                    A   A   A

This analysis is perfectly compatible with that of Ko (2012), who, building on Kim (1993) and work by others, argues for an RTR-based analysis as in (9), where we have added the element-based representations.

(9) i [cor] |I| ɨ [ ] | | u [lab] |U|
                       ʌ [RTR] |A| o [lab], [RTR] |U A|
                       ə [low] |A|
                       a [low], [RTR] |A A|

A clear advantage of this analysis is that it accounts for the above-mentioned 'minimal' character of the vowels /ɨ/ and /ə/ in Middle Korean and earlier stages of the Korean language. A problem of this analysis from the viewpoint of RCVP, however, is that the only specification of the vowel /ʌ/ is the secondary element |A|. In RCVP, a secondary element is only allowed if a primary element is present too (van der Hulst 2020: 79). To solve this problem, we propose that this constraint only holds at what van der Hulst (2018) calls the 'non-cyclic' or word level, where the insertion of the element |ⱴ| is triggered in vowels that are not specified for |A|, as in (10). Angled brackets are used to indicate that the element is inserted.

(10)   i   ɨ   u   ə   ʌ   o   a
                         A   A
                   U   U
       I
                         A   A   A
       <ⱴ> <ⱴ> <ⱴ> <ⱴ> <ⱴ>

The insertion of |ⱴ| can be thought of as following from a constraint that forces any segment to contain a manner element. The reason why |ⱴ| rather than |A| is inserted is that |A| has already been used contrastively, and therefore is no longer available. Importantly, a constraint along the lines of (11) is necessary anyway to ensure that the vowels with only a contrastive 'color' element |I| or |U| surface with a manner element, a condition which can be derived from the fact that the manner node is the head of the segment.

(11)   V → A, ⱴ

In this analysis, the additional |ⱴ| element allows us to account for the 'minimal' status of [ɨ] and [ʌ], without having to lift the RCVP restriction on surface phonological forms without a manner element.

What still remains to be accounted for is the fact that [i] is neutral in MiK vowel harmony. The most straightforward to way to deal with this is by simply positing a constraint that prevents it from being combined with secondary |A|, causing it to be neutral:

(12)   I → ¬ A

As discussed above, co-occurrence constraints are part and parcel of phonological systems, so an analysis based on such a constraint is more than reasonable.

3 Development to Modern Korean

In this section, we will discuss the differences between the MiK vowel system and that of MSK, showing that, apart from differences in the vowel inventory, the vowels of the two varieties can be analyzed in essentially identical ways in RCVP.

According to Ahn and Iverson (2007), in the late nineteenth and early twentieth century, Early Modern Seoul Korean had the following ten monophthongs.

(13) Early Modern Seoul Korean
    i   y   ɨ   u
    e   ø   ə   o
    ɛ   a

In Modern Seoul Korean (MSK), the vowels /y/ and /ø/ have been broken into the diphthongs /wi/ and /we/, and the vowels /e/ and /ɛ/ have merged, resulting in the system of simple vowels in (14) (Ahn and Iverson 2007):[5]

(14) Modern Seoul Korean
    i   ɨ   u
    e/ɛ ə   o
          a

In the more conservative variety of MSK described in the literature, vowel harmony in mimetic words is based on the distinction between the 'bright' vowels /a o ɛ/, and the 'dark' vowels /ə e u i ɨ/. Examples from mimetic words taken from Lee and Yoshida (1998) are given in (15).

(15) Vowel harmony in MSK mimetic words (adapted from Lee and Yoshida 1998)
    a. Harmonic patterns:

	bright-bright	dark-dark	
	kaŋcʰoŋ	kəŋcʰuŋ	'skipping'
	cʰals'ak	cʰəls'ək	'lapping'
	p'ɛcok	p'icuk	'protruding'
	c'ɛlkaŋ	c'ilkəŋ	'chewing'

    b. Non-initial high vowels:

	bright-dark	dark-dark	
	kaŋcʰuŋ	kəŋcʰuŋ	'skipping'
	omcuk	umcuk	'shivering'
	paŋkɨs	pəŋkɨs	'smiling'
	p'ɛtul	p'itul	'zigzag'

---

[5] Henceforth, we will ignore the vowels /y/ and /ø/, which historically were derived from /u/+/i/ and /o/+/i/. In any case, a priori the analysis we propose below seems compatible with the proposal of harmony as pertaining to the secondary *A* element, which is absent in /y/, and present in /ø/.

c. Initial high vowels: *dark-bright*   *dark-dark*

*c'ilkaŋ	c'ilkəŋ	'chewing'
*p'icok	p'icuk	'protruding'
*sukt'ak	sukt'ək	'whispering'
*t'ɨk'am	t'ɨk'ɨm	'stinging'

The forms in (15a) show morphophonological alternations between /a/ and /ə/, /o/ and /u/, and /ɛ/ and /i/. As shown in (15b), high vowels may appear freely after any vowel. However, when a high vowel appears in an initial syllable, as in (15c), it may not be followed by a bright vowel. Based on these forms, we may say that any bright vowel in non-initial position must be preceded by an initial bright vowel. Therefore, leaving aside for the moment the question of which element or feature should be used to describe bright vowels, non-initial syllables may only contain a bright vowel if the initial syllable contains the same feature.[6]

The examples of infinitival verbal forms in (16), adapted from Hong (2008), show another morphophonological pattern involving vowel harmony. As shown in (16a) and (16b), if the stem-final vowel is /a/ or /o/, the allomorph with the bright vowel /a/ is selected, whereas in verbs with a stem-final dark vowel (/u/, /e/, /i/, or /ɨ/) the allomorph with the dark vowel /ə/ is selected. The verbs in (16c) evidence the merger of /e/ and /ɛ/ in verbs: the allomorph -ə rather than -a is selected even if the stem contains the bright vowel /ɛ/.

(16)   Infinitive   Imperative
- a.   pat-a   pat-ala   'receive'
       nol-a   nol-ala   'play'
- b.   sum-ə   sum-əla   'hide'
       mək-ə   mək-əla   'eat'
       k'ɨl-ə   k'ɨl-əla   'pull'
       mit-ə   mit-əla   'believe'
- c.   pe-ə   pe-əla   'cut'
       p'ɛs-ə   p'ɛs-əla   'take away'

It is worth noting that in colloquial speech even verbs whose final syllable contains /a/ or /o/ may take the allomorph -ə, depending on factors like the stem-fi-

---

[6] The brief discussion here does not do justice to the complex patterns of vowel harmony in mimetic words; for more details, see Lee and Yoshida (1998), Park (1990) and Kim (2003).

nal vowel and the presence and quality of a stem-final consonant (Hong 2008; see also S. Park 1990; Kang 2012; Jang 2020).

Although there are complicating factors like stratum-specific behavior and ongoing changes in verbal forms, we would like to focus on what kind of elemental distinctions would enable a distinction between the reflexes of the MiK bright and dark vowels in MSK. Building on the analysis proposed in Poppe (2020), we propose the representations in (17), where /ɛ/ is given with |A| between parentheses to deal with the fact that /e/ and /ɛ/ is only relevant phonologically in mimetic words (Park 1990). Thus, |A| is only specified for /ɛ/ in mimetic words, although the phonetic realization of |A A I| may be the same as |A I|. Only the contrastive elements are given; we will discuss the specification of redundant elements below.

(17)

	Modern Seoul Korean		Middle Korean	
	i	|I|	i	|I|
	ɨ	| |	ɨ	| |
	-	-	ʌ	|A|
	u	|U|	u	|U|
	o	|U A|	o	|U A|
	ə	|A|	ə	|A|
	a	|A A|	a	|A A|
	e	|A I|	ə + i	|A|+ |I|
	ɛ	|A (A) I|	a + i	|A A| + |I|

The representations of the MSK vowels are almost identical to those of Middle Korean; the main difference is that the MiK diphthongs /əi/ and /ai/ have become the monophthongs /e/ and /ɛ/. The obvious appeal of this analysis is that we can analyze the vestiges of vowel harmony in MSK in terms of the same secondary element |A| which was already active as such in MiK. The difference between MiK and MSK then boils down to a matter of degree of generality: in MiK, both simple and complex words showed a high tendency to follow the vowel harmony pattern, while in MSK it can only be observed in certain inflected verbs and in mimetic words.[7]

Although the phonological representations proposed for MSK in (17) are basically identical to those of MiK, when we compare the vowel spaces proposed for MiK by Kim (1993) (and cited in Ko 2012) and for MSK in Ahn and Iverson (2007), we see that the vowels for which we have used identical phonetic symbols are distributed differently within the vowel space.

---

[7] In J.-K. Kim (2000), vowel harmony in MSK is analyzed by means of both [RTR] and [low], whereas only [RTR] is used for MiK.

(18) a. Middle Korean   b. Modern Seoul Korean

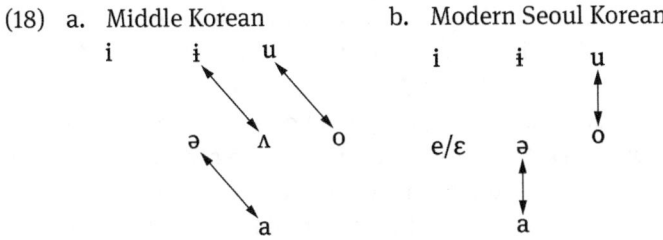

Comparing (18a) with (18b), we could say that the phonetic interpretations of the phonological representations are different: whereas in MiK secondary |A| functions as [RTR], in MSK it functions as [low]. Moreover, the interpretation of [low] is relative rather than absolute: when secondary |A| occurs together with a primary |A|, the result is a low vowel, as in /a/, but when it is the only instance of |A|, which is the case in /o/, it stands for non-high. In other words, it represents 'lower than' rather than 'low'. Now, once we consider the phonetic interpretation of |A| to be relative [low] rather than absolute [low], the distinction between [low] and [RTR] becomes unnecessary; in both cases, the vowels with A are lower than those without A.[8] The slightly different locations in the vowel space, then, involve low-level phonetic details that have not (yet) caused phonological reinterpretation of element structure.

We can now turn to the full specification of the MSK vowels. For MiK, the phonetically high vowels /i ɨ u/ and two of the three phonetically mid vowels /ʌ o/ were all assigned the default element |∀|. The insertion of this redundant element was motivated by the constraint in (11) which forces any segment to contain a head manner element. This constraint is inextricably related to the architecture of RCVP, and therefore is presumed to be active in any language, including MSK. The MSK vowels /i ɨ u o/ then can also be considered to be specified for |∀|. One may wonder, however whether the front /e/ shouldn't be a assigned the same element as well. This is an option in RCVP because two different elements may enter into dependency relations within the primary manner head node. A constraint that would motivate the assignment of |∀| to any front or back mid vowel is given in (19). According to the constraint, which is presented by van der Hulst (2020: 348) as one of an open-ended list of possible co-occurrence constraints, any segment with a colour element |I| or |U| also has the element |∀|.

(19) Colour → ∀

---

[8] We would like to thank a reviewer for drawing our attention to this point.

However, this constraint will also assign the element |ᴧ| to the vowel /ɛ/; the next question is then whether there is any phonological or phonetic motivation for adding |ᴧ| to the surface representation of this vowel. In the variety in which /e/ and /ɛ/ have at least phonetically, and partly phonologically, merged, it is of course no problem to assign |ᴧ| to /ɛ/. And even in the more conservative variety in which /ɛ/ is lower than /e/, it could be argued to contain |ᴧ| as it is not as low as [a]. The difference between /e/ and /ɛ/ forms no problem either, as the latter vowel has an additional secondary |A| element which is absent in the former. Interestingly, both the analysis in which /e/ and /ɛ/ contain |ᴧ|, as well as the analysis in which they lack it are compatible with the phonetic data. To understand this, a more fine-grained diagram of the MSK vowel space based on Shin, Kiaer, and Cha (2013: 102–104) is displayed in (20).

(20) Modern Seoul Korean (fine-grained)

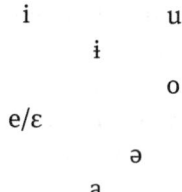

As can be seen in the above diagram, /o/ is higher than /e/ and /ɛ/, which in turn is higher than /ə/ and /a/. Whether we assign |ᴧ| to /e/~/ɛ/ or not thus does not seem to be crucial; it could even be the case that both representations are allowed. Also relevant is the fact that /ə/ is indeed lower than both /o/ and /e/~/ɛ/, which would be reflected in the analysis by the fact that /ə/ lacks |ᴧ|. In any case, in the absence of clear support for the presence of |ᴧ| in /e/~/ɛ/, we adopt the representations in (21) for which we do not need the constraint in (19).

(21) i   e   ɛ   ɨ   u   ə   o   a
              A   A   A   A
                                      U   U
      I   I   I
                      (A)   A   A
      <ᴧ>   <ᴧ>   <ᴧ>   <ᴧ>

4 Conclusion

In this paper we have analyzed some aspects of the development of the Korean vowel system. Both Middle and Modern Korean show vowel harmony, although this has become unproductive in the modern language. We have proposed a new view on the MiK vowel system, cast in RCVP, which allowed us to sketch out a natural development of the vowel system itself and the rules to which this was subject (not only vowel harmony, but also palatalization). The RCVP model was capable of this, in part because of its introduction of the 'fourth' element, |∀|, which may be obligatory in three-height vowel systems with multiple central vowels. The proposed analysis involves a distinction between contrastive and redundant elements, the latter of which were difficult to determine for some vowels because the position one takes depends on the amount of freedom of phonetic interpretation one is willing to accept with respect to phonological representations. Problems related to this, as well as the details of the Korean vowel harmony processes we abstracted away from in this paper deserve more scrutiny.

References

Ahn, Sang-Cheol & Gregory K. Iverson. 2007. Structured imbalances in the emergence of the Korean vowel system. In Joseph C. Salmons & Shannon Dubenion-Smith (eds.), *Historical Linguistics 2005. Selected Papers from the 17th International Conference on Historical Linguistics, Madison, Wisconsin, 31 July–5 August 2005* (Current Issues in Linguistic Theory 284), 275–294. Amsterdam/Philadelphia: John Benjamins.

Backley, Phillip & Toyomi Takahashi. 1998. Element activation. In Eugeniusz Cyran (ed.), *Structure and Interpretation: Studies in Phonology*, 13–40. Lublin: Folium.

Hong, Sung-Hoon. 2008. Variation and exceptions in the vowel harmony of Korean suffixes. *The Journal of Studies in Language* 24(2). 405–428.

Hulst, Harry van der. 1988. The dual interpretation of |i|, |u| and |a|. *Proceedings of the North East Linguistic Society (NELS)* 18, 208–222.

Hulst, Harry van der. 2018. *Asymmetries in Vowel Harmony: A Representational Account* (Oxford Linguistics). Oxford: Oxford University Press.

Hulst, Harry van der. 2020. *Principles of Radical CV Phonology* (Edinburgh Studies in Theoretical Linguistics 4). Edinburgh: Edinburgh University Press.

Ito, Chiyuki. 2013. Korean accent: Internal reconstruction and historical development. *Korean Linguistics* 15(2). 129–198.

Jang, Hayeun. 2020. Segmental factors in variations of Korean vowel harmony: A corpus approach. *Korean Journal of Linguistics* 45(3). 651–669.

Kang, Hijo. 2012. *Diachrony in synchrony: Korean vowel harmony in verbal conjugation*. Stony Brook, NY: Stony Brook University PhD dissertation.

Kim, Jong-Kyoo. 2000. *Quantity-sensitivity and feature-sensitivity of vowels: A constraint-based approach to Korean vowel phonology*. Bloomington: Indiana University PhD dissertation.

Kim, Jong-Kyoo. 2003. Positional neutrality in Korean vowel harmony. *Studies in Phonetics, Phonology and Morphology* 9(2). 327–351.

Kim, Juwon. 1993. *Moum cohwa uy yenkwu* [A study of vowel harmony]. Gyeongsan: Yeungnam University Press.

Kim, Juwon. 2000. Kwuke uy pangen pwunhwa wa paltal [Bifurcation and development of Korean dialects]. In The Institute of Korean Cultural Studies (ed.), *Hankwuk mwunhwa sasang taykyey* [Compendium of Korean culture and thought], 151–185. Gyeongsan: Yeungnam University Press.

Ko, Seongyeon. 2012. *Tongue root harmony and vowel contrast in Northeast Asian languages*. Ithaca, NY: Cornell University PhD dissertation.

Lee, Duck-Young & Shohei Yoshida. 1998. A-head alignment: The case of vowel harmony in Korean. In Eugeniusz Cyran (ed.), *Structure and Interpretation: Studies in Phonology*, 195–204. Lublin: Folium.

Lee, Ki-Moon & S. Robert Ramsey. 2011. *A History of the Korean Language*. Cambridge: Cambridge University Press.

Martin, Samuel E. 1992. *A Reference Grammar of Korean: A Complete Guide to the Grammar and History of the Korean Language*. Rutland, VT: Charles E. Tuttle.

Park, Jong-Hee. 1994. Cwunglip moum /i/ uy poncil kwa moum cohwa [The nature of the neutral vowel /i/ and vowel harmony]. In Essay Collection Publication Committee (ed.), *Wulimal yenkwu uy saymthe* [A fountain of research on our language], 134–153. Seoul: Pagijong Press.

Park, Sayhyon. 1990. Vowel harmony in Korean. *Language Research* 26(3). 469–499.

Poppe, Clemens. 2020. Head, dependent, or both: Dependency relations in vowels. In Kuniya Nasukawa (ed.), *Morpheme-Internal Recursion in Phonology* (Studies in Generative Grammar 140), 267–306. Berlin/New York: Mouton de Gruyter.

Shin, Jiyoung, Jieun Kiaer & Jaeeun Cha. 2013. *The Sounds of Korean*. Cambridge: Cambridge University Press.

Whitman, John B. 1985. *The phonological basis for the comparison of Japanese and Korean*. Cambridge, MA: Harvard University PhD dissertation.

Whitman, John B. 1994. The accentuation of nominal stems in Proto-Korean. In Young-Key Kim-Renaud (ed.), *Theoretical Issues in Korean Linguistics*, 425–439. Stanford: CSLI Publications.

Eugeniusz Cyran
How Much Phonology in 'Laryngeal Phonology'?

Abstract: Phonetically observed voicing phenomena cannot be unambiguously and exhaustively identified with laryngeal phonology, in which phonetic properties such as voicedness or voicelessness are directly translated into phonological categories, and in which phenomena such as voicing assimilation are necessarily viewed as phonological spreading. This much became clear with the advent of privative representations, which cannot capture, for example, phonetically observable symmetrical voicing assimilations as symmetrical spreading. This paper attempts to demonstrate that the laryngeal phonology of Polish *per se* is very small and can be reduced to strictly privative representation with substance free categories and positional licensing as the only instance of phonological computation. This minimal phonological component allows us to understand a complex set of voicing phenomena in Polish, including positional and dialectal variation. What is required, however, is an increased role of the language specific phonetic knowledge in the process of acquisition and in phonetic interpretation. Additionally, the relation between phonetics and phonology must be viewed as arbitrary.

Keywords: laryngeal phonology, substance free categories, language specific phonetics, voicing assimilation, sandhi

1 Introduction

The term 'laryngeal phonology' should in principle refer to phonology, deeming the question posed in the title pointless. However, it is often understood in a broader sense, synonymous with laryngeal phenomena, or voicing patterns in a given language, thus assuming a more phonetic meaning. This shift often goes unnoticed in the phonological models which use binary features, and assume, for example, that any instance of phonetic voicing is phonologically classifiable as [+voice] (e.g. Itô, Mester, and Padgett 1995; Rubach 1996). With most phonetic distinctions and observable phenomena directly encoded in the phonology, laryngeal phonology and voicing patterns become tantamount. For example, in

---

Eugeniusz Cyran, John Paul II Catholic University of Lublin, Poland.

https://doi.org/10.1515/9783110730098-009

Rubach's (1996) analysis of Regressive Voice Assimilation (RVA) in Polish, the symmetrical phonetic facts – Polish has both voicing and devoicing assimilation between obstruents – are described as spreading of [+voice] or [–voice], respectively, e.g. *liczba* /lits-ba/ > [lʲidẓba] 'number', *ławka* /waw-ka/ > [wafka] 'bench'.

By contrast, recent privative frameworks, for example, Laryngeal Realism (Beckman, Jessen, and Ringen 2013; Harris 1994, 2009; Honeybone 2002; Iverson and Salmons 1995, 2003) make some distinction between observable voicing patterns and their representation in the phonology. Given that two-way contrast languages possess only one laryngeal category, RVA patterns in Polish must be analysed as asymmetrical phonologically: the voicing assimilation involves spreading of the laryngeal category [voice], or some equivalent category, e.g. element |L|, while the devoicing RVA is restricted to delaryngealization of the first obstruent in a sequence (Gussmann 2007). In other words, the laryngeal phonology of Polish and the voicing patterns do not match directly. However, Laryngeal Realism seems to follow the traditional practice of taking certain phonetic properties of segments as unambiguously indicating particular laryngeal categories in the phonological representation. For example, the division into 'voice' and 'aspiration' languages, which is clearly a phonetic observation, is assumed to correspond to specific phonological representations: full voicing, as in Polish, is marked with [voice]/|L|, while aspiration, as in English, is marked with [spread glottis], or |H|, leaving the voiceless unaspirated series unmarked in both systems (Harris 1994, 2009). Thus, by classifying phonetic pre-voicing and aspiration as phonologically marked, Laryngeal Realism also confuses laryngeal phonology with phonetic facts. This approach has some other unwelcome consequences, too. Firstly, it entails a non-privative analysis of languages like Swedish, in which the two-way voicing distinction is that between fully voiced and aspirated obstruents (Helgason and Ringen 2008). Secondly, and more importantly, it is unable to account for the well-known dialectal variation in Polish, without compromising one of the main tenets of privativity – that sonorants are not specified for [voice]. Specifically, the Cracow-Poznań dialect, unlike the Warsaw dialect, has pre-sonorant sandhi voicing, e.g. *brat ojca* /brat ojtsa/ > [brad ojtsa] 'father's brother'. A successful privative account of these facts is impossible within the Laryngeal Realism (Gussmann 2007).

A solution to the dialectal problem in Polish, and, more importantly, to the unwelcome direct relation between phonetic VOT values and phonological representation is offered in Cyran (2011, 2014) in the form of the proposal called Laryngeal Relativism. It claims that there is no direct relation between pre-voicing in Polish and the presence of a laryngeal category, and that the two dialects of Polish in fact have the opposite marking of the two series of obstruents. Details of this proposal are reviewed below. What is important at this stage is the fact that laryngeal patterns, as observed in a given language, are now fully divorced from laryngeal phonology, and we can rephrase the initial question as: how much phonology in the observed laryngeal patterns?

This paper argues that, with some strict theoretical assumptions about phonological representation, computation, and mechanisms of implementation, it is possible to define the minimal amount of phonology which is required to understand the laryngeal patterns of Polish. The role of phonology in the description of laryngeal phenomena may be broadly defined in terms of two aspects: the representation of the laryngeal contrast(s) and the computation that to some extent reflects the voicing patterns observed on the surface. However, no less important in a given voicing system is the nature of the relation between phonology and the language specific phonetics. The following assumptions are made about phonological representation, computation, and implementation.

(1) *Minimal theoretical assumptions*
    a. Strictly privative and substance-free representation of laryngeal contrasts (C^{Lar} - C^{o})
    b. Computation is limited to positional licensing of the laryngeal category
    c. Spell-out is a reversal of arbitrary relations established in acquisition

The phonological model assumed in this discussion is the Strict CVCV version of Government Phonology (Kaye, Lowenstamm, and Vergnaud 1990; Scheer 2004, 2014). There are only two crucial points that need to be mentioned at this stage. Firstly, a phonetic sequence of two obstruents [CC] contains an empty nucleus phonologically /CØC/. This fact is important because the distribution of laryngeal categories, at least in Polish, follows from the licensing relation that nuclei establish with the phonologically adjacent preceding consonants. In brief, phonetically realised nuclei, vowels, license the laryngeal distinctions in their onsets, while empty nuclei do not (Cyran 2017). Secondly, there is no surface phonological representation. The phonological representation after computation is fully interpretable phonetically (Harris and Lindsey 1995). Both the marked obstruents (C^{Lar}) and the unmarked ones (C^{o}) are fully pronounceable.

In what follows, we will look at the laryngeal system of Polish from the perspective of the division of labour between phonology and phonetics that follows from the restrictive assumptions given in (1). The decision as to what is phonological and what is phonetic will allow us to provide a clearer picture of the kind of phonological and phonetic knowledge that must be acquired to learn such a system.

2 Polish Voicing

The basic Polish voicing facts are well known. Irrespectively of dialectal divisions, there is a two-way contrast between fully voiced obstruents and voiceless unaspirated ones, e.g. *koza / kosa* [kɔza / kɔsa] 'goat/scythe', or *data / tata* [data / tata] 'date/father'. All dialects exhibit the same main processes, that is, final obstruent devoicing (FOD), e.g. *żaba / żab* [ʐaba / ʐap] 'frog, nom.sg./gen.pl.' and regressive voicing assimilation (RVA), word-internally and across the word boundary, e.g. *ława / ławka* [wava / wafka] 'bench, nom.sg./dim.' and *brat Basi* [brad baɕi] 'Barbara's brother' (Bethin 1984, 1992; Cyran 2014; Gussmann 1992, 2007; Rubach 1996, 2008).[1]

However, the most theoretically challenging phenomenon, at least for strictly privative and minimalist models, is that of pre-sonorant sandhi voicing which occurs in Cracow-Poznań Polish (CPP), as opposed to Warsaw Polish (WP) (Cyran 2014). For example, in CPP *brat ojca* 'father's brother' and *sad ojca* 'father's orchard' are both pronounced with a voiced obstruent, that is, [brad ojtsa] and [sad ojtsa], while in WP both phrases are pronounced with a voiceless obstruent [brat ojtsa] and [sat ojtsa]. Lexically, the words *brat* and *sad* end in a voiceless and a voiced obstruent, respectively.

3 The Relevance of Phonetics

From the acquisitional perspective the laryngeal system begins with phonetics, which, for our purposes, can be simply defined as consisting of some linguistic knowledge which follows from universal phonetics (UP), that is, the constraints and principles determining the articulation and perception of speech sounds (e.g. Stevens 1972), and the language specific phonetics (LSP). The latter is understood as knowing and producing the major allophones and allophonic variation of a given system (cf. Kingston 2019: 389). This LSP knowledge is not restricted to the types of surface segments in a given system, but, crucially, it includes knowing contextual alternations as well as variation. In most cases, the variation to be discussed below does not refer to barely distinguishable differences which can be established by reference to precise measurements and statistical testing. It is

---

[1] There are a number of other voicing issues that are normally included in the general picture, but they will be left aside. These include progressive voicing assimilation (PVA), e.g. *bitewny / bitwa* [bitevnɨ / bitfa] 'battle-like / battle', or the transparency and opacity of sonorants, e.g. *Jędrek / Jędrka* [jendrek / jentrka] 'Andrew, nom.sg./gen.sg.' (Rubach 1996; Cyran 2018).

rather the kind of variation which is overtly present and consciously experienced by learners in contact with the ambient language. This may include awareness of the incompleteness of neutralization.

With respect to laryngeal systems, UP is rather probabilistic in nature as it provides more potential distinctions than may be utilised – pronounced and perceived as categorical – in a given system. For example, there are three potential phonetic categories [d-t-tʰ], which are commonly utilised in linguistic systems to express laryngeal contrasts (Cho and Ladefoged 1999), but only two of them are utilised in two-way contrast systems. These phonetic categories, which can be described in terms of quantal regions along the VOT continuum (Lisker and Abramson 1964) are characterised by displaying phonetic distance, that is, they exhibit sufficient distinctions in articulation, acoustic effects and perception that allows for their contrastive usage in linguistic systems.

3.1 LSP Choices and LSP Knowledge

It is an established fact that out of the three phonetic categories provided by UP, linguistic systems which have a two-way contrast typically utilise two adjacent, rather than two extreme categories. Thus, for example, the so-called 'voicing' languages select the [d-t] distinction, while 'aspiration' languages select [t-tʰ]. With some notable exceptions, such as Swedish (Helgason and Ringen 2008), the extreme dispersion of the contrast along the VOT continuum is not selected. This is in keeping with the findings in phonetic theory which support the idea of sufficient rather than maximal dispersion of contrasts in linguistic systems (e.g. Liljencrants and Lindblom 1972; Schwartz, Boë, and Abry 2007). The scheme in (2) illustrates the language specific choices made in 'voicing' and 'aspiration' languages from the available three categories along the VOT continuum.

(2) *LSP choice of laryngeal distinctions*

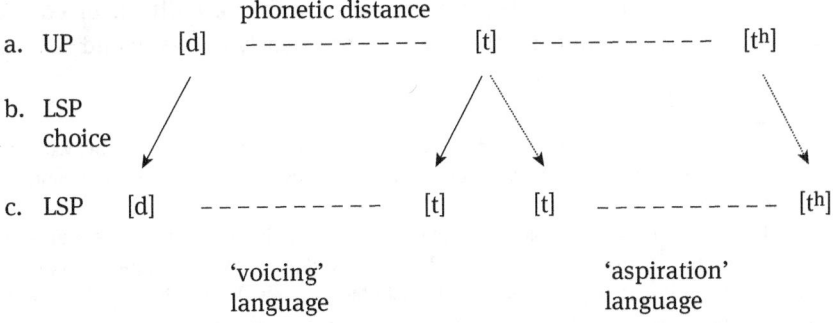

The first point that needs to be made is that the choice of the phonetic categories to express the laryngeal contrast in a two-way system is purely phonetic and to a great extent diachronic. It is phonetic in the sense that it respects the principle of sufficient distance, and diachronic in the sense that this choice is not made by learners but rather inherited in the ambient language. Another point is that learners of a given system, for example, a 'voicing' one such as Polish, are not familiar with the third possibility along the VOT continuum, that is, the aspirated series. This is important to emphasize because one of the arguments for claiming that the voiceless unaspirated plosives are unmarked is based on the fact that this phonetic object is present in both types of systems. In fact, it is also present in systems with no laryngeal contrast, and in those with three- and four-way contrasts (Harris 1994). The idea, then, is that the full voicing and aspiration require marking with a laryngeal category because they are active deviations from the 'neutral', that is, ostensibly, from the phonologically unmarked object. This argument is phonetically correct, but it need not be correct phonologically. The direct and non-arbitrary translation of phonetic effort to phonological markedness has its attractions and has become part and parcel of some theoretical models, for example, Laryngeal Realism (Beckman, Jessen, and Ringen 2013; Harris 1994, 2009; Honeybone 2002; Iverson and Salmons 1995, 2003). It has been shown, however, that this direct relation fails to capture the voicing facts from Polish which were alluded to above.

The two phonetically dispersed major allophones [d – t] in (2c) constitute only a fraction of what we can call LSP knowledge. A more complete picture of what a speaker of Polish knows is presented in (3). For example, the contrast is likely to be the most robust in the context _V (3a).[2] It is the only context in Polish in which the laryngeal categorical distinction is displayed properly. Elsewhere, that is, in the phonetic contexts (3b–d) it appears to be either lost or masked, yet often recoverable through alternations, and, in some contexts, on the basis of the presence of variation, which will be shown below. It should be noted that the pre-vocalic context itself is not devoid of some variation, which concerns the voiced series.[3] These obstruents may be partially unvoiced or even voiceless under certain conditions, which are clearly phonetic and sometimes

---

[2] In Polish, the context should perhaps be described as _(R)V, that is, pre-vocalic, with or without an intervening sonorant. The simpler formulation is used here because what counts is the presence of the vowel.

[3] For the purpose of this discussion the scope of this variation is illustrated as scales [b>b̥>p] or [p>b̥>b], with the first object on the left being most likely or expected in a given position in relatively unmonitored fast speech, and the last object is most likely when such monitoring is present, or when some phonetic or pragmatic conditioning is at play (see footnote 4).

pragmatic.[4] The phonetic basis of variation in the voiced series is quite unsurprising in obstruents given the aerodynamics of voicing and the complexity of articulatory gestures that need to be coordinated during the production of voiced obstruents (e.g. Halle and Stevens 1971). The learner of Polish, thus, somehow works out that the distinction is that between voiced vs. voiceless unaspirated, and that it is most faithfully expressed in pre-vocalic context (3a). She also learns about linguistically irrelevant context-independent variation which is related to the inherent phonetic properties of some segments.

The data in (3b–d) expose the child to another aspect, namely, context-dependent alternations, which are also accompanied by some variation. Although the distinction between variation and alternation is a neat one, it would be a mistake to assume that this is where the line between phonology and phonetics can be drawn. It seems that variation of the type observed in (3) can indeed be excluded from phonological considerations. The question is whether all types of alternations are encoded in phonology and how. In what follows, the contexts are phonetic rather than phonological. '_C$^{-\alpha\,voi}$' reads: followed by an obstruent of opposite voicing, '_C$^{\alpha\,voi}$' followed by an obstruent of the same voicing, '>' phonetically interpreted as.

(3)   *LSP knowledge (both Polish dialects)*

    a.   Context: _V, major allophones [d]-[t], some variation of the lexically voiced
        domek [domek] 'house'   /D/   > [d>d̥>t]
        Tomek [tomek] 'Tom'   /T/   > [t]

    b.   Context: _C$^{-\alpha\,voi}$, loss of identity, symmetrical regressive assimilation (RVA),
        symmetrical variation, alternation [d~t] and [t~d]
        ślad kultury [ɕlat kulturɨ] 'trace of culture'   /D/   > [t>d̥>d]
        świat dziecka [ɕfjad dʑetska] 'child's world'   /T/   > [d>d̥>t]

    c.   Context: _C$^{\alpha\,voi}$, voicing agreement, still some variation of the lexically voiced
        ślad dzika [ɕlad dʑika] 'trace of a boar'   /D/   > [d>d̥>t]
        brat taty [brat taty] 'father's brother'   /T/   > [t]

---

[4] For example, words spoken in anger often do not show much voicing word-initially, which is due to the muscle stiffening. One example of pragmatic conditioning is the blocking of FOD in the word *dób* 'day and night, gen.pl.' which prevents homophony with the rude word *dup* [dup] 'arse, gen.pl.'.

d. Context: _#, final obstruent devoicing (FOD), some variation of the lexically voiced, alternation [d~t]
   wada ~ wad [vada ~ vat] 'flaw, nom.sg./gen.pl.'   /D/   > [t>d̥>d]
   świat [ɕfjat] 'world'   /T/   > [t]

As signalled earlier, the phonetic contexts in (3b–d) can be viewed collectively as elsewhere cases to the pre-vocalic one in (3a). The second context, (3b), is rather complicated. We observe both the loss of identity of the first obstruent as a result of regressive voicing assimilation (RVA), and some variation related to that phenomenon. RVA is found both word-internally, e.g. *ława / ławka* [wava / wafka] 'bench, nom.sg./dim.' and across word boundaries. The voiced nature of the final obstruent in *ślad* [ɕlat] 'trace' is recoverable from alternations, e.g. *ślady* [ɕladɨ] 'trace, pl.'. The voiceless final obstruent in *ślad* is the most probable phonetic realization in this context because it is word-final, a context for FOD, and followed by a voiceless obstruent, which is a context for RVA. The variation in this context is virtually limited to slow and controlled speech, and not so much to phonetic pauses. A pause may eliminate RVA, but instead, it triggers FOD. In the other example, *świat dziecka*, there is evidence from inflected forms that this is a lexically voiceless obstruent, e.g. *światy* [ɕfjatɨ] 'world, pl'. The observed variation depends on the amount of phonetic voicing in the following obstruent and the speech rate. Putting aside the variation in (3b), the learner is confronted with a lot of evidence that she is dealing with some sort of assimilation and symmetrical alternations that follow from it, that is, [d~t, t~d]. We can only hypothesize how the symmetrical assimilations are going to be internalized into the phonological module. A particular proposal is given in the following section.

    The context in which the two obstruents share the same specification, as in (3c), is an extension of the previously discussed situation in (3b). Two obstruents typically exhibit voicing agreement, especially root-internally, e.g. *gdy* [gdɨ] 'when', *który* [kturɨ] 'which'. Some variation concerns the word-final voiced obstruent and is connected with the tempo of speech and the amount of voicing in the following obstruent (Gussmann 2007; Cyran 2014).

    Finally, the word-final context, (3d), is characterized by asymmetry, both in terms of alternations and variation. The LSP knowledge related to this context is two-fold. Firstly, this is where the learner observes voicing alternations of the type *wada ~ wad* [vada ~ vat] 'flaw, nom.sg./gen.pl.', that is, [d~t]. Secondly, she learns about quite robust, asymmetrical and easily detectable variation which is related to final devoicing. The phenomenon is often incomplete ([wad̥]), and sometimes non-existent ([wad]). While the former case may be due to the tempo and style of speech, the latter is usually conditioned by pragmatics (Cyran in press).[5]

There are two important conclusions that follow from the above discussion with respect to the nature of the LSP knowledge of the laryngeal sound patterns in Polish, which are relevant for the phonological acquisition. Firstly, we are dealing with a two-way contrast which must be represented phonologically in a privative way, as we assume. Secondly, the sound patterns seem to involve both contextual alternations between major allophones, and a fair amount of overt variation which depends on the context, the lexical origin of the target obstruent, and other phonetic and pragmatic causes. More generally, it can be observed that variation seems to be present in those cases where the target is lexically voiced, or if not, it is followed by a voiced obstruent.

Given the complexity of the LSP knowledge related to contrast, alternations and variation, we can hypothesize that what is phonologised as computation depends on the treatment of the alternations and variation. Earlier, it was mentioned that this neat distinction may constitute the basis for the decision as to which phenomena are phonological and which ones are not. However, we would like to pursue a more restrictive hypothesis given in (4b) below.

(4) *Phonology – phonetics divide*
    a. Hypothesis I (soft version)
       Phonological computation is responsible for alternations but not variation

    b. Hypothesis II (hard version)
       Phonological computation is not responsible for variation or alternations which can be explained at the level of phonetics

4 What Is Minimally Phonological

The phonological side of a sound system is always a theoretical construct which depends on initial assumptions. Given that the child opts for strict privativity, only one series of obstruents is marked phonologically and enters the system of phonological computation related to this category. It may be claimed that from

---

[5] The so-called incomplete neutralization (e.g. Slowiaczek and Dinnsen 1985), which is often argued for on the basis of statistical testing and perceptual experiments is thus a mere fraction of the observed variation.

the phonological point of view it does not matter which series is marked. What matters is that one of them is. However, the choice must be consistent with the way the entire system operates. Cyran (2011) argues that the alignment of the phonetic categories [d – t] with the phonological distinction (C^{Lar} – C^{o}) depends on dialect; in WP (5a), C^{Lar} is aligned with [d], and C^o with [t], while the reverse alignment is found CPP (5b). If this is the case, then we can talk about the arbitrariness of the spell-out relation between the phonological category and its phonetic correlates, which basically means that the phonological representation itself can be viewed as substance-free: both /d^{Lar} – t^o/ and /d^o – t^{Lar}/ are possible representations in laryngeal systems called 'voicing' languages.

(5) *The lexicalisation of the LSP distinction*

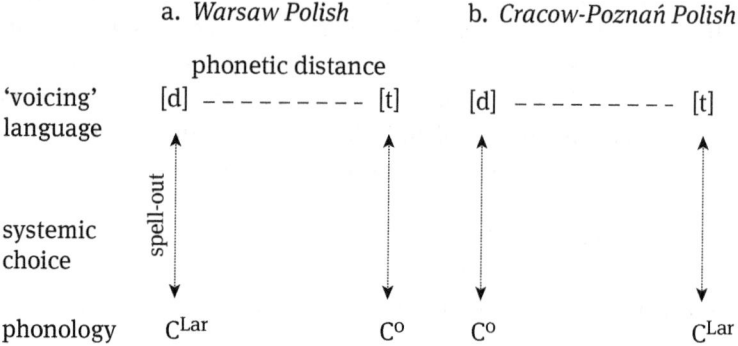

The systemic decision to mark the voiced series of obstruents in WP (5a) automatically creates a spell-out relation for the marked object (C^{Lar} ↔ [d]), but also for the unmarked one (C^o ↔ [t]). The same mechanisms are at play in CPP (5b), except that the marking is reversed. For example, the phonological representation of *rasowy* [rasovɨ] 'thoroughbred' is /ras°ovɨ/ in WP, but /ras^{Lar}ovɨ/ in CPP. On the other hand, the representation of *razowy* [razovɨ] 'wholemeal' is /raz^{Lar}ovɨ/ in WP, and /raz°ovɨ/ in CPP. An important consequence of the different alignments between phonetic categories and phonological contrasts is that what is marked phonetically is not necessarily the same as what is marked phonologically.

It is important to bear in mind that the LSP knowledge presented in (3), which includes contextual phonetic alternations and variation shared by both dialects, does not include the evidence for the reversed marking. This evidence, alluded to earlier, concerns the phenomenon of pre-sonorant voicing in sandhi and will be returned to below. However, it is important to demonstrate that the reversed marking is also able to account for the patterns which are common to both dialects, thus revealing the relativity of the relation between voicing patterns and their potential phonological description. This is what we intend to do below, by first looking at how two alternative analyses can account for the same RVA and FOD effects, and then, by pointing to the different predictions that the systems with reversed marking make.

The postulated phonological representations necessarily ignore a lot of variation and possibly some of the alternations. Thus, spell-out will need to be supplemented with positional phonetic implementation. It follows, that what is called phonetic interpretation in GP (Harris and Lindsey 1995) is in fact a more complex mechanism. Spell-out is an interface mechanism of a lexicalised translation (e.g. Scheer 2014), possibly designating one relevant major allophone as target, whereas another aspect of phonetic interpretation takes place in LSP, that is, in the phonetics, and may mask the target of spell-out in various ways and to varying degree. This point will be elaborated on below.

Turning now to phonological computation, let us make the theoretical assumption that the distribution of |Lar| is restricted to positions in which it is licensed by a phonologically adjacent full vowel. It will become clear below that the pre-vocalic context has a different function at the level of phonetics than in phonology. While phonological adjacency is important for licensing and what is spelled out, that is, submitted to phonetic interpretation of the obstruents, the phonetic adjacency is only important for the phonetic interpretation. In the elsewhere cases in (3b–d), that is, in the pre-obstruent and word-final contexts the obstruents find themselves in front of an empty nucleus (Ø), which is not a laryngeal licenser in Polish (Cyran 2014, 2017).[6] Thus, in the contexts for FOD and RVA, the target obstruent can only be neutral, while in front of a full vowel they can be neutral or marked. The only possible licensing configurations are therefore /$C^{Lar}V$/, /$C°V$/, and /$C°Ø$/.

As for RVA, in binary feature analyses, e.g. Rubach (1996), first, the target obstruent in C_1 is de-laryngealized, which is followed by spreading of [±voice] from C_2. This directly expresses the symmetry of assimilations which is found in Polish, e.g. *liczba* /litṣ-ba/ > [lʲidẓba] 'number', *ławka* /wav-ka/ > [wafka] 'bench' (cf. also 3b, c). In a privative system of representation the phonological computation may involve de-laryngealization of the target, but this can be followed by spreading only from the marked trigger. Thus, the phonological computation is inherently asymmetrical. Given that acquisition is based on privativity, this is the

---

6 The CVCV version of Government Phonology, which is assumed here, renders the phonetic contexts _#, _C phonologically identical, that is, as _Ø.

point at which the child learns that what is observed on the surface as an instance of assimilation need not be represented as spreading of properties.

In this paper, we will go one step further by assuming that de-laryngealization of C_1 in Polish RVA is the only phonological computation that takes place, and it is obligatory, which will become apparent when we discuss the pre-sonorant sandhi voicing below. On the other hand, no spreading of the laryngeal categories from C_2 is needed, and the observed effects can be neatly explained by the nature of spell-out and LSP. Firstly, let us return to the distinction between spell-out and phonetic interpretation, which is normally not made within GP. It will be recalled that, e.g. in WP, /C^{Lar}/ is spelled out as voiced, while /C^o/ is spelled-out as voiceless in pre-vocalic context, which is the only context licensing the laryngeal distinction. The pre-vocalic context has a different phonological and phonetic function. Phonologically, it is a laryngeal licensing context in which the distinction will have to be spelled out, e.g. /U,ʔ,Lar/ ↔ [b], and /U,ʔ/ ↔ [p] and phonetically interpreted as such. The fact that pre-obstruent and word-final obstruents can only be neutral /C^o/ will not affect the spell-out, but the phonetic interpretation of that object may differ from the targeted [p] in WP. The phonetic interpretation will take into account the phonetic (not phonological) context and the LSP knowledge of alternations and variation.[7] Most crucially, the interpretation of that object will be subject to influence following from articulatory planning. The latter will be assumed to work in the following way: active gestures may be anticipated and overlap to various degrees with the articulation of the neutral obstruent. Additionally, the following sonorants, which are characterized by the so-called spontaneous voicing will only enhance the typical target of spell-out in a given system.[8] In other words, we assume that a neutral obstruent in a non-neutralizing context /C^oV/ may be phonetically interpreted in a different way than the same neutral object in a neutralizing context /C^oØ/.[9] The representations in (6) below illustrate the interaction between licensing of |Lar| (phonology), spell-out (interface), and phonetic interpretation (co-articulation, LSP) that account for RVA in both dialects.

---

[7] In this sense, we agree with Ernestus and Baayen (2006), Kohler (2012), and Port and O'Dell (1985) that incomplete neutralization need not be resolved at the level of phonology.

[8] An illustration of this point has to be delayed till the discussion of pre-sonorant voicing in CPP below.

[9] This becomes clear in languages in which empty nuclei are laryngeal licensers, e.g. Ukrainian (Bethin 1987). This system has no FOD, e.g. *plid* [plid] 'fruit' vs. *plit* [plit] 'fence', and RVA is limited to voicing, cf. *pros'ba* [proz^{j}ba] 'request' vs. *ridko* [ridko] 'rarely'.

In (6a), *prośba* [proẓba] 'request', which alternates with *prosić* [proɕitɕ] 'to ask', has a lexically neutral obstruent /ɕ°/. Additionally, it finds itself in a laryngeally unlicensed phonological context – before an empty nucleus – and in the phonetic context, in which its phonetic interpretation is most likely to be influenced by surrounding sounds. The following /b/, on the other hand, is lexically marked and licensed by a filled nucleus. Here, the phonetic context favours the full interpretation of the target of spell-out, that is, the fully voiced [b]. Thus, in WP, the spell-out should produce a sequence *[ɕb], but the phonetic interpretation, taking into account co-articulation, yields the correct [ẓb], or in fact a variation [ʐ>ẓ>ɕ], with the fully voiced fricative as most likely. In CPP (6b), the phonologically marked /ɕLar/ is de-laryngealized. This means that the target of spell-out is [ẓ], and the surrounding context only supports this phonetic interpretation. It will be shown below, in the discussion of FOD, that this phonetic support is crucial.

Turning now to *tchu* [txu] 'breath, gen.sg.', alternating with *dech* [dex] 'breath, nom.sg.', the analysis in WP (6c) involves de-laryngealization of the lexically marked /dLar/. Hence, the target of spell-out of /d°/ is [t], which is pronounced as such, given the voiceless phonetic context. In CPP (6d), the lexical representation of the first obstruent is neutral, which, as we assume, is spelled out as a voiced obstruent if the phonetic context permits. In this example, the voicing has no phonetic support and the consonant is phonetically interpreted as voiceless.

(6) *RVA in Polish dialects*

    Warsaw Polish   *Cracow-Poznań Polish*
a. *prośba* [proẓba] 'request'   b. *prośba* [proẓba] 'request'
    co-articulation '((('   de-laryngealization and co-articulation

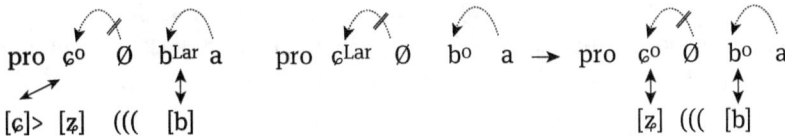

c. *tchu* [txu] 'breath, gen.sg.'   d. *tchu* [txu] 'breath, gen.sg.'
    de-laryngealization and   co-articulation
    co-articulation

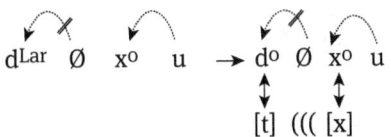 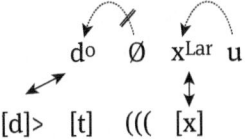

It is interesting to note that the analyses in (6), which are devoid of phonological spreading, seem to work regardless of the type of marking used in a given dialect. This also sheds some light on the nature of alternations such as [d~t] in *dech / tchu* [dex ~ txu] 'breath, nom.sg./gen.sg.' or [ɕ~ʑ] in *prosić / prośba* [proɕitɕ ~ proʑba] 'to ask / a request'. Namely, the change of identity of C_1, which was alluded to in (3b), is always dependent on the phonetic context and co-articulation, rather than phonological spreading (cf. Jansen 2007). This co-articulation yields the variation shown in (3), whose range is strongly correlated with the existence of alternations and structural differences: variation is least observed root-internally (*dech / tchu*), more variation is observed across morpheme boundaries within the word (*prosić / prośba*), and most variation is found across the word boundary (*świat dziecka*). The correlation between the amount of variation and phonetic distance strongly suggests that the assimilations are to a great extent phonetic, rather than phonological.

Let us now turn to FOD. It must be noted that although the phonetic facts related to this phenomenon, including variation, are identical in both dialects, the systemic analysis must be slightly different given the reversed marking. Phonologically, both dialects have de-laryngealization in this context, which means that there is no phonetic enhancement of the distinction voiced / voiceless. On the one hand, in WP, the spell-out of the neutral /C°/ yields a voiceless target automatically, as it were, because that is the spell-out and interpretation of that object in pre-vocalic position and word-finally. On the other hand, in CPP, FOD must be viewed as a contextual realization of the neutral /C°/ in a neutralizing context. In other words, we are dealing with a coincidence of two factors militating against a voiced object. Firstly, no phonological distinction is possible in this context (/C°Ø/), and secondly, there is no phonetic (interpretational) context for /C°/ to be interpreted as voiced. This is because LSP enhancement of the distinction between, say, [b] and [p] can only occur in pre-vocalic context. Thus FOD in CPP is partly phonological (laryngeally unlicensed position) and largely phonetic (LSP). This distinction leads to an interesting prediction to which we return below.

(7) *FOD in WP and CPP*
    a. WP   *ras* 'race, gen.pl.'
                              /ras°Ø/ ↔ [ras] > [ras]
        raz 'once'
        /raz^{Lar}Ø/ → /raz°Ø/ ↔ [ras] > [ras] + variation

b. CPP *ras* 'race, gen.pl.'
/ras^{Lar}Ø/ → /ras°Ø/ ↔ [raz] > [ras]
raz 'once'
/raz°Ø/ ↔ [raz] > [ras] + variation

→ de-laryngealization, ↔ spell-out, > contextual phonetic interpretation

Under this analysis, the uniformity of the word-final variation concerning the lexically voiced obstruents in both dialects can only have its basis in the LSP knowledge shown in (3), and not in the phonological representation or computation. In other words, the existence of the variation is related to the existence of phonetic alternations of the type [z] ~ [s] as in *dwa razy* [dva razɨ] 'twice' vs. *jeden raz* [jeden ras] 'once', which has some phonological basis in WP, but none in CPP.

The distinction into spell-out and phonetic interpretation in LSP in fact means that the target of spell-out, say /C°/ ↔ [b] in CPP, is subject to contextual interpretation. However, it is potentially [b] if the phonetic conditions are met. We predict, then, that in CPP, the change in the phonetic context to pre-vocalic could yield a voiced obstruent when interpreting /C°/. On the other hand, this is impossible in WP, in which a pre-vocalic /C°/ must be voiceless. This is exactly what happens in the sandhi context. It is important to note that the phonetic interpretation of /C°/ in both dialects is consistent with the word-internal one as shown in (8). The sequence of symbols '↔,>' means that the obstruent is spelled out and interpreted in the same way. This is because of the pre-vocalic context.

(8) *CPP and WP final obstruents in sandhi context*
  a. CPP /C°/ ↔,> [voiced] / _V, _#V

   ras obronnych 'defensive races'
   /ras^{Lar}Ø/ → /ras°Ø obronnɨx/ ↔,> [raz obronnɨx]

   = *raz obronił* 'defended once'
   /raz°Ø/ /raz°Ø obroɲiw/ ↔,> [raz obroɲiw]

   = *razowy* 'wholemeal' (intervocalic word-internal)
   /raz°ovɨ/ ↔,> [razovɨ]

b. WP /C°/ ↔,> [voiceless] / _V, _#V

    ras obronnych 'defensive races'
    /ras°Ø/ /ras°Ø obronnɨx/   ↔,> [ras obronnɨx]

  = *raz obronił* 'defended once'
    /raz^{Lar}Ø/ → /raz°Ø obroɲiw/   ↔,> [ras obroɲiw]

  = *rasowy* 'racial' (intervocalic word-internal)
                      /ras°ovɨ/   ↔,> [rasovɨ]

The pre-sonorant sandhi voicing in CPP appears to disambiguate a number of systemic choices. First of all, it should be borne in mind that in this dialect both lexically voiced and lexically voiceless obstruents are voiced before the following word beginning with a sonorant (8a). Thus, some sort of neutralization of the laryngeal distinction is required, as assumed above. In WP, the situation is similar but the opposite, in that both types of obstruents are realized as voiceless in the sandhi context (8b). This is where the reversed representation and indeed the reversed interpretation of the unmarked /C°/ becomes apparent and the effects come for free. It may be claimed, that the acquisitional decision as to the reversed marking in the two dialects is based on the sandhi patterns.

The above survey of the laryngeal patterns in Polish shows that the phonological component is very small. The representation must be privative, while the decision as to which property – voicing or voicelessness – is marked is systemic. Additionally, the only phonological computation that is required to understand the voicing patterns involves licensing of the laryngeal distinction by melodically filled nuclei and de-laryngealization elsewhere. No separate phonological mechanisms are required to understand the pre-sonorant sandhi voicing in CPP, except for assuming that this dialect has the opposite laryngeal marking. The rest follows from lexicalized list-based spell-out and contextual phonetic interpretation based on the LSP knowledge.

5 Neutralization and Enhancement

One of the possible alternative choices in the process of acquiring phonological computation that was not mentioned so far is that the child might not postulate de-laryngealization as a phonological process. As a consequence, she would not need to postulate any licensing mechanism either. All the targets of RVA and FOD (3) would maintain their lexical identity, but assume different phonetic identity in some way. A proposal to this effect is put forward in van der Hulst

(2015) working within the model of Radical CV Phonology (RcvP) (van der Hulst 2005, 2020). One of the premises of the proposal is that the representation of the two-way distinction in voicing languages like Polish and in aspiration languages like English is the same, in that one of the series of obstruents is always marked as [fortis]. The distinction into voicing and aspiration systems follows from different phonological language specific enhancement rules. In Polish, the unmarked obstruents are phonologically enhanced with the gesture [voiced] in pre-vocalic position, while in English, the [fortis] series is additionally enhanced with the gesture [spread] in the relevant contexts. FOD in Polish, then, is a result of the absence of enhancement in final position rather than a case of de-laryngealization. Thus, the two series are still distinct word-finally, but remain unenhanced, that is, voiceless. This is a welcome result, given the incompleteness of neutralization in this context (e.g. Slowiaczek and Dinnsen 1985).

There are two obvious differences between the analysis discussed in this paper and the proposal in van der Hulst (2015). One of them is that enhancement in RcvP is phonological, which enforces a view of phonology with two distinct levels resembling traditional underlying and surface representations. This leads to a situation in which the lexicon is privative and simple, but the phonology is not. The other difference concerns the absence of neutralization as a phonological process. The obvious question in the light of our discussion is whether the enhancement rules indeed have to be phonological. But a more important question is whether van der Hulst's approach is able to account for the dialectal distinction in Polish irrespective of where enhancement belongs.

On the one hand, voiced obstruents require enhancement, and on the other, it seems that the CPP sandhi voicing cannot be generated by phonological enhancement rules. Even if we assume that the pre-vocalic context across a word-boundary can trigger phonological enhancement of the word-final obstruents, we would expect /C°/ to be enhanced as [voiced], while /C$^{[\text{fortis}]}$/ should remain voiceless. This is because the whole idea of phonological enhancement is that implementation should follow directly from it. Alternatively, it may be proposed that some enhancement is also present at the implementation stage, that is, in LSP. It would then need to override the unenhanced phonological distinctions. This is possible in RVA contexts, that is, when followed by a voiced obstruent, e.g. *świat dziecka* [ɕfjad dʑetska] 'child's world'. The word-initial obstruent is phonologically enhanced as voiced and can affect the preceding word-final obstruent. Then it does not matter whether RVA is phonological – [voice] spreading – or phonetic, that is, co-articulatory. However, for this analysis to work for the pre-sonorant sandhi context, sonorants in CPP, but crucially not in WP, would have to be enhanced with [voice] and spread it too, as a phonological process. A phonetic explanation based on co-articulation is even more difficult to refer to because sonorants are spontaneously voiced and do not require special gestures that could then be used to explain co-articulation. Needless to say, such sonorants in CPP would have to be different phonetically from those in WP, where pre-sonorant voicing does not occur. In conclusion, either way, it looks like the analysis without laryngeal neutralization and reversed specification has to resort to voice specification of sonorants, which resembles the standard binary feature analysis of Rubach (1996).

6 Conclusions

The voicing phenomena in Polish, including the dialect variation, can be understood if a couple of restrictive assumptions are made about the phonological and the phonetic parts of the system, and about the relation between these parts. Phonologically speaking, the representation of the laryngeal contrast is privative and substance-free. It is also minimal, in that sonorants are never marked with laryngeal properties. The computational aspect of phonology is reduced to one mechanism of laryngeal licensing, which is discharged by melodically filled nuclei, but not by empty nuclei. The latter trigger de-laryngealization in Polish in pre-obstruent and word-final position. The phonological module must reflect the sound patterns, but the two do not need to be in a one-to-one relationship. The postulation of phonological categories to express the laryngeal distinction and the computation to go with it may look quite different from the overt patterns. For example, we saw that the data in (3) can be given two alternative systemic interpretations with opposite marking of the two-way laryngeal contrast. Neither FOD, nor RVA require one particular analysis. Additionally, the symmetrical effects of RVA need not involve phonological spreading of laryngeal features (6). In fact, this is quite impossible in a privative model.

Crucial in the understanding of the Polish voicing patterns is the place of language specific phonetics (LSP) in the laryngeal system. Given the acquisitional perspective, LSP knowledge involves knowing the major allophones and their contextual distribution, alternations and variation. These phonetic sound patterns constitute the basis for the systemic choice / acquisition of the phonological representation and computation that generalize the patterns in the mind. But, phonology works according to its own principles, such as privativity of representation, licensing, etc. In this sense, phonological categories and phonological computation cannot be based on what is referred to as 'phonological behaviour' (e.g. Odden nd). Firstly, the very idea that phonological categories and computation can be discovered by looking at the phonological behaviour involves circularity. Secondly, the term 'phonological behaviour' comes very close to the wrongly understood concept of 'laryngeal phonology' described in the introduction above.

As for the relationship between LSP and phonology, the establishment of a phonological category generalizing over a set of phonetic objects is viewed as a simultaneous establishment of the spell-out relation. Since phonological categories are abstractions of phonetic patterns and align according to the phonological principles, it follows that the spell-out relations are arbitrary in nature. Hence, the laryngeal categories may be called substance-free. Clearly the arbitrariness here is of the same nature as the relation between the word *chair* and the meaning 'a piece of furniture on which one can sit'. The spell-out targets are lexicalized as linked to particular phonological representations and stay put. Thus, arbitrariness really means that it is not immediately obvious which of the two series of obstruents is going to be marked in acquisition. It must be emphasized, however, that the choice of marking is not entirely arbitrary and free. It must be consistent with all the aspects of a given system, that is, the representation, the spell-out relations and the phonetic interpretation, all yielding the observed phonetic patterns.

In this paper, the familiar concept of direct phonetic interpretation used in GP (Harris and Lindsey 1995) is explicitly unfolded into two aspects: spell-out and phonetic interpretation. The former is a lexicalized relation between a phonological category and a spell-out target, which is established during acquisition. At this point, we may somewhat naively perhaps assume that this target is the major allophone found in the licensing/pre-vocalic context. Once it is put in the phonetic context of LSP, e.g. during articulatory planning, it may be affected in various phonetically natural ways yielding effects of RVA and FOD. For these reasons, /C°/ in CPP is voiceless word-finally but voiced pre-vocalically, both word-internally and in sandhi. In this sense, both alternations and variation, including incomplete neutralization, are to a great extent governed by LSP. It is in this module, or level, that enhancement has its place. The role of LSP is clearly becoming more important, and this aspect of sound systems needs further systematic study, for example, with respect to the function of contexts at this level as opposed to the phonological one. One example mentioned above concerned the difference between the phonological context /_V/ and the phonetic context [_V]. While the former is responsible for licensing of laryngeal distinctions, the latter is responsible for phonetic interpretation of the outcome of spell-out.

To conclude, laryngeal phonology proper is very small, and, although it is very different from the observed voicing patterns, it makes little sense outside the specific system for which it is established in acquisition.

References

Beckman, Jill, Michael Jessen & Catherine Ringen. 2013. Empirical evidence for laryngeal features: Aspirating vs. true voice languages. *Journal of Linguistics* 49(2). 259–284.

Bethin, Christina. 1984. Voicing assimilation in Polish. *Journal of Slavic Linguistics and Poetics* 29. 17–32.

Bethin, Christina. 1987. Syllable final laxing in Ukrainian. *Folia Slavica* 8. 185–197.

Bethin, Christina. 1992. *Polish Syllables: The Role of Prosody in Phonology and Morphology*. Columbus, OH: Slavica.

Cho, Taehong & Peter Ladefoged. 1999. Variation and universals in VOT: Evidence from 18 languages. *Journal of Phonetics* 27. 207–229.

Cyran, Eugeniusz. 2011. Laryngeal realism and laryngeal relativism: Two voicing systems in Polish? *Studies in Polish Linguistics* 6. 45–80.

Cyran, Eugeniusz. 2014. *Between Phonology and Phonetics: Polish Voicing*. Berlin/New York: De Gruyter Mouton.

Cyran, Eugeniusz. 2017. Hocus bogus? Licensing paths and voicing in Polish. In G. Lindsay and A. Nevins (eds.), *Sonic Signatures*, 34–62. Amsterdam: John Benjamins.

Cyran, Eugeniusz. 2018. Sonorant opacity without opaque segments. In B. Czapliski, B. Łukaszewicz & M. Opalińska (eds.), *Phonology, Fieldwork and Generalisations*, 105–127. Berlin: Peter Lang.

Cyran, Eugeniusz. In press. Production bias and acquisitional amnesia: Voicing retention and other 'statistically significant' phenomena in Polish. In F. Breit (ed.), *Government, Licensing, and Elements*. London: University College London Press.

Ernestus, Mirjam & Harald Baayen. 2006. The functionality of incomplete neutralization in Dutch: The case of past-tense formation. In L. M. Goldstein, D. H. Whalen & C. T. Best (eds.), *Laboratory Phonology* 8, 27–49. Berlin: Mouton de Gruyter.

Gussmann, Edmund. 1992. Resyllabification and delinking: The case of Polish voicing. *Linguistic Inquiry* 23. 29–56.

Gussmann, Edmund. 2007. *The Phonology of Polish*. Oxford: Oxford University Press.

Halle, Morris & Kenneth Stevens. 1971. A note on laryngeal features. *MIT Quarterly Progress Report* 101. 198–212.

Harris, John. 1994. *English Sound Structure*. Oxford: Blackwell.

Harris, John. 2009. Why final obstruent devoicing is weakening. In K. Nasukawa & P. Backley (eds.), *Strength Relations in Phonology*, 9–45. Berlin/New York: Mouton de Gruyter.

Harris, John & Geoff Lindsey. 1995. The elements of phonological representation. In J. Durand & F. Katamba (eds.), *Frontiers of Phonology: Atoms, Structures, Derivations*, 34–79. London/New York: Longman.

Helgason, Pétur & Catherine Ringen. 2008. Voicing and aspiration in Swedish stops. *Journal of Phonetics* 36. 607–628.

Honeybone, Patrick. 2002. Germanic obstruent lenition: Some implications of theoretical and historical phonology. Newcastle upon Tyne: University of Newcastle upon Tyne PhD Dissertation.

Hulst, Harry van der. 2005. The molecular structure of phonological segments. In P. Carr, J. Durand & C. Ewen (eds.), *Headhood, Elements, Specification and Contrastivity*, 193–234. Amsterdam: John Benjamins.

Hulst, Harry van der. 2015. The laryngeal class in RcvP and voice phenomena in Dutch. In J. Caspers, Y. Chen, W. Heeren, J. Pacilly, N. O. Schiller & E. van Zanten (eds.), *Above and Beyond the Segments: Experimental Linguistics and Phonetics*, 323–349. Amsterdam: John Benjamins.

Hulst, Harry van der. 2020. *Principles of Radical CV Phonology: A Theory of Segmental and Syllabic Structure*. Edinburgh: Edinburgh University Press.

Itô, Junko, Armin Mester & Jaye Padgett. 1995. Licensing and underspecification in Optimality Theory. *Linguistic Inquiry* 26. 571–613.

Iverson, Gregory & Joseph Salmons. 1995. Aspiration and laryngeal representation in Germanic. *Phonology* 12. 369–396.

Iverson, Gregory & Joseph Salmons. 2003. Laryngeal enhancement in early Germanic. *Phonology* 20. 43–74.

Jansen, Wouter. 2007. Dutch regressive voicing assimilation as a 'low level phonetic process': Acoustic evidence. In J. van de Weijer & E. J. van der Torre (eds.), *Voicing in Dutch: (De)voicing – Phonology, Phonetics, and Psycholinguistics*, 125–151. Amsterdam/Philadelphia: John Benjamins.

Kaye, Jonathan, Jean Lowenstamm & Jean-Roger Vergnaud. 1990. Constituent structure and government in phonology. *Phonology* 7. 193–231.

Kingston, John. 2019. The interface between phonetics and phonology. In W. F. Katz & P. F. Assmann (eds.), *The Routledge Handbook of Phonetics*, 359–400. London: Routledge.

Kohler, Klaus. 2012. Neutralization?! The phonetics-phonology issue in the analysis of word-final obstruent voicing. In D. Gybbon, D. Hirst & N. Campbell (eds.), *Rhythm, Melody and Harmony in Speech: Studies in Honour of Wiktor Jassem*, 171–180. Poznań: Polish Phonetic Association.

Liljencrants, Johan & Björn Lindblom. 1972. Numerical simulation of vowel quality systems: The role of perceptual contrast. *Language* 48(4). 839–862.

Lisker, Leigh & Arthur Abramson. 1964. A cross-language study of voicing in initial stops: Acoustical measurements. *Word* 20. 384–422.

Odden, David. nd. Radical substance free phonology and feature learning, Ms.

Port, Robert & Michael O'Dell. 1985. Neutralization of syllable-final voicing in German. *Journal of Phonetics* 13. 455–471.

Rubach, Jerzy. 1996. Non-syllabic analysis of voice assimilation in Polish. *Linguistic Inquiry* 27. 69–110.

Rubach, Jerzy. 2008. Prevocalic faithfulness. *Phonology* 25. 433–468.

Scheer, Tobias. 2004. *A Lateral Theory of Phonology: What Is CVCV, and Why Should It Be?* Berlin: Mouton de Gruyter.

Scheer, Tobias. 2014. Spell-out, post-phonological. In E. Cyran & J. Szpyra-Kozłowska (eds.), *Crossing Phonetics-Phonology Lines*, 255–275. Newcastle upon Tyne: Cambridge Scholars Publishing.

Schwartz, Jean-Luc, Louis-Jean Boë & Christian Abry. 2007. Linking Dispersion Focalization Theory and the maximum utilization of the available distinctive features principle in a Perception-for-Action-Control Theory. In M.-J. Solé, P. Beddor & M. Ohala (eds.), *Experimental Approaches to Phonology*, 104–124. Oxford: Oxford University Press.

Slowiaczek, Louisa & Daniel A. Dinnsen. 1985. On the neutralizing status of Polish word-final devoicing. *Journal of Phonetics* 13. 325–341.

Stevens, Kenneth. 1972. The quantal nature of speech: Evidence from articulatory-acoustic data. In P. B. Denes & E. E. David Jr. (eds.), *Human Communication: A Unified View*, 51–66. New York: McGraw Hill.

Krisztina Polgárdi
The Representation of Nasal + Stop + Obstruent Clusters in English: Stop Insertion or Stop Deletion?

Abstract: The medial stop of English nasal+stop+obstruent clusters is present only optionally (indicated by italics or superscript in the transcription, following Wells 2008): e.g. *sphincter* [ˈsfɪŋktə] and *concert* [ˈkɒnˢət]. The question then arises if the stop is deleted or inserted in this context. I argue that in fact both processes exist, accounting for the differences between them. I propose a Government Phonological analysis, where deletion is caused by lack of proper government, whereas insertion involves creation of a contour structure. I show that the latter process applies at the stem level, while the former belongs to the word level. The analysis is then extended to a third process of optionally reducing affricates to fricatives after nasal or oral stops (as in *angel* [ˈeɪndʒəl] and *actual* [ˈæktʃuəl]), represented as loss of the affricate's stop half.

Keywords: cluster simplification, emergent stop, government, contour structure, Strict CV, Element Theory

1 Introduction

The occurrence of CCC-clusters is severely limited in English, unless C_2C_3 form a possible branching onset (as in *country* [ˈkʌntri]). If this is not the case, then either C_2 must be [s] (as in *substitute* [ˈsʌbstɪtjuːt]), or a homorganic nasal+stop cluster is followed by an obstruent. The medial stop of such nasal+stop+obstruent clusters is present only optionally, indicated by italics or superscript in the transcriptions of (1a) vs (1b), following Wells (2008). (Data in this paper have

---

Acknowledgements: This paper is dedicated to Harry van der Hulst, to express my gratitude for everything I have learned from him and for all the fun we have had discussing phonology and other important questions of life. I would also like to thank Péter Siptár, Jeroen van de Weijer, an anonymous referee, and audiences of presentations at the 6th Fonologi i Norden Meeting, and at the 28th Manchester Phonology Meeting, for valued comments on previous versions of this paper.

Krisztina Polgárdi, Hungarian Research Centre for Linguistics

https://doi.org/10.1515/9783110730098-010

been collected from the electronic database of Lindsey and Szigetvári (2013), and all examples cited have been checked in Wells 2008.)

(1) nasal+stop+obstruent clusters
    a. empty   ['em*p*ti]   b. concert   ['kɒnᵗsət]
        tincture ['tɪŋ*k*tʃə]   infant   ['ɪnᵗfənt]
        sphincter ['sfɪŋ*k*tə]   length   [leŋᵏθ]
        function ['fʌŋ*k*ʃən]   hamster ['hæmᵖstə]

The question then arises if the stop is deleted or inserted in this context. Szigetvári (2020) proposes to analyse both cases as insertion. However, I will show that important differences between the two types remain unexplained under such an analysis. Therefore, I will argue that there is both deletion and insertion (in (1a) and (1b), respectively, as suggested by the transcriptions of Wells), and I will provide a Government Phonological analysis, in terms of Strict CV (Lowenstamm 1996) and Element Theory (Backley 2011). I will also extend the analysis to a third process, the reduction of affricates to fricatives, applying optionally after nasal or oral stops (as in *angel* ['eɪndʒəl] and *actual* ['æktʃuəl]). This cannot be analysed as insertion either because it does not happen in forms like *action* ['ækʃən].

2 Deletion vs Insertion

Comparing (1a) and (1b), the following differences between the two types can be identified. (i) In (1b), C₃ is always a fricative, while in (1a), C₃ is mostly a stop or an affricate. (ii) When the third consonant in the cluster is a fricative, the alternation does not occur in the context of a following stressed vowel (e.g. *concert* (noun) ['kɒnᵗsət] vs *concert* (verb) *[kənᵗˈsɜːt]), whereas in case of a stop the alternation is also found pretonically (e.g. *punctilious* [pʌŋkˈtɪliəs]). (iii) An optional [t] can be found before a fricative (e.g. *infant* ['ɪnᵗfənt]), but never before a stop (e.g. *melancholy* *['melənˈkəli]). As a coronal stop cannot occur in a word-internal coda in English (words like *chapter* [pt] and *doctor* [kt] exist, but the reverse clusters, [tp] and [tk], are ruled out), this difference between (1a) and (1b) can be explained if the nasal+stop+stop clusters in (1a) must be underlying but the [t] in forms like *concert* ['kɒnᵗsət] in (1b) is excrescent in some way. (iv) [ŋ] is normally only permitted before a velar plosive morpheme internally at the stem-level, which would be contradicted by forms of type (1a) if the [k] was not underlying. (v) Finally, voiceless stops are also optionally deleted in the parallel forms containing the word-level suffixes *-s* and *-ed*: e.g. *jumped* [dʒʌmpt], *prints* [prɪnts], and *thanks* [θæŋks], where an insertion analysis is not feasible, shown by the fact that the stops are also present in the unsuffixed form (where there is no alternation). Therefore, I maintain that forms in (1a) involve deletion of the medial stop, while forms in (1b) exhibit insertion.

3 Analysis of Deletion

Deletion of the medial stop in (1a) can be easily understood in a Strict CV analysis (following Lowenstamm 1996). In this approach, syllable structure consists of strictly alternating C and V positions. As a consequence, the representation of closed syllables, geminate consonants and long vowels involves an empty position, as shown by the hypothetical forms in (2).[1]

(2) *Strict CV* (Lowenstamm 1996)
  a. *closed syllable*   b. *geminate consonant*   c. *long vowel*

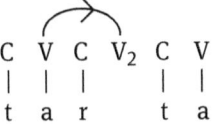 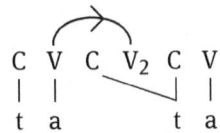 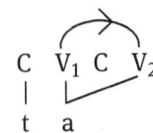

Geminates and long vowels are built up of two CV units. In a geminate the consonantal melody straddles an empty V position, while in a long vowel the vocalic melody straddles an empty C.

Following Rowicka (1999a, 1999b), I employ trochaic (left-to-right) proper government instead of the more usual right-to-left type,[2] as defined in (3) (argued for extensively in Polgárdi 2012, 2015a, 2015b).

(3) *Trochaic (left-to-right) Proper Government* (Rowicka 1999a, 1999b)
  A nuclear position *A* properly governs a nuclear position *B* iff
  (a) *A* governs *B* (adjacent on its projection) from left to right
  (b) *A* is not properly governed

---

1 In this approach, there is no syllabic structure above the skeleton, all we have are the CV units, with some positions potentially remaining empty. For ease of exposition, I will keep using expressions like rhyme, closed syllable, branching onset etc., but only as descriptive terms, referring to specific configurations in the data, which then will receive a CV-analysis.
2 Iambic proper government was proposed by Kaye (1990), and Kaye, Lowenstamm, and Vergnaud (1990), and it has been employed by most proponents of Government Phonology. Advocates of trochaic proper government include Gibb (1992) and Yoshida (1999).

Government is a binary, asymmetric relation between skeletal positions. Proper government, indicated by a curved arrow in (2), is a special form of government, which works in conjunction with the Empty Category Principle, given in (4).

(4) *Empty Category Principle (ECP)* (Kaye, Lowenstamm, and Vergnaud 1990: 219)
A position may be uninterpreted phonetically if it is properly governed.

As a result, an empty V position may remain silent if it is properly governed, as shown by V_2 in (2a–b) above. According to Rowicka (1999a, 1999b), the relationship between the two halves of a long vowel is also one of proper government, as shown in (2c). The difference between this case and the one in (2a–b) is that in (2c) the C position between V_1 and V_2 is unfilled, and therefore the governing relationship is manifested by spreading the melodic content of V_1 into V_2, in Rowicka's proposal. The ECP permits properly governed positions to remain uninterpreted, but it does not demand that they do so. Therefore, the realisation of V_2 in (2c) does not contradict the ECP.

Deletion of the medial stop in forms like (1a) can then be analysed as presented in (5).

(5) *deletion of ungoverned CV unit*

$$C\ V_1\ C\ V_2\ <C_3\ V_3>\ C\ V_4$$
$$|\quad |\quad\quad |\quad\quad\quad |\quad |$$
$$e\quad m\quad\quad p\quad\quad\quad t\quad i$$

In this representation, V_1 properly governs the empty V_2 inside the homorganic cluster, thus enabling it to remain silent. Being properly governed, however, V_2 can now not govern V_3.[3] Therefore, it is no surprise that the cluster is optionally simplified, by deleting the C_3V_3 sequence (indicated by angle brackets).[4] Note that

---

[3] The situation seems to be the same when the consonant cluster occurs word-finally, as in *lamp* [læmp], but in this case no alternation is found. To take care of the second empty nucleus in the sequence, either domain-final licensing of empty nuclei is proposed to be permitted parametrically (e.g. Yoshida 1999), or a Loose CV approach is adopted which dispenses with inaudible domain-final empty nuclei altogether (e.g. Polgárdi 2015a).

[4] What is surprising, though, is why this deletion only happens optionally and not obligatorily. While I do not have a satisfactory answer for this question at the moment, note that similarly surprising forms are also sometimes (optionally) created by syncope, as in *comp(a)ny* ['kʌmpni] and *vict(o)ry* ['vɪktri], where the third consonant following the coda-onset cluster is of course a sonorant (Polgárdi 2015a).

with iambic proper government, V_3 would be governed by the following filled V position. In that situation, we would not expect that CV unit to delete, but rather the previous one, contrary to what actually happens.

4 Analysis of Insertion

As the lexical representation in (5) is ill-formed, we do not expect another process to create it. The appearance of a stop in (1b) thus cannot result from segment insertion. I propose that a contour structure is created, similar to that of the two root node analysis of affricates by Harris (1994) (see also Clements 1987).

To represent this process, I use Element Theory, as introduced for example in Backley (2011). In this version, there are three resonance elements and three manner/laryngeal elements, all monovalent, presented in (6a–b).

(6) *Element Theory* (Backley 2011)
   a. *resonance elements*
                acoustic pattern
      I   [i]   *dIp*: low F_1, high F_2 merged with F_3
      A [a]   *mAss*: high F_1 merged with F_2
      U [u]   *rUmp*: lowered formants
   b. *manner / laryngeal elements*
                acoustic pattern
      ʔ   [ʔ]   *stop*: sudden and sustained drop in acoustic energy
      H [h]   *noise*: raised F_0, aperiodic noise (continuous/transient)
      L [ũĩ] *nasal*: low frequency energy, murmur

The list in (6) gives the representation of the element in bold, its phonetic interpretation when it constitutes a segment by itself (in a V position in (6a) and in a C position in (6b)), followed by the name of the element in italics, and a brief description of the acoustic pattern it is mapped onto. All elements can occur in both V and C positions, although their interpretation differs depending on the position.

In the case of vocalic expressions, the resonance element |I| occurs in front vowels, |A| in non-high vowels, while |U| in rounded vowels. The unmarkedness of the vowels [i a u] is expressed by their simplex nature, that is, that they are made up of a single element. Elements can also combine, resulting in compound expressions, mapping onto composite spectral patterns, comprising the acoustic characteristics of contributing elements. For example, the mid vowel [ɛ] is represented by the compound |A I|, combining the openness of |A| with the frontness of |I|. In addition, following Dependency Phonology (Anderson and Ewen 1987), the notion of headedness is also employed. This gives an element acoustic prominence or strength (as in the contrast between [e] |A I̲| as a lowered front vowel vs [æ] |A̲ I| as a fronted low vowel). As we shall see below, non-headed expressions and expressions with more than one head are also allowed.

Turning to the manner/laryngeal elements, the stop element |ʔ| occurs as non-headed in oral and nasal stops (and affricates) and in creaky vowels, and as headed in ejectives. Non-headed |H| can be found as noise in fricatives and released stops (and affricates), while headed |H̲| is interpreted as voicelessness or aspiration in languages such as English, where a phonologically active voiceless series of obstruents contrasts with a phonologically neutral series of voiced obstruents lacking a laryngeal property. Conversely, in languages like French, where the phonologically active obstruent series is voiced, this series possesses the headed element |L̲|, representing voicing, in contrast to the neutral series, again lacking an active laryngeal element. Non-headed |L|, on the other hand, stands for nasality, in both consonants and vowels. In addition to aspiration and voicing in obstruents, headed |H̲| and |L̲| in vowels represent high and low tone, respectively.

The elemental representation of the English consonant system is given in (7), except for the laryngeal distinction. (The non-headed |H| in (7) represents neutral obstruents, and it is replaced by headed |H̲| in their voiceless counterparts.) The articulatory labels are provided for ease of reference here, and they might not always match the phonetic details. The representational classes in Element Theory are based on phonological behaviour and not simply on articulatory properties.

(7) *representation of consonants in English, voicing disregarded*

		lab	dent	alv	pal-alv	pal	vel	glott
		U	A I	A	A I̲	I	U	–
stop	ʔ H	p b	t d		tʃ dʒ		k g	(ʔ)
fric	H	f v	θ ð	s z	ʃ ʒ			h
nasal	ʔ L	m		n			ŋ	
approx	–	w	l	ɹ		j		

Affricates and stops are treated as phonologically identical, only distinguished by their resonance properties (resulting in a difference in release phase in their phonetic interpretation). Place of articulation is defined by the resonance elements, with variation in headedness again representing a difference in the strength of their acoustic cues. The parallelism with vowels is quite clear in the case of headed |U| standing for labials, non-headed |U| for velars, and headed |I| for palatals. The coronal area is more complex, and it also shows more language-specific variation. Palato-alveolars may share a class with palatals or they may be separate, as proposed here, bearing the specification |A I|. Dentals and alveolars may be represented by non-headed |I|, |A|, or |A I|, depending on their behaviour. I have chosen to represent [t d θ ð] in English as |A I| to be able to formulate the restriction against homorganicity within branching onsets in a straightforward way (i.e. *[tl dl θl] vs [tɹ dɹ θɹ]),[5] but nothing hinges on this with respect to the story of nasal+stop+obstruent clusters. (Headed |A| is used for uvulars and pharyngeals, or for retroflexes, in languages that have these types of consonants.) Finally, glottals lack a resonance element altogether.

The representation of stop "insertion" is provided in (8), on the example of the medial cluster in *hamster* [ˈhæmᵖstə].

(8) *creation of a contour structure*

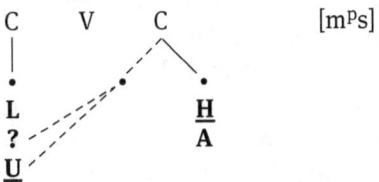

Here, [m] is built up of the nasal element |L|, the stop element |?|, and the place element |U| (for labial), while [s] comprises the headed |H| element, standing for voicelessness and noise, and the place element |A| (for alveolar). During the process, the stop and place elements of the nasal spread to the following fricative (expressing extension of oral closure), and an additional root node (•) is created to host them, producing a contour structure (see also Clements 1987). This representation is similar to that proposed by Harris (1994) for affricates, except that here the two root nodes bear separate place specifications.[6] Analysing the emergent stops of (1b) as part of a contour structure makes the prediction that they should be shorter than the underlying stops of (1a). In fact, there has been some experimental evidence for this, measured in pairs of minimally distinct words like *dense* [denᵗs] vs *dents* [dents] (Fourakis and Port 1986).

---

5 Note that *[ðl] and *[ðɹ] are ruled out independently because voiced fricatives cannot occur in complex onsets in English.
6 In Backley's (2011) system, affricates are not contour segments, as shown in (7), an issue that I will come back to in Section 5.

The process only applies when the fricative is voiceless (e.g. *hamster* [ˈhæmᵖstə] vs *crimson* *[ˈkrɪmᵇzən]) which, therefore, always bears headed |**H**|. In my view, this element does not need to spread to the root node of [p] because neutral obstruents in languages like English only exhibit passive voicing when they are surrounded by voiced sounds (essentially vowels and/or sonorant consonants), whereas next to a voiceless obstruent passive voicing is blocked (Iverson and Salmons 1995). Or if |**H**| does spread, I think, this should be an automatic consequence of a general requirement on root nodes within the same segment to share their laryngeal specifications, and it should not be specified as a separate part of this process.

A question that arises at this point concerns the motivation for this process: in what sense is the sequence [mᵖs] better than the sequence [ms]? Nasals like to be homorganic with a following obstruent, but this does not suffice as an explanation because the process also applies in homorganic nasal+fricative clusters (as in *comfort* [ˈkʌmᵖfət]). The motivation provided in the literature is rooted in the challenging nature of the relative timing of articulatory gestures during the production of this sequence: closure of the velum and release of the oral closure for the nasal must be synchronised to produce a neat transition between the nasal and the fricative. If release of the oral closure lags behind, an epenthetic stop is produced (e.g. Ali, Daniloff, and Hammarberg 1979; Ohala 1997; see Page (1997) for an overview and further references). I propose to represent this extension of oral closure of the nasal in Government Phonology as in (8). Both the two root node analysis and the idea that this process is not motivated by syllable structure are supported by the finding of Solé (2007) that an epenthetic stop also occurs in the mirror image fricative+nasal context (i.e. when the cluster /sm/ is realised as [sᵖm], e.g. in *Christmas* [ˈkrɪsᵖməs]). In this case, oral closure for the nasal precedes lowering of the velum. Because such emergent stops are nasally released, they are perceptually much less salient than the ones occurring in nasal+fricative clusters (and they are not indicated in Wells (2008)).

Having an articulatory motivation might suggest that the process applies at a very low, perhaps even phonetic, level. This is, however, not the case. One argument against this is provided by the fact that it is lexically variable: that is, in the same prosodic and melodic context, epenthesis applies in one word (e.g. *infant* [ˈɪnˈfənt]), but not in another (e.g. *infamous* *[ˈɪnˈfəməs]), showing that the process must belong to the lexical phonology.[7] In fact, it can be demonstrated that it is

---

7 One factor involved in this difference is probably relative usage frequency of lexical items.

restricted to the stem level, as it applies before stem-level suffixes (e.g. *month* [mʌnᵗθ]) but not before word-level ones (e.g. *painful* *[ˈpeɪnᵗfəl]). Stem-level status of *-th* is evidenced by shortening of the stem vowel to conform to phonotactic restrictions characterising monomorphemic items. The lack of such shortening testifies to word-level status for *-ful*. (For a discussion of the stem vs word level distinction, see Harris 1994; Kaye 1995 in Goverment Phonology; Kiparsky 1982; Borowsky 1993 in Lexical Phonology; and Kiparsky 2000; Bermúdez-Otero 2012 in Stratal OT.)

This leads us to the question of how the few items like *length* [leŋᵏθ] can be derived. That suffixation of *-th* has applied at the stem level is also clear from umlaut of the stem vowel. However, simplification of /ŋg/-clusters is restricted to domain final position at this level, as in *long* [lɒŋ] vs *longitude* [ˈlɒŋgɪtjuːd]. The /g/ of /leŋgθ/, therefore, cannot be deleted by it. The only way I see to analyse this form is to assume that the /g/ has been devoiced, standing next to a voiceless obstruent, and it is optionally deleted, similarly to the parallel forms in (1a). Thus, it does not exemplify epenthesis. If emergent stops turn out to be systematically shorter than underlying stops, then the validity of this analysis could be tested by measuring the duration of the alternating stop.

As discussed in Section 2, insertion of an epenthetic stop fails to occur preceding a stressed vowel: e.g. *inference* [ˈɪnˈfərənᵗs] vs *infer* *[ɪnᵗˈfɜː]. The representations of the medial clusters are given in (9a–b).

(9) *no spreading across a foot boundary*
    a. *inference* [ˈɪnˈfərənᵗs]   b. *infer* *[ɪnᵗˈfɜː]

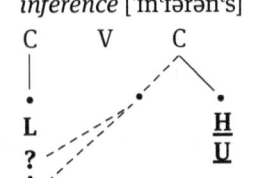
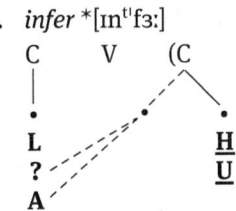

The difference involves presence or absence of a foot boundary (indicated by a parenthesis on the CV-tier in (9b)) between the trigger and target of spreading. The generalisation thus seems to be that spreading cannot cross a foot boundary, while it is allowed to apply within the same foot. In fact, this restriction is not specific to the emergence of epenthetic stops, but it can also be found with respect to another stem-level process, syllabic consonant formation (Polgárdi 2015a), which is also prohibited pre-tonically: e.g. *shibboleth* [ˈʃɪbəˌlɛθ]/[ˈʃɪbələθ]/[ˈʃɪbl̩əθ], where a syllabic [l̩] is only possible when the following vowel is reduced. Relevant parts of the representations are given in (10).

(10) *English syllabic consonant formation*

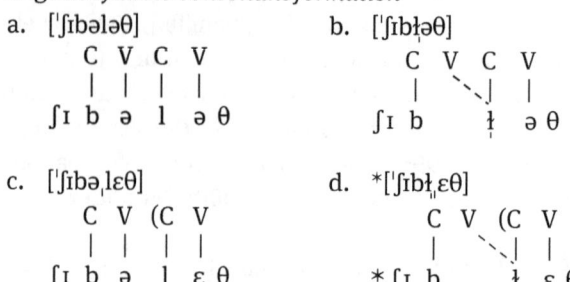

Syllabic consonants in English are analysed in Government Phonology as resulting from spreading of the melody of the consonant to a preceding V position (Szigetvári 1999; Scheer 2004; Polgárdi 2015a), accounting for their alternation with a schwa plus non-syllabic consonant sequence, as in (10a–b). The representations in (10c–d) show that such spreading is illicit when it would involve crossing a foot boundary, similarly to what we have seen in the case of emergent stops. In fact, if these emergent stops were analysed as resulting from regular epenthesis (i.e. insertion of a CV unit), then this restriction would remain unexplained, as the explanation crucially relies on the involvement of spreading to the C position of the fricative.

5 Reduction of Affricates

Finally, there is an interesting further process in English that applies in a partly overlapping context (which I have not seen discussed in the literature), whereby affricates following nasal or oral stops optionally reduce to fricatives, as illustrated in (11a–b).

(11) *reduction of affricates*
 a. nasal+affricate clusters
  angel ['eɪndʒəl]
  century ['sentʃəri]
 b. stop+affricate clusters
  actual ['æktʃuəl]
  capture ['kæptʃə]

This process is not the exact reverse of that exemplified in (1b), not only because it applies after oral stops too, but also because it affects voiced affricates as well, although only when they follow a nasal (e.g. *subjugate* *['sʌbʒəgeɪt]). Another difference is that here the stop part of the affricate of course shares its place properties with the fricative part, and not (necessarily) with the preceding nasal or stop. This reduction is lexically variable in the context of an oral stop (e.g. *structure* [ˈstrʌkʃə] vs *stricture* *[ˈstrɪkʃə]), but after a nasal no such variation is found. In addition, the process is prevented from applying by a following stressed vowel (e.g. *angel* [ˈeɪnʒəl] vs *angelic* *[ænˈʒelɪk]).

It is not entirely obvious how to analyse this process. If affricates are represented as contour structures, then their reduction is sort of the reverse of stop insertion in (8), given in (12a), by losing their stop half (including one of their root nodes).

(12) *reduction of affricates: angel* [ˈeɪndʒəl]
   a. *affricate as a contour structure*   b. *affricate as a stop*

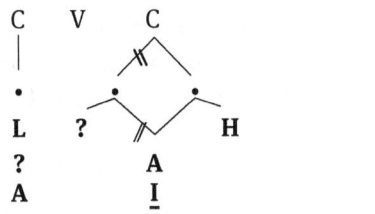
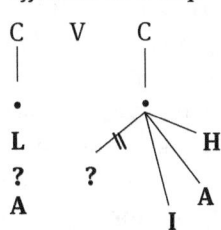

However, in Backley's (2011) system, affricates are generally treated as phonologically identical to stops, in which case reduction simply means loss of their stop element, without further simplification of the structure, as in (12b). Restriction to non-pretonic position can be explained by the nature of the process as a type of lenition which we do not expect to apply in a strong position, as the one preceding a stressed vowel.

The question then is why two processes with the exact opposite result would apply in (almost) the same context. I think, the reduction of affricates might be a natural extension of the stop "insertion" process. As the latter applies optionally, a form like *censure* will sometimes appear with a nasal+fricative sequence, as [ˈsenʃə], and at other times with a nasal+"affricate" sequence, as [ˈsenˈʃər]. It then will be easy for speakers to extend the alternation to forms like *venture* [ˈventʃə] with a nasal+affricate sequence and pronounce it sometimes with a nasal+fricative sequence, as [ˈvenʃə]. In this way, the surface forms become completely analogous, even though coming from different sources.[8] Perhaps this "conspiracy" provides an argument in favour of the two root node analysis of

---

[8] It might, of course, also be that the chronology of these developments was the reverse, or that they happened at the same time. My point here is simply that they were probably related.

affricates. Extending the pattern further, to stop+affricate clusters, is interesting because in stop+fricative sequences like *action* ['ækʃən] emergent stops are not found. Perhaps what helps here is that underlyingly stop+stop+fricative clusters (such as [ktʃ]) are also illicit in English because the second stop should be a [t] which, however, cannot occur in an internal coda (as mentioned in Section 2).

6 Summary

In this paper, I have examined the alternation exhibited by the medial stop of nasal+stop+obstruent clusters in English. I have argued for the existence of two separate processes: deletion of an underlying stop between a nasal and an obstruent (mostly a stop), and formation of an emergent stop in a nasal+fricative context. These are supplemented by a third process, reducing an affricate to a fricative after a nasal or oral stop.

I have analysed deletion of an underlying stop in a Strict CV framework, as caused by lack of proper government of the relevant CV unit. The representation of emergent stops in a nasal+fricative context involves creation of a contour structure, by spreading the stop and place elements of the nasal to the following fricative. This spreading is restricted to apply only within the domain of a foot, a parallel of which can be observed in syllabic consonant formation. Both of these processes apply at the stem level, whereas deletion of an underlying stop applies at the word level, evidenced by the fact that it can also be triggered by word-level suffixes. Finally, the reduction of affricates is analysed as a process which is sort of the reverse of the one creating emergent stops, by loss of the affricate's stop half. An insertion analysis is not possible in this case either, as it would overgenerate in stop+fricative sequences like *action* *['ækᵗʃən].

References

Ali, Latif, Ray Daniloff & Robert Hammarberg. 1979. Intrusive stops in nasal-fricative clusters: An aerodynamic and acoustic investigation. *Phonetica* 36. 85–97.
Anderson, John M. & Colin J. Ewen. 1987. *Principles of Dependency Phonology*. Cambridge: Cambridge University Press.
Backley, Phillip. 2011. *An Introduction to Element Theory*. Edinburgh: Edinburgh University Press.
Bermúdez-Otero, Ricardo. 2012. The architecture of grammar and the division of labour in exponence. In Jochen Trommer (ed.), *The Morphology and Phonology of Exponence*, 8–83 (Oxford Studies in Theoretical Linguistics 41). Oxford: Oxford University Press.

Borowsky, Toni. 1993. On the word level. In Sharon Hargus & Ellen M. Kaisse (eds.), *Phonetics and Phonology*, vol. 4: *Studies in Lexical Phonology*, 199–234. San Diego, CA: Academic Press.

Clements, G. N. 1987. Phonological feature representation and the description of intrusive stops. *Papers from the Twenty-third Meeting, Chicago Linguistic Society*, vol. 2, 29–50. Chicago: CLS.

Fourakis, Marios & Robert Port. 1986. Stop epenthesis in English. *Journal of Phonetics* 14. 197–221.

Gibb, Lorna. 1992. *Domains in phonology: With evidence from Icelandic, Finnish and Kikuyu*. Edinburgh: University of Edinburgh dissertation.

Harris, John. 1994. *English Sound Structure*. Oxford: Blackwell.

Iverson, Gregory K. & Joseph C. Salmons. 1995. Aspiration and laryngeal representation in Germanic. *Phonology* 12. 369–396.

Kaye, Jonathan. 1990. 'Coda' licensing. *Phonology* 7. 301–330.

Kaye, Jonathan. 1995. Derivations and interfaces. In Jacques Durand & Francis Katamba (eds.), *Frontiers in Phonology: Atoms, Structures, Derivations*, 289–332. London: Longman.

Kaye, Jonathan, Jean Lowenstamm & Jean-Roger Vergnaud. 1990. Constituent structure and government in phonology. *Phonology* 7. 193–231.

Kiparsky, Paul. 1982. Lexical Morphology and Phonology. In In-Seok Yang (ed.), *Linguistics in the Morning Calm*, 3–91. Seoul: Hanshin.

Kiparsky, Paul. 2000. Opacity and cyclicity. *The Linguistic Review* 17. 351–365.

Lindsey, Geoff & Péter Szigetvári. 2013. *Current British English searchable transcriptions*. http://seas3.elte.hu/cube.

Lowenstamm, Jean. 1996. CV as the only syllable type. In Jacques Durand & Bernard Laks (eds.), *Current Trends in Phonology: Models and Methods*, 419–441. Paris: CNRS.

Ohala, John J. 1997. Emergent stops. In *Proceedings of the 4th Seoul International Conference on Linguistics*, 84–91. Seoul: Linguistic Society of Korea.

Page, B. Richard. 1997. Articulatory phonology as a tool for explanation in historical phonology: The case of stop epenthesis in Germanic. In Irmengard Rauch & Gerald F. Carr (eds.), *Insights in Germanic linguistics II: Classic and Contemporary*, 175–188. Berlin/New York: Mouton de Gruyter.

Polgárdi, Krisztina. 2012. The distribution of vowels in English and trochaic proper government. In Bert Botma & Roland Noske (eds.), *Phonological Explorations: Empirical, Theoretical and Diachronic Issues*, 111–134 (Linguistische Arbeiten 548). Berlin/New York: Mouton de Gruyter.

Polgárdi, Krisztina. 2015a. Syncope, syllabic consonant formation, and the distribution of stressed vowels in English. *Journal of Linguistics* 51. 383–423.

Polgárdi, Krisztina. 2015b. Vowels, glides, off-glides and on-glides in English: A Loose CV analysis. *Lingua* 158. 9–34.

Rowicka, Grażyna. 1999a. On trochaic proper government. In John Rennison & Klaus Kühnhammer (eds.), *Phonologica 1996: Syllables!?*, 273–288. The Hague: Holland Academic Graphics.

Rowicka, Grażyna. 1999b. *On Ghost Vowels: A Strict CV Approach*. The Hague: Holland Academic Graphics.

Scheer, Tobias. 2004. *A Lateral Theory of Phonology: What Is CVCV, and Why Should It Be?* Berlin/New York: Mouton de Gruyter.

Solé, Maria-Josep. 2007. The stability of phonological features within and across segments: The effect of nasalization on frication. In Pilar Prieto, Joan Mascaró & Maria-Josep Solé (eds.),

Segmental and Prosodic Issues in Romance Phonology, 41–65. Amsterdam/Philadelphia: John Benjamins.

Szigetvári, Péter. 1999. *VC Phonology: A theory of consonant lenition and phonotactics*. Budapest: Eötvös Loránd University & Hungarian Academy of Sciences dissertation.

Szigetvári, Péter. 2020. Emancipating lenes: A reanalysis of English obstruent clusters. *Acta Linguistica Academica* 67(1). 39–52.

Wells, J. C. 2008. *Longman Pronunciation Dictionary*, 3rd edn. Harlow: Longman.

Yoshida, Shohei. 1999. Inter-nuclear relations in Arabic. In John Rennison & Klaus Kühnhammer (eds.), *Phonologica 1996: Syllables!?*, 335–354. The Hague: Holland Academic Graphics.

Norval Smith
A Perfect Mess in Ancient Greek: The Story of -*ka*

Abstract: This article is by no means the first to attempt an explanation of the various expressions of the Perfect in Ancient Greek. The two recognized allomorphs of the first person singular form are -*ka* and -*a*, to which I have added a third -*ha*. This last was hitherto termed the Aspirate(d) Perfect and was not directly evidenced in much more than about 20-odd verbs. The source of -*ka* has never been satisfactorily explained. The source of the -*ha* Perfect has generally been assumed to be analogical.

What is new about my contribution is that I explore the possibility that these suffix-variants were due to a lengthy history of language contact with Carian, and possibly Lycian, two closely related extinct languages. -*ka* and -*ha* are, I suggest, allomorphs of a single morpheme, with -*ka* originally the allomorph employed in post-vocalic position, while -*ha* was originally the allomorph employed in post-consonantal position. -*ka* has been a success story in Greek, spreading to some sonorant consonant cases, while the *ha*-allomorph is extremely recessive.

I cite a number of sources indicating that in cases of intimate language contact small portions of morphology can be borrowed. I suggest that this is another such case.

In conclusion I show that there is tentative evidence from Carian that the suffix -*ka* existed in that language. There is ample evidence from Lycian.

Keywords: The aspirated perfect (in Ancient Greek), language contact, Carian, compensatory lengthening, deportation (Caria/Lycia to Greece)

Acknowledgements: I would like first of all to acknowledge the fruitful years during the 1980s when Harry van der Hulst and I were partners in phonology. Not just in terms of articles and edited collections, but also in terms of discussions with each other on every aspect of phonology, as well as the joint organization of regular informal discussion groups on phonology with other Dutch phonologists. Thank you, Harry.

A second person whose influence I would like to acknowledge here is that of Dr. Betty Knott, my tutor in the Classics Department at the University of Glasgow. It was at her suggestion that I ended up at the School of Oriental and African Studies, the home of Firthian linguistics. I have never lost interest in the linguistic study of Classical languages, and I hope that this article would meet with her approval. Thank you again, Betty.

Norval Smith, Amsterdam Center for Language and Communication

https://doi.org/10.1515/9783110730098-011

1 Introduction

This article has as its topic the unsolved problem of the origin of the *ka*-perfect and the *aspirated* perfect in Ancient Greek, which last I will refer to as the *-ha* perfect, and which I claim have the same source in Carian, an extinct language of the Luwian subgroup of the Anatolian branch of the Indo-European language family (Melchert 2004; Adiego 2007). Some few *a*-perfects can also only be explained as former *ha*-perfects, as I attempt to show.

A large number of linguists have given their solutions to this problem, often leaning to a large extent on the use of analogy. There is strong disagreement about which forms are based on which analogy. Analogy is a last resort solution, especially in morphophonology. If a unified phonological solution can be provided, that is better.

I quote Cowgill's reaction to a suggestion by Sturtevant (1940b: 273–284, 1942: 87–89):

(1) "His explanation of the Greek verbs with κ-extensions in aorist and perfect requires that the κ originated in the 1st sg. perfect of roots ending in two of his four laryngeals, where the combination of root-final laryngeal with the ending *-Ae resulted in Indo-European *-ka. It is in my opinion practically impossible that the *k* could have spread from here to other persons of the perfect active singular; if anything, one would expect to have been reanalyzed and exploited as a mark of the 1st person singular. No Indo-European language has a first singular perfect in *-ka opposed to other persons without *k; ..." (Cowgill 1965: 175).

Now, however, two encouraging developments have taken place. Firstly, Kloekhorst (2018), has proposed new phonetic equivalents for the Lycian reflexes of the two "laryngeals" of Hittite and Luwian – fortis /χː/ and lenis /χ/. These are respectively /k/ and /x/, he suggests (see Table 1). Furthermore, the decipherment of Carian has revealed a language which according to Kloekhorst is clearly related to Lycian. He now posits what he calls the Proto-Caro-Lycian group of Anatolian languages.

The 1st person preterite marker in Lycian was *-ka*. The /k/-value for Carian was only established for initial position by Kloekhorst. But see Section 7.

It would be stretching the truth to claim that much is so far known about the Carian verbal system. However the Lycian verbal system has been studied in some detail (e.g. Billing (2019); Serangeli (2018)). I will return to this point in Section 7.

I will now present my transcription scheme for Greek phonology, followed by an analysis of aspiration.

Table 1: Proto-Anatolian.

PIA[1] /*h₂/	PAnatolian	Carian	Lycian	Luwian	Hittite
fortis	*q:	k	k	χː	χː
lenis	*q	?	x	χ	χ

1.1 Transcription

I first want to say a few words on the transcription of Ancient Greek. I will make use of a simpler transcription system for the indication of accent. This has the advantage that all high-toned vowels are indicated in the same fashion.

(2) Vowel accentuation: Acute accent: V́, VV́; Circumflex accent: V́V.[2]

My transcription of the Ancient Greek vowels is fairly conservative. It deviates from the later Attic fronting of /u/ to /y/[3] and raising of /oo/ to /uu/, as these only complicate the symmetry of vocalic relationships.

Table 2: Vocalic values based on Allen (1968).

Vox Graeca values				
Alphabetic <...>	Phonetic Allen's description [..]	Phonetic Allen's diagram [..]	Phonological /../	Later Attic realisations /../
ι	i	i	i	
ι	ii	ii	ii	
ε	ε	ε/ẹ[4]	e	
ει	ee	ee	ee	
η	εε	εε	εε	
α	a	a	a	
α	aa	aa	aa[5]	

---

1 PIA = Proto-Indo-Anatolian. Anatolian languages include Hittite, Luvian (Luwian), Lycian, Lydian, Carian and other lesser known languages.
2 Greek scholars will no doubt shudder at my non-use of the circumflex symbol. But for a more general public it is clearer just to mark the location of the accented vocalic element.
3 I.e. /ü/.
4 By this symbolization I refer to the short true mid vowel representation of Allen on his vowel diagram
5 In general, unless preceded by certain vowels or /r/, this is pronounced as η ([εε]).

Table 2 (continued)

Vox Graeca values				
Alphabetic <...>	Phonetic Allen's description [..]	Phonetic Allen's diagram [..]	Phonological /../	Later Attic realisations /../
υ	u	u	u	y
υ	uu	uu	uu	yy
ο	ɔ	ɔ̝/ǫ	o	
ου	oo	oo	oo	uu
ω	ɔɔ	ɔɔ	ɔɔ	
αι	ai	ai	ai	
αυ	au	au	au	
ευ	eu	eu	eu	
οι	oi	oi	oi	
υι	ui	ui	ui	

It is extremely importatant to realise that my "transliterations" are infact not transliterations but phonological representations. The difference from a work like Sommerstein (1973) is that I utilise the Ancient Greek of a rather earlier period, and do not try to incorporate the later Attic phonological changes marked here in the final column. The shaded values are very important.

Ancient Greek had three stop series in syllable initial position.[6]

(3) p   t   k   (plain)
     b   d   g   (voiced)
     pʰ   tʰ   kʰ   (aspirated)

The aspirated series is often inherited from Indo-European aspirates, and correspond (at least in a more traditonal view) to a voiced aspirated series in Proto-Indo-European (i.e. *bʰ, dʰ, ǵʰ gʰ, gʷʰ).

I will transcribe the aspirated stops in Ancient Greek as /ph, th, kh/ for the simple reason that various processes combining /p, t, k/ with a following /h/ also result in an "aspirated stop."

Other consonants are as follows, first sonorants:

(4) m n l r

---

6 Mycenaean Greek had a fourth, labiovelar, series.

and fricatives:[7]

(5) s h

I will now return to the question of the "aspirated stops" and address the question of their representation. To clear the ground for the further discussion of these stops, I will first illustrate three well-known processes involved in the *synchronic creation* of such stops.

2 Classical Greek Processes of Aspiration

There are various synchronic processes deriving aspirated stops. The first we can call *Phrasal elision*, usually referred to by grammar writers just as *Elision*. The second we can call *Lexical elision*. This refers to similar processes operating within the word. The third process is traditionally referred to as *Crasis* or "blending." These will be discussed in turn.

2.1 Phrasal Elision

The term *Phrasal Elision* describes a process whereby a word-final short vowel may be dropped (*elided*) before an initial vowel in the following word. This has different effects, depending on what is meant by the "initial *vowel*." If a word begins with an ordinary vowel, then this is marked a so-called "smooth breathing" (indicated with a closing inverted comma).

However, more relevant for our purposes is what happens when a short vowel preceded by a stop is elided before a so-called vowel with a "rough breathing." This term refers to an initial /h/ followed by a vowel (written with an opening inverted comma), as illustrated in (6).

(6) Examples of Phrasal Elision
    a. apo   híppɔɔn
          ἀφ'   ἵππων
          aph   ippɔɔn
          'from horseback' (Plat. Rep. 328 A)

---

[7] The semivowels /w, j/ do not play a role of any significance in this article.

b. kata   helláda
   καθ'   Ἑλλάδα
   kath   elláda
   'throughout Greece'   (Aesch. Ag. 578)

c. núkta   holeen
   νύχθ'   ὅλην
   núkhth   óleen
   '(the) whole night long'   (Eub. 53. 1)

2.2 Lexical Elision

This takes place in so-called "compound verbs" where *h*-initial verb stems follow certain prefixes. These cases resemble what we have seen under (6) in that they involve truncated forms of (prepositional) prefixes, but differ in their Greek spelling in that there is no double marking of aspiration, due to their single word status.

(7)   Examples of Lexical Elision
   a. *apo-hiíɛɛ-mi   > ap-hiíɛɛ-mi   > aphiíɛɛmi   = ἀφίημι
      'send forth'

   b. *hupo-hiíɛɛ-mi   > hup-hiíɛɛ-mi   > huphiíɛɛmi   = ὑφίημι
      'lower'

   c. *kata-hupo-hiíɛɛ-mi > kat-hup-hiíɛɛ-mi > kathuphiíɛɛmi = καθυφίημι
      'compromise, let drop'

W. S. Allen sums things up succinctly in his section on Aspirated Plosives (1968: 17–18):

(8) "In such cases a spelling of the type καθ' ἡμέραν [kath hɛɛméran, 'day by day,' NS], with the aspiration also marked on the following vowel, is strictly speaking, redundant, since the aspiration is transferred to the consonant; it is a normalizing tradition in Byzantine practice, but is not general in the inscriptions which otherwise indicate the rough breathing . . .,[8] just as it is not in compounds such as καθημέριος [katheemérios 'daily,' NS]."

---

[8] More details in Allen (1968: 50ff).

2.3 Crasis

Allen (1968: 18) also gives parallel examples of *Crasis* (lit. 'blending'). *Crasis* is a running-together of a monosyllabic grammatical word with a following vowel-initial word. The term 'vowel-initial' can also here include words that begin with *rough breathings* (i.e. /h/ followed by a vowel). He gives the following examples [my transliterations, N.S.]:

(9)   Crasis
    a. τῇ + ἡμέρᾳ   >   θἠμέρᾳ
        tέɛ + hɛɛméra   >   thέɛméra
        'on the day'

    b. καὶ + ὅπως   >   χὥπως
        kai + hópɔɔs   >   khɔ́pɔɔs
        'and how'

Note here that the original *breathings* at the beginnings of words *are* indicated in Greek script with a placeholder following the original initial aspirated stops.

2.4 Interpretation

From this we conclude that Ancient Greek treated aspirated stops as units in underlying phonology, but as clusters in surface phonology. In the next section I turn to the Ancient Greek *-ha*, where I will treat the "aspiration" as part of an allomorph of a separate *perfect* allomorph, rather than as part of the verb-stem.

3 Ancient Greek Aspirated Perfects

Sturtevant (1940a) fails to come up with a convincing account for medio-passive forms with aspirates. However, he does suggest a parallel for the active perfect aspirates, in the form of the 1st person singular ending *-ḫḫi* in Hittite. In hindsight, a Luwic language would be more suitable here, as these all have a *preterite* in, or derived from, Luwian *-ḫ(ḫ)a* (e.g. Friedrich 1960: 192). We are still dependent on a theory involving analogies here, but I will explain things in different terms later.

Sturtevant (1940b) attempts to build a similar story for the Greek *-ka* perfect, which most frequently occurs with vowel verb stems in Ancient Greek perfects.

Sturtevant, and others, suggest associating the Greek perfect marker with a Tokharian suffix -*ka*. This he sees as related to the -*ki* in Latin *feci* 'I did, and *ieci* 'I threw'.

In fact I will claim later that Greek perfect markers also derive from a form related to the Luwian preterit -ḫ(ḫ)a.

Only Georgiev (1992: 7–9) has attempted to follow Sturtevant (1940 a, b). In section III of his article he deals with the Greek Aspirated Perfect and the Greek *ka*-perfect., while in section IV he treats the *ka*-perfect and the *ka*-aorist.

I will not discuss either proposal in any detail as I think they are both wrong. I think they are both correct however in proposing a common source for the Aspirated Perfect and the *ka*-Perfect.

3.1 Goodwin (1892)

Goodwin (1892: 154–155) had the following section on Aspirated Perfects.

(10)   §692. (*Aspirated Second Perfects.*) Most stems in *p* or *b* change these to *ph*, and most ending in *k* or *g* change these to *kh*, in the second perfect, *if a short vowel precedes*. Those in *ph* and *kh* make no change.

Only Sommerstein (1973) appears to have noticed Goodwin's rule.[9]

I now present a list of short vowel aspirated perfects. Note the restriction to short vowels is only applicable to stems that end in *a single* consonant. As far as this is concerned, Goodwin's formulation is imprecise, but his meaning is clear from the examples he gives. Under section §692, he includes the following verbs. I give the last column of Table 3 pre-analysed in my terms for as much clarity as possible:

Table 3: Conditions for Aspirated Perfects.

-(C)VC		
example	stem	perfect
blápt-ɔɔ	blab-	bé-blap-ha
kópt-ɔɔ	kop-	ké-kop-ha
alláss-ɔɔ	allag-	e-éllak-ha
but not		
plɛέss-ɔɔ	plɛɛg-	pé-plɛɛg-a
stérg-ɔɔ	sterg-	é-storg-a
lámp-ɔɔ	lamp-	lé-lamp-a

---

9 Sommerstein cites the 1894 edition.

From this it is clear that what Goodwin actually means by "*if a short vowel precedes*" is "*if a short vowel directly precedes.*" Consider *lámpɔɔ* 'I shine.' This does not result in a perfect *lé-lamp-ha* 'I shone.' On this basis we can identify a list of about twenty[10] regular verbs with short vowels preceding a *single* labial or velar stop which result in an aspirated stop in their perfect form. These are illustrated in Table 4.

Table 4: Provisional list of Aspirate Perfects.

-(C)VC

Only Active Perfect forms are listed here. Pluperfects, where available, behave in a parallel fashion.

no.	stem	reference[11]	act. perf. 1 sg.	meaning	authors (incl. cpds)
1	ag-	ág-ɔɔ	é-ek-ha	lead	Xen., Dem.
2	allag-	alláss-ɔɔ	e-éllak-ha	change	Xen., Dem.
3	blab-	blápt-ɔɔ	bé-blap-ha	damage	Dem., Aristot.
4	blep-	blép-ɔɔ	bé-blep-ha	steal	Antip. ap. Stobaeus
5	enok-	[phér-ɔɔ]	en-ɛénok-ha[12]	bear	Dem., Pl.
6	klep/klop-	klépt-ɔɔ	ké-klop-ha	steal	Pl., Aristop.
7	kop-	kópt-ɔɔ	ké-kop-ha	cut	Xen., Pl.
8	krub-	krúpt-ɔɔ	ké-krup-ha	hide	Hipp.
9	lap-	lápt-ɔɔ	lé-lap-ha	lap	Aristop.
10	leg/log-	lég-ɔɔ	-eélok-ha[13]	gather	Dem.
11	mag-	máss-ɔɔ	mé-mak-ha	knead	Aristop.
12	meeg/mig-	meég-nuu-mi	mé-mik-ha	mix	(Polyb.)
13	oruk-	orúss-ɔɔ	or-ɔɔruk-ha	dig	Pherec., Xen.
14	phulak-	phulátt-ɔɔ	pe-phúlak-ha	guard	Xen., Pl., Dinarch.
15	plek/plok-	plék-ɔɔ	dia-pé-plok-ha	interweave	Hipp.
			em-pé-plek-he	entwine	Hipp.

---

10 This is not completely exhaustive, but is sufficient to make my point.
11 The examples in this column that appear to involve two consonants actually contained a stem-final suffix /*j/, which had become absorbed in the present tense stem. So *klep-j-ɔɔ, *phulak-j-ɔɔ etc.
12 I base myself on Beekes (1969: 121) where he identifies the process causing the lengthening of the second syllable vowel (originally a Proto-Indo-European laryngeal) with the same lengthening in the case of the negative adjectival prefix allomorph (1969: 107). An epenthetic vowel was inserted in each case.
13 See Melazzo (1993: 32), who does not exclude the possibility that "an original formation such as either *se-slog- or *se-sloǵ- changed by phonetic transition into *eéokha* (dissimilated < *heélokha) [My phonetic transcription, NS]. Beekes with van Beek (2010: 841) stick to an analogical explanation.

Table 4 (continued)

-(C)VC

Only Active Perfect forms are listed here. Pluperfects, where available, behave in a parallel fashion.

no.	stem	reference	act. perf. 1 sg.	meaning	authors (incl. cpds)
16	tag-	táss-ɔɔ	té-tak-ha	arrange	Xen., Pl.
17	thliib-	thliíb-ɔɔ	té-thlip-ha	squeeze	(Polyb.)
18	trep/trop/ trap-	trép-ɔɔ	té-trop-ha té-trap-ha	turn	Aristop., Soph. Dem., Dinarch.
19	triib-	triíb-ɔɔ	té-trip-ha	rub	Eub., Aristop, Pl., Iso.

In Table 4 we can see a number of *o*-grade perfects, sometimes as an option to a reduced grade (18) or a full grade (15).

Goodwin (1892) notes a number of exceptions to his rule in section §693, including the following (see Table 5):

Table 5: Exceptional Aspirate Perfects.

stem	reference	act. perf. 1 sg.	meaning
pemp/pomp-	pémp-ɔɔ	pé-pomp-ha	send
ptɛɛk-	ptɛέss-ɔɔ	é-ptɛɛk-ha	cower

-*ka* seems to be the preferred choice in post-vocalic position, following directly on long vowels, short vowels and diphthongs (see Table 6). This was observed a long time ago.

Table 6: Post-vocalic *ka*-perfects.

stem	reference	act. perf. 1 sg.	meaning
praa-	pi-praá-sk-ɔɔ	pé-praa-ka	sell
stuge-	stugé-ɔɔ	e-stúgɛɛ-ka	hate
luu-	luú-ɔɔ	lé-lŭ-ka	loose
pneu-	pné-ɔɔ	pé-pneu-ka	blow

There are only a very restricted number of apparent exceptions to this rule. One example is given in Table 7.

After liquids and nasals, we find both -*a* and -*ka*. See below for some special -*a* cases.

Table 7: An apparent exception to the rule in Table 6.

stem	reference	act. perf. 1 sg.	meaning
akou-	akoú-ɔɔ	ak-ɛɛko-a[14]	hear

Older medio-passive Aspirate Perfect forms are sometimes found in the 3pl. perfect and pluperfect with consonant stems. Because of the context /..C-ntai/ or /..C-nto/, the nasal was necessarily syllabic, and was replaced by /a/, as was the normal reflex in Ancient Greek. In Attic and other dialects, such forms were replaced by a participial periphrastic form, presumably because of the irregular morphology. This is illustrated in Table 8.

Table 8: Medio-passive Aspirate Perfects.

-(C)VC					
Various Medio-Passive forms with short vowel in the relevant cases are given here. Both Perfect 3rd Plural (*-hatai*) and 3rd Pluperfect forms (*-hato*) are provided where found.					
no.	stem	reference	medio-passive	meaning	authors (incl. cpds)
8	krub-	krúpt-ɔɔ	ké-krup-hatai	*hide*	Hipp., Hes.
12	meeg/mig-	meég-nuu-mi	ana-me-mík-hatai	*mix*	Herod.
16	tag-	táss-ɔɔ	te-ták-hatai	*arrange*	Thuc., Xen.
			dia-te-ták-hato		Herod.
18	trep/trap-	trép-ɔɔ	te-tráp-hatai	*turn*	Herod, Hom. (Il.)
19	triib-	triíb-ɔɔ	te-tríp-hatai	*rub*	Herod.
20	heerg-/eerg-	heérg-nuu-mi/	érk-hatai	*shut in*	Hom. (Il.)
		eérg-ɔɔ -(etc.)	érk-hato		Hom. (Il.)
			e.érk-hato		Hom. (Od.)
21	he(e)lik-	he(e)líss-ɔɔ	heelík-hato	*turn*	Herod.
22	oreg-	orég-ɔɔ	or-ɔɔrék-hatai	*reach*	Hom. (Il.)
			or-ɔɔrék-hato		Hom. (Il.)
23	sag-	sáss-ɔɔ	e-se-sák-hato	*load, pack*	Herod.

The fact that Attic has regular active aspirated perfects, *and* that Ionicizing texts have passive aspirated perfects in the *same* environment suggests that both go back to a model in which *both* were regular. Explanations where the one acted as the model for the other, or vice versa, are unconvincing

---

[14] Not really an exception as the root originally ended in a *digamma* <ϝ> (/w/). This is also a case illustrating Attic Reduplication.

3.2 An Explanation for Aspirated Perfects

What could be the explanation for these patterns? The long-short correlation noted by Goodwin has an obvious explanation. If we take the short:aspirated::long:unaspirated relationship seriously this can be interpreted as an old dissimilation effect. I interpret aspirated perfects as representing original sequences of single stem-final consonant plus a following laryngeal:

(11) ...CVC + *laryngeal-a*   e.g. bé-blap-ha

and non-aspirated long-vowel perfects as representing:

(12) ...CV-laryngeal-C + ~~laryngeal~~-*a*   e.g. pé-pleeg-a

Then we have Goodwin's correlation, or a part of it. We haven't explained *lé-loip-a, lé-lamp-a* or *pé-pheug-a*, for instance. Conceivably, at a later stage, the original rule was reinterpreted in terms of syllable weight.[15]

3.3 The Problem of Coronal Stops

A problem is why verbal roots in coronal stops /t, d/ did not develop aspirated perfects. There were next-to-no verb stems in /t/. But there were stems in /d/. A single conceivable example does not aspirate.

Table 9: Non-aspiration with active dentals.

-(C)VC					
No aspiration.					
no.	stem	reference	act. perf. 1 sg.	meaning	authors (incl. cpds)
1.	khed/khod-	khéz-ɔɔ[16]	-ke-khod-a	*shit*	Aristop.

Interestingly, all three *underlying* aspirate root-finals – *including coronal* – are encountered. These preserve their aspiration in the active perfect, whatever the length of the vowel.

---

[15] Obviously I am not referring to the individual cases here, but to the general pattern.
[16] *khéd-j-ɔɔ.

Table 10: Final aspiration preserved in all roots, including dentals.

-(C)VC					
Aspirate roots.					
no.	stem	reference	act. perf. 1 sg.	meaning	authors (incl. cpds)
1.	graph-	gráph-ɔɔ	gé-graph-a	write	-
2.	arkh-	árkh-ɔɔ	é-erkh-a	rule	-
3.	briith-	briíth-ɔɔ	bé-briith-a	be heavy	-

In Section 4 I illustrate a number of cases where languages have borrowed morphological material from other languages under conditions of close contact.

4 Small-Scale Language-Contact Phenomena

The following examples illustrate small-scale phenomena that have occurred under intense language contact. The point of this section is to demonstrate that *very small chunks of grammar can* be transferred if two languages are in intimate contact.

4.1 Saramaccan

Saramaccan is a mixed English-Portuguese lexifier creole, spoken by one of the six maroon groups living in Surinam, South America. I will mention a feature of Saramaccan, displaying influence from the language of the Fon people (FonGbe) of Benin, a West African country, on what was formerly called the *Slave Coast*.

A peculiarity of Saramaccan is the way it marks focus. Other English-lexifier creole languages spoken in the Caribbean area use a focus-marker *(n)a* positioned *before* the focused element (Smith 1996). This includes other creole languages spoken in Surinam. However Saramaccan uses a *low-toned* focus-marker *wɛ* positioned *after* the focused element.

(13) a. 1805 translation Acts 7–35[17]
    [ambeh-weh] bi putta ju vo Heddiman effi krottuman
    WHO-FOC PAST put YOU FOR master OR judge
    'who was it created you lords and judges?'

---

[17] Schuchardt (1914: 17).

b. Wycliffe NT Luke 9–30/31
[de   wɛ] ko   ta   fan   ku   Masa   Jesosi dɛ
THEY   FOC come PROG speak WITH Master Jesus   THERE
'*it was them* who came to talk with Lord Jesus there.'

c. Wycliffe NT John 12–33
nɔɔ [pindja   wɛ] a   ta   pindja   dee   sɛmbɛ   fu ..
AND squeeze   FOC HE PROG squeeze DEF.PL people TO ..
'.. and *squeeze* the people he did to in order to ..'

In FonGbe we find precisely the same patterns with a low-toned marker *wɛ*. Cf. the following sentences from Lefebvre and Brousseau (2002)

(14) a. (72a)
àtín wɛ̀
tree FOC
'it's *a tree*'

b. (72b)
Masɛ̀ vì   lɛ́ wɛ̀   wá
Massè child PL FOC arrive
'it's *the people of Massè* who have arrived'

c. (72c)
lɔ́n   wɛ̀   súnû ɔ́   lɔ́n
jump FOC man   DEF jump
'it was *jump* that the man did'

While *wɛ̀* in Saramaccan has a more limited range of uses than in FonGbe, the contrastive focus usage is exactly the same.

4.2 Berbice Dutch

My second example comes from Berbice Dutch, a recently extinct Dutch-lexifier creole language of Guyana, which, however, has a full description in Kouwenberg (1994). Smith, Robertson, and Williamson (1987) identified the African substrate language as the Eastern Ijọ language of Nigeria, a language with relatively few speakers.

A striking feature of Berbice Dutch is the fact that it possesses a number of cases of Eastern Ijọ inflectional verbal and nominal morphology. Morphology is not unknown in Atlantic creoles, but in general this comes from the superstrate (colonial) language. In the case of Berbice Dutch, these suffixes came from Eastern Ịjọ, including two verbal aspectual markers, and a plural marker on nouns and pronouns. See Kouwenberg (1994: 230) for an overview. The Eastern Ịjọ plural marker is -apụ, while the Berbice Dutch plural marker is *ap(u)*.

(15) matjap   'friends'   < mati-apu   (p. 238)
     sosərapu   'sister'   < sosro-apu (p. 239)
     tantijapo   'aunt and family'   < tanti-apu (p. 239)
     gutwap   'things'   < gutu-apu   (p. 67)
     bɛrap   'stories'   < bɛrɛ-apu   (p. 39)

4.3 Island-Carib Men's Language

Taylor and Hoff (1980: 301–312) discovered that the linguistic situation of the Island-Carib, who were famed as having had separate men's and women's languages in the 17th century, was more complex than had been assumed. The Island-Carib language was spoken till about 1900 on the Caribbean islands of St Vincent and Dominica by so-called Red Caribs. In addition the 18th century British government got rid of part of the Island-Carib population of St Vincent by banishing them to Central America, where the Black Carib language is still spoken.

What has been called the women's language was in fact the native language of both sexes, conclude the authors, and is basically an Arawak language. This contains a sizeable Carib (Karina) element – about 22% of basic vocabulary (Taylor 1977: 44–99), but is still more correctly classified as an Arawak language. There are historical reasons for the name, dating from the wars of the Caribs against the Arawaks.

Males only learnt the Karina men's language later on for use as a secret Men's Language.

(16) "the [17th century, N.S.] "men's language" had retained a (Carib) Karina lexicon, but had also almost completely lost the abundant morphology of Karina and had made up for this loss by using native Arawakan morphology in its place." (Taylor and Hoff 1980: 301)

For this reason Taylor and Hoff describe the 17th century Men's Language as a pidgin. This "pidgin" is virtually extinct today. Taylor and Hoff's only source for the Island-Carib Men's Language is Breton (1665, 1666, 1667).[18]

---

[18] Around 1000 pages: two dictionaries and a grammar.

The main relevance for our study is to be found in the second of four types of fates of former Karina grammatical morphemes in the *17th century Men's Language.*

(17) "(2) A morpheme of K[arina] provenance is productive; it has completely lost its original semantic value, but has acquired a new function. This has happened to two personal prefixes of the finite verb, that is, K[arina] si- *I/him* [transitive] and ni- *he* [intransitive]. In ICM [Island-Carib Men's Language, N.S.] both have lost these semantic values and have become markers of transitivity and intransitivity (e.g., transitive, with reflex of si-, chirámain- *to bring back*; intransitive, with reflex of ni-, nirámain- *to come back*). (Taylor and Hoff 1980: 303)

Other examples are:

(18) a. chi-tikae LI-Á-TINA   he has frightened me   small caps: Arawak
     b. ni-ticae áo   I am afraid   lower case: Karina

We see in example (18a) a form *chi-tikae*, which in true Karina had a prefix *chi-* meaning '1st.p. subject, 3rd.p. object' while *tikae* meant 'frighten, afraid.' The meaning of the prefix had been bleached to 'any subject, any object,' i.e. 'transitive.' The actual grammatical relationships were expressed in the Men's Language by means of the Arawak auxiliary verb LI-Á-TINA:

(19) LI-Á-TINA   3rd.Pers.Subj.-perfective-1st.Pers.Obj. (perf.)

The actual meaning of the Karina part of (18a) was 'I frighten him,' nearly the opposite of what it actually meant in Island Carib Men's Language!

In example (18b) the prefix *ni-* indicated '3rd person subject' in true Karina. This meaning had been bleached to 'intransitve.' The 1st person reference in this example now required to be explicitated with a free pronoun, in this case a loan from true Karina.

(20) áo   free Ist person Karina pronoun.

In the original Karina, *ni-ticae* meant 'he is afraid.'

This is illustrative that borrowing languages can expand the meanings of person suffixes to vaguer interpretations, or even misanalyses.

Clearly this kind of broadening of scope in the use of a borrowed verbal morpheme is of highly relevant for the case I want to make here in connection with the Carian Preterite-Ancient Greek Perfect case. In the Island Carib case, two specific *singular* person forms are reinterpreted as having scope over all person-number combinations.

In Section 5 we turn again to Ancient Greek.

5 Ancient Greek Perfect Conjugation

To link to the case in question, let us consider a typical set of regular Ancient Greek active perfect endings.

(21)

	ka-perfect	*ha*-perfect	*a*-perfect
1.sg.	-ka	-ha	-a
2.sg.	-ka-s	-ha-s	-a-s
3.sg.	-k-e	-h-e	-e
2/3.du.	-ka-ton	-ha-ton	-a-ton
1.pl.	-ka-men	-ha-men	-a-men
2.pl.	-ka-te	-ha-te	-a-te
3.pl.	-k(a)-aasi	-h(a)-aasi	-(a)-aasi

In Table 3 we saw that Aspirated Perfects are basically limited to stems with *short vowels* followed by *a single stop*. I assume that aspiration represents *suffix*-forms with an initial *lenis* consonant /*-xa/, borrowed from Carian (although only found in Lycian so far). Other consonant-final *long vowel* stems may exhibit laryngeal dissimilation with the result /-a/ (see section 3.2). The stems in final "aspirated" consonants also have /-a/ (see Table 10).

Stems ending in vowels have a Perfect in /k/.[19] This represents the borrowed *fortis* correspondent /*-ka/ (Kloekhorst 2018).

What about sonorant-consonant finals?

To find that out, it is necesssary to examine *s*-aorists with sonorant-final roots first. These are numerous, and they exhibit a very specific kind of historical behaviour when the root comes into direct contact with the *s*-aorist suffix.

Let us now look at some s-aorist examples:

---

[19] In some verbs the /k/-forms (e.g. he-stee-ka) are restricted to the singular. This suggests that the /k/-perfect originated in a singular form.

Table 11: A possible historical development of sonorant-final s-aorists. (= means *no further change*).

Stem	Reference	*s-Aorist	*h-Aorist[20]	Comp.Length.	Aorist Form	Meaning
agal-	agáll-ɔɔ	e-ágal-sa	ɛ-égal-ha	ɛ-égaal-a	ɛ-égɛɛl-a	honour
sar-	sair-ɔɔ	é-sar-sa	é-sar-ha	é-saar-a	é-sɛɛr-a	grin
man-	maín-ɔɔ	é-man-sa	é-man-ha	é-maan-a	é-mɛɛn-a	madden
nem(e)-	ném-ɔɔ	é-nem-sa	é-nem-ha	é-neem-a =	é-neem-a	swim
angel-	angéll-ɔɔ	e-ángel-sa	ɛ-éngel-ha	ɛ-éngeel-a =	ɛ-éngeel-a	announce
ager-	ageér-ɔɔ	e-áger-sa	ɛ-éger-ha	ɛ-égeer-a =	ɛ-égeer-a	collect
huphan-	huphaín-ɔɔ	he-úphan-sa	hu-úphan-ha	hu-úphaan-a	hu-úphɛɛn-a	weave
gam(e)-	gamé-ɔɔ	é-gam-sa	é-gam-ha	é-gaam-a	é-gɛɛm-a	marry

/s/ in these forms goes to /h/ (see for a partial derivation see, FN 20). *Comp. Length.* is the important development. This stands for Compensatory Lengthening. What this means is that, firstly the reconstructed **h-Aorist* forms have a second-last syllable that is heavy. And secondly the *Comp.Length.* forms also have a second-last syllable that is heavy. In the first case, we have a CVC syllable, and in the second a CVV syllable. In other words, the onset-/h/ of the final syllable, which makes the preceding consonant into a coda is lost. To *compensate* for this – to preserve what we can call the *syllable-weight structure* – the vowel of the preceding syllable is *lengthened*. The result is that the former coda consonant becomes the onset of the following syllable.

Now, there are some *Perfect forms* with sonorant-final stems that appear also to show traces of compensatory lengthening. Several of these forms are the subject of notes in Beekes with van Beek (2010). I give a list of those cases I have identified so far in Table 12. In the third column I provide Aorist forms for comparison.

Table 12: Perfect verb forms derived with Compensatory Lengthening.

Stem	Reference	(Aorist form)	*ha-Perfect	Comp.Length.	Output	Meaning
man-	maín-ɔɔ	(é-mɛɛn-a)	mé-man-ha	mé-maan-a	mé-mɛɛn-a[21]	madden
mel, mal-	mél-ɔɔ	–	mé-mal-ha	mé-maal-a[22]	mé-mɛɛl-e[23]	care for
phan-	phaín-ɔɔ	(é-phɛɛn-a)	pé-phan-ha	pé-phaan-a	pé-phɛɛn-a[24]	show
sar-	sair-ɔɔ	(é-sɛɛr-a)	sé-sar-ha	sé-saar-a	sé-sɛɛr-a	grin
thal-	tháll-ɔɔ	(é-thɛɛl-a)	té-thal-ha	té-thaal-a	té-thɛɛl-a[25]	bloom

---

20 Cf. in a different morphological context /*akowsā > *akowhā/ in the derivation of ἀκοή (Beekes with van Beek 2010: 55, ἀκούω). [ἀκοή (verbal noun) = ako-εέ; ἀκούω = akoó-ɔɔ].

So far I have found five such cases. There are a number of striking aspects here. The most obvious is the number of interesting footnotes (four) that were required to explain these forms. I will treat the separate footnotes (FN) in detail.

Firstly, for (FN 19: 892) it is claimed by Beekes with van Beek that this formation took place *in Greek*. That is what I claim too, in different terms. That the *ha*-Perfect is merely an allomorph of the *ka*-Perfect, and these forms can be described in the same way as sonorant-stem *aorists*.

Secondly, for (FN 21: 929) their claim is that this form displays a *remarkable lengthened grade*. If however the lengthening of the vowel is merely due to regular Compensatory Lengthening (with the aim of preserving the syllable-strength relationships), then this seems like a simpler solution. Note that the suffix has to begin with a consonant first for this to work – in this case the /h/ of the "aspiration."

Their third footnote of relevance for this issue, in (FN 22: 1545), concerns the point that the *ka*-Perfect, *pé-phan-ka*, is a later Attic formation than the other perfect, *pé-phɛɛn-a*, which is also found in Doric (Doric did not undergo the general Attic raising of /aa/ to /ɛɛ/). This form was originally *pé-phan-ha. Note that Grassman's law does not apply in this case. My standpoint is that there were originally two allomorphs of the *ka*-Perfect: *-ka* after vowels, *-ha* after consonants. This last was hidden from sight by the general loss of /h/ after sonorants.

Their fourth relevant footnote (FN 23: 530) affirms the later creation of an Aorist form of the verb *thall-ɔɔ* ('bloom') than the Perfect. This rules out any possible claim that the Perfect form was modelled on an already existing Aorist form. The function of the Aorist was, as Beekus with van Beek indicate, performed by a "second" aorist *é-thal-on*.

No Aorist parallel seems to exist for *mél-ɔɔ* either. Here we have another related pair of forms, however, Aorist *e-mélɛɛ-sa* and Perfect *me-melɛɛ-ka*.

Theoretically there is a lot of scope for confusion between vowel-initial and s-initial identical forms of aorists and perfects. However, there is also a lot of scope for avoiding this with the help of different Indo-European grades and available

---

21 Beekes with van Beek 2010: 892 "Formations that arose *in Greek* are μῆνασθαι < PGr. **man-s-* and μέμηνα (after τακῆναι : τέτηκα, etc.)". [μέμηνα = *mé-mɛɛn-a*, my emphasis, N.S.].
22 Cf. perfect participle (Pindar) *me-maal-ótas* (Doric).
23 Beekes with van Beek 2010: 929 "Beside the full-grade thematic root-present μέλω, the perfect μέμηλα has a *remarkable lengthened grade*." [μέμηλα = *mé-mɛɛl-a*, my emphasis, N.S.].
24 Beekes with van Beek 2010: 1545 ".. [Perf.] act. intr. πέφηνα (IA), Dor. πέφᾱνα (Sophr.), trans. πέφαγκα (*later* Att.), .." [πέφηνα = *pé phɛɛn-a*; πέφᾱνα = *pé-phaana*; πέφαγκα = pé-phan-ka, my emphasis, N.S.].
25 Beekes with van Beek 2010: 530 "perf. with present meaning τέθηλα, ..; *later* forms s-aor. ἀν-έθηλα (Ael.), .." [τέθηλα = *té thɛɛl-a*; ἀν-έθηλα = an-é-thɛɛl-a, my emphasis, N.S.].

alternate vowel-stems, not to mention the greater infrequency of the perfect as such. And if all is lost -*ka* can just be attached to the perfect form, as in Table 13.

Table 13: Resolving possible confusion between Aorist and Perfect with -*ka*.

Stem	Reference	*s-Aorist	Aorist outpt	*ha-Perf.	*Perf. output	Perf. output	Meaning
angel-	angéll-ɔɔ	e-ángel-sa	ɛ-ɛ́ngeel-a	e-ángel-ha	*ɛ-ɛ́ngeel-a	ɛ-ɛ́ngeel-*ka*	announce
er-	eér-ɔɔ	é-er-sa	é-(e)er-a	é-er-ha	*é-(e)er-a	é-(e)er-*ka*[26]	join
aar-	aír-ɔɔ	é-aar-sa	ɛ́-(ɛ)ɛr-a	é-aar-ha	*ɛ́-(ɛ)ɛr-a	ɛ́-(ɛ)ɛr-*ka*	raise

We see that the underlying *ka*-morpheme has as it were made a second appearance here. Due to the identity of -*ka*'s allomoph -*ha* to a stage in the deletion of the *aorist* suffix -*sa*, the distinction between the aorist and the perfect threatened to disappear. The solution for these examples? Stick -*ka* in again – the Perfect is the least frequent of the two tenses, and loses out here.

6 Mycenaean Times

Important Achaean/Mycenaean centres in Greece were Mycenae, Thebes, Argos, Pylos, Tyrins and Crete. These have left most (known) Linear B records. Other "palace" centres, like Iolcos, Athens and Menelaion in Mainland Greece and Miletus/Millawata/Millawanda[27] in Western Anatolia have not left such records, or at least not as many, due no doubt to the vagaries of history.

In this brief summary of possible avenues of language contact and its possible effects I will contrast very briefly aspects of the work of two researchers: Hajnal and Herda. I will refer to their main English-language articles on this issue, Hajnal (2018)[28] and Herda (2013).

---

[26] Trimoraic vowels with identical vowel quality are disallowed in 5th century Ancient Greek. The output always defaults to a double (long) vowel.
[27] In Caria.
[28] Apparently based on "Die griechisch-anatolischen Sprachkontakt zur Bronzezeit" (Hajnal 2014).

6.1 Hajnal

In terms of archaeology Miletus is a centre of Mycenaean "presence" from ca. 1450 to 1100 BC. The zone of intense Mycenaean settlement extended to Halicarnassus. In historical terms Miletus often features as a point of conflict between the Hittite Empire and the *Aḫḫiya(wa)*, now generally identified in this period with the collectivity of Mycenaean palace-centered states of the *Akhai(w)oi* or Achaeans (Hajnal 2018: 2038).

(22) "The Pylian A-series lists a group of female textile workers from Milet [Miletus] (mi-rati-ja /Milatiai/) or, possibly, Halicarnassus (ze-pu2-ra3 /dzephurai/)" (2018: 2038).

This kind of thing if repeated on a large scale would provide opportunities for language-contact. The question is if this actually occurred (2018: 2038–2040).

Hajnal looks at a similar verbal issue to one we are studying here- the question of *sk*-iteratives/distributives in Greek and Hittite, but decides that there is no necessary requirement for a relation (2018: 2047)

Hajnal's conclusion is that "the range and intensity" of language contacts was insufficient to have resulted in significant influence on either language (2018: 2050).

6.2 Herda

In his FN66 Herda remarks that Hajnal underestimates the impact of deportation of larger groups of people from Western Asia Minor to the Mycenaean homeland in Greece. He provides the example of 7,000 Lukka-people (closely related Lycians), abducted by Piyamaradu in the mid-thirteenth century (Herda 2013: 437).

Herda states that the Carians lived in a close symbiosis with the Greeks, first the Mycenaeans, and then particularly the Ionians, for more than a 1000 years (2013: 471). He (FN66) quotes Hajnal as saying that the Greeks' "close contact with Carians" only left "small traces" in Greek (2013: 437).

6.3 Conclusion

If my hypothesis is anything like correct the effect seems to have been significantly larger.

7 A Clue

I mentioned above that while little is known about Carian verbs in general, much more is known about Lycian verbs.

Billing (2019: 18) gives the Lycian 1st Preterite ending as *-(x)xa*, *-ga*, with the geminate ending *-xxa* occurring with consonant-final stems. In terms of Kloekhorst (2018) *-(x)xa* would implie *-(k)ka*.

A possible occurrence of a Carian preterite verb form in *-ka* has been found in one inscription so far. This inscription was published in Türkteki and Tekoğlu (2012: 99–113), an article about a brief Carian inscription on a wine-jar from Hydai, which is now in the Sadberk Hanim Museum, in Istanbul. The authors assign the find to the 7th century BC. According to Adiego (2019: 25) this is "the oldest unequivocally Carian inscription found in Caria proper."

Türkteki and Tekoğlu (2012: 102) give the transcription as follows:

(23) ⟨Carian script⟩

Using Adiego's modernized symbol-equivalents gives us the following transliteration, reading the symbols from right to left, and adjusting one word-division:

(24) dmounś leos mlane ýšrot | balja yšraka

Türkteki and Tekoğlu identify two possible words in support of their analysis, *dmounś*, a name occurring in an inscripton in Memphis (E.Me 18b) in the form *idmuonś*, interpereted as a proper name in the genitive case, and *mlane*, a form of uncertain meaning. They also remark that there are possibly two verbs, the first a 3s preterite verb and the other a 1s preterite. Adiego revises their hypothesis by altering the division between the last two words to the form I have quoted in (24), but their hypothesis still stands.

This gives us the following analysis:

(25) dmoun-ś   leos   mlane   ýšro-t | balja   yšra-ka
      name-GEN   ?   ?   verb$_i$-3S.PRET?   ?   verb$_i$-1S.PRET?

Adiego's revision introduces the possibity that what we might have here is the same verb stem with two possible inflections, one of which is conceivably the same *-ka* that we find in Ancient Greek.

8 Conclusions

For a Carian morphological element to have embedded itself in Ancient Greek, this must have occurred in Mycenaean times, when the Achaeans had a significant West Asian "bridgehead" at Miletus and neighbouring islands, and a possibly substantial number of Carians/Lycians were "imported" as slaves.

A reading of Beekes and van Beek's (2010) etymological dictionary of Ancient Greek suggests that the Ancient Greek verb had undergone a large amount of restructuring. This would create a prime situation for the introduction of a new *borrowed* morpheme.

The original distribution of the Carian-origin cases is assumed to be -*ka* with vowel- stems, and -*ha* with consonant-stems. The few sonorant consonant-stems that can be identified lose the /h/, with the only trace of this being vowel length due to Complementary Lengthening.

Note that my example from Island Carib demonstrates clearly that political superiority by no means guarantees linguistic superiority.

Abbreviations

Aesch.	Aeschylus
Antip.	Antiphanes
Aristop.	Arisophanes
Aristot.	Aristotle
Dem.	Demosthenes
Dinarch.	Dinarchus
Eub.	Eubulus
Herod.	Herodotus
Hes.	Hesiod
Hipp.	Hippocrates
Hom.	Homer
Il.	Iliad
Iso.	Isocrates
Men.	Menander
Od.	Odyssey
Pherec.	Pherecrates
Plat./Pl.	Plato
Polyb.	Polybius
Thuc.	Thucydides
Xen.	Xenophon

References

Adiego, I. J. [I.-X.] 2007. *The Carian Language*. With an appendix by Koray Konuk. Leiden: Brill.
Adiego, I. J. [I.-X.] 2019. 'Archaic' Carian. In Oliver Henry & Koray Konuk (eds.), *Karia Arkhaia. Le Carie, des origines à la périoe pré-hékatomnide (4émes Rencontres d'Archéologie de l'IFÉA, 2013)*, 23–43. CNRS: Institut Français d'Études Anatoliennes Georges Dumézil.
Allen, W. S. 1968. *Vox Graeca: The Pronunciation of Classical Greek*. Cambridge: Cambridge University Press.
Beekes, R. S. P. 1969. *The Development of the Proto-Indo-European Laryngeals in Greek*. The Hague/Paris: Mouton.
Beekes, R. S. P. with L. van Beek. 2010. *Etymological Dictionary of Greek*. Vols. 1, 2. Leiden/Boston: Brill.
Billing, N. O. P. 2019. Finite verb formation in Lycian. Leiden: Universiteit Leiden Research M.A. thesis.
Breton, R. 1665. *Dictionaire Caraibe-Francois*. Auxerre: Gilles Bouquet.
Breton, R. 1666. *Dictionaire Francois-Caraibe*. Auxerre: Gilles Bouquet.
Breton, R. 1667. *Grammaire Caraibe*. Auxerre: Gilles Bouquet.
Cowgill, W. 1965. Greek evidence. In W. Cowgill (ed.), *Evidence for Laryngeals*, 141–180. The Hague: Mouton.
Friedrich, J. 1960. *Hethitisches Elementarbuch*. 1. Teil. Heidelberg: Cartl Winter.
Georgiev, V. I. 1992. Ide. Media asp. oder Tenuis asp. aus Media oder Tenuis + Laryngal und die Herkunft griechischen aspirierten Perfekts, des κ-Perfekts bzw. des κ-Aorists. *Orpheus. Journal of Indo-European and Thracian Studies* 2. 5–10.
Goodwin, W. W. 1892. *A Greek Grammar*. Boston: Ginn & Company.
Hajnal, I. 2014. Die griechisch-anatolischen Sprachkontakte zur Bronzezeit – Sprachbund oder loser Sprachkontakt? *Linguarum Varietas* 3. 105–116.
Hajnal, I. 2018. Graeco-Anatolian contacts in the Mycenaean period. In J. S. Klein, B. D. Joseph, M. Fritz & M. Wenthe (eds), *Handbook of Comparative and Historical Indo-European Linguistics*, vol. 3, 2037–2055. Berlin/Boston: De Gruyter Mouton.
Herda, A. 2013. Greek (and our) views on the Karians. In A. Mouton, I. Rutherford & I. Yakubovich (eds), *Luwian Identities*, 421–506. Leiden: Brill.
Kloekhorst, A. 2018. Anatolian evidence suggests that the Indo-European laryngeals *h2 and *h3 were uvular stops. *Indo-European Linguistics* 6. 69–94.
Kouwenberg, S. 1994. *A Grammar of Berbice Dutch Creole*. Berlin/New York: Mouton De Gruyter.
Lefebvre, C. & A.-M. Brousseau. 2002. *A Grammar of Fongbe*. Berlin/New York: Mouton De Gruyter.
Melazzo, L. 1993. On the Ancient Greek εἴλοχα/εἴλεγμαι. *Glotta* 71. 30–33.
Melchert, M. H. 2004. Carian. In Roger D. Woodward (ed.), *The Cambridge Encyclopedia of the World's Ancient Languages*, 609–613. Cambridge: Cambridge University Press.
Schuchardt, C. L. 1914. Die Sprache der Saramakkaneger in Surinam. *Verhandelingen der Koninklijke Akademie van Wetenschappen te Amsterdam. Afdeeling Letterkunde*. Nieuwe reeks, 14(6).
Serangeli, M. 2018. Lykische s-Verben und ske/o-Bildungen im Anatolischen. In Elisabeth Rieken with Ulrich Geupel & Theresa Maria Roth (eds.), *100 Jahre Entzifferung des Hethitischen. Morphosyntaktische Kategorien in Sprachgeschichte und Forschung. Akten der Arbeitstagung der Indogermanischen Gesellschaft vom 21. bis 23. September in Marburg*, 319–328. Wiesbaden: Reichert Verlag.

Smith, N. S. H. 1996. Focus-marking wɛ in Saramaccan: Grammaticalization or substrate. In P. Baker & A. Syea (eds), *Changing Meanings, Changing Features: Papers Relating to Grammaticalization in Contact Languages*, 113–128. London: University of Westminster Press.
Smith, N. S. H., I. E. Robertson & K. Williamson. 1987. The Ịjọ element in Berbice Dutch. *Language and Society* 16. 49–90.
Sommerstein, A. H. 1973. *The Sound Pattern of Ancient Greek* (= Publications of the Philological Society 23). Oxford: Blackwell.
Sturtevant, E. H. 1940a. The Greek aspirated perfect. *Language* 16. 179–182.
Sturtevant, E. H. 1940b. The Greek κ-perfect and Indo-European -k(o)-. *Language* 16. 273–284.
Sturtevant, E. H. 1942. *The Indo-Hittite Laryngeals*. Baltimore: Linguistic Society of America.
Taylor, D. 1977. *Languages of the West Indies*. Baltimore: Johns Hopkins University Press.
Taylor, D. & B. J. Hoff. 1980. The linguistic repertory of the Island-Carib in the seventeenth century: The men's language – a Carib pidgin. *IJAL* 46. 301–312.
Türkteki, S. & R. Tekoğlu. 2012. Une inscription carienne sur œnochoé au Musée de Sadberk Hanim. *Kadmos* 51. 99–113.
Wycliffe Bible Translators. 2009. *Gadu Buku. Het Nieuwe Testament in het Saramaccaans*.

Claartje Levelt, Eline van den Brink, and Josefine Karlsson
Prompted Self-Repairs in Two-Year-Old Children

Abstract: Previous work has shown that young children can be prompted to revise an utterance by an unspecific prompt like "hm?" or "what?". In a game setting this technique is re-introduced with two-year-old children who name pictures on cards that they collect to put on a game-board. The pictures elicit words that start with an onset cluster, like /tr/, /kl/, /st/, which are often reduced to singleton consonants by two-year-old speakers. The prompt is assumed to trigger their self-monitoring system, which could highlight a mismatch between the uttered word – with a reduced cluster – and the intended target – with a full cluster – if this full cluster is indeed part of the young speaker's segmental representation of the word. We compared the initial production and the prompted repeated productions of 20 children and studied the changes that were triggered by the prompt. Results show that (1) the technique works very well with these young speakers and triggers repeats in most cases, (2) changes involve improvements in most cases, ranging from segmentally more accurate productions and signs of knowledge of an initially absent additional consonant, to full consonant cluster productions, (3) the technique can help to disentangle word-form encoding errors from errors resulting from the stored segmental representation.

Keywords: word production, language development, self-monitoring, self-repairs, toddlers, onset clusters

1 Introduction

In order to produce words, a young language learner needs to simultaneously acquire a lexical representation, a (phonological) grammar, and the means to construct a motor program in real time. It is well-known that it takes time to accomplish this and that during this time children's word productions often

---

Claartje Levelt, Leiden University, Leiden University Centre for Linguistics. Leiden Institute for Brain and Cognition
Eline van den Brink, Hanze University of Applied Sciences, School of Business Management
Josefine Karlsson, Örebrö University, School of Humanities, Education and Social Sciences

https://doi.org/10.1515/9783110730098-012

deviate from the adult target. Because of this simultaneous development at different levels, it is not always so clear *what* exactly causes deviations from the target or *where* in the speech production process a deviation arises. Take for example young children's attempts at producing words that start with a consonant cluster, the focus of this paper. In (1) are examples of such productions, of the Dutch child Robin at the age of 1;9, from the CLPF database (Fikkert 1994; Levelt 1994) available in Phonbank (Rose and MacWhinney 2014).

(1) Attempts at word-onset consonant cluster productions

		Target	Robin (1;9)
a.	trein *train*	/ˈtrɛin/	[ˈdœn]
b.	stoel *chair*	/ˈstul/	[ˈtuːl]
c.	school *school*	/ˈsχol/	[ˈzoː]
d.	groot *big*	/ˈχroˑt/	[ˈzːoˑt]
e.	brommer *moped*	/ˈbrɔmər/	[ˈbuːmɪ]
f.	slapen *sleep*	/ˈslapə/	[ˈpaːpɪ]
g.	clown *clown*	/ˈklɑun/	[ˈtœun]

In all of the productions in (1), in addition to segmental deviations from the target word, the onset cluster of the attempted word is reduced to a singleton consonant. Several accounts have been proposed for this cluster reduction phenomenon, usually in terms of a developing syllable structure grammar, like the presence of a fixed CV(C) syllable template (Menn 1978; Fikkert 1994), or a constraint banning clusters, like*CC or *Complex-Onset (Jongstra 2003; Levelt, Schiller, and Levelt 2000). Usually, the most sonorant segment from the target cluster is omitted to meet the restriction on onset clusters. However, even though a developing syllable structure grammar is a plausible account for cluster reduction in child language, other feasible error sources, like the lexical representation, phonetic encoding, and articulation, should be considered too; the child language data that we study are *utterances* after all.

In this paper we present a study on child language productions, specifically productions of target adult words containing consonant clusters in word onsets, which takes this broader speech production perspective. The study centers around the (re)introduction of an experimental method, self-repair prompting, that will be shown to provide a window on the developing speech production mechanism. Before turning to this method and the resulting data, however, let us shortly introduce the language production model assumed in this work, and the notions of self-monitoring and self-repair that underlie the method.

2 Language Production Model

Our understanding of language production in adults is at an advanced state, and there is general consensus on the big picture of the language production mechanism, based on extensive experimental evidence (Levelt, Roelofs, and Meyer 1999; Indefrey and Levelt 2004; Indefrey 2011; McQueen and Meyer 2019). The model of word production in Figure 1 below, based on the full model of speech production presented in Levelt, Roelofs, and Meyer (1999), focuses on word-form encoding and will be used in the present study.

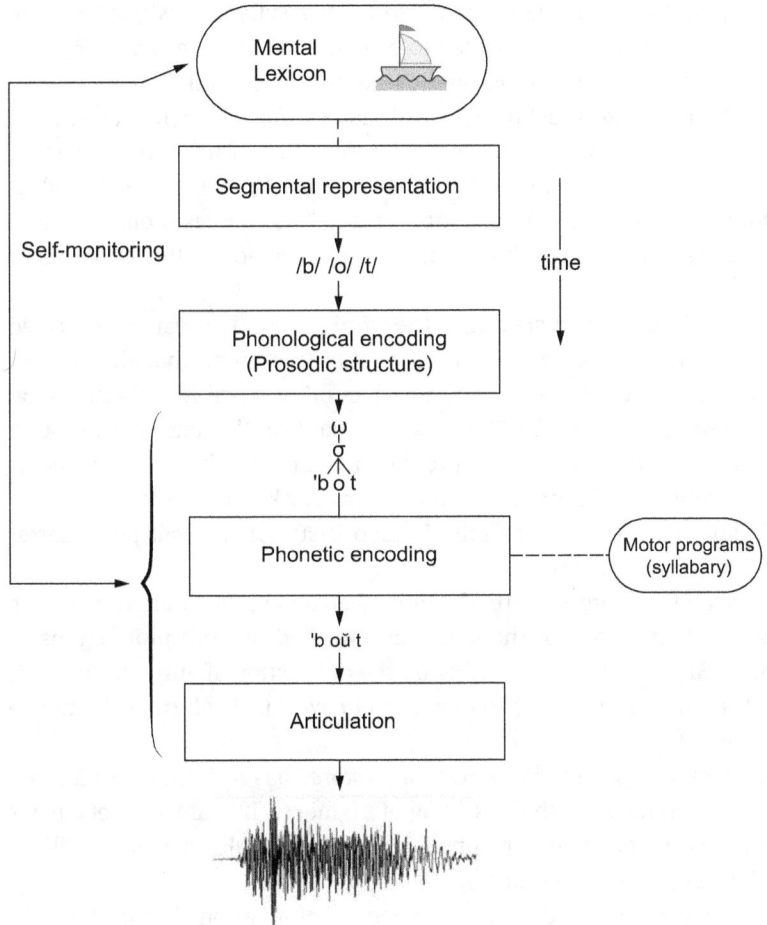

Figure 1: Word-form encoding model (based on Levelt, Roelofs, and Meyer 1999).

Word forms are stored in the *mental lexicon*. In order to prepare the articulatory program that will in the end be executed by the articulators, the phonological representation of a word is retrieved from the mental lexicon. That is, the segmental structure is accessed, as well as word properties that will not be discussed here like the morphological structure and non-predictable metrical structure. In the *phonological encoding module*, the retrieved segmental information will then be spelled out; the segments become available one by one and are grouped into syllables, following both universal and language-specific rules of syllabification. Gestural scores for the syllables are subsequently computed in the *phonetic encoding module*. For mature speakers it has been proposed that gestural scores for (frequent) syllables are stored in a 'syllabary' where they can be accessed directly, so they do not need to be constructed on the fly every time a syllable needs to be articulated. Phonetic fine-tuning is required to smoothen syllable transitions and to adjust the gestural scores to specific contexts. Finally, the gestural score is executed by the *articulatory system*. During the encoding process, speakers monitor their so-called internal speech, that is, the phonological and phonetic representations that are formed. This enables them to correct erroneous representations even before they are executed by the articulatory system.

Up until now it is far from clear how the word production system described here develops in young children. It is reasonable to assume that this system requires a certain period of maturation, just like other cognitive modules (e.g. Dehaene-Lambertz and Spelke 2015), but is it available in this form to the young language learner from the start of word production? And, if fully available, does it perform in the same way? Up until now, hardly any work that takes this perspective on child language data is available (Wijnen 1990, 1992; Levelt 1998; Carter and Gerken 2004; Gulian 2017).

In a fully available word-form production mechanism, the different modules could all form potential *loci* for the deviations we find in word productions of young children. Since we will be focusing on the production of onset clusters, let us take the deviating production ['zoː] for *school* /'sχol/ (*school*) from (1c) above to illustrate this:

- *The lexical representation*: the word form is *stored* as /zo/, due to perceptual difficulties or problems with the storing of segments. If a target onset cluster is represented with a singleton consonant, only a single consonant will be encoded in the production process.
- *Phonological encoding*: even if the segmental information that is stored in the mental lexicon contains all segments, /s/ /x//o/ /l/, syllabification at the level of phonological encoding could be restricted to CV syllable structures.

This would leave no room for the segments /x/ and /l/, which become 'stray erased' as a consequence. This results in a phonologically encoded syllable /so/, which is subsequently phonetically encoded and receives a gestural score. This scenario subsumes previous phonological accounts of cluster reduction in child language, in which fixed syllabic templates or constraints on syllable structure play an important role.
- *Phonetic encoding*: if phonological encoding has been able to supply the complete syllable /sxo(l)/ – focusing on the onset cluster – this syllable now needs a gestural score. However, constructing a plan with a combination of two consecutive consonantal gestures could be problematic: the gestural scores for [s] and [o] could, for example, overlap, largely masking the score for [x]. The listener is therefore not aware of a [x] sound in the production, but an acoustic analysis could reveal a trace of [x] in the vowel.
- *Articulation*: this scenario is very much like the one for *phonetic encoding*, except that the source of the cluster reduction now lies in the execution of the gestural score rather than in the gestural score itself. The execution of [x] could be masked by an articulatory overshoot of [s] (Shaw et al. 2011).

What kind of information could be used to determine the source of specific deviations and to find out about the developmental state of the speech production mechanism? We could look at the nature of deviations from adult target words in longitudinal child language data. In case some deviation is stable for a period of time, that is, the same error shows up every time a child attempts to produce a specific word, it is likely that the source for the error lies either in the lexical representation or in the phonological encoding module – constrained by the developing phonological grammar. More variable errors are expected if the source lies in the phonetic encoding module or in articulation. We could get more information about the level of segmental detail in young speakers' lexical representations by performing perception experiments, e.g. preferential looking (Swingley 2003, 2005; White, Morgan, and Wier 2005). Acoustic analyses of the produced words could reveal if target segments that seem to be missing from the produced form are indeed completely absent or turn out to be partly realized, revealed by acoustic traces in the signal that are hard to pick up by ear (Gulian 2017). Finally, ultrasound measures could help determine the motor execution abilities of the child (Gibbon 1999). In the present study, however, we will use information provided by a production experiment that revives the method of inducing self-repairs, as used in work by, among others, Gallager (1977) and Käserman and Foppa (1981).

3 Self-Monitoring and Self-Repairs

Self-monitoring entails comparing the encoded, or articulated speech form – here we focus on words – to the intended form, i.e. the perceptual standard of a speaker. If the speaker detects a mismatch between these forms, a correction is made. Self-repairs, or the absence thereof, can provide an important source of information on the state of the production mechanism. First of all, it tells us if children pay attention to their own speech, that is, if the self-monitoring mechanism is in place (see Figure 1) and functioning. Slobin (1978), based on an observation of his daughter at the age of 3;1,[1] remarks that self-monitoring is probably relatively late to develop. However, Jaeger (2005) reports on spontaneous phonological self-repairs in two-year olds acquiring American English, as in: "A blue [pʰa.wi] ... no ... [wa.wi.pʰap] (lollipop)" by Alice, 2;4.2. Of the 198 errors recorded by Jaeger in this age group, 38.5% were self-corrected (Jaeger 2005). Gallagher (1977) is to our best knowledge the first study using prompts to induce revisions. The study involved 18 subjects between 20 and 29 months old. In a one-hour play and read session with individual children, an unspecific prompt "what?" was uttered 20 times by the experimenter, independent of the correctness of the child's utterance. These prompts led to revisions in 77% of the cases. Gallagher observed a high frequency of phonetic changes in the youngest group, like in the following interaction. *Child*: "He kit ball" *experimenter*: "What?", *child*: "He kick ball." These phonetic revisions, although they did not always result in the correct target form, were consistently unidirectional, i.e. in the direction of the adult model. According to Gallagher this showed that the child's reaction to "what?" is not merely an attempt to repeat his or her utterance, with some accidental segmental variability due to his or her immature phonological system. Gallagher concludes that *"[. . .] the phonetic changes are revisions within a language system so primitively organized that other structural options are not as readily available."* The unidirectionality of phonetic revisions by these young children was also found by Käsermann (1980), who showed that sounds in words were changed more often towards an adult model than away from it in situations where the mother showed signs of incomprehension. From both these studies it can be concluded that self-monitoring is functioning in children younger than 3 years old. In Käsermann and Foppa (1981) the assumption is, indeed, that the revision behavior of even these young children is guided by their awareness of standard word-forms, and they designed a study to investigate what kind of standards

---

[1] "If her verbal formulations are not at once understood, she lies on the floor and cries or screams – but doesn't attempt to reformulate her statement" (Slobin 1978: §12).

determined children's systematic revisions. In their study, again a 1 hour play and read session, with 4- to 5-year old children, they intervened now and then with an unspecific "*hm?*," which they call a "modification-provoking non-understanding signal." Their hypothesis was that both the occurrence – does the child reformulate or not – and the type of revision a child would make would tell us something about their postulated linguistic standards of correctness and completeness. For this purpose, the utterance before the "hm?" was compared to the utterance prompted by "hm?". Since the children in this study were older, the focus of this study was on grammatical structures rather than on phonological segments. An important conclusion of the study, however, is that triggered repairs are dependent on the existence of certain linguistic standards, that is, on the child's present linguistic knowledge.

Thus, a child's utterance prompted by "hm?" or "what?" can tell us whether an initial, erroneous utterance is or is not in accord with the perceptual standard of this developing speaker. This is important to know, especially in the case of young language learners, who are simultaneously developing competence at different levels. If the initial, deviating, production is in accord with the speaker's perceptual – phonological – standard, suggested by a prompted repetition that does not contain any segmental changes, the error locus is probably situated in the lexical representation, while if it is not in accord with the perceptual standard, suggested by a revised utterance with some segmental change, the source of error should be sought in the form-encoding mechanism. The ability to make self-repairs indicates that children have representations of language forms that are more developed than their productions reveal, but not necessarily adult-like. Self-monitoring thus appears to be an important requisite for language development: only by comparing one's own production to his or her perceptual standard the learner can become aware of discrepancies that necessitate changes in either the lexical representation or the form-encoding system (Clark and Andersen 1979).

In addition to inducing self-monitoring the "hm?" prompt can also be understood as a form of repetition priming (Wheeldon and Monsell 1992; Jacobs et al. 2015; Tsuboi, Francis, and Jameson 2020). In studies with adult speakers, it has been found that repeated productions are facilitated and can have shorter durations. Repetition priming studies with adults have not made use of a prompt but have combined reading or listening to a prime with a subsequent picture-naming task. Up until now it has not been possible to robustly assess the accuracy of picture-naming after a produced prime, due to very low error rates in the primes produced by adult speakers. Shorter durations of primed repetitions were only found when the prime had been overtly articulated (Jacobs et al. 2015), and this was thought to be the effect of priming of the production component through the processing of auditory feedback. According to Tsuboi, Francis, and Jameson (2020) all processes that are not overlearned are susceptible to the repetition priming effect, and more difficult processes will show stronger repetition priming effects. While in the case of adult speakers the articulation of phonological sequences can, in most cases, be called 'overlearned', this is certainly not the case for the developing speakers in our study who are targeting consonant clusters. If the mechanism functions like in adult speakers, we can thus expect a strong repetition priming effect, i.e. possibly more accurate and faster post-prompt productions. However, the effect of more accuracy in the post-prompt repetition is at least partially dependent on the segmental information available in the lexical representation.

4 Experiment

Inspired by the work discussed above, we set out to use the unspecific question method in a more restricted way to study the relation between produced form and perceptual standard in the case of consonant clusters in word onsets. Since previous work had shown that the method worked with children as young as 20 months old, we could target the age group that is still struggling with consonant clusters in production, namely children between 24 and 30 months old. This would provide the opportunity to find pairs of initial incorrect productions and induced self-repairs. Below we describe the experimental method, and we will then present two types of analyses of the data, a more quantitative analysis and a more qualitative analysis of a set of systematic repairs, which tells us more about the locus of the initial error in the speech production mechanism.

5 Method

5.1 Participants

We analyzed the data of 20 children from different age groups. In the younger age group there were four boys and six girls between 23 and 25 months old, with a mean age of 24 months. In the older age group there were four boys and six girls between 27 and 31 months old, with a mean age of 30 months. Two more recordings are not analyzed here: data of one 24-month-old girl was not included because it was difficult to recognize individual segments in her speech, and data of one 30-month-old girl was not included in the analysis because her younger sister participated in the experiment, and it was hard to keep their voices apart in the recording. All children had at least one native Dutch-speaking parent. Parents were asked about their children's hearing-, language- and cognitive development; no parent reported any abnormalities. All children were familiar with the pictures-to-be-named during the recording session as the pictures had been sent home to the parents a week before and parents had been asked to show the pictures to their child and encourage the child to name the pictures.

5.2 Stimuli

The test stimuli were Dutch words starting with consonant clusters (/bl, br, dr, kl, kn, kr, fl, xl, vl, vr, sx, sl, sn, sp, st, tr/). One third of the words that could be elicited consisted of phonologically less complex control words, in order to prevent possible frustration with the task. All the words that were used as stimuli had been produced by toddlers in the Dutch-CLPF corpus (Levelt 1994; Fikkert 1994) available in PhonBank (Rose and MacWhinney 2014), indicating that the chosen stimuli were not beyond the possibilities for children at this age. For a list of all the words that could be elicited see Appendix 1.

5.3 Procedure

The experiment was conducted in a quiet room in the Babylab at Leiden University. In order to motivate the children to produce words, and to get a natural setting for self-repair prompts, the test was designed as an interactive game.[2] The child was encouraged to collect nine cards with pictures in color, which fitted on a 3x3 game-board that contained the same nine pictures in black and white. There were 7 different game-boards to choose from, with pictures of well-known animals, household objects, pieces of clothing, or food items. Both the experimenter and the child had a game-board and a stack of cards and they had to ask each other for the card they wanted to fit on the game-board. The main purpose of the game was to elicit specific words, so for some children the card collecting game had to be slightly modified, e.g. some children wanted to collect the cards in the card box instead of on the game-board. When the child named a picture of a word starting with an onset cluster, the experimenter pretended that she had not understood the child and uttered a non-specific request for repetition such as "hm?". If the child did not react to this prompt the experimenter more specifically

---

[2] Thanks to Frank Wijnen for suggesting this!

asked the child to repeat the word by asking "Can you say it again?" or "What did you say?". There were seven different sets of nine pictures and the aim was to prompt minimally four repeated utterances per set, which was not always possible. All sessions were audio-recorded with a mobile digital recorder (M-AUDIO microtrack II) using a table microphone (RØDE NTG-2 microphone and NC fxx PROEL cable).

5.4 Analysis

All recordings were entered in Phonbank. For the analysis we focused on word-pairs that were produced before and after the prompt, meeting the following criteria: (1) the target word had to contain an onset cluster, (2) the repair could not be a direct imitation of the experimenter's utterance – since this would not show the self-monitoring effect – and (3) the audio files of both utterances – the original utterance and the repeat – had to be clear, i.e. free from intervening voices or other noise. The data set that fulfilled the above criteria consisted of 236 word-pairs – out of 314 initial productions that were followed by a repetition – produced by the 20 children described above, ranging from 4 to 27 word-pairs per child. Only in 21 cases a prompt did not trigger a repetition.

The utterances were phonetically transcribed by two of the authors, making use of Praat (Boersma and Weenink 2020) to help focus on details of the productions and to compare the pairs of utterances directly.[3] In addition, the durations of the productions before and after the prompt were measured. This was done to check whether, especially in cases where no segmental or structural change could be detected in the prompted production, the repetition priming effect would be noticeable in a faster repeated production after the prompt.

We compared the phonetic transcriptions of each before-after-prompt word-pair, focusing on the realization of the target consonant cluster, and determined whether or not a segmental change had occurred. Regarding consonant cluster development, detailed research by Gulian (2017) had revealed 7 stages in the production of target /Cr/ onset clusters: (1) Complete cluster reduction to a single consonant, (2) Cluster reduction to C_1, with an acoustic trace of C_2 in the following vowel, (3) Cluster vocalization, i.e. production of C_1 and vocalization of C_2, (4) Epenthesis between C_1 and C_2 substitute, (5) C_1+substituted C_2 without epenthesis, (6) Epenthesis between C_1 and correct C_2, (7) Correct cluster realization. While

---

[3] The data are available through CHILDES/Phon and OSF (Data repository of "Prompted Self-repairs in Two-year-old Children", https://osf.io/kdqa3/).

these stages were not necessarily all encountered in the developmental data of the individual children studied by Gulian, subsets of the stages would always appear in this order. These stages – except for stage 2, because our data was too sparse to robustly establish the presence of acoustic traces – formed the basis to determine whether the prompted repetition involved an improvement or a deterioration in the realization of the target cluster compared to the initial spontaneous word production. In order to classify all the changes we encountered, it was necessary to add some substages; in two cases the target cluster had been completely deleted in the initial production and was improved to a reduced cluster after the prompt. We therefore added a Stage Ø. The single consonant in the cluster reduction stage, Stage 1, could either be the target C_1, the target C_2, or a substitute consonant (C_{sub}). Some of the post-prompt productions involved a change from one type of single C to another type of single C, where a change from C_{sub} to either C_1 or C_2 was regarded as an improvement. Finally, in three cases the production changed from a single C to a very long version of this C. This was interpreted as a variant of the vocalized cluster, Stage 3 in Gulian (2017). This brings us to the following set of stages in the production of target onset clusters:[4]

Stage 0: Ø
Stage 1a: C_{subst}
Stage 1b: C_1
Stage 1c: C_2
Stage 2a: CV
Stage 2b: C::
Stage 3: CVC_{subst}
Stage 4: CC_{subst}
Stage 5: $CVC_{correct}$
Stage 6: $CC_{correct}$

Finally, changes could also affect other parts of the word. These were not analyzed in detail, but just classified as either improvements or deteriorations.

6 Results and Discussion

6.1 Aggregated Findings

Of the 236 word-pairs, the vast majority, 166 (70.3%) contained some change in the repeated production (see Table 1 below). In 109 of these cases (46%) a change took place in the production of the target cluster, of which more than half, 62 (56.9%), were clear improvements, in the sense that the production of the target cluster in the repetition belonged to a more advanced developmental stage than

---

[4] One category that is still unaccounted for in this system is a single C that merges feature information from both target consonants, like [m] for /br/.

the one produced initially. In 18 cases (7.6%) the repeated production was even corrected from a singleton onset in the initial production to a (correct) cluster. In 6 cases the target cluster remained reduced to a single segment but changed to the other consonant from the target cluster. In 7 cases a single substituted consonant changed to one of the target cluster consonants. In 25 cases (22.9%) the production of the cluster deteriorated after the prompt, that is, the speaker reverted to a production from a less advanced developmental stage after the prompt. In the remaining cases some segmental change occurred, but this could neither be classified as an improvement, nor as a deterioration.

In 92 out of the 236 repeated productions (39%) there was a change in a different part of the word (too), with 40 (43.5%) clear improvements and 21 (22.8%) clear deteriorations. Deteriorations, in this case, involved for instance the dropping of a coda consonant that was correctly produced before the prompt, the production of an additional consonant or vowel – not related to the production of the target cluster and also not present in the target word – or a change from a correct to an incorrect consonant or vowel. In 18 cases the sentence structure (also) changed after the prompt: words were added, an article was added or removed, or the word was changed from or to a diminutive or plural form.

In 67 (28.4%) of the 236 word-pairs there was no segmental or structural change at all in the repeated production – but sometimes the repeated utterance was either produced in a softer voice, or it became louder or more emphatic.

In terms of duration, in 78 (74.3%) out of the 105 cases in which the before and after production had similar (numbers of) segments, and were produced in similar sentence positions, the duration of the repeated production was shorter (mean 211ms shorter, range 3ms–1047ms), while in 25 (23.8%) cases it was longer (mean 191.2ms longer, range 10ms–1412ms).

The 24-month-olds produced more repetitions that contained changes than the 30-month-olds (in 77.4% vs. 62.5% of the repetitions), and these changes also involved the production of the cluster more often (50.8% vs 38.4% of the repetitions). Almost 70% of the changes in the repeated production of the cluster were improvements in the 30-month-olds, while for the 24-month-olds changes were improvements in 54% of the cases. A higher percentage of the changes in the repeated production of the cluster involved deteriorations for the 30-month-olds than for the 24-month-olds (27.9% vs. 17.5%). These numbers can be understood when we look at the initial productions of the target clusters in the two groups. Here a major, and expected, difference was found in the percentage of onset clusters produced (correctly) in the initial production: 13.7% (4.8%) for the 24-month-olds versus 42.9% (29.5%) for the 30-month-olds. For the 24-month-olds there is thus more room for improvement, while the 30-month-olds have a higher risk of deteriorations in their cluster production. The higher percentage of changes in general in the 24-month-olds could signify a less robustly operating word-production mechanism. However, this requires further study.

From the numbers above we can conclude that the method successfully triggers self-monitoring; the prompt triggers a repetition, which in the majority of cases involves a change. In comparable before-after pairs, the repeated word was also produced with a shorter duration in most cases, a repetition priming effect. In 56.9% of the changes in repeated target cluster productions, and in 43.5% of the changes elsewhere in the word the rendered production was more accurate, showing that – at least in these cases – self-monitoring indeed functioned in a mature way, as it signified errors and led to self-repairs. Let us now turn to the data in more detail.

7 Changes in the Prompted Productions of Target Clusters

7.1 Overview

In Table 1 below all the different types of changes in the repeated production of the target onset cluster, i.e. improvements, denoted by x, and deteriorations, denoted by o, are tallied. The grey cells denote "no changes" which we ignore here.

Three main observations can be made. The first one is that most improvements occur when the initial spontaneous production is from Stage 1a or 1b. While at first sight this is only logical, because there are simply many ways in which a Stage 1 production can be improved, it is actually highly informative with respect to the question whether the initial productions were produced according to the perceptual standards of the participating developing speakers. The answer in these cases is "no": these speakers can correct themselves, triggered by the prompt, indicating that more information is stored in their lexical representations than the initial productions would lead us to believe.

The second observation is that pre-prompt productions belonging to Stage 2 do not appear to change very often. At this stage the speaker is clearly targeting more than a single consonant, pointing to a lexical representation that contains information about both consonants from the target cluster. The fact that we do not find many changes could of course simply be an effect of the fact that we have a constrained set of data from this stage. However, it could also point to a production solution that developing speakers feel comfortable with for some time: both

Table 1: Status of the productions of target clusters of all 20 participants before and after the prompt. Cells contain production tokens. An x denotes an improvement, an o denotes a deterioration in the repetition.

before → after ↓	Stage 0: ∅	Stage 1: C$_{sub}$	Stage 1: C$_1$	Stage 1: C$_2$	Stage 2: CV	Stage 2: C::	Stage 3: CVC$_{subst}$	Stage 4: CC$_{subst}$	Stage 5: CVC$_{correct}$	Stage 6: CC$_{correct}$
Stage 0: ∅										
Stage 1: C$_{sub}$			o							
Stage 1: C$_1$	xx		ooo		oo		oo	oo	o	ooo
Stage 1: C$_2$		x	xxxxx							
Stage 2: CV		x	xxxxxx					o	o	
Stage 2: C::			xxx							
Stage 3: CVC$_{subst}$					xx		xxxxx			
Stage 4: CC$_{subst}$		xxxx	xxxxxx					xx	o	o
Stage 5: CVC$_{correct}$			x				x			
Stage 6: CC$_{correct}$		xxxx		xx				xxxxxx	xxxxx	

consonants are realized, while the unmarked core syllable structure CV is still observed: a win-win situation. This hypothesis awaits further testing.

The final observation is that when the initial production is from Stage 3, 4 or 5, changes go both ways. Here the prompt either leads to a more accurate production, or it triggers developing speakers to revert to productions from an earlier stage with which they have more experience. This could be related to speakers' familiarity with the particular stage. In case speakers have just entered the stage, they might revert to a more comfortable previous stage after the prompt, while if speakers are about to reach the next stage the prompt might function as a boost to attain this next level production. This could not be tested with the present set-up of the study. To do this, experiments with prompted repetitions should be repeated over time with a group of developing speakers, while their spontaneous speech is collected at regular intervals over this longer period as well. In this way it can be determined whether a speaker has just entered a specific developmental stage or has been there for a while, and whether this affects the type of change in a prompted repetition.

Let us now discuss actual examples of word productions before and after the prompt.

7.2 Hidden Knowledge

There are several types of changes that reveal that a young speaker who produced a reduced cluster in the word production before the prompt, has more detailed information about the target cluster available in the lexical representation. That is, there is knowledge, initially hidden, about the full target cluster that is revealed by the post-prompt production. Below in (2) are examples of a C_1-C_2 swap: the speaker produced one of the two consonants, or a regular substitute for that segment, of the target cluster before the prompt and reverted to the other consonant, or a regular substitute for that segment, in the production after the prompt.

(2) Hidden knowledge I: C_1-C_2 swap

	Target	Gloss.	IPA target	Before prompt	After prompt	Participant
a.	stoel	chair	/stul/	[tˢʊ]	[sʊ]	N24
b.	broodje	bun	/brotjə/	[doʃə]	[loʃə]	H24
c.	kraan	faucet	/kran/	[kan]	[lan]	A24
d.	slang	snake	/slɑŋ/	[tˢɑn]	[lan]	D24

In (3) are examples of cases where the speaker again produced only one of the two consonants, or a regular substitute for that segment, of the target cluster before the prompt, but added (partial) information about the other consonant in the repeated production. In these examples the initial part of the repeated utterance is still CV, but now the V is either a vocalized version of the target C_2, or an epenthesized vowel followed by C_2 – or a consonant substituting this consonant.

(3) Hidden knowledge II: A vocalized or epenthesized cluster after the prompt

	Target	Gloss	IPA target	Before prompt	After prompt	Participant
a.	broek	trousers	/bruk/	[bux]	[puu:x]	A24
b.	fles	bottle	/flɛs/	[fɛs]	[fiɛs]	N24
c.	druifje	grape (dim)	/drœyfjə/	[ʋœyçʲə]	[tĭœysʲə]	H24
d.	brood	bread	/brot/	[poˑt]	[puoːt]	T24

In (4), finally, are cases where a speaker produced one of the two consonants, or a regular substitute for that segment, of the target cluster before the prompt and a full-fledged consonant cluster after the prompt.

(4) Hidden knowledge III: full-fledged clusters after the prompt

	Target	Gloss	IPA target	Before prompt	After prompt	Participant
a.	sleutel	key	/sløtəl/	[toto]	[klotoŭ]	A24
b.	sleutel	key	/sløtəl/	[lɔtɔ]	[tlotɔ]	L30
c.	sloffen	slippers	/slɔfə/	[sˑafɔ]	[sˑlæ̆ufɛ]	C24
d.	slang	snake	/slɑŋ/	[θɑŋ]	[tlɑŋ]	H24
e.	klok	clock	/klɔk/	[lɔk]	[klɔk]	R27
f.	broek	trousers	/bruk/	[puːk]	[bʀuk]	N30
g.	schoen	shoe	/sxun/	[xu]	[sxun]	L30

The target clusters in (4a–e) all have /l/ as the target C_2 and a [Cl] cluster is produced in the repeated productions. The participants who produced these remarkable improvements all had other instances of [Cl] realizations in their recorded data. For example, C24 produced [pɬːœt] for target *brood* (bread), substituting target C_2 /r/ with [l], but in this recording also produced epenthesized clusters, like in [kɑlʌk] for *klok* (clock), and reduced target /Cl/ clusters, like in [paː] for *bloem* (flower). Participant C24 is clearly working on the realization of this specific cluster type and this also applies to the other participants in (4a–e). There is, thus, some articulatory experience with the production of a [Cl] cluster, and the repetition seems to provide the speaker with the opportunity to supply the information that was missing from the original reduced pre-prompt production. The same applies to the example in (4f), but here involving /r/ as the target C_2; instead of correct [Cl] clusters, N30 produced several instances of correct [Cr] clusters in initial productions. The example in (4g), finally, involves a target /sx/ cluster, produced by L30 who already produced both target /Cl/ and /Cr/ clusters correctly.

The pairs of productions discussed in this section clearly show that the source of the reduced clusters in the pre-prompt productions does not lie in the stored lexical representation of the words. That is, it is not the case that the cluster reduction in the pre-prompt production results from a lexical representation that contains a single consonant instead of a consonant cluster at the word onset. The post-prompt production demonstrates that information about both consonants of the cluster in the target word is – at least partially – available in the lexical representation. The source of the deviating production must therefore lie at the level of phonological encoding or at the phonetic-articulatory level.

In the case of the before-after productions in (2) and (3) above, constraints at the phonological encoding level could play a role. The production of the target cluster structurally deviates in both the production before and the production after the prompt, in the sense that instead of CCV sequences only CV sequences are realized. If syllables with complex onsets cannot be construed in the phonological encoding module, due to a constraint that only allows for the construction of CV syllables, then a /C_1C_2V/ sequence retrieved from the lexicon must be accommodated in some way: by encoding only one of the consonants, C_1V or C_2V, by vowel epenthesis, C_1VC_2V, or by assigning the C_2 to the V position, which results in a vocalized cluster, CVV, as in 3a–d above.

In the case of the before-after productions in (4) above, however, the error locus must lie at the articulatory-phonetic level. The fact that a full cluster is produced after the prompt shows that the syllable spell-out at the phonological encoding level is not constrained to single onset positions. Two scenarios can be considered to account for the production variation illustrated in (4). In one, two motor plans are activated for the target /CCV/ sequences, the old [CV] plan and a new [CCV] plan. Since the speaker has more experience with the old plan, this will be activated above the threshold level first and is executed. The activation of the executed old plan subsequently drops, and the prompt and resulting self-monitoring now provide the new plan – that has still retained some activation – with the opportunity to cross the threshold level for execution. In the second scenario the locus of the variation lies in the execution of a single motor plan, containing the gestural scores for both consonants. In the initial execution of this plan the motor coordination of the gestures is off, resulting in the – perceptual – masking of one of the consonants. The prompted self-monitoring correctly identifies the problem, and in the repetition the coordination is improved. At this point, and on the basis of the sparse data available in this study, it is not possible to decide which of the two scenarios is most likely.

7.3 Full Knowledge-Lack of Knowledge

In 27.5% of the repetitions after the prompt no noticeable segmental change occurred. For some children the repeated production was softer, or even whispered, while for other children it was louder, or more emphatic. While there might be all kinds of reasons why nothing changed, like a lack of attention or increasing fatigue, here we consider two possible causes related to the development of the speech production mechanism.

One child was clearly bored with the repetition procedure.[5] This child was one of the 30-month-olds and produced almost all the target clusters correctly in the initial spontaneous production. In this case, the prompted self-monitoring procedure comes up with nothing to correct or improve. The production mechanism appears to be fully developed: the lexical representation is fully specified, word-form encoding applies accurately – the motor program might have been stored in the syllabary – and there is apparently enough articulatory experience with the motor program to execute it flawlessly every time.

On the flip side, some children produced mostly reduced clusters in the initial production and repeated this without a change after the prompt. In these cases, too, the prompted self-monitoring appears to come up with nothing that can be corrected or improved. However, because both the initial production and the repetition deviate in the same way from the adult target, in these cases knowledge seems to be lacking somewhere in the mechanism. The two most likely sources are the lexical representation and the phonological encoding module. The reduced cluster in both productions either originates in the lexical representation of the target word, which would lack the specification for one of the onset consonants, or results from the presence of constraints on complex onsets at the level of phonological encoding. Alternatively, the self-monitoring system could be the source, leaving errors unnoticed. However, in our data all children produced at least some self-repairs, making this option less likely. In one case, L30, the mechanism did seem to be particularly immature, as 9 out of 11 initial productions contained reduced clusters, 6 prompts led to unchanged repetitions and 4 out of 7 repetitions had longer rather than shorter durations. Again, we would need more information to decide on the exact locus, and this could differ for individual children. For example, an additional perception experiment could, in a future study, determine whether both consonants from target words with onset clusters are specified or not.

---

5 In one case E30 emphasized this by adding the word "poep" (poop) to the repeated word!

8 Conclusions

Two main conclusions can be drawn from this study. First, the method, using prompts to trigger repetitions, is highly suitable to perform with two-year-olds and provides highly informative data. The prompt almost always leads to a repetition and appears in most cases to successfully trigger self-monitoring, resulting in self-repairs. These repairs provide us with a window on the developing speech production mechanism, and we can conclude that the method adds to our understanding of children's development of language production, by disentangling representational from form-encoding immaturity.

Second, the fact that the source of deviating productions could be located at the lexical representation, at the level of phonological encoding, or at the level of phonetic encoding/articulation, demonstrates that studies of child language development cannot do without a detailed speech production model.[6] Self-monitoring appeared to function, and shorter durations of the repeated productions, an effect of repetition priming, were found. Together with the different sources for error in the model that could be established, this seems to indicate that the basic layout of the word-form encoding part of the speech production mechanism is available to the developing speakers.

Finally, we hope that the promising prompted repetition method re-introduced here will help to revive the use of production experiments to study, in particular, early typical child language development. Especially when performed in tandem with perceptual or articulatory studies they can provide us with still much needed and robust information on the developmental state of the language production system.

Appendix I: Stimuli

Test items (consonant cluster in onset)	Distractors (no consonant cluster in onset)
Animals	
schaap *sheep*	poes *cat*
vlinder *butterfly*	aap *monkey*
slang *snake*	kip *chicken*

---

[6] And in order to fully understand the contribution of the lexical representation to production deviations, the same necessity applies to a model of speech perception.

(continued)

Test items (consonant cluster in onset)	Distractors (no consonant cluster in onset)
krokodil *crocodile*	beer *bear*
spin *spider*	
Clothes	
broek *trousers*	jas *coat*
knoopjes *buttons*	sokken *socks*
trui *sweater*	pet *cap*
schoen *shoe*	
slab *bib*	
sloffen *slippers*	
In the house	
stoel *chair*	bed *bed*
klok *clock*	telefoon *phone*
kraan *faucet*	tafel *table*
trap *stairs*	kast *cupboard*
	bad *bath tub*
Transportation	
trein *train*	auto *car*
graafmachine *excavator*	fiets *bicycle*
slee *sled*	boot *boat*
vliegtuig *airplane*	
tractor *tractor*	
vrachtauto *truck*	
Food	
snoepjes *candy*	appel *apple*
druiven *grapes*	taart *cake*
brood *bread*	kaas *cheese*
fles *bottle*	banaan *banana*
spaghetti *spaghetti*	
Play	
glijbaan *slide*	ballon *balloon*
trommel *drum*	konijn (knuffel) *rabbit*
schommel *swing*	pop *doll*
knuffel *cuddle toy*	puzzel *puzzle*
blokken *blocks*	boek *book*
trompet *trumpet*	

(continued)

Test items (consonant cluster in onset)	Distractors (no consonant cluster in onset)
Other items	
bril *glasses*	kam *comb*
sleutel *key*	kaars *candle*
bloem *flower*	hamer *hammer*
ster *star*	ijsje *ice-cream*

References

Boersma, Paul & David Weenink. 2020. Praat: Doing phonetics by computer [Computer program]. http://www.praat.org/.

Carter, A. & L. Gerken. 2004. Do children's omissions leave traces? *Journal of Child Language* 31. 561–568.

Clark, E. V. & E. S. Andersen. 1979. Spontaneous repairs: Awareness in the process of acquiring language. *Papers and Reports on Child Language Development* 16. 1–12.

Dehaene-Lambertz, G. & E. Spelke. 2015. The infancy of the human brain. *Neuron* 88(1). 93–109. DOI: 10.1016/j.neuron.2015.09.026. PMID: 26447575.

Fikkert, P. 1994. *On the acquisition of prosodic structure*. Leiden: Leiden University Doctoral dissertation. (HIL Dissertation Series 6). The Hague: HAG.

Gallagher, T. M. 1977. Revision behaviors in the speech of normal children developing language. *Journal of Speech, Language, and Hearing Research* 20(2). 303–318.

Gibbon, F. 1999. Undifferentiated lingual gestures in children with articulatory/phonological disorders. *Journal of Speech, Language, and Hearing Research* 42. 382–397.

Gulian, M. E. 2017. *The development of the speech production mechanism in young children: evidence from the acquisition of onset clusters in Dutch*. Leiden: Leiden University LOT Dissertations in Linguistics.

Indefrey, P. 2011. The spatial and temporal signatures of word production components: A critical update. *Frontiers in Psychology* 2. Article 255. DOI: 10.3389/fpsyg.2011.00255.

Indefrey, P. & W. Levelt. 2004. The spatial and temporal signatures of word production components. *Cognition* 92. 101–144.

Jacobs, C., L. Yiu, D. Watson & G. Dell. 2015. Why are repeated words produced with shortened durations? Evidence from inner speech and homophone production. *Journal of Memory and Language* 84. 37–48.

Jaeger, J. 2005. *Kids' Slips. What Young Children's Slips of the Tongue Reveal about Language Development*. Mahwah, NJ/London: Lawrence Erlbaum Associates.

Jongstra, W. 2003. *Variation in reduction strategies of Dutch word-initial consonant clusters*. Toronto: Toronto University Doctoral dissertation. Toronto University Working Papers.

Käsermann, M. 1980. *Spracherwerb und Interaktion*. PhD Dissertation. Bern: Hans Huber.

Käsermann, M. & K. Foppa. 1981. Some determinants of self correction: An interactional study of Swiss-German. In W. Deutsch (ed.), *The Child's Construction of Language*, 97–104. London: Academic Press.

Levelt, C. 1994. On the acquisition of Place. Leiden: Leiden University Doctoral dissertation. (HIL Dissertation Series 8). The Hague: HAG.

Levelt, W. 1998. The genetic perspective in psycholinguistics. Or: where do spoken words come from? *Journal of Psycholinguistic Research* 27(2). 167–180.

Levelt, C., N. Schiller & W. Levelt. 2000. The acquisition of syllable types. *Language Acquisition* 8(3). 237–264.

Levelt, W., A. Roelofs & A. Meyer. 1999. A theory of lexical access in speech production. *Behavioral and Brain Sciences* 22. 1–75.

McQueen, J. M. & A. S. Meyer. 2019. Key issues and future directions: Towards a comprehensive cognitive architecture for language use. In P. Hagoort (ed.), *Human Language: From Genes and Brain to Behavior*, 85–96. Cambridge, MA: MIT Press.

Menn, L. 1978. Phonological units in beginning speech. In A. Bell & J. Hooper (eds.), *Syllables and Segments*, 157–172. Amsterdam: North Holland.

Rose, Y. & B. MacWhinney. 2014. The PhonBank Project: Data and software-assisted methods for the study of phonology and phonological development. In J. Durand, U. Gut & G. Kristoffersen (eds.), *The Oxford Handbook of Corpus Phonology*, 380–401. Oxford: Oxford University Press.

Shaw, J., A. Gafos, P. Hoole & C. Zeroual. 2011. Dynamic invariance in the phonetic expression of syllable structure: A case study of Moroccan Arabic consonant clusters. *Phonology* 28(3). 455–490.

Slobin, D. 1978. A case study of early language awareness. In A. Sinclair, R. J. Jarvella & W. J. M. Levelt (eds.), *The Child's Conception of Language*, 45–54. (Springer Series in Language and Communication 2). Berlin/Heidelberg: Springer. DOI: 10.1007/978-3-642-67155-5_3.

Swingley, D. 2003. Phonetic detail in the developing lexicon. *Language and Speech* 3. 265–294.

Swingley, D. 2005. 11-month-olds' knowledge of how familiar words sound. *Developmental Science* 8(5). 432–443.

Tsuboi, N., W. Francis & J. Jameson. 2020. How word comprehension exposures facilitate later spoken production: Implications for lexical processing and repetition priming. *Memory* 29(1). 39–58. DOI: 10.1080/09658211.2020.1845740.

Wheeldon, L. & S. Monsell. 1992. The locus of repetition priming of spoken word production. *Quarterly Journal of Experimental Psychology* 44A(4). 723–761. DOI: https://doi.org/10.1080/14640749208401307.

White, K., J. Morgan & L. Wier. 2005. When is a *dar* a car? Effects of mispronunciation and referential context on sound-meaning mappings. In A. Brogos, R. Clark-Cotton & S. Ha (eds.), *Proceedings of the 29th Annual Boston University Conference on Language Development*, 651–662. Somerville, MA: Cascadilla Press.

Wijnen, F. 1990. The development of sentence planning. *Journal of Child Language* 17. 651–676.

Wijnen, F. 1992. Incidental word and sound errors in young speakers. *Journal of Memory and Language* 31. 734–755.

Glyne Piggott
Deriving Variable Phonological Visibility from Word Structure

Abstract: In certain languages, a particular set of morphemes displays variable phonological behaviour, varying between being visible or invisible to some phonological process. For example, subject prefixes in the Austronesian language, Mangap-Mbula, vary in terms of their visibility to stress assignment, while functionally similar affixes in the Papuan language, Maybrat vary in terms of their visibility to a process of schwa epenthesis. Typical phonological descriptions stipulate the reason for the variable visibility, ex post facto. Appeals to extrametricality and similar labels fall into such a category. In this paper, I propose to derive such variable phonological behaviour from the way phonology applies to the cyclic spell-out of word structure, assuming the framework of Distributed Morphology (DM) (Halle and Marantz 1993, 1994). I build on the observation that application of many phonological processes is restricted to word-internal domains.

Keywords: Cyclicity, spellout, phases, interfaces, Distributed Morphology, minimal word

1 Introduction

Cyclic derivation has been a remarkable constant in generative phonological analysis since Chomsky and Halle (1968). However, there have been few attempts to provide a principled characterization of cycles. Phases as defined by Chomsky (2001, 2008) in combination with Distributed Morphology (DM) (Halle and Marantz 1993, 1994) help to remedy this deficiency, at least, in some cases. Phase theory postulates that derivation proceeds by sending certain chunks of syntactic structure to the LF and PF interfaces (i.e. Spell-out) where they are assigned semantic and phonetic interpretation. Various elaborations of phase theory in the syntactic literature (e.g. Bošković and Lasnik 1999; Legate 2003; Heck and Zimmermann 2004; Svenonius 2004; Matushansky 2005; Adger 2006b) recognize that phrases headed by elements such as complementizers (CP), verbs (vP), determiners (DP) and number (NUMP) qualify as phases. According to DM, phases are also properties of words, because the same computational system that gener-

Glyne Piggott, McGill University

https://doi.org/10.1515/9783110730098-013

ates phrases and sentences also generates words. DM postulates that categories such as nouns, verbs and adjectives are derived by merging category-defining little-*x* heads (*v, n, a*) with root morphemes. These little-*x* elements are recognized in several publications (e.g. Marantz 2000; Marvin 2002; Di Sciullo 2003; Newell 2004 and 2008; Arad 2005; Embick and Marantz 2008; Embick 2010) as phase heads. Word-internal structures like *v*P, *n*P and *a*P are therefore phases.

The transfer of material to the two interfaces is regulated by certain principles. One of these blocks the process if the relevant chunk contains deficiencies, identified as uninterpretable features. The presence of such features in a candidate for transfer would force a delay in its spell-out until they are checked. For example, roots, considered to be category-deficient by DM, cannot be interpreted alone and must combine with the category-defining element before Spell-out. Another principle of delayed Spell-out is advocated by Svenonius (2004) and Bobaljik and Wurmbrand (2013), respectively. It allows elements to be extracted from a phase (XP), if they are required to satisfy the needs of a higher head. To meet such a requirement, the transfer of a phase (XP) would always have to be frozen until the merger of the next head (Y). If Y is needy, X can be extracted from XP to satisfy the needs of Y (i.e. [Y [..X..$_{XP}$]$_{YP}$] ⇒ [X+Y [..X..$_{XP}$]$_{YP}$]).[1] Such a view of delayed Spell-out or phase extension allows a phase head to escape from a phase and be spelled out later in a derivation in combination with another head.[2]

Each instance of transfer to the interfaces obviously constitutes a cycle of a derivation, forming a sound-meaning pair. Mapping to the LF interface might straightforwardly yield a semantic interpretation, but the abstract syntactic structure of a phase that is mapped to PF cannot be readily assigned a phonological interpretation, because phonology cannot interpret abstract syntactic features. Assuming that phonology is fundamentally word-centric (Ewen and van der Hulst 2001), it must have access to a unit that qualifies as a word.[3] Newell (2008) and Newell and Piggott (2014) propose a mechanism that parses the transferred

---

[1] There are slight differences between the proposal by Svenonius (2004) and that of Bobaljik and Wurmbrand (2013). Another advocate of delayed Spell-out, described as phase extension, is Den Dikken (2007).
[2] I believe that the appearance of globalism in the description of delayed Spell-out, pointed out by an anonymous critic, can be addressed by considering the higher head (Y) as a necessary licenser for the trigger of Spell-out. Investigation of this possibility would, of course, have to be explored further but is beyond the scope of this paper.
[3] This assertion does not mean that phonology never applies to domains larger or smaller than the word.

structure into words at the PF interface. Incorporated into the principles of DM, the mechanism applies after vocabulary items are inserted in the terminal nodes of the syntactic structure.

(1) *Word(ω)-Projection*
At Spell-out, exponents of morphemes in a head position are organized as a word (ω), if they contain a root.[4]

The first cycle in a derivation at PF must, therefore, contain a word and the outputs of subsequent cycles are merged into this word until the Spell-out of the final cycle/phase (i.e. CP, DP, AP, etc.) is reached.

Cyclic spell-out predicts the possibility of morpheme invisibility. A phonological process that applies to the spell-out of a phase would not routinely encompass elements that emerge in another phase, because phase internal conditions are not necessarily replicated across phases. Mangap-Mbula, an Austronesian language of New Guinea (Bugenhagen (1995), is but one of a number of languages that illustrate the invisibility effect. In this language, trochaic stress assignment produces patterns like those in (2).

(2) a. (mólo)lo   'long (plural objects)'
    b. (náka)(bàsi) 'axe'
    c. to(mó:)to   'man'

The first syllable of each of the examples in (2a, b) is stressed because foot parsing is left to right. This mode of stress assignment routinely skips a light initial syllable if the second syllable is heavy (2c). However, the first syllable of the examples in (3), each of which is a realization of a morpheme that marks the subject, is not stressed.

(3) a. ti-(ménder)   'they stand'   *(tí-men)der
       3PL-STAND

    b. aŋ-bo(bó:)bo   'I am calling'   *(áŋ-bo)(bò:bo)
       1-CALL

---

4 See Embick and Noyer (2001) for the assumption that the difference between a root and non-root morpheme is lexically represented.

There is no principled phonological reason for skipping the first syllables of the examples in (3). The only plausible reason for the non-parsing of these syllables is their status as realizations of a subject prefix.[5]

A particularly striking effect of morpheme invisibility comes from Maybrat, a language from the Papua Province of Indonesia (Dol 2007). This language has five subject prefixes, which, when realized, take the form of bare consonants. When these subject morphemes are morphologically affixed to certain consonant-initial verbs, they are invisible to a process, informally described as schwa epenthesis, that normally (and, perhaps, uniquely) simplifies word-initial clusters. Morpheme invisibility in this instance takes the form of ineffability.

(4) a. t-kapuk [kapuk] 'I close my eyes' *[təkapuk]
    1-CLOSE EYES

   b. n-kapuk [kapuk], 'you close your eyes' *[nəkapuk]
    2-CLOSE EYES

The ineffability of subject prefixes under conditions like those in (4) means that person-marked forms in verb paradigms are not phonetically distinguished. In other words, there is considerable homophony. In the following sections, I will demonstrate how cyclic spell-out accounts for the invisibility of subject morphemes in Maybrat and in Mangap-Mbula. Afterwards, I will discuss how a phonological condition on words (i.e. word minimality) can override the invisibility effects of cyclicity.

2 DM and Cyclic Spell-Out

As mentioned above, DM does not consider entities such as nouns, verbs and adjectives to be primitive word categories. Instead, these are derived by combining root morphemes, unspecified for category, with category-defining functional elements (*n, v, a*). I assume that head movement (Travis 1984), adjoining the root to a functional element, is the mechanism that allows category to be assigned to the root before it is spelled out. Application of this mechanism would yield configurations like those in (5a) and (5b), underlying nouns and verbs, respectively.

---

[5] The prefix label is used descriptively to refer to the exponent of a functional element in a pre-radical position. Consequently, it covers elements that would be analyzed in the literature as proclitics. The subject morphemes in Mangap-Mbula and Maybrat are probably best treated as clitics, but the syntactic case for such treatment is beyond the scope of this paper.

(5) a. Noun structure   b. Verb structure

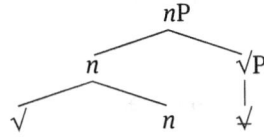
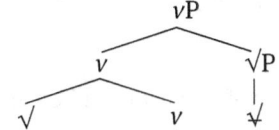

Since these structures contain phase heads, they are candidates for transfer to the interfaces, when the conditions described by principles of delayed Spell-out are satisfied. Each would constitute the first phase of a derivation. Further elaboration of (5a) would minimally require the addition of a determiner morpheme (D), resulting in DP phase that would be spelled out as a second and final cycle. Verb structure is somewhat more complex. A verb requires the merger of at least one argument and may also be inflected for tense. The argument that qualifies as the subject is generally considered to emerge when the CP phase is spelled out. The derivational structures of both nouns and verbs, therefore, minimally contain two phases and two cycles. A bi-phasal derivation plays a crucial role in explaining morpheme invisibility.

2.1 Subject Prefix Invisibility in Mangap-Mbula

As pointed out above, stress in Mangap-Mbula is assigned by trochaic parsing. The evidence is reintroduced below, with additional examples.

(6) a. (mólo)lo   'long (plural objects)'
       (náka)(bàsi)   'axe'
       (páza)(ŋàna)   'something planted'

    b. to(mó:)to   'man'
       bo(bó:)bo   'you (sg.) are calling'

The presence and location of unparsed syllables in the above examples are readily accounted for by the leftward orientation of foot parsing and the inherent properties of the trochaic foot. The canonical trochee is left-headed, binary and bimoraic. Consequently, a monomoraic syllable at the end of some of the examples in (6) must be unparsed. The initial syllable in (6b) is skipped, because it is followed by a heavy (i.e. bimoraic) syllable which must be parsed as the head of the foot, generally referred to as the weight-sensitivity condition.

None of the explanations for the occurrence of unparsed syllables in (6) can be extended to the presence of such syllables at the beginning of verbs containing a subject-marking prefix.

(7) The invisibility of subject morphemes to stress assignment:
    a. ti-(ménder) 'they stand' *(tí-men)der
        3PL-STAND

    b. ti-(pómbol) 'they cause to be strong' *(tí-pom)bol
        3PL-CAUSE TO BE STRONG

    c. aŋ-bo(bó:)bo 'I am calling' *(áŋ-bo)(bò:bo)
        1-CALL

    d. aŋ-ga(ráu) 'I approach' *(áŋ-ga)(ràu)
        1-APPROACH

There is no obvious reason for parsing to overlook the first syllable in (7). The second does not qualify as heavy, because consonant positions in Mangap-Mbula do not contribute weight. The realization of stress in (7c, d) is very informative. The first two syllables are ignored in each case, although routine parsing would yield optimal binary trochees. Consequently, under seemingly ideal conditions for assigning stress, the subject morphemes are still ignored. In the framework of this paper, their invisibility to stress follows readily from the spell-out of the subject markers in CP, roughly in the configuration illustrated in (8).

(8)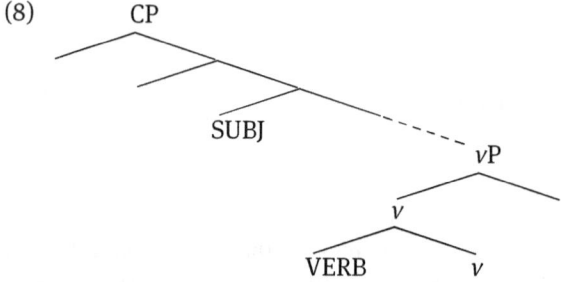

If there is no post-syntactic adjustment to this structure (see Marantz 1988; Embick and Noyer 2001; Adger 2006a), cyclic spell-out of the *v*P phase followed by the CP phase would result in a hierarchical phonological structure in which the subject prefix and the verb would be realized in different (prosodic) words. Stress would therefore be assigned to (7c) in the representation below.

(9)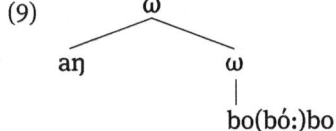

Word-centric foot structure could not span the boundary between the prefix and the exponent of the verb. The invisibility of Mangap-Mbula subject prefixes to stress assignment therefore follows directly from phase-based cyclic spell-out.

Subject markers are not the only pre-radical morphemes in Mangap-Mbula. This set also includes those listed in (10) (Bugenhagen 1995: 61).

(10) Transitivity affixes[6]
 a. p/pa (Causative)
 b. m/ma (Detransitive)
 c. par (Reciprocal)

These affixes appear between the subject marker and the verb root and are never invisible to stress assignment.

(11) Stressed transitivity affixes
 a. tipárpamòtoto 'they are making each other afraid'
    ti-par-pa-mototo
    3P-REC-CAUS-FEAR

 b. ipámiliŋ 'he accidentally spilled something'
    i-pa-m-liŋ
    3S-CAUS-DETR-POUR

 c. imíliŋ 'it spilled'
    i-m-liŋ
    3S-DETR-POUR

Notice that stress falls on the reciprocal in (11a), the causative in (11b) and the detransitive in (11c). Their phonological behaviour is consistent with their emer-

---

6 The realizations of the causative and detransitive morphemes are, respectively, subject to morphologically-controlled allomorphy, and one of the allomorphs is a bare consonant. In Mangap-Mbula, whenever the exponent of a morpheme is a bare consonant, it must be followed by a copy of the following vowel, as shown in (11b, c).

gence when the *v*P phase is sent to Spell-out. They are not separated from the verb by a boundary that is impermeable to stress assignment.[7]

2.2 Subject Prefix Invisibility in Maybrat

Let us now show how the structure of the preceding analysis of Mangap-Mbula accounts for the invisibility and ultimate ineffability of subject prefixes in Maybrat, identified by Dol (2007: 49) as those listed below.

(12) Maybrat pronominal subject markers
    a. t '1st Singular'   d. j '3rd Singular (masculine)'
    b. p '1st Plural'   e. m '3rd Unmarked'
    c. n '2nd Singular/Plural'

As observed earlier, when these subject markers are introduced before consonant-initial verbs, they are phonetically undetectable. Additional data are included in (13).

(13) Omission of subject markers before consonants
    a. t-kapuk   [kapuk]   'I close my eyes'
        t-samuox   [samuox]   'I am heavy'
        t-periet   [periet]   'I divide'
    b. n-kapuk   [kapuk]   'you close your eyes'
        n-samuox   [samuox]   'you are heavy'
        n-periet   [periet]   'you divide'

Routinely, we would expect these subject markers to appear, if Maybrat tolerated initial consonant clusters (CC) or if such clusters could be simplified by epenthesis. The evidence points to an absolute prohibition against initial CC clusters. On the other hand, there is both direct and indirect evidence for a process of schwa epenthesis with the sole function of simplifying initial CC clusters.

    Consider, first, the indirect evidence for schwa epenthesis. Dol (2007: 35) points out that schwa has a unique distribution in Maybrat; it "invariably occurs

---

[7] In the framework of delayed Spell-out adopted in this paper, the analysis of the causative, detransitive and reciprocal morphemes are exponents of *v* would ensure their realization within the first phase. Another possible analysis is that these morphemes are root modifiers (cf. Steriopolo and Wiltschko 2007).

between two Cs in word-initial position". While there appear to be some superficial exceptions, this statement is fundamentally valid. The restricted distribution of schwa contrasts with the relative freedom of occurrence of the other five (basic) vowels of Maybrat (i.e. /i, e, a, o, u/). Schwa also differs from the other vowels in that it is does not display allophony. For example, the realization of underlying /o/ ranges over the set [o, ʌ, ɔ, ʊ]. Dol (2007: 35) infers from its distribution that schwa "does not have phonemic status". If it is non-phonemic, the only other source is via epenthesis. The direct support for this conclusion is introduced later. The obvious question now is why does this process fail to rescue consonant exponents of the subject morphemes.

Given the syntactic location of subject morphemes sketched in (8), the phonological representation that underlies the form /t-kapuk/ [kapuk] 'I close my eyes' would be the nested word structure in (14).

(14)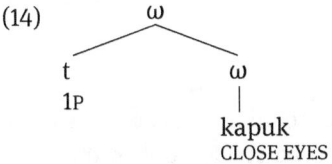
kapuk
CLOSE EYES

In this representation, the stranded consonant (i.e. /t/) that is the exponent of the 1st Person Subject might become effable only if it could be supported by an epenthetic vowel. Schwa in Maybrat cannot discharge such a function, given Dol's description of distribution of this vowel; the consonants that are separated by schwa must be strictly within the same word.

There are cases where single consonants that emerge in a representation like (14) are rescued by an epenthetic vowel. Support for this claim comes from Nivkh, a language spoken in the Russian Far East. According to Shiraishi (2006: 38), the possessor argument in a possessive construction is realized by one of the following prefixes.

(15) Nivkh pronominal possessor
    a.   1st Person   ɲ-
    b.   2nd Person   cʰ-
    c.   3rd Person   i̯-
    d.   Reflexive   pʰ-

These prefixes are realized before vowels and consonants in inalienable possessive constructions.

(16) Nivkh inalienable possessive constructions
  a. pʰ-acik 'one's own younger sister'
     pʰ-umgu 'one's own wife'
  b. pʰ-naχ   'one's own eyes'
     pʰ-nanak 'one's own older sister'

However, in an alienable possessive construction, a consonant exponent of the possessor argument is invariably followed by an epenthetic vowel /i/, whether the following noun root begins with a vowel or a consonant.

(17) Nivkh alienable possessive constructions
  a. pʰi-eɲ   'one's own skis'
     pʰi-oq   'one's own coat'
  b. pʰi-naχ 'one's own bed'
     pʰi-caqo 'one's own knife'

Dobler (2008) and Newell and Piggott (2014) propose an analysis of possessive constructions that requires an inalienable noun to be spelled out in the same phase as the possessor argument. In contrast, the noun and possessor in an alienable possessive construction are spelled out in different phases. The necessary properties of the latter construction are captured by the following structure.

(18)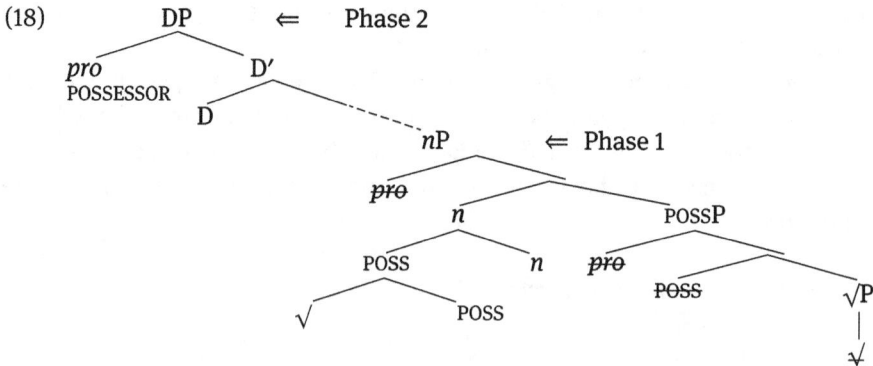

The spell-out of the *n*P phase and subsequently the DP phase in this structure guarantees that a consonant would be stranded in the derivation of /pʰi-naχ/ 'one's own bed'.

(19)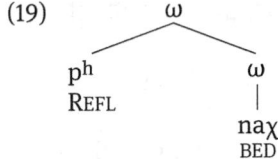

Nivkh makes use of the option of a particular epenthesis process to guarantee the realization of the consonant in (19) that would otherwise be stranded. Maybrat, in contrast, has no mechanism to support the stranded consonant in (14). The Maybrat equivalent is invisible to schwa epenthesis and, consequently, ineffable.

3 Variability in Morpheme Visibility

Ceteris paribus, given the argument that the structures in (8) and (18) underlie morpheme invisibility, we would expect the correlation to hold throughout the grammar with respect to a particular phonological process. However, this expectation must be tempered by the fact that DM allows representations to undergo post-syntactic adjustments. Some of these operations fall under the general umbrella of *Morphological Merger* (Marantz 1988) and include *Lowering* and *Local Dislocation* (Embick and Noyer 2001; Adger 2006a). There is no principled reason to restrict post-syntactic adjustments to purely morphological operations. Newell and Piggott (2014) argue that phonological representations that emerge at PF from the mapping between syntax and phonology are also subject to post-Spell-out adjustment. They propose a mechanism called *Phonological Merger* that is described in (20).

(20) *Phonological Merger (P-Merger)*
[X [. . . . . .$_\omega$]$_\omega$] → [✘ [. . .X. . . .$_\omega$]$_\omega$], where X is the exponent of a functional element.

Independent justification for positing such a mechanism is the phenomenon of infixation which locates the exponent of an affix within a phonologically defined domain. *P-Merger* would target a structure like that in (8) and effectively flatten it. Because this mechanism applies within phonology proper, it has to be conditioned by well-defined phonological constraints. It can be invoked to explain why the exponents of subject prefixes are sometimes visible to stress in Mangap-Mbula and to schwa epenthesis in Maybrat.

3.1 Subject Prefix Visibility in Mangap-Mbula and Maybrat

When subject morphemes in Mangap-Mbula merge with verbs that have monosyllabic, monomoraic exponents, the prefixes are not invisible to stress. Visibility is shown by the assignment of stress to the first syllable, bringing the stress pattern on such words in line with that on unprefixed words like those in (6a), as illustrated by the following examples.

(21) a. tíla   'they do'   *tilá
        ti-la
        3P-DO

    b. áŋdu   'I cross'   *aŋdú
        aŋ-du
        1-CROSS

When the syntactic structure that underlies (21a) is mapped to phonology, cyclic spell-out to PF would produce the nested structure in (22).

(22)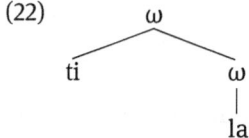

Stress on the first syllable of the word in (21a) cannot be derived from the above representation. The structure must be flattened to combine the prefix and the verb into a simple (rather than complex) word. *P-Merger* in this instance would be the response to a well-known condition on word-size, the preference for a word to contain at least two syllables or moras.

(23) MINIMAL WORD (MINWD)
     A word contains more than one syllable (or mora).

When the boundary between the two constituents in (22) is eliminated, the two syllables can be parsed into an optimal trochaic foot, allowing initial stress to emerge.

(24) a. [3PL[DO_vP]...cP]
    [ti[la_ω]_ω]   Spell-out at PF

b. [3PL[DO_vP]...cP]
    [t̶i̶[ti-la_ω]_ω]   P-Merger

c. [3PL[DO_vP]...cP]
    [t̶i̶[(tíla)_ω]_ω]   Stress assignment

Notice that the MINWD constraint would have no flattening effect on the derivation of words in (7). Subject prefixes must remain invisible to stress in such words.

MINWD is also active in Maybrat. It forces consonants that realize subject morphemes to combine with monosyllabic verb roots within a simple word. In this re-arrangement of constituents, schwa epenthesis would be triggered and the effability of the exponents of subject morphemes would be assured. The data set in (25) shows the results.

(25) Retention of subject markers before monosyllabic verbs
   a. t-po   [təpo],   *[po]   'I hold'
      t-se   [təse],   *[se]   'I place'
   b. p-po   [pəpo],   *[po]   'we hold'
      p-se   [pəse],   *[se]   'we place'

The following derivation underlies the realization of the prefix-verb combination /t-po/ [təpo] 'I hold'.

(26) a. [1[HOLD_vP]...cP]
    [t[po_ω]_ω]   Spell-out at PF

b. [3PL[HOLD_vP]...cP]
    [t[t-po_ω]_ω]   P-Merger

c. [3PL[HOLD_vP]...cP]
    [t[təpo_ω]_ω]   Schwa epenthesis

The obligatory application of schwa epenthesis produces the disyllabic output that satisfies the MINWD requirement.[8]

---

[8] In Government Phonology (Kaye, Lowenstamm, and Vergnaud 1990) or in the Radical CV theory of Scheer (2004, 2012), the exponents of subject morphemes in Maybrat are not just consonants but CV syllables in which the V position is empty. *P-Merger* would therefore produce a

4 Conclusion

The central claim of this paper is that cyclic spell-out creates relatively impermeable boundaries between spell-out domains that block certain phonological relations. Hence, the exponent of morpheme that merges after a phase has already been spelled out might be invisible to a phonological process that applies to the earlier phase. Specific adjustment to the structure that emerges from cyclic spell-out is required to overcome the invisibility. An important outcome of the analysis of variable visibility is the assertion that the types of morphemes that might display this behaviour are not randomly distributed. Candidate affixes in verbs include markers of subject and tense that are spelled out in the CP phase, while candidates in nouns include possessor markers and determiners that are spelled out in the DP phase. Swedish appears to provide evidence for the invisibility of determiners to a phonological process. Swedish words bear one of two accents, usually correlated with the difference between monosyllabic and polysyllabic types (Lahiri, Wetterlin, and Jönsson-Steiner 2005). The two patterns are informally referred to as Accent 1 (monosyllabics) and Accent 2 (polysyllabics). The affixation of the plural morpheme to a monosyllabic root (e.g. *häst-ar* 'horses') qualifies a word as polysyllabic and a bearer of Accent 2. In contrast, both a monosyllabic singular (e.g. *häst* 'horse') and the disyllabic definite form (e.g. *häst-en* 'the horse') are treated in the same manner; they are both bearers of Accent 1. Evidently, the Swedish definite morpheme is invisible to accent assignment.

References

Adger, David. 2006a. Post-syntactic movement and the Old Irish Verb. *Natural Language and Linguistic Theory* 24. 605–654.
Adger, David. 2006b. Stress and phasal syntax. Ms., Queen Mary College, University of London.
Arad, Maya. 2005. *Roots and Patterns: Hebrew Morpho-syntax.* (Studies in Natural Language and Linguistic Theory 63). Dordrecht: Springer.
Bobaljik, Jonathan & Susi Wurmbrand. 2013. Suspension across domains. In Ora Matuschansky & Alec Marantz (eds.), *Distributed Morphology Today: Morphemes for Morris Halle*, 185–198. Cambridge, MA: MIT Press.
Bošković, Zeljko & Howard Lasnik. 1999. How strict is the cycle? *Linguistic Inquiry* 30. 691–703.

---

disyllabic output, even before schwa epenthesis applies. The context for the realization of the empty position by schwa would then be formulated as a requirement that there be a preceding and following consonant. The exact details of the analysis are beyond the scope of this paper.

Bugenhagen, Robert. 1995. *A Grammar of Mangap-Mbula: An Austronesian Language of Papua New Guinea*. Canberra: Australian National University, Pacific Linguistics.
Chomsky, Noam. 2001. Derivation by phase. In Michael Kenstowicz (ed.), *Ken Hale: A Life in Language*, 1–52. Cambridge, MA: MIT Press.
Chomsky, Noam. 2008 On phases. In Robert Freidin, Carlos Otero & Maria-Luisa Zubizarreta (eds.), *Foundational Issues in Linguistic Theory: Essays in Honor of Jean-Roger Vergnaud*, 133–166. Cambridge: MIT Press.
Chomsky, Noam & Morris Halle. 1968. *The Sound Pattern of English*. New York: Harper and Row.
Den Dikken, Marcel. 2007. Phase extension: Contours of a theory of the role of head movement in phrasal extraction. *Theoretical Linguistics* 33. 1–41.
Di Sciullo, Anna-Maria. 2003. Morphological phases. In Huang-Jin Yoon (ed.), *Generative Grammar in a Broader Perspective: Proceedings of the 4th GLOW in Asia*. Korean Generative Grammar Circle & Cognitive Science, Seoul National University, 113–137.
Dobler, Eva. 2008. One DP, two phases: Evidence from phonology. Ms., McGill University.
Dol, Philomena. 2007. *A Grammar of Maybrat*. Canberra: Australia National University.
Embick, David. 2010. *Localism versus Globalism in Morphology and Phonology*. Cambridge, MA: MIT Press.
Embick, David & Alec Marantz. 2008. Architecture and blocking. *Linguistic Inquiry* 39. 1–53.
Embick, David & Rolf Noyer. 2001. Movement operations after syntax. *Linguistic Inquiry* 32. 555–595.
Ewen, Colin & Harry van der Hulst. 2001. *The Phonological Structure of Words*. Cambridge: Cambridge University Press.
Halle, Morris & Alec Marantz. 1993. Distributed morphology and pieces of inflection. In Kenneth Hale & Samuel Keyser (eds.), *The View from Building 20: Essays in Linguistics in Honor of Sylvain Bromberger*, 111–176. Cambridge, MA: MIT Press.
Halle, Morris & Alec Marantz. 1994. Some key features of distributed morphology. In Andrew Carnie & Heidi Harley (eds.), *Papers in Phonology and Morphology. MITWPL* 21. 275–288.
Heck, F. & M. Zimmermann. 2004. DPs as phases. Ms., Universität Leipzig and HU Berlin.
Kaye, Jonathan, Jean Lowenstamm & Jean-Roger Vergnaud. 1990. Constituent structure and government in phonology. *Phonology* 7. 193–231.
Lahiri, Aditi, Allison Wetterlin & Elisabet Jönsson-Steiner. 2005. Lexical specification of tone in North Germanic. *Nordic Journal of Linguistics* 28(1). 61–96.
Legate, Julie. 2003. Some interface properties of the phase. *Linguistic Inquiry* 34. 506–516.
Marantz, Alec. 1988. Clitics, morphological merger, and the mapping to phonological structure. In Michael Hammond & Michael Noonan (eds.), *Theoretical Morphology*, 253–270. San Diego: Academic Press.
Marantz, Alec. 2000. Words. Handout of WCCFL presentation. UCLA.
Marvin, Tatiana. 2002. *Topics in stress and the syntax of words*. Cambridge, MA: MIT Doctoral dissertation.
Matushansky, Ora. 2005. Going through a phase. In Martha McGinnis & Norvin Richards (eds.), *Perspectives on Phases. MIT Working Papers in Linguistics* 49. 157–181.
Newell, Heather. 2004. The phonological phase. *McGill Working Papers in Linguistics* 18(2).
Newell, Heather. 2008. *Aspects of the morphology and phonology of phases*. Montreal: McGill University Doctoral Dissertation.
Newell, Heather & Glyne Piggott. 2014. Interactions at the syntax-phonology interface: Evidence from Ojibwe. *Lingua* 150. 332–362.

Scheer, Tobias. 2004. *A Lateral Theory of Phonology*. Vol. 1: *What Is CVCV, and Why Should It Be?* Berlin: Mouton de Gruyter.

Scheer, Tobias. 2012. *Direct Interface and One-Channel Translation: A Non-Diacritic Theory of the Morphosyntax-Phonology Interface*. Vol. 2 of *A Lateral Theory of Phonology*. Berlin: Mouton de Gruyter.

Shiraishi, Hidetoshi. 2006. *Topics in Nivkh phonology*. Groningen: Groningen Dissertations in Linguistics 61.

Steriopolo, Olga & Martina Wiltschko. 2007. Parameters of variation in the syntax of diminutives. *Annual Meeting of the Canadian Linguistic Association*, University of Saskatchewan, May 26–29, 2007.

Svenonius, Peter. 2004. On the edge. In David Adger, Cécile de Cat & George Tsoulas (eds.), *Peripheries: Syntactic Edges and Their Effects*, 261–287. Dordrecht: Kluwer.

Travis, Lisa de Mena. 1984. *Parameters and effects of word order variation*. Cambridge, MA: MIT Doctoral dissertation.

Tobias Scheer
Recursion in Phonology: Anatomy of a Misunderstanding

Abstract: The absence of recursion in phonology is a long-standing observation: linguists have always wondered why there is such a fundamental difference between morpho-syntax and phonology. The chapter is about the claim often made in phonology that phonological patterns are recursive in the sense of what syntacticians call recursion, that is self-embedding. The endless debate on whether this is the "correct" definition of recursion (there are a number of others out there) is irrelevant: this is the one used in syntax, and the question pursued is whether alleged phonological recursion is the same, or comparable, to what we know form morpho-syntax. Is the formal status of recursion the same on both sides? The chapter shows that the answer is a clear *no*. What some call recursion in phonology is quite different from morpho-syntactic recursion, both regarding the linguistic facts (phenomena) and their formal status. The structures that phonologists call recursive are embedding, but not *self*-embedding. The ubiquitous claim that there is recursion in phonology, often made in order to abide by syntactic standards or to show that morpho-syntax and phonology are not that different after all (in the debate on modularity), is thus prone to a misconception of what syntactic recursion is. This is also the case for the foot- and syllable-internal structures that Harry van der Hulst has developed: they embed, but do not self-embed items, and thus have nothing to do with recursion as understood in syntax.

Keywords: recursion (in syntax), recursion (in phonology), embedding, self-embedding, phonological word

1 Introduction

The absence of recursion in phonology is a long-standing observation: linguists have always wondered why there is such a fundamental difference between morpho-syntax and phonology (Nespor and Vogel 1986: 2; Kaye, Lowenstamm, and Vergnaud 1990: 193; Hauser, Chomsky, and Fitch 2002; Carr 2000: 90, 2006: 642ff; Idsardi 2018).

Tobias Scheer, Université Côte d'Azur, CNRS 7320

https://doi.org/10.1515/9783110730098-014

Pinker and Jackendoff (2005: 211) write that

(1) "Recursion consists of embedding a constituent in a constituent of the same type, for example a relative clause inside a relative clause (*a book that was written by the novelist you met last night*), which automatically confers the ability to do so ad libitum (e.g. *a book [that was written by the novelist [you met on the night [that we decided to buy the boat [that you liked so much]]]]*). This does not exist in phonological structure: a syllable, for instance, cannot be embedded in another syllable." (italics in original)

Before anything may be said about recursion, we must define what we are talking about.[1] Coolidge, Overmann and Wynn (2010: 547) recall that "there is no single, universally accepted definition of recursion. Its definition varies across disciplines (e.g., mathematics, logic, computer science, and linguistics), and it varies within these disciplines, particularly within linguistics". Tomalin (2011: 298) adds that "the notion of 'recursion' was fundamentally ambiguous when it began to be used by linguists in the 1950s, and [. . .] these ambiguities have persisted to the present day. This unfortunate (and needless) perpetuation of imprecision has had a deleterious impact upon recent discussions of the role of recursion in linguistic theory." In concluding his historical survey, Tomalin (2011: 307) identifies nine distinct interpretations of "recursion" that were running in the adult sciences by the time Syntactic Structures appeared (1957). Lobina (2014a, 2014b, 2014c) distinguishes "four distinct senses of the term recursion that can appropriately be applied, or so it will be argued here, to four well-defined theoretical constructs of the cognitive sciences" (Lobina 2014c: 151). In fact there are two much debated questions: 1) what is the actual definition of recursion in the formal (adult) sciences (namely mathematics and computer science), and 2) how do linguistic (in fact: syntactic) phenomena and theorizing relate to that? The former question is addressed in Watumull et al. (2014) and Lobina (2014a) (the latter challenging the former), but we have seen that there does not appear to be a single or "correct" answer. The latter issue is even more eclectic, due to the many different ways in which recursion was used by (especially generative) linguists, that is to say, by syntacticians.

A significant distinction that runs through this literature is the difference between computation and structure. The former is about "defining a function by specifying each of its values in terms of previously defined values" (Cutland 1980: 32), while the latter concerns a static (arboreal) structure that encodes domina-

---

[1] See Idsardi (2018) for another review of the questions discussed below.

tion (e.g. a CP contained in a CP). Linguists tend to equate both since the former may generate the latter: at first by virtue of rewrite rules (*Syntactic Structures*, Chomsky 1957), then through Merge in minimalist times (Chomsky 1995). This is misleading, though, as the literature reminds us (e.g. Lobina 2014c: 152): only a function can be recursive in mathematics, where the notion of structure and dominance does not exist. Lobina (2014c: 163) thus distinguishes (computational) recursion (a function) and its (structural) implementation:[2] "[g]ranted, linguistic expressions also exhibit a binary tree structure, and it is certainly the case that Merge effects this geometry, but crucially it does not do so in the way of a recursive implementation. Recursive generation (successor function) and recursive implementations are different things, even if they may result in similar 'forms'". In his writings, Lobina insists that Chomsky was remarkably consistent in his computational use of recursion: "generative grammar recursively enumerates structural descriptions of sentences" (Chomsky 2006 [1966]: 165), or in the Minimalist Programme: "the operations of C_{HL} [that is, Merge] recursively construct *syntactic objects* from items in N [the Numeration, i.e. lexical items] and syntactic objects already formed" (Chomsky 1995: 226, emphasis in original). But Tomalin (2011: 306) shows that Chomsky has used both computational and structural definitions since his earliest writings: in LSLT, Chomsky (1975 [1955–1956]: 171) says that "certain rules may have a recursive character. Thus *noun phrase* (NP) might be analyzed in such a way that one of its components may be an NP" (emphasis in original).

This intricate debate about terminological confusion which, it seems, is not set to produce much of a consensus, is very much orthogonal to the question pursued in the present contribution. When linguists talk about recursion in phonology, they want to know whether this alleged phonological recursion is the same, or comparable, to what we know form morpho-syntax: is the formal status of recursion the same on both sides? I set out to show that the answer is a clear *no*. What some call recursion in phonology is quite different from morpho-syntactic recursion, both regarding the linguistic facts (phenomena) and their formal status.

In this context, it does not matter whether the word *recursion* is used "correctly" or according to mathematical or whatever other standards. I will take the liberty to use this word in order to refer to what syntacticians (mistakenly or not) believe it characterizes: the goal is not to talk about words and their meaning or usage, but rather to compare syntactic phenomena and analyses with their pho-

---

[2] This contrast appears to be reminiscent of the difference between competence and performance.

nological counterparts. Given this goal, the computational definition of recursion is not operational since, as dwelled on in greater detail in Section 4, there is no concatenation (Merge) in phonology (phonological computation does not glue together pieces originating in long term memory). Therefore, syntax and phonology are incommensurable on the computational side. This is reflected by the fact that alleged phonological recursion is always about structure (see Sections 2 and 3): some item dominates some other item in an arboreal structure.

Therefore, the only means to compare what syntacticians call recursion with what phonologists call recursion is structural in kind. The structural definition of what syntacticians believe to be recursion is provided by the quote under (1) (see also Watumull et al. 2014): a structure is called recursive in morpho-syntax iff it contains two items, A and B, which meet two requirements: 1) they are embedded (one dominates the other) and 2) they are of the same type. The handy term *self-embedding* expresses both conditions (Lobina 2014c). It is shown in Section 3.2 that the structures which phonologists call recursive are embedding, but not *self*-embedding: phonologists who talk about phonological recursion use this word in reference to syntax, but are prone to a misconception of what syntactic recursion is.

Van der Hulst (2010) surveys the growing body of literature where, starting with Ladd (1986), phonologists talk about recursion in phonology. The pages below mean to show that this is a misunderstanding: while phonologists intend a parallel with syntax when using the word *recursion*, the phenomena, structures and analyses they appeal to have nothing to do with what is known from syntax. To show that, three arguments are made in Section 3. First, the linguistic facts are quite different: nobody has ever seen a recursive *phenomenon* in phonology. What we have seen are recursive *analyses* of non-recursive phenomena (Section 3.1). Second, embedding is not recursion, and projection could not possibly be recursion: alleged recursion in phonology involves embedding, but never of the same type of items, i.e. which have identical domination properties) (Section 3.2). Finally, alleged cases of phonological recursion always have limited depth (Section 3.3). The core of the arguments made in the two latter subsections have appeared elsewhere (Vigário 2010; Vogel 2012, 2020; Downing and Kadenge 2020; Golston 2021).

Section 3 is fed by Section 2, which introduces and illustrates what phonologists call recursion: some historical background is discussed, the motivation of alleged phonological recursion is identified, and illustration of particular or widespread analyses is provided.

Finally, Section 4 mentions a particular theory, Strict CV, where dominance relationships in phonology are not expressed in terms of trees, but rather by the genuine contribution of Government Phonology to the field: lateral relations (government and licensing). The rationale for deforestation is that phonology does not concatenate pieces taken from long term memory and therefore has no tree-building device: concatenation, i.e. Merge, is the only source of arboreal structure in syntax. Instead, a core input condition of phonology is linearity, which (minimalist) syntax lacks. Arboreal structure being thus unavailable to phonology, hierarchy is expressed by a different means, which concords with its linear conditions: lateral relations. If there are no trees in phonology, of course the existence of recursion is excluded. No concatenation, no trees – no trees, no recursion.

The broad idea that the cognitive system in general, or language in particular, tends to replicate its workings, rather than to implement distinct devices, is present in some quarters, and, under the heading of Structural Analogy, specifically in the Dependency Phonology tradition that Harry van der Hulst is committed to. Structural Analogy (on which more below) thus holds that the replication of devices across distinct linguistic domains (modules: morpho-syntax, phonology, semantics etc.) and more broadly the cognitive system is the default, and that strong arguments are needed to make the existence of different devices plausible. The present contribution thus (re)produces relevant arguments to this end regarding "recursion", in an attempt to convince Harry.

2 Recursive Analyses of Phonological Phenomena

2.1 Past and Current Practice

Van der Hulst (2010) offers an informed survey of how recursive structure is used in phonology (see also Vogel 2012: 42ff, 2020: 19ff). The general picture is that the higher up a given constituent is in a phonological arboreal structure, the more likely it is to have been analyzed as recursive. Working on intonation, Ladd (1986) has introduced what is held to be recursion in phonological arboreal structure. Especially since in the new OT environment Selkirk (1996) has given up on the Strict Layer Hypothesis (that banned recursion, Selkirk 1981) by demoting nonrecursivity to a violable constraint, the literature abounds in recursive analyses of higher items of the Prosodic Hierarchy: intonational phrases contain intonational phrases, prosodic words contain prosodic words, etc. (e.g. Booij 1996; Hall 1999; Itô and Mester 2007). As stretches become smaller when moving down the Prosodic Hierarchy, recursive analyses of the relevant items become rarer, and once they are below the syllable level, they are almost absent: syllables do not contain syllables, codas do not contain codas. As far as I can see, below the segment, they do not occur at all: nobody has ever argued that in a feature geometric tree, say, V-Place is dominated by another instance of V-Place, or that laryngeal prime dominates laryngeal[0]. Save one exception: Nasukawa's Precedence-free Phonology (Nasukawa 2015, 2017; Backley and Nasukawa 2020), on which more in Section 3.2 and note 9.

This tendency is formalized by Kabak and Revithiadou (2009), who argue that only items at and above the Prosodic Word may be recursive. This is, they contend, because recursive morpho-syntactic structure is mirrored in the phonology. Items below the Prosodic Word (moras, syllables, feet) do not originate in morpho-syntactic structure and therefore are not recursive.

2.2 Van der Hulst's Motivation

The replication of recursive morpho-syntactic structure in the phonology is also one of the two reasons that van der Hulst (2010: 303) believes motivate recursion in phonology: "at higher levels of organization, phonotactic structure tries to match (be isomorphic to) morphotactic structure [...]. This stimulates recursion wherever the morphotactic structure is recursive." The other reason he mentions is the widely held assumption that structure is binary, i.e. that constituents can only have two daughters: this restriction faces the need to incorporate stray items. The typical instance of this dilemma are so-called ternary feet where three syllables need to be parsed (see Section 3.1). If binary branching (here binary feet) is to be respected, a way out is to make the third syllable the daughter of a foot that dominates a foot: $[[\sigma\ \sigma]_{foot}\ \sigma]_{foot}$. Van der Hulst (2010: 304) thus recaps his take on recursion: "I will argue that phonotactics *does* produce recursive structures to (a) incorporate stranded units and (b) achieve isomorphy with morphotactic and thus semantic structure" (emphasis in original).

A deeper motivation for van der Hulst's position regarding recursion in phonology is his Dependency Phonology background. A founding statement of this theory is Structural Analogy: in the words of Durand (1990: 281), Structural Analogy is "[t]he idea is that we should expect the same structural properties to recur at different levels and that very strong support is required to motivate properties which are unique to a given level" (in dependency parlance, *levels* or *planes* are modules: syntax, morphology, phonology, etc.). Structural Analogy was introduced by Anderson (1985) and developed in a sizeable body of literature, among which two book-length syntheses by Anderson 1992, 2011: vol. 3). Here is the opening sentence of an article entitled "Why phonology is the same" by van der Hulst (2005): "In this short contribution, I would like to discuss and defend the idea that phonology and (morpho-)syntax are organized in parallel ways. Thus, I take issue with views that explicitly regard phonology as different, or implicitly adopt different theoretical models in both domains."

Structural analogies have been argued for properties from different modules, claiming that they have the same essence. Such pairs include case relations (theta roles) and phonemic systems, which Anderson (1986: 86, 1992: 58ff) holds to be expressions of contrast. Also, adjuncts in syntax (circumstantials in DP vocabulary) are argued to instantiate the same "stray argument" structure as extrametrical consonants in phonology (Anderson, 1986: 88, 1992: 66ff).

Regarding the specific issue of recursion, van der Hulst (2010: 302) writes: "I will promote the idea that recursion is part of the 'tactic planes' of language. Being within the reach of our human cognitive capacities, both phonotactics and morphotactics make use of it, albeit it [sic] to different degrees." What he means is that there is less recursion in phonology than in morpho-syntax because the desire to mimic morpho-syntactic recursive structure is moderated by phonetic substance: "what would perhaps be optimal recursion in phonology (from the view point of achieving maximal isomorphy) is counterbalanced (i.e. flattened) by the inherent sequential, rhythm and iterative drive of the phonetic substance" (van der Hulst 2010: 304).

2.3 Van der Hulst's Take on Infra-syllabic Recursion: Syllables in Syllables

Although on van der Hulst's view there is less recursion in phonology than there is in morpho-syntax, he takes exception with the idea that there is no recursion of items that are syllable-sized or smaller. He especially rejects the idea that there are no syllables in syllables, as Pinker and Jackendoff contend under (1).

As far as I can see, the very rare analyses where alleged recursion occurs below the syllable node follow the idea introduced by Levin (1985) whereby syllabic constituents are projections of the syllable centre, the nucleus. That is, the syllable is an instantiation of syntactic X-bar structure where the nucleus is X^0, the rhyme X' and the syllable N". The onset adjoins to N", while the coda plugs into X': the regular structure [[onset [nucleus coda]$_{rhyme}$]$_{syll}$ is thus reinterpreted as [[onset [N^0 coda]$_{N'}$]$_{N''}$. Although on syntactic standards this is about projection, not recursion (items are embedded, but not of the same kind), and although there cannot be any recursion in a projection-based structure (see Section 3.2), Levin's take introduced what phonologists (erroneously) thought was syntactic recursion. Smith (1999) follows this logic, and so does GP2.0 (Pöchtrager 2006; Pöchtrager and Kaye 2013) as well as van der Hulst (2010). Consider van der Hulst's (2010: 310) take on sub-syllabic recursion under (2)a.

(2) a. syllable   b. foot

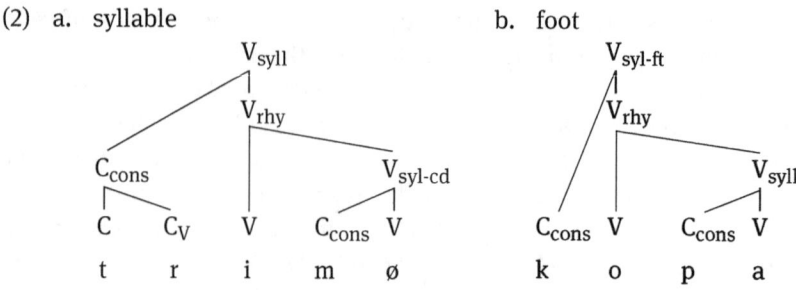

In van der Hulst's view, the structure is recursive since a C may be dominated by another C (note that C_V "C over V" is the Dependency notation for a sonorant, i.e. here the second member of a branching onset), and a V may be dominated by another V. Van der Hulst subscribes to the Strict CV idea that the phonological identity of coda consonants is to be followed by an empty nucleus (while onset consonants are followed by a filled nucleus, Lowenstamm 1996; Scheer 2004). Therefore the final consonant of *trim* is followed by an empty nucleus. Given the presence of the empty nucleus, this Cø unit must somehow be a syllable following the logic that syllables are headed by nuclei. But since the nucleus of Cø is empty, van der Hulst considers it somehow unsuited to stand on its own feet. Therefore, instead of assigning it its own independent syllable node, he makes the syllable node dominating Cø a dependent of the rhyme. This is thus a compromise of Strict CV where coda consonants are followed by an empty nucleus, and the canonical syllable structure where they are a dependent of the rhyme. Or, in other words, codahood is expressed twice.

Given this situation where an empty-headed syllable Cø (which van der Hulst assigns an extra label, $V_{syl\text{-}coda}$, knowing that V_{syll} is the syllable node) is dominated by a syllable whose head is filled (V_{syll}), van der Hulst concludes that "[i]t is precisely this possibility that invokes the kind of recursion that is generally held impossible: a syllable inside a syllable."

The structure under (2)b is van der Hulst's take of a (trochaic) foot: the only difference with (2)a (save the non-branching onset) is that the second V is filled. Regular feet dominate two syllables, but van der Hulst takes a different view: the prominence of the leftmost syllable in a trochaic foot is marked by the fact that the dependent syllable is dominated by the rhyme of the dominant syllable. Thus, van der Hulst (2010: 311) concludes, "'feet' are syllables that happen to *contain* another syllable" (emphasis in original).

3 What Is Called Recursion in Phonology Has Nothing to Do with Recursion in Morpho-syntax

3.1 Recursive Phenomena vs. Recursive Analyses of Non-recursive Phenomena

As far as I can see, all cases of alleged phonological recursion are due to a decision made by the analyst, in presence of alternative analytical options. The typical pattern is this: there is some principle that needs to be obeyed, but data do not fit. In order to avoid the violation of the principle, an extra layer is introduced in the arboreal structure that is dubbed X' where X is the regular layer at hand. Thus foot binarity requires that a foot dominates exactly two syllables. In case a word has an uneven number of syllables, a stray syllable begs the question (3)a: a ternary foot could be built as under (3)b, in violation of foot binarity (Rice 1992). Such a violation can be avoided if the analyst decides to introduce an extra arboreal layer where the stray syllable attaches to, as under (3)c. Since the whole operation is about grouping syllables into feet, the constituent of the extra layer must somehow be a foot, and this is how foot prime (or whatever the label, e.g. superfoot) comes into being. This is a widespread analysis (see Martínez-Paricio and Kager 2015).

(3) a. stray syllable   b. ternary foot   c. layered feet

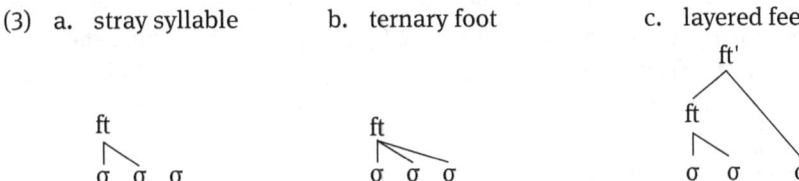

There is reason to believe that this pattern is general: recursive structure in phonology only exists in order to satisfy some theoretical purpose, which on van der Hulst's take may be either the incorporation of stray items into an otherwise binary structure, or the mimicking of morpho-syntactic recursive structure (see Section 2.2). If the theory were different, i.e. if there were no principle of foot binarity or the idea that phonological structure mimics morpho-syntactic structure, there would be no recursion. In other words, alleged phonological recursion is always theory-born: it is created by the analyst in order to satisfy some specific assumptions.

There is no phonological *phenomenon*, though, that is recursive in any pre-theoretical or pre-analytical sense, or which would suggest or demand recursive structure. By contrast in morpho-syntax, recursive phenomena abound: this is what Pinker and Jackendoff (2005) refer to under (1). Thus a clause may occur within another clause and in many languages an overt complementizer marks this subordination (*Peter thinks [that John says [that Amy believes [that . . .]]]*); or a PP dominates another PP (*Jil wants to read [[in the book [on the shelve]]*), or a morpheme is repeated (Czech *děl-at* "to do", *děl-áv-at* "to do repeatedly/often", *děl-áv-áv at* "to do even more often", *děl-áv-áv-áv-at* "to do really really often", etc.). Here recursion owes nothing to any theoretical principle, or the avoidance of a violation thereof. It is a descriptive fact of the language, pre-theoretical and pre-analytical. It is also independent of the choices or theoretical inclination of the analyst: whatever they are, there is no way to avoid a recursive structure for these items – a CP dominating a CP, a PP dominating a PP, a given suffix dominating a copy of the same suffix, etc.[3]

All this is absent from phonology: there is no overt manifestation of recursion, there is no recursive phenomenon. In morpho-syntax, recursion is a fact about language, while in phonology alleged cases of recursion are a fact about the analyst.

A consequence of the purely analytic nature of recursion in phonology is that recursive analyses of non-recursive phenomena may be and actually are challenged by competing, non-recursive analyses. Thus Vigário (2010), Vogel (2012) and Downing and Kadenge (2020) argue against the recursion of prosodic words (ω dominated by ω') on the grounds that the different ω's of layered prosodic words have different formal properties and thus represent distinct prosodic constituents above (the prosodic word group PWG on Vigário's, the composite group on Vogel's take, this item being reminiscent of Nespor and Vogel's 1986 original clitic group), or below the prosodic word (the phonological stem PStem, Downing and Kadenge).

In the same way, based on the languages that are quoted as the strongest case for ternary rhythm, Golston (2021: 10) "show[s] that none of these languages requires ternary feet if we assume that some mechanism keeps the number of feet minimal." Regarding the language Tripura Bangla, Golston (in press: 4) writes: "[t]he source for Tripura Bangla, Das 2001, shows that Tripura Bangla alternates binary, ternary, and quaternary stress and his analysis shows that none of it requires ternary feet".

Also, recursive analyses of non-recursive phenomena may be and actually are challenged on empirical grounds. Thus Golston (2021: 10) regarding layered feet

---

3 Coming from the quarters of psychology and computer science, though, some argue that recursion does not exist in language, or is unnecessary: according to Paap and Partridge (2014), descriptions can do or are better off with no recursion, and this way the trouble caused by the infinity issue disappears.

(3)c: "[p]ublished work on this important dialect of Yupik is based on Leer (1985a, 1985b, 1985c). Leer (1993/1994) updates the data and generalizations, however, leading him to reject major parts of his earlier work including ternary feet."

Finally, recursive analyses of non-recursive phenomena may be and actually are challenged with respect to their predictions: Golston (2021: 23) argues that recursive feet "predict too many prosodic domains [. . . and] too many feet."

Try to imagine an equivalent in syntax: would anybody venture to challenge the existence of recursive structure in syntax as such by proposing competing non-recursive analyses? Or on empirical grounds? Or regarding the predictions made? I am not aware of any such attempts, which are absent because recursion is a linguistic fact in syntax, but only an analytic option in phonology. On occasion, recursive and non-recursive analyses of syntactic data may compete (this was the case of the Pirahã debate, Everett 2005; Nevins, Pesetsky, and Rodrigues 2009), but nobody has challenged the very existence of syntactic recursion in natural language. This is what the literature mentioned intends regarding alleged phonological recursion, tough, based on analytic, empirical and predictive grounds.

3.2 Confusion of Recursion and Embedding

Recursion and embedding are not the same thing. Similar-looking items that dominate each other may or may not instantiate recursion. To illustrate, consider the three-layer X-bar structure under (4)a,b that was imported from syntax (see Section 2.3). This structure does not instantiate any recursion, neither in syntax nor in its phonological adaptation. Recall that recursion is about different copies of a given item in a tree where one dominates the other. Crucially, we are talking about copies of the *same* item (*self*-embedding). In case different items are in a dominance relationship, they are simply embedded and there is no recursion.

An X-bar structure contains three perfectly distinct items that have idiosyncratic properties: X_0, X' and XP, as under (4)a. They are defined by their position in the structure, i.e. by their mothers, sisters and daughters. X_0 dominates a lexical item and is the daughter of X'. X' directly dominates X_0 as well as its complement (a lower XP), and is the daughter of its own XP. Finally, XP is the mother of X' and Spec (another XP); it is dominated by the X' of a higher XP. None of these items can occur anywhere else in the structure, or have any other mothers, sisters and daughters. They are different individuals with quite distinct properties and thus *not* copies of the same item. But they are in a projection relationship: X_0 projects X' and XP. All of this also applies to the phonological avatar of (4)a, the X-bar syllable under (4)b.

A situation where two copies of the *same* item are in a dominance relation is shown under (4)d: a CP containing a CP. Note that both copies of the CP have the exact same properties: they have the same mother, sister and daughter, that is, they may occur in the exact same positions in the tree. This is not the case for, say, N′ under (4)b, which obviously cannot occur in the position of N or N″. The same goes for, say, X⁰ under (4)a, which is not interchangeable with X′ or XP.

Chris Golston has pointed out another argument to me: in syntax, two copies of the same XP cannot directly dominate each other, i.e. stand in a mother-daughter relationship. That is, the lower CP under (4)d is separated from the higher CP by other constituents. In phonology, though, this is the standard situation of alleged recursion: a V directly dominates another V (2)a,b (even if different descriptive labels are added: V_{rhy}, V_{syll}, $V_{syl\text{-}ft}$, $V_{syl\text{-}cd}$ etc.), a foot directly dominates a foot (3)c, a syllable directly dominates another syllable (4)c, an I directly dominates another I (4)e. This also shows that alleged recursion in phonology is quite different from the recursion that occurs in morpho-syntax.

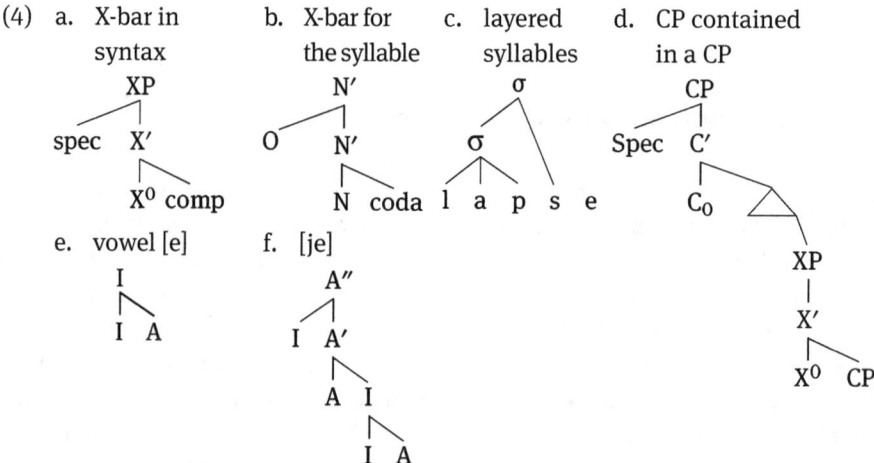

Therefore syntacticians would not venture talking about X_0, X′ and XP as versions of the same object: projection is the transmission of some property, but this does not make the items involved identical or interchangeable. Thus no syntactician would say that X_0, X′ and XP entertain a recursive relationship. But this is what phonologists do when considering equivalent structures.

Note that all this is still the case in minimalist times where rigid X-bar structure as such is abandoned, giving way to individual Merge operations that build constituents only if needed (e.g. Fukui and Narita 2014). Whatever the projecting and the projected item (and no matter how Merge, projection or labelling exactly work), they are not identical, not interchangeable and do not instantiate recursion.

The graphical resemblance of items that dominate each other, and typically are understood as projections of one another, as under (4)b,c or the layered feet under (3)c, though, is enough for phonologists to believe that the structure at hand is recursive and thus that phonology has recursion just the way syntax does. This is a misconception: projection is not recursion, and embedding isn't either. Phonologists do not consider the crucial question whether the items at hand have the same or different properties, i.e. are copies of the same object or distinct objects. A projection relationship as under (4)a–c and (3)c could not possibly represent recursion: this is excluded by definition since the properties of the items at different levels of projection are distinct.

Thus under (4)b, N' is just another word for rhyme: it has the exact same properties, can only dominate a nucleus and a coda, and can only be dominated by the syllable node (or its code name N"). Changing the graphical appearance of labels in the attempt to indicate that they entertain a projection relationship does not change anything to their essence or properties: a rhyme aka. N' is a rhyme, and its properties are distinct from those of all other items under (4)b. The same of course goes for N", and also for the layered feet under (3)c. The item called ft necessarily dominates two syllables and its mother is ft'. By contrast, ft' can only dominate ft and a syllable (Martínez-Paricio and Kager 2015: 465 are explicit on that: they do not allow ft' to dominate two ft). This is just more of the same: phonologists wish to express that both items are somehow feet, i.e. relevant for stress, and thus decide to use the same label "ft" while making one the projection of the other. But their properties are perfectly distinct.

The same goes for van der Hulst's representations under (2): there are many "V"s, suggesting resemblance and embodying the wish to express projection (the straight line relating V, V_{rhy} and V_{syll} and/or $V_{syl\text{-}ft}$) or the idea that a somehow dependent syllable (having an empty nucleus under (2)a, being unstressed under (2)b) is dominated by a V since all syllables are V-dominated. All of these V-items (V, V_{rhy}, V_{syll}, $V_{syl\text{-}cd}$, $V_{syl\text{-}ft}$) are very different, though: they can only occupy the specific place in the tree that they appear in, defined by mothers, sisters and daughters. That is, they are just regular rhymes, syllable nodes etc. under a different code name. Therefore the structures under (2) illustrate embedding and maybe projection, but certainly not recursion.

This is also the case of (4)e and (4)f, which are taken from Nasukawa (2015: 232f). The former represents the vowel [e]: Nasukawa expresses the traditional GP notion of headedness by dominance (or projection). The two Elements that make the vowel, I and A, produce a projection that defines the dominant item: I is dominated by another I under (4)e to produce [e] (if A projects another A, the result is [ɛ]). Under (4)f, the structure of (4)e is the most embedded piece, which is dominated by A' that represents the nucleus. A" is the syllable node, whose dependent is the I representing the onset [j]. Thus A, the baseline timbre in Nasukawa's approach, projects A' and A" where A' is the rhyme and A" the syllable node. Again there is multiply embedded A, but no recursion anywhere since the different As are distinct objects with contrasting dominance relations which for that reason are not interchangeable.

Next consider (4)c, which was proposed by McCarthy (1979: 453) for the analysis of Classical Arabic heavy syllables (bearing a long vowel or a short vowel plus a consonant) that are followed by another consonant and the end of the word (here represented by the English word *lapse*). Things are as before: phonologists have established some principle (nothing can be added to the right edge of a heavy syllable, either universally or in a specific language, and final consonants cannot be onsets) and then face adverse evidence which somehow needs to be accommodated. Adjoining the stray item to a projection of the basic constituent is a solution. McCarthy may have stood alone (in the generative realm) with this analysis in these early days of generative syllable structure (where there was no syllable-internal constituency yet), and the same empirical situation was quickly accounted for by other means that do not involve recursion: an edge-specific constituent (coming in various guises: appendix, termination etc.) or extrasyllabicity. Also note that like in the previous example involving feet, the dominating σ (which McCarthy does not note as σ': he says it is Chomsky-adjoined to the lower σ) has quite different properties with respect to the dominated σ: it can only dominate another σ and a consonant, while the lower σ dominates a CVC or a CVV string.

In account of this, Golston (2021: 30) says that calling internally layered feet (ILT), i.e. (3)c, recursive in the syntactic sense "would require that the Xs have the same properties, that they be the same kind of thing, and this is clearly not the case. [. . .] ILT footing is simply embedding (which is ubiquitous in phonology), but not *self*-embedding" (emphasis in original).

In the same way, Vogel (2012) observes that

> [a]ccording to the definition of recursion, the embedded PWs should be the same type of constituent as the ones in which they are embedded, and thus exhibit the same properties. The rule of Intervocalic s-Voicing (ISV) in northern varieties of Italian shows that this view is problematic. ISV results in the pronunciation of intervocalic 's' as [z] between vowels within a PW, so if all PWs are the same type of constituent, we would expect ISV to apply to the various instances of 's' in (3). This prediction is incorrect, however (i.e. *[lo *[z]i ri [*[z]ostitu-isce]$_{PW}$]$_{PW}$, [[gira]$_{PW}$ [*[z]ole]$_{PW}$]$_{PW}$*). Thus, despite the claim that such structures are recursive, the fact that the properties of the inner and outer PWs are different conflicts with the usual definitions of recursion and constituent. That is, we do not observe the 'embedding [of] a constituent in a constituent of the same type.' Vogel (2012: 45)

In a more recent overview of proposals that do away with the Strict Layer Hypothesis, i.e. with the prohibition of recursion, Vogel (2020) notes this:

> [i]t is usual to account for the similarity in linguistic behavior of different types of strings by analyzing them as the same type of constituent (C); strings that show distinct types of behavior are analyzed as different types of constituents. Thus, in a recursive structure in which a particular type of constituent C is embedded within another C of the same type, it would be expected that both Cs would exhibit the same behavior. As seen above, however, proposals have been advanced in which the same constituent label is used for structures with divergent properties. Vogel (2020: 24f)

Let us now return to the two motivations for phonological recursion that van der Hulst has identified (Section 2.2): isomorphism with morpho-syntactic structure and the adjunction of stray items. As far as I can see, all cases of the latter are instances of the pattern described: motivated by some theory-internal principle, phonologists choose a particular tree structure and in an attempt to express some phonological properties, decide to label nodes in such a way that they look graphically akin.

The other source of alleged recursion in phonology, isomorphism with morpho-syntactic structure, is interesting insofar as it shows that the confusion between recursion and embedding (or projection) also extends to the morpho-syntactic side. The argument made by Selkirk (1996: 204f) takes the following shape. Object cliticization in English is optional: *need him* may be pronounced either with a full (*need* [hɪm]) or a reduced (*need* [m]) clitic. Optional cliticization occurs in syntax, which outputs two distinct structures: [V [Det]$_{DP}$]$_{VP}$ and [V Pro]$_V$. Alignment and other constraints convert the former into the regular non-recursive prosodic structure ((need)$_{PWd}$ (him)$_{PWd}$)$_{PPh}$ where *him* remains unreduced in account of its independent PWd status. By contrast, the latter is converted into ((need)$_{PWd}$ him)$_{PWd}$ where a PWd is dominated by another PWd and *him* is reduced because it is not protected by a PWd of its own. The reason for this phonological recursion of prosodic words, Selkirk argues, is simply the syntactic recursive structure that it was born from through faithful mapping (high ranking alignment constraints): [V Pro]$_V$ where V is dominated by a V. This is what van der Hulst (2010: 303f) and Kabak and Revithiadou (2009) mean when they say that one raison d'être of recursion in phonology is the faithful replication of recursive morpho-syntactic structure.

The problem is that, as was shown, there is no recursion on the phonological side: the domination of a PWd by another PWd is embedding (or projection), but not recursion. The fact that what is mistakenly interpreted as recursion in phonology is said to stem from a recursive structure in syntax shows that phonologists also export their misconceived idea of recursion to its home module, syntax: [V Pro]$_V$ where a V dominates another V is not any more recursive in syntax than ((need)$_{PWd}$ him)$_{PWd}$ is in phonology.

More generally regarding the idea that phonology somehow replicates or the recursion of syntactic structure, Idsardi (2018) shows that this may not be replication, but rather inheritance. That is, phonology is not doing anything to mimic syntactic recursion (there is no recursive mechanism in phonology): it just inherits recursive structure from syntax. This "eliminate[s] the need for recursive structure within the phonology, accomplishing the necessary marking within the recursive Merge calculation while maintaining non-recursive phonological structures" (Idsardi 2018: 217).

3.3 Unlimited Depth of Recursion

A basic property of recursion in morpho-syntax is its unlimited depth. This follows from the definition of recursion: the ability to embed an item in another item of the same kind. As Pinker and Jackendoff note in the quote under (1) (or Watumull et al. 2014: 4), the number of iterations of this operation is unrestricted: nothing in the operation itself imposes any limits.

Restrictions on the depth of recursion are rooted in factors that lie outside of grammar, such as memory (see Koopman 2014; Stabler 2014). Speakers lose track after two or three levels of recursion: *Mary said that Paul thought that Amy considered that David asked Helen to buy the car*, or center embedded *John whom June whom Paul whom Jean whom Dick hates adores prefers detests loves Mary*.[4]

It is thus to be expected that the alleged cases of phonological recursion, were they real instances of recursion, follow the same pattern. But they do not: the depth of phonological recursion is implicitly or explicitly restricted to one or two levels, but never for grammar-external reasons as in morpho-syntax. Instead of these factors, grammar-internal reasons are invoked.

Most often authors call a given structure recursive but do not address the question why the maximum depth of the particular recursive item is one, i.e. why further recursion of the item is impossible (or does not occur). At other times, authors explicitly set a limit of recursion, to one level of depth. This is the case of Martínez-Paricio and Kager (2015: 465): "[r]ecursion at the foot level is minimal: feet display maximally one layer of recursion." On p. 494, the authors motivate this move against expected unboundedness by the fact that unlike higher constituents starting with the prosodic word, feet are not born from a mapping of

---

[4] Karlsson (2007, 2010) has studied the depth of recursion (in its various guises: initial, final and nested, the latter known as center-embedding) in actual speech production (oral and written corpora) and identified a number of factors that limit recursive depth. In his data, the maximum depth of recursion is three (but even instances of three are very rare).

morpho-syntactic structure, which may be itself recursive. Items below the word level thus do not inherit possible recursion from morpho-syntax and are therefore not or only mildly recursive (this is along the lines of Kabak and Revithiadou 2009).[5] Golston (2021: 29) remains unconvinced, though: "recursion elsewhere (in phonology, syntax, semantics, math, computer science) is never limited to 'maximally one layer', which seems like a contradiction in terms."

Another restriction of the depth of embedding is due to the import of syntactic X-bar structure mentioned in Section 2.3: X_0 is supposed to project an X' and an XP, or *maximal* projection. Following this logic which restricts embedding to maximally two levels, Itô and Mester (2007, 2013) allow the phonological word ω and the phonological phrase Φ to project twice until the maximal projection is reached (in their view, by adding a prosodic adjunct at each level; note the intended parallel with syntactic adjunction).[6]

4 No Concatenation, No Trees – No Trees, No Recursion

In morpho-syntax, dominance and hence arboreal structure are the consequence of concatenation, i.e. the fact of drawing pieces from long term memory and gluing them together. In minimalist times, this operation is called Merge.[7] Note that in morpho-syntax, concatenation is the *only* source of dominance and arbo-

---

[5] The authors do not mention that more than one level of recursion does not appear to make sense given the phonological properties of feet. Adding a level of recursion would produce [[[σ σ]ft σ]ft' σ]ft'', but the principle of foot binarity which is at the origin of ft' that accommodates a "stray" syllable will of course warrant two binary feet for the four syllables at hand: [σ σ]ft [σ σ]ft. That is, no embedding or recursion of any kind is needed. Therefore in this case (as well as in van der Hulst's structures under (2)), the very principles creating an allegedly recursive structure may also be responsible for the maximum depth of recursion, "set" to one.
[6] The typologically oriented work by Schiering, Bickel, and Hildebrandt (2010) argues that eight or more layers of the prosodic word are needed for descriptive purposes, but acknowledges that items on each layer are different objects: demarcative word, culminative word, harmonic word, metrical word etc. These objects are thus estranged from the ambition of self-embedding that is found elsewhere: they have different properties and hence are not of the same kind.
[7] This is also true if labelling and the hierarchical relationship of the items merged are determined independently of the bare merge operation (Chomsky 2013; Collins & Stabler 2016: 64f; Cecchetto & Donati 2015). No dominance or hierarchy can exist without items having been merged. Note that here and below the term *concatenation* only refers to the operation whereby items taken from long term memory are glued together. Syntax does that, but phonology does not.

real structure. No domination relation or arboreal structure ever occurs that does not involve a (prior) merge operation.

In phonology and semantics, there is no concatenation: in production, these modules work on the string that was pieced together by morpho-syntax. Neither phonology nor semantics ever access long term memory in order to retrieve pieces and glue them together.[8] This distinction between a concatenative (morpho-syntax) and two interpretative (phonology, semantics) computational systems, ordered in the way discussed (in production), is the very foundation of generative grammar: the inverted T model was introduced in Aspects (Chomsky 1965: 15ff) and ever since stands unchallenged in generative quarters.

If there is no concatenation in phonology, and if the only source of trees is concatenation, how then could there be any phonological trees at all? No concatenation, no trees. But if there are no trees in phonology, how could there be recursion? No trees, no recursion. Since recursion as defined under (1) is about dominance in a tree, no item can possibly dominate any other item in absence of trees (Scheer 2004: xliv, 2011: §§45f, 2013).

It thus appears that dominance / trees in morpho-syntax and in phonology, should they exist in the latter, are quite different objects. If phonological trees exist in absence of concatenation, what are their properties? And how do they come into being? Certainly nothing can be inferred from the properties of morpho-syntactic trees: there is no reason why branching should be binary for example. And there is no way to import labelling of non-terminal nodes from its workings in syntax (Chomsky 2013; Cecchetto and Donati 2015). But the crucial difference of phonological trees with respect to their morpho-syntactic cousins is the fact that they are built on an input string that comes in one single piece: the trees that occur in the phonological literature are built on a linearized string of items (say, segments, or Elements / features[9]) over which an arboreal structure is

---

8 Making up new words is combining segments taken form long term memory. But this is a practice restricted to the creation of nonce words: regular new words (acronyms etc.) always come in through an auditory (or visual) stimulus. In production phonology, i.e. where strings that are online-created by morpho-syntax are interpreted, no concatenation of pieces taken from long-term memory occurs. And this is also true for nonce words made up by the speaker, which need to be lexicalized before they undergo production phonology and then behave just like any other lexical item.

9 In Nasukawa's Precedence-free Phonology (Nasukawa 2015, 2017; Backley and Nasukawa 2020), the phonological structure of morphemes based on a linear string of phonological primes (Elements), rather than of segments (the latter have no phonological status). There is thus a mechanism that builds structure based on phonological items (results are shown under (4)a,f), but these 1) are linearized beforehand (there is no way to predict linearity from anything: *tea* and *eat* are different), 2) do not originate in the lexicon (they are defined in perception by the

erected, i.e. where dominance relationships are defined. This never ever occurs in morpho-syntax: items are not linearized, and arboreal structure is never established over a single piece.

Therefore, a minimal conclusion should be that phonological trees are quite different from morpho-syntactic trees. And that, consequently, the latter cannot serve as motivation, justification or example for the existence of the former. Phonological trees, should they exist, have different workings. Chris Golston has pointed out to me that hierarchical structure elsewhere in the cognitive system is probably not due to syntactic Merge: hierarchy occurs in vision (Martins, Martins, and Fitch 2016) or higher cognitive functions where e.g. individuals are grouped into a family, or are part of social hierarchies (Fitch and Martins 2014). This is certainly true and it would be very interesting to see whether the trees known from the analysis of phonology share properties with non-linguistic hierarchical structure in the cognitive system. As far as I can see, no-one has tried to look into that for the time being. But as was shown in Sections 2 and 3, phonologists constantly take morpho-syntactic trees as a reference when building phonological trees. It should be understood that this is misguided.

Now consider an established alternative to the arboreal encoding of hierarchy in phonology: in Government Phonology (Kaye, Lowenstamm, and Vergnaud 1990; Kaye 1990), syllable structure is not expressed in terms of a syllabic arborescence, but rather in terms of lateral relations, i.e. government and licensing. For example, a coda consonant is not defined by its affiliation to a coda constituent which itself is dominated by the rhyme, but rather by the lateral relation that it entertains with the following syllabic item: a coda consonant is a consonant that occurs before a (governed) empty nucleus, while an onset consonant is followed by an (ungoverned) filled nucleus. It displays coda (weak) properties because its nucleus, being governed and empty, is unable to license or govern it (while ungoverned nuclei can govern and license their onset).

The programme of Strict CV (Lowenstamm 1996; Scheer 2004) is to take this lateral perspective on phonological hierarchy to its logical end, an entirely flat phonology (Scheer 2013). The absence of arboreal structure also extends to items of the prosodic hierarchy (Scheer 2008, 2011: §§45f, 2012).

In this perspective, hierarchical structure is thus implemented in module-specific ways: concatenation in syntax (Merge) produces trees, while linearity in phonology is the source of lateral relations. Note that concatenation and

---

auditory stimulus of the to-be-lexicalized morphemes) and 3) are not the result of concatenation. Nasukawa (2015: 219) says that the primes at hand are combined into structure by "a syntax-like structure-building operation in phonology", but it is unclear what exactly is syntax-like if the string over which the operation works is linearized and not the result of concatenation.

linearity are necessary design properties of their respective modules. There is no grammar in absence of the concatenation of pieces that are independently stored in long-term memory, and there is no speech without linearity: linguistic structure needs to be linearized in order for speakers to be able to encode it physically, i.e. in the vocal or signed modality.

The absence of linearity from syntax is a leading idea of the minimalist programme: syntax is about hierarchy, not linearity. Linearity is imposed upon speech by interface conditions: it must not be part of the computational system that creates hierarchical structure over lexical items by piecing them together (Chomsky 1995: 334).

Concatenation and linearity are thus in complementary distribution: concatenation is present in syntax but absent from phonology, while linearity is an input condition of phonology that is unknown in syntax. This correlates with the existence of different means to express hierarchy: phonology has no trees because it does not concatenate anything; there cannot be any lateral relations in syntax in absence of linearity. That is, trees in syntax and lateral relations in phonology are two ways of expressing hierarchy that are adapted to the design properties of their environment.

Quite independently of the preceding, Neeleman and van de Koot (2006) arrive at the same conclusion, i.e. the absence of trees in phonology. Trees have certain formal properties that make predictions regarding the type of phenomena that should be found in a tree-bearing environment. These include projection, long-distance dependencies and recursion. The authors show that phonological phenomena do not display these properties. They thus conclude that the presence of trees in phonology overgenerates: arboreal structure predicts things that are absent from the record.

References

Anderson, John. 1985. Structural analogy and dependency phonology. *Acta Linguistica Hafniensia* 19. 5–44.
Anderson, John. 1986. Structural analogy and case grammar. *Lingua* 70. 79–129.
Anderson, John. 1992. *Linguistic Representation: Structural Analogy and Stratification*. Berlin/New York: Mouton de Gruyter.
Anderson, John. 2011. *The Substance of Language. Vol. 1: The Domain of Syntax. Vol. 2: Morphology, Paradigms, and Periphrases. Vol. 3: Phonology-Syntax Analogies*. Oxford: Oxford University Press.
Backley, Phillip & Kuniya Nasukawa. 2020. Recursion in melodic-prosodic structure. In Kuniya Nasukawa (ed.), *Morpheme-Internal Recursion in Phonology*, 11–35. Berlin: de Gruyter.

Booij, Geert. 1996. Cliticization as prosodic integration: The case of Dutch. *The Linguistic Review* 13. 219–242.
Carr, Philip. 2000. Scientific realism, sociophonetic variation, and innate endowments in phonology. In Noel Burton-Roberts, Philip Carr & Gerard Docherty (eds.), *Phonological Knowledge: Conceptual and Empirical Issues*, 67–104. Oxford: Oxford University Press.
Carr, Philip. 2006. Universal grammar and syntax/phonology parallelisms. *Lingua* 116. 634–656.
Cecchetto, Carlo & Caterina Donati. 2015. *(Re)labeling*. Cambridge, MA: MIT Press.
Chomsky, Noam. 1957. *Syntactic Structures*. Mouton: La Haye.
Chomsky, Noam. 1965. *Aspects of the Theory of Syntax*. Cambridge, MA: MIT Press.
Chomsky, Noam. 1975 [1955–1956]. *The Logical Structure of Linguistic Theory*. New York: Plenum.
Chomsky, Noam. 1995. *The Minimalist Program*. Cambridge, MA: MIT Press.
Chomsky, Noam. 2006 [1966]. *Language and Mind*. Cambridge: Cambridge University Press.
Chomsky, Noam. 2013. Problems of projection. *Lingua* 130. 33–49.
Collins, Chris & Edward Stabler. 2016. A formalization of minimalist syntax. *Syntax* 19. 43–78.
Coolidge, Frederick L., Karenleigh A. Overmann & Thomas Wynn. 2010. Recursion: What is it, who has it, and how did it evolve? *WIREs Cognitive Science* 2. 547–554.
Cutland, Nigel. 1980. *Computability: An Introduction to Recursion Function Theory*. Cambridge: Cambridge University Press.
Downing, Laura & Maxwell Kadenge. 2020. Re-placing PStem in the prosodic hierarchy. *The Linguistic Review* 37. 433–461.
Durand, Jacques. 1990. *Generative and Non-linear Phonology*. London/New York: Longman.
Everett, Daniel L. 2005. Cultural constraints on grammar and cognition in Pirahã: Another look at the design features of human language. *Current Anthropology* 46. 621–646.
Fitch, Tecumseh & Maurício Dias Martins. 2014. Hierarchical processing in music, language, and action: Lashley revisited. *Annals of the New York Academy of Sciences* 1316. 87–104.
Fukui, Naoki & Hiroki Narita. 2014. Merge, labeling, and projection. In Andrew Carnie, Yosuke Sato & Daniel Siddiqi (eds.), *The Routledge Handbook of Syntax*, 3–23. New York: Routledge.
Golston, Chris. 2021. No stress system requires recursive feet. *Catalan Journal of Linguistics* 20. 9–35.
Hall, Tracy. 1999. The phonological word: A review. In Tracy Hall & Ursula Kleinhenz (eds.), *Studies on the Phonological Word*, 1–22. Philadelphia: Benjamins.
Hauser, Marc, Noam Chomsky & Tecumseh Fitch. 2002. The faculty of language: What is it, who has it, and how did it evolve? *Science* 298. 1569–1579.
Hulst, Harry van der. 2005. Why phonology is the same. In Hans Broekhuis, Norbert Corver, Riny Huybregts, Ursula Kleinhenz & Jan Koster (eds.), *Organizing Grammar: Studies in Honor of Henk van Riemsdijk*, 252–262. Berlin: Mouton de Gruyter.
Hulst, Harry van der. 2010. A note on recursion in phonology. In Harry van der Hulst (ed.), *Recursion and Human Language*, 301–341. Berlin: de Gruyter.
Idsardi, William. 2018. Why is phonology different? No recursion. In Ángel J. Gallego & Roger Martin (eds.), *Language, Syntax, and the Natural Sciences*, 212–223. Cambridge: Cambridge University Press.
Itô, Junko & Armin Mester. 2007. Prosodic adjunction in Japanese compounds. *MIT Working Papers in Linguistics* 55. 97–111.
Itô, Junko & Armin Mester. 2013. Prosodic subcategories in Japanese. *Lingua* 124. 20–40.

Kabak, Baris & Anthi Revithiadou. 2009. An interface approach to prosodic and word recursion. In Janet Grijzenhout & Baris Kabak (eds.), *Phonological Domains: Universals and Deviations*, 105–133. Berlin: Mouton de Gruyter.

Karlsson, Fred. 2007. Constraints on multiple center-embedding of clauses. *Journal of Linguistics* 43. 365–392.

Karlsson, Fred. 2010. Syntactic recursion and iteration. In Harry van der Hulst (ed.), *Recursion and Human Language*, 3–67. Berlin: de Gruyter.

Kaye, Jonathan. 1990. 'Coda' licensing. *Phonology* 7. 301–330.

Kaye, Jonathan, Jean Lowenstamm & Jean-Roger Vergnaud. 1990. Constituent structure and government in phonology. *Phonology* 7. 193–231.

Koopman, Hilda. 2014. Recursion restrictions: Where grammars count. In Tom Roeper & Margaret Speas (eds.), *Recursion: Complexity in Cognition*, 17–38. London: Springer.

Ladd, Robert. 1986. Intonational phrasing: The case for recursive prosodic structure. *Phonology* 3. 311–340.

Levin, Juliette. 1985. *A metrical theory of syllabicity*. Cambridge, MA: MIT PhD dissertation.

Lobina, David J. 2014a. When linguists talk mathematical logic. *Frontiers in Psychology* 5. Article 382.

Lobina, David J. 2014b. What linguists are talking about when talking about . . . *Language Sciences* 45. 56–70.

Lobina, David J. 2014c. "A running back" and forth: A review of *Recursion and Human Language*. *Biolinguistics* 5. 151–169.

Lowenstamm, Jean. 1996. CV as the only syllable type. In Jacques Durand & Bernard Laks (eds.), *Current Trends in Phonology: Models and Methods*, vol. 2, 419–441. Salford, Manchester: ESRI.

Martínez-Paricio, Violeta & René Kager. 2015. The binary-to-ternary rhythmic continuum in stress typology: Layered feet and nonintervention constraints. *Phonology* 32. 459–504.

Martins, Maurício Dias, Isabel Pavão Martins & W. Tecumseh Fitch. 2016. A novel approach to investigate recursion and iteration in visual hierarchical processing. *Behavior Research Methods* 48. 1421–1442.

McCarthy, John. 1979. On stress and syllabification. *Linguistic Inquiry* 10. 443–465.

Nasukawa, Kuniya. 2015. Recursion in the lexical structure of morphemes. In Marc van Oostendorp & Henk van Riemsdijk (eds.), *Representing Structure in Phonology and Syntax*, 211–238. Berlin: de Gruyter.

Nasukawa, Kuniya. 2017. Extending the application of Merge to elements in phonological representations. *Journal of the Phonetic Society of Japan* 21. 59–70.

Neeleman, Ad & Hans van de Koot. 2006. On syntactic and phonological representations. *Lingua* 116. 1524–1552.

Nespor, Marina & Irene Vogel. 1986. *Prosodic Phonology*. Dordrecht: Foris.

Nevins, Andrew, David Pesetsky & Cilene Rodrigues. 2009. Pirahã exceptionality: A reassessment. *Language* 85. 355–404.

Paap, Kenneth R. & Derek Partridge. 2014. Recursion isn't necessary for human language processing: NEAR (Non-iterative Explicit Alternatives Rule) grammars are superior. *Minds & Machines* 24. 389–414.

Pinker, Steven & Ray Jackendoff. 2005. The faculty of language: What's special about it? *Cognition* 95. 201–236.

Pöchtrager, Markus. 2006. *The structure of length*. Vienna: University of Vienna PhD dissertation.

Pöchtrager, Markus Alexander & Jonathan Kaye. 2013. GP2.0. *SOAS Working Papers in Linguistics and Phonetics* 16. 51–64.

Rice, Curtis Calvin. 1992. Binarity and ternarity in metrical theory: Parametric extensions. Austin, TX: University of Texas at Austin PhD dissertation.

Scheer, Tobias. 2004. *A Lateral Theory of Phonology.* Vol. 1: *What Is CVCV, and Why Should It Be?* Berlin: Mouton de Gruyter.

Scheer, Tobias. 2008. Why the prosodic hierarchy is a diacritic and why the interface must be direct. In Jutta Hartmann, Veronika Hegedüs & Henk van Riemsdijk (eds.), *Sounds of Silence: Empty Elements in Syntax and Phonology*, 145–192. Amsterdam: Elsevier.

Scheer, Tobias. 2011. *A Guide to Morphosyntax-Phonology Interface Theories: How Extra-Phonological Information Is Treated in Phonology since Trubetzkoy's Grenzsignale.* Berlin: Mouton de Gruyter.

Scheer, Tobias. 2012. *Direct Interface and One-Channel Translation: A Non-Diacritic Theory of the Morphosyntax-Phonology Interface.* Vol. 2 of *A Lateral Theory of Phonology.* Berlin: de Gruyter.

Scheer, Tobias. 2013. Why phonology is flat: The role of concatenation and linearity. *Language Sciences* 39. 54–74.

Schiering, René, Baltahsar Bickel & Kristin Hildebrandt. 2010. The prosodic word is not universal, but emergent. *Journal of Linguistics* 46. 657–710.

Selkirk, Elisabeth. 1981. On the nature of phonological representation. In J. Anderson, J. Laver & T. Meyers (eds.), *The Cognitive Representation of Speech*, 379–388. Amsterdam: North Holland.

Selkirk, Elisabeth. 1996. The prosodic structure of function words. In James Morgan & Katherine Demuth (eds.), *Signal to Syntax: Bootstrapping from Syntax to Grammar in Early Acquisition*, 187–213. Mahwah, NJ: Erlbaum.

Smith, Norval. 1999. A preliminary account of some aspects of Leurbost Gaelic syllable structure. In Harry van der Hulst & Nancy Ritter (eds.), *The Syllable, Views and Facts*, 577–630. Berlin/New York: de Gruyter.

Stabler, Edward P. 2014. Recursion in grammar and performance. In Tom Roeper & Margaret Speas (eds.), *Recursion: Complexity in Cognition*, 159–177. London: Springer.

Tomalin, Marcus. 2011. Syntactic structures and recursive devices: A legacy of imprecision. *Journal of Logic, Language and Information* 20. 297–315.

Vigário, Marina. 2010. Prosodic structure between the prosodic word and the phonological phrase: Recursive nodes or an independent domain? *The Linguistic Review* 27. 485–530.

Vogel, Irene. 2012. Recursion in phonology? In Bert Botma & Roland Noske (eds.), *Phonological Explorations: Empirical, Theoretical and Diachrnic Issues*, 41–61. Berlin: de Gruyter.

Vogel, Irene. 2020. Life after the strict layer hypothesis. In Hongming Zhang & Youyong Qian (eds.), *Prosodic Studies: Challenges and Prospects*, 9–60. London: Routledge.

Watumull, Jeffrey, Marc D. Hauser, Ian G. Roberts & Norbert Hornstein. 2014. On recursion. *Frontiers in Psychology* 4. Article 1017.

Aida Talić
Phases and Accent Assignment Domains

Abstract: The theory of syntactic domains capturing limits on syntactic interactions between elements and the model of grammar where phonology follows syntax have raised questions about whether syntactic domains may limit phonological interactions as well. While previous research provides various studies showing that syntactic domains do correspond to phonological domains in many contexts (Dobashi 2003; Kratzer and Selkirk 2007; Elfner 2012; Talić 2018 a.o.), the idea that syntactic spell-out determines prosodic domains has not remained unchallenged (e.g., Cheng and Downing 2011). In this chapter, I discuss two Bosnian/Croatian/Serbian (BCS) accent assignment rules from this perspective and show that while syntactic spell-out domain boundaries do seem to limit these accentual rules in some case, it is less clear that they do so in others. I review three different contexts where accent assignment may be expected to be affected by phases: the clausal domain (CP), the phasehood within PPs, and the adjectival domain. I show that accent assignment rules do show sensitivity to spell-out domain boundaries. If a spell-out domain does not create a prosodic constituent large enough to trigger accent assignment, then an accent domain spans over the material from two spell-out domains.

Keywords: phases, spell-out, pitch accent, accent assignment domain, clitics, High tone

1 Introduction

The advancement of the theory of syntactic domains delimiting syntactic dependencies between elements in the structure (see e.g., Chomsky 1986, 2000) and assuming a model of grammar – where phonological computations follow syntactic ones, raises questions about whether those same syntactic domains at least partially delimit phonological interactions between elements as well. Various researchers have offered evidence from many languages suggesting that syntactic spell-out domains correspond to (map onto) certain prosodic domains – phonological phrase or major phrase – in many contexts (Dobashi 2003; Kahnemuyipour 2004; Kratzer and Selkirk 2007; Elfner 2012; Talić 2018 among others; cf. Nespor and Vogel 1986). In a similar vein, within the Distributed Morphology framework, cate-

---

Aida Talić, University of Illinois at Urbana-Champaign

https://doi.org/10.1515/9783110730098-015

gory defining heads v^0, n^0, a^0 have been argued to delimit domains for phonological processes such as stress assignment (Marantz 2001; Marvin 2002). However, the idea that syntactic spell-out fully determines prosodic domains has not remained unchallenged (see e.g., Cheng and Downing 2016 for a discussion of Bantu tone).

In this chapter, I address two Bosnian/Croatian/Serbian (BCS) accent assignment rules from this perspective (High-tone spreading and default initial High-tone insertion, see e.g., Inkelas and Zec 1988) and show that while syntactic spell-out domain boundaries do seem to limit these accentual rules in many cases, it is less clear that they do so in others. I will review three different domains where accent assignment may be expected to be affected by phases. First, I will consider the clausal domain and discuss whether an element spelled out within the complement of the C head can interact with the accent of the element at the edge of the CP. Second, I will turn to phasehood within PPs and discuss the interaction between the head P and elements within its complement. Lastly, I discuss phasehood and accent in the adjectival domain.

2 Clause Phasehood

The idea that clausal boundaries may form locality domains for syntactic operations has been around longer than assumptions that such domains are formed within smaller constituents (Ross 1967; Chomsky 1986, 2000). In this section I turn to this most typical phase and discuss how it interacts with accentual rules in BCS.

Under the standard approach to phases (Chomsky 2000, 2001), CPs and strong vPs are phases; the heads C^0 and v^0 induce spell-out of their complement, after which only the edge of CP or vP remains accessible to further operations. In this sense, phasehood is an inherent property of particular syntactic categories. In contrast, under more recent contextual approaches to phases, any syntactic phrase may be a phase depending on its syntactic context and it is the highest projection in every domain that is a phase (Bobaljik and Wurmbrand 2005, 2013; Bošković 2005, 2013). Thus, only when a phrase XP merges with a head Y^0 from the next higher domain, it is determined that XP is a phase and its complement undergoes spell-out. The number of projections within the same phase may vary cross-linguistically and in the different constructions in the same language, which leads to the same category being a phase in some contexts but not in others. What matters here is that the topmost projection of a clause is treated as a phase under both types of accounts.

To show whether the CP phase delimits accentual domains in BCS (i.e. domains of High-tone spreading and initial High-tone insertion), we need to see whether accentual interaction is possible between an element spelled out within the complement of C and an element at the edge of CP, either the head C or the specifier of CP. As pointed out by Talić (2018), contexts for testing this are quite rare because High-tone spreading and High-tone insertion apply within a prosodic word, so no interactions across word boundaries are expected. Nevertheless, if we find two elements that are prosodically light enough to not constitute prosodic words on their own, we might expect some accentual interactions between such elements when they are linearly adjacent and in the same domain. Interestingly, BCS does indeed offer two such situations in the context of enclitics and a limited set of light hosts. In what follows, I offer a brief sketch of the phenomenon and refer the reader to the work cited for a detailed description and analysis.

In BCS words, one syllable gets prominence and either a falling or a rising accent. A falling accent can arise in two ways – either the leftmost lexical High tone is on the initial syllable in the accentual domain ($dî^H{:}vna^H$ – 'wonderful.F.SF'), or a default initial High tone is inserted in the absence of any lexical High tones ($grà^H{:}d$ – 'city/town. M'). In contrast, a rising accent results from a High tone on a non-initial syllable, which spreads onto the preceding syllable and gives it prominence ($grá{:}dnja^H$ – 'construction.F') (see e.g., Inkelas and Zec 1988).[1] The domain of the default High tone insertion is the minimal prosodic word and if no lexical High tone is present in this domain, this rule will apply. Crucially, if a lexical High tone is present on at least one element in the accentual domain (the minimal prosodic word), the default rule of initial High tone insertion does not apply. The rule of High tone spreading can apply within prosodic words of any size, as long as there is a syllable preceding a High tone.

Thus, to illustrate the effect of the CP phase on accent assignment in BCS, we need to consider a toneless host and enclitics that have a lexical High tone and that can occur either high or lower in the syntactic structure depending on the context. It turns out that all BCS enclitics, except for 3rd person singular auxiliary *je*, have a lexical High tone i.e. they occur in at least some contexts where they are preceded by a rising accent, which indicates that they have a High tone that undergoes spreading. Crucially, this happens when the toneless host and the enclitic are both within the CP edge. Before turning to the pattern of accent interactions with enclitics, note that there is evidence based on constituent extraction and ellipsis that BCS second position clitics do not all move to C in all constructions (see Stjepanović 1998; Bošković 2001). Rather, in the syntax, they

---

[1] There are also Low tones that get inserted to all moras that do not have a winning High tone, which leads to the final contour (see e.g., Inkelas and Zec 1988), but since rising and falling accents can be predicted by simply tracking the distribution and interaction of High tones, I will only focus on those for ease of exposition.

occupy positions where satisfy their syntactic properties (auxiliaries are in T or C, pronominal clitics in their argument positions in the verbal domain), while their second position placement results from post-syntactic processes. Consider now the following contexts.

In (1), the wh-words are in SpecCP, while the auxiliaries are moved to C^0, given that these are questions. The dative clitic in (1b) actually has a lower syntactic position, but it linearizes before the auxiliary *je* because this is the only BCS auxiliary that has to follow all other clitics.[2] What we see here is that enclitics with a High tone, which are syntactically in C^0 or which have to precede an element in C^0 for independent phonological reasons, do interact with the accent of a toneless host in SpecCP, i.e. the High tone from the enclitic spreads onto the host and the host gets a rising accent.

(1) a. Štá **su** mi rekli?[3]
    what are me.DAT said
    'What did they tell me?'

  b. Štá m**i** je rekla?
    who me.DAT is said.F
    'What did she tell me?'

Note that a High tone can only spread from an element in C^0 that is an enclitic, which does not constitute a prosodic word by itself. As illustrated in (2), if a full non-clitic verb is in C^0, its initial High tone cannot spread onto the element in SpecCP, and the wh-word gets a default initial High tone and a falling accent.[4]

---

[2] Note: This requirement to follow all enclitics is an idiosyncratic phonological requirement of this particular auxiliary, triggering linearization of other clitics before it. Its syntactic behavior has been argued to be the same (see Bošković 2001; Talić 2018) or similar (Franks 2017) as that of other auxiliaries. Crucially, all auxiliaries do raise to C^0 in questions. Furthermore, BCS enclitics have to follow a strict order: Q+Aux+Dat+Acc/Gen+{se, je}.

[3] In all examples, I will use an acute accent mark to indicate a rising accent (e.g. [á]) and a grave accent mark to indicate a falling accent (e.g. [à]); vowel length will be marked by [:]. The vowel with the leftmost High tone in the accentual domain, responsible for the falling or rising accent, will be bolded. This will be the vowel following the accent mark in words with a rising accent, and the vowel with the accent mark (i.e. the initial vowel) in words with a falling accent. I will only use accent and length diacritics on words under consideration since the spelling system of BCS does not mark accents or length.

[4] Being in the same spell-out domain seems to be a necessary, but not sufficient condition for High-tone spreading to take place from an element in C to an element in SpecCP. In addition to that, it needs to be possible for the two elements to map to prosody as one prosodic word. This can happen if one of the elements is a clitic, but not with two non-clitic elements given that the

(2) Štà hòćeš da mi kažeš?
    what want that me.DAT say
    'What do you want to tell me?'

Another toneless host that allows such interaction with enclitics is the complementizer *da*, which occurs in a variety of contexts. Crucially, when it occurs in the same complex head C⁰ with some enclitics, it gets a rising accent, as a result of High-tone spreading. This takes place in yes-no questions, where *da* shares the head C⁰ with the question particle *li* (3a) and in desiderative constructions in (3b), where it shares the same head with the auxiliary *je* and the dative clitic *mi* linearizes between them at PF.

(3) a. Dá li su otputovali?
       Comp Q are traveled?
       'Did they leave on a trip?'

    b. Dá mi je putovati.
       Comp me.DAT is travel.INF
       'I wish I could travel.'

Thus, the lexical High tone on an enclitic spreads onto its toneless host when both are within the CP-edge, either the host is in SpecCP and the clitic is in C⁰ or both are in the head C⁰.

Crucially, when there is no syntactic motivation for the clitics to move to the CP layer, in identical linear sequences of hosts followed by clitics, High-tone spreading from the clitic within the TP to the host in SpecCP or in C⁰ is not possible. In (4a), the wh-host is in SpecCP and the dative clitic stays within the TP since there is no *je* which would bring it into the CP-layer at PF. In the embedded declaratives in (4b–c) and the conditional in (4d), the complementizer is in C⁰ and the clitics also stay within the TP since there is no motivation for them to undergo raising to C.

(4) a. Štà mi kaže?   *štá_mi
       who me.DAT tell
       'What is (s)he telling me?'

---

two would not be dominated together by a prosodic word level category at PF and that the domain of application of High tone-spreading.

b. Znam da su otputovali. *dá_su
   know Comp are traveled
   'I know they left on a trip.'

c. Znam da mi je rekao istinu. *dá_mi_je
   know Comp me.DAT is said truth.ACC
   'I know you will tell me the truth.'

d. Da mi je rekao istinu, vjerovala *dá_mi_je
   Comp me.DAT is said truth.ACC trusted
   bih mu.
   would him.DAT
   'If he had told me the truth, I would have believed him.'

Therefore, the CP phase does seem to participate in delimiting accentual domains in BCS. In particular, if an enclitic with a High tone is on the same side of the spell-out domain boundary introduced by C^0, it can spread its High tone onto the host (5a–b). If it is spelled-out within the complement of C^0 and the host is at the edge of CP, then the High tone on the enclitic does not get realized at all (5c–d).

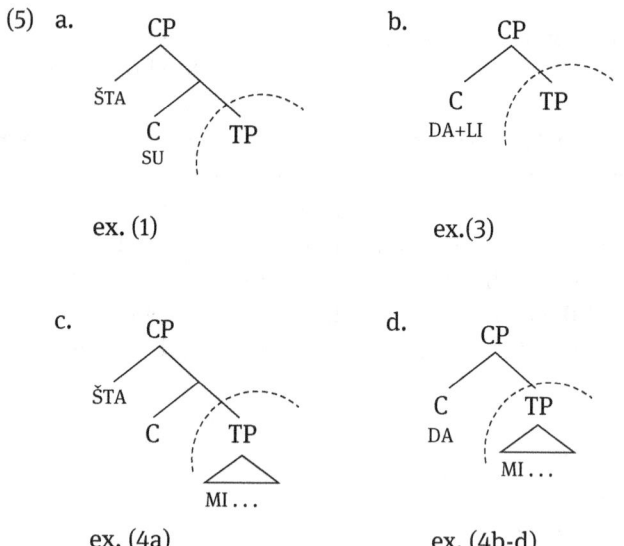

Finally, with non-clitic words that are capable of spreading their accent to a preceding proclitic in other contexts (i.e. words with an initial High tone), High-tone spreading does not take place to the complementizer, since these are inevitably within the TP, either in SpecTP or in T^0, or even in a lower position.

(6) a. Znam da sòba ima dovoljno prostora. *dá_soba
       know Comp room has enough space
       'I know the room has enough space.'

   b. Znam da vòliːš kafu. *dá_volːiš
       know Comp love coffee
       'I know you love coffee.'

Taking into consideration phases in domains other than CP under the contextual approach to phases discussed above, in the examples in (6), the complementizer is likely separated from *sòba* and *vòliš* by another phasal projection: NP in (6a) and vP in (6b).

3 PP Phasehood

I now turn to the domain with a less established phasehood status. While under the standard approach to phases, only CP, strong vP, and later DP are phases (Chomsky 2000, 2001), Matsubara (2000) extends this approach to PPs and argues that this domain too contains a functional phasal head p^0 (parallel to C^0, v^0, D^0). Discussing cross-linguistic differences in the availability of P-stranding between languages like English that allows it (7a) and languages like BCS that does not (7b), Abels (2003) parametrizes the phasehood of PP, suggesting that PP is a phase in BCS, but not in English. As a result, movement of the complement of P^0 either through SpecPP or without stopping there would be a locality violation.

(7) a. What$_i$ are you talking about t_i?
   b. *Čemu$_i$ pričaš o t_i?
       what talk.3.PRES about

Furthermore, given that under contextual approaches to phases the highest projection in every domain is a phase, it follows that the highest projection in the domain of P^0 is a phase as well (Bošković 2013). While it is not completely clear whether P^0 is a lexical category (Jackendoff 1973) or a functional one (Abney 1987; Grimshaw 1991, 2005), this does not affect the phasal status of PP. It is either a phase as the highest projection in its own domain, or as the highest projection in the nominal domain. Crucially, either under parametrized phasehood approach or under the contextual approach, BCS PP is a phase.

Note also that accent assignment in complex prosodic words is expected to apply multiple times, where the information established at earlier cycles is retained and detectable after accent assignment rules at later cycles apply. This is similar to English stress assigned at earlier cycles being retained as secondary stress, after stress rules at later cycles have applied (e.g. *oríginal* – *orìginálity*; Marantz 2001; Marvin 2002). In BCS, given that initial High-tone insertion is the default rule that applies when no lexical High tone is present in the accentual domain, we expect that even toneless roots would gain a High tone if they have gone through a cycle of accent assignment. At a later cycle, that High tone could undergo spreading to a preceding toneless syllable, but crucially, that High tone blocks default initial High tone insertion at later cycles.

As in the previous section, this raises a question whether elements spelled out within the complement of P⁰ can interact with the accent of an element at the edge of PP. I will again consider the contexts with clitics. Crucially, most BCS prepositions are proclitics and they do not constitute a prosodic word on their own. If P⁰ is spelled out separately from its complement, we expect the accentual rules to apply to the complement before P⁰ is spelled out. To see what accent we might expect if P is in or outside of the accentual domain of its host, consider first the accent of the prefix *ne* 'not' when it attaches within the minimal prosodic word of the toneless noun *ra:d* 'work' (8a–b) and when it attaches to the noun *ra:dni:k* derived from the noun *ra:d* (8c–d). In (8a), default initial High tone insertion applies and yields a falling initial accent. In (8b), *ne* is within the accent assignment domain of its host *ra:d*, so it gets the default initial High tone, which is realized as a falling accent on *ne*. In (8c–d), the derivational suffix closes the lower accentual domain, so again a default initial High tone is inserted to *ra:d* and results in an initial falling accent in (8c). Crucially, when *ne* is spelled out in (8d), its host already has a High tone form the earlier cycle, which blocks initial High tone insertion, so *ne* does not get a High tone and a falling accent. Instead, the High tone from *ra:d* spreads, which yields a rising accent on *ne*. Recall, that the domain of the High tone insertion is the smallest prosodic word where no lexical High tone is present, while the rule of High tone spreading can apply within prosodic words of any size, as long as there is a syllable preceding a lexical High tone or a High tone inserted before further prefixation takes place (8d).

(8) a. (rà:d)_ω   *falling*   c. ((rà:d)ni:k)_ω   *falling*
       'work'   'worker'

    b. (nèra:d)_ω   *falling*   d. (né((ra:d)ni:k)_ω)_ω   *rising*
       'inactivity'   'botcher/lazy person'

Thus, if BCS P⁰ can enter the smallest accent assignment domain of its host, we expect it to get a falling accent in front of a host that lacks any lexical High tones (parallel to the prefix *ne* in (8b)). If such a host constitutes an accentual domain and gains a default initial High tone before P⁰ enters, but if P⁰ can still become a part of the same larger prosodic word, we expect P⁰ to get a rising accent (parallel to the prefix *ne* in (8d)). And if P⁰ is not in the prosodic word of the host at all, we do not expect it to have any accent since it would be completely outside the domain of both accent assignment rules. Now, if P⁰ is a phase head and its complement is spelled out before P⁰ is, we may expect P⁰ to either get: (i) no accent, which would be parallel to the behavior of the complementizer *da* in declarative clauses (see the previous section); or (ii) a rising accent, which would indicate that P⁰ cliticized to a host that has undergone spell-out and gained a default initial High tone (same as the prefix *ne* in (8d)).[5]

While there are BCS dialects that do not allow any accent interactions between P⁰ and its complement, which would support that all accent assignment rules apply to the spelled-out complement before P⁰ is spelled out, there are several dialects where such interaction is available with some structural restrictions (Talić 2019).[6] Consider the examples in (9) illustrating a lexically toneless host *puːt* in a variety of contexts. In (9a), the noun occurs without a derivational suffix or a postnominal modifier. Instead of the noun receiving a default initial High tone, which occurs when it is not preceded by a preposition or a prefix, the preposition preceding it receives the High tone and a falling accent. This indicates that P⁰ can be incorporated into the smallest accentual domain of this noun. In (9b), there is a derivational suffix on *puːt* and the preposition now gets a rising accent. This shows that the noun and the suffix belong to the first accentual domain where the default initial High tone insertion applies to the syllable *puːt*, and that the preposition is still within the larger prosodic word since the High tone inserted at the first cycle can now spread to P⁰. Finally, (9c–d) show that if the NP has a postmodifier, then P⁰ remains unaccented even when it linearly precedes the same nouns,[7] which indicates that it is neither enter the smallest accentual domain ((9a) vs. (9c)) in the absence of a derivational suffix, nor the larger accentual domain ((9b) vs. (9d)) when the noun combines with the suffix first.

---

[5] The latter would be similar to secondary stress in English as a reflex of stress assignment rules applied at an earlier cycle (Marantz 2001; Marvin 2002).
[6] For the purposes of this chapter, I discuss a subset of contexts with accent shifts to prepositions found in central, southern, and northeastern Bosnia and Herzegovina. For a more detailed description and discussion, see Riđanović and Aljović (2009) and Talić 2019; a subset of basic examples was also discussed by Zec and Inkelas (1991), Selkirk (1996), Zec (2005).
[7] The blocking effect of post-nominal modifiers on the accent shift to proclitics was first observed by Riđanović and Aljović (2009).

(9) a. zà_puːt   c. za pùːt u Zenicu
for_trip   for trip to Zenica

b. zá_puːtniːka   d. za pùːtniːka iz Zenice
for_traveler   for traveler from Zenica

As mentioned above, the outcomes in (9b) and (9c–d) are expected if PP is a phase. Crucially, with simple nouns (9a), the preposition is present at the first accent assignment cycle (the smallest prosodic word), which is surprising if P^0 is a phase head and spell-out domains always correspond to accent assignment domains. If the noun is spelled out within the complement of P^0, it should be structurally equally far from P^0 in both (9a) and (9c), as well as in both (9b) and (9d). There is no motivation to posit any syntactic or post-syntactic movement in (9a–b) that we would not posit in (9c–d) as well.

However, rules within any module of grammar cannot apply before their structural description is met. It has been long recognized that certain prosodic constituents have a general tendency to be binary (see e.g., McCarthy and Prince 1993; Ito and Mester 1992). Crucially, even if the complement of P^0 is spelled out when this phase is completed in (9a), the phonological content inserted at that level is monosyllabic. Assuming that one syllable does not constitute an ideal prosodic word in these dialects, the complement of P^0 here does not get mapped onto one and as a result accentual rules do not apply. At the next spell-out, the insertion of the preposition adds the syllable needed to build a prosodic word and accent assignment rules can apply (10a). In (9b), the complement of P^0 has to be mapped onto a prosodic word, since this constituent is unambiguously of the right size, which triggers initial High-tone insertion to apply before P^0 is inserted. Now, given that phonological phrases in these dialects need at least two prosodic words (Talić 2019), when PP is spelled out at the next phase, the P^0 clitic adjoins to the prosodic word created earlier instead of PP mapping onto a phonological phrase.[8] At the level of this larger prosodic word, accentual rules apply again. High-tone insertion is blocked by the presence of the High tone inserted earlier (which explains why *za* in (9b) cannot get a falling accent), but High-tone spreading applies and gives *za* a rising accent (10b). When the complement of P^0 is spelled out in (9c–d), the postnominal PP maps onto a prosodic word same as

---

8 For a distinction between internal (incorporated), affixal (adjoined) and free clitics, see Selkirk (1996). In short, internal clitics are fully incorporated into the minimal prosodic word of the host; affixal clitics are adjoined as sisters to the prosodic word of the host, creating a larger prosodic word; and free clitics are sisters to the prosodic word of the host, but they create a phonological phrase with it.

(9a) or (9b) and the NP containing N and the postnominal PP maps onto a phonological phrase. Given that the noun is not a clitic, adjoining *puːt* in (9c) to the prosodic word of the postmodifier is not an option, and as a last resort *puːt* becomes a prosodic word, triggering High tone insertion.[9] The same phonological phrase is built in (9d), except that it has a heavier noun which constitutes a prosodic word in any context. Finally, when the entire PP in (9c–d) undergoes spell-out, it maps onto a phonological phrase given that it already contains a constituent of that size within. The preposition remains within the phonological phrase as a free clitic and since it is not immediately dominated by a prosodic word, it is not in the domain of any accent assignment rules (10c).

(10) a. PP [P NP [N]] $(za_\sigma\ puːt_\sigma)_\omega$

b. PP [P NP [N]] $(za_\sigma\ (puːtniːka)_\omega)_\omega$

c. PP [P NP [NP PP]] $(za_\sigma\ (puːtniːka)_\omega\ (iz Zenice)_\omega)_\phi$

Crucially, a spelled-out complement of P^0 in BCS delimits an accentual domain if and only if enough phonological material is inserted to build at least a prosodic word. When this condition is not met, accent assignment rule application is delayed until the next spell-out. Finally, what counts as "enough" to build a prosodic word or a phrase may vary cross-dialectally, i.e., different dialects could differ in whether they are sensitive to the binarity requirement for prosodic constituents. In a dialect where prosodic words can freely have just one syllable, we expect that accent shifts of this sort would be unattested, which could be what is responsible for complete lack of accent shift to proclitics in the Belgrade dialect discussed by Zec (1993).

---

9 An anonymous reviewer wonders when this mechanism of last resort kicks in, so I would just like to clarify a couple of points. I am making a distinction here between clitics (weak words that cannot become full prosodic words on their own as last resort without an additional phonological process) and words like *put*, which are not clitics, but in some contexts they fail to map as full prosodic words. Based on the pattern here, the latter seem to not map as prosodic words only when they are the only material in a spell-out domain. The presence of modifiers brings in enough additional phonological material to not allow for a delay of prosodic mapping at that spell out, and as last resort, words like *put* map as prosodic words since they are not clitics and have no other choice.

4 AP Phasehood

Turning now to another domain that was not immediately considered a phase under the standard approach to phases, but for which more recent work has provided some evidence for phasehood, let us consider APs. APs are not on the list of phasal categories, under the standard approach to phases. However, under the contextual approach to phases, it follows that the highest projection in the domain of A is a phase (see Bošković 2013; Talić 2015). Furthermore, in DM, on a par with phrases headed by categorizing heads little v^0, little n^0, those headed by little a^0 are considered phases at the word level (Marantz 2001; Marvin 2002) and are expected to affect word prosody. Given that in the presence of multiple High tones in an accentual domain in BCS the leftmost one is always realized, such contexts obscure the effects of any High tones present to the right of the root, so I will be discussing only adjectives with lexically toneless roots whose prosody is affected by High tones to the right.

BCS has long form adjectives and short form adjectives, which are differentiated primarily by prosodic means (Aljović 2002; Talić 2020). For instance, in (11), the accusative suffix has a lexical High tone. This tone spreads onto the preceding syllable in short-form adjectives (11a–b), yielding a rising accent on that syllable. However, in long-form adjectives, High-tone spreading from the suffix is not possible because the stem itself has an extra High tone on the syllable preceding the suffix. Given that this tone is not present in the short form in adjectives like *pla:v* and *zelen*, it is not a lexical tone of the root, but it surfaces throughout the rest of the derivation.

(11)   short   long
a. plá:vo:g   c. plà:vo:g
   blue.ACC.SF   blue.ACC.LF
b. zeléno:g   d. zéleno:g
   green.ACC.SF   green.ACC.LF

Regarding the phasehood in the adjectival domain in BCS in particular, Talić (2015) argues that the size of phrases projected by the two forms of adjectives differs, in that long-form adjectives have an extra functional layer XP above AP.[10] Thus, as the highest projection in APs projected by short-form adjectives, the AP itself is a phase. On the other hand, XP is the highest projection and a phase in long-form adjectives. The consequence of this is that extraction of AP-adjoined

---

10 For the purposes of this paper, it does not matter what feature this functional projection is associated with, so I will put aside discussing it in the interest of space.

modifiers is blocked from XPs (12b), but not from APs (12a) (for an account and more details, I refer the reader to the work cited; a similar contrast has been observed for the nominal domain regarding left-branch extraction, which is possible when no functional layer is present above NP, and impossible when a DP is projected (Bošković 2013)).

(12) a. Izuzetno$_i$ su kupili [t$_i$ skup] automobil.
    extremely are bought expensive.SF car
    'They bought an *extremely* expensive car.'

   b. *Izuzetno$_i$ su kupili [t$_i$ skupi] automobil.
    extremely are bought expensive.LF car

Crucially, regarding the accent in the two forms, lexically toneless stems in long-form adjectives have a stem-final High tone (11c–d), which is lacking in parallel short-form adjectives (11a–b). Given that AP is considered to be a phase in short-form adjectives, the complement of A (if any) is spelled-out when the AP is built, while the head A and the edge of AP are spelled out when the next phase head (α) sends its complement to spell-out. XP is a phase in long-form adjectives, and its complement AP is spelled out when XP is completed (see the discussion after (14) below). This raises the question whether the presence of the extra functional phase head in the structure of long-form adjectives is responsible for the emergence of this extra High tone. There are two ways we may expect this functional head to contribute the extra High tone: (i) by closing off an accentual domain, so that accent assignment rules trigger High-tone insertion in the absence of a lexical High tone, or (ii) by providing an exponent with a lexical High tone.

Interestingly, the accent pattern illustrated in (11) provides evidence against the former and for the latter. If the adjectival stem created a separate accent assignment domain (being spelled out within the complement of X^0) in long-form adjectives, but not in short-form adjectives, we would expect the toneless stems in long-form adjectives to always receive a default High tone. However, the default High tone in BCS is *initial*, which would predict all long-form adjectives with toneless roots to have an initial falling accent. As shown in (11d), this is not what happens with polysyllabic stems. Instead, all of these stems have a High tone on the syllable preceding the agreement suffix, which blocks High-tone spreading from the agreement suffix to the stem that takes place in short-form adjectives. Talić (2020) argues that this High tone is actually the exponent of the functional head X^0 within long-form adjectives. Such tonal affixes have been observed in many languages (e.g., see recent work by Yu (2021) on a High tone marking absolutive case in Samoan) and they often result from a language change where a particular exponent loses segmental content and only the tone remains. Similarly, long-form inflection in Old-Church Slavonic stems from a pronominal element that had segmental content (Schenker 1993: 91). In contemporary BCS, the segmental content of long-form inflection is not there, but the High-tone surfaces as the exponent of this functional head.

Following Harley and Tubino Blanco (2013), I assume the following order of operations applying to a syntactic representation at spell-out (the bolded ones matter for the discussion here):[11]

(13) **Lowering**/Linearization → **Dissociated Morphemes Inserted** → Impoverishment/ Fission/ Fusion → **Vocabulary insertion** → Readjustment rules → **Phonological Rules**

Regarding the adjectival complex head in BCS, I argue that it is assembled in PF by: (i) lowering the functional head X and adjoining it to the adjectival stem A; (ii) inserting a dissociated morpheme AGR. It is argued that lowering and dissociated morpheme insertion take place before inserting exponents, while phonological rules can only apply after the exponents have been inserted.

The structures in (14) illustrate short-form adjectives and long-form adjectives at the point when the head A^0 undergoes spell-out and the relevant post-syntactic operations apply.

(14) a. short-form structure   b. long-form structure

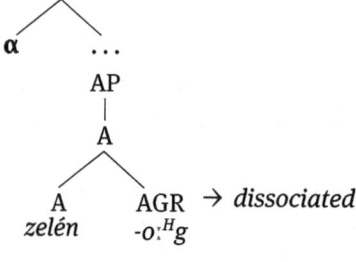
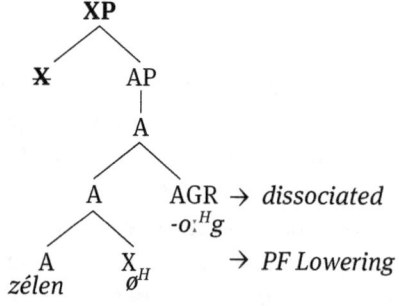

---

11 See Harley and Tubino Blanco (2013), as well as Embick and Noyer (2001) for more discussion about these individual operations. For our purposes here, we simply need to allow for: (i) some movement operations taking place after the syntax has sent the structure to PF – in this case lowering; and (i) insertion of some nodes within a complex head to take place at PF if they are not interacting with semantics, i.e. dissociated morphemes (e.g. nodes that carry concord features AGR).

In (14a), XP is not present, so the AP undergoes spell-out when the next phase head enters. At PF, a dissociated AGR node is inserted, followed by vocabulary insertion. The toneless adjectival stem is in the same domain as the agreement suffix that has a lexical High tone, so High tone spreading can take place. In (14b), XP is present in the adjectival domain and induces spell-out. At spell-out the head X^0 lowers to A^0, after which AGR node gets inserted to the resulting complex A^0 head. After vocabulary insertion, the toneless stem precedes the [$ø^H$] exponent of the head X^0. Given that the High tone contributed by X^0 is not inherently linked to a vowel, it links to the closest vowel available (the final vowel of the stem). With polysyllabic stems, it undergoes further spreading and results in a rising accent. Thus, the High tone contributed by the exponent of the phase head X^0 does interact with the accent of its host. Crucially, this is possible because the head X^0 undergoes PF lowering at spell-out before the AGR node is inserted (see (13)), which leads to the observed order of exponents ADJ-X-AGR.[12] Note that if we assume that the head A^0 undergoes syntactic rising to X^0 instead of X^0 lowering at PF, we would predict that only long-form adjectives precede their adverb modifiers, while short-form adjectives follow them. This is not what we find. Instead, the functional head X^0 syntactically behaves as if it is High in the adjectival structure, blocking syntactic movement (12b), but phonologically it shows that it undergoes lowering.

While it may seem that a simpler assumption for capturing the prosodic contrast between the two adjectival forms would be to assume that a phase is not projected in the domain of A at all, and that both short-form adjectives and long-form adjectives are spelled out when the next phase head higher in the structure enters, this would not capture why the functional layer XP has a blocking effect on syntactic extractions (12b), which follows straightforwardly if XP is a phase.[13]

Finally, I did not represent the categorizer *a* in the structures above since it has no effect on prosody. Crucially, even if we assume that the stem A splits into the root *zel* and the phase *a* head *-en* and that the root undergoes spell-out before *a* does, the root still does not become an accentual domain on its own. The reason for this could be the same as what we have seen with simple monosyllabic nouns

---

[12] The idea that a phase head can undergo PF-lowering into its complement here is similar to D-lowering in Bulgarian proposed by Embick and Noyer (2001), i.e., even though the complement of the phase undergoes spell-out, the head remains accessible for certain operations at this point.

[13] This could also be another case of domain suspension, where spell-out of the complement of X would be delayed until a higher head sends the head X itself to spell-out, similar to those discussed by Bobaljik and Wurmbrand (2013).

as complements of P in Section 3, the root is too small to become a prosodic word in PF before -*en* is spelled out.

5 Conclusion

In sum, we have seen that accent assignment rules, High-tone insertion and High-tone spreading in Bosnian/Croatian/Serbian do show sensitivity to spell-out domain boundaries in most contexts, i.e., spell-out domains may delimit accentual domains. However, if a spell-out domain does not create a prosodic constituent large enough to trigger accent assignment rules (i.e., if vocabulary insertion at PF does not provide enough material to build a prosodic word), then an accent domain spans over the material from two spell-out domains. We have also seen that phase heads may exhibit different behavior. If a phase head sends its complement to spell-out without undergoing incorporation via PF lowering (e.g., the complementizer *da*), then its prosody is not affected by its complement and vice versa. If a phase head undergoes PF lowering into its complement (e.g., the functional head in the adjectival domain), then its exponent can interact with the accent of its host. Thus, while phases partially inform PF about domain boundaries, the phonological shape of vocabulary items and PF-specific rules determine the final shape of accent domains.

References

Abels, Klaus. 2003. *[P clitic]!–Why? *Linguistik International*, 443–460. Frankfurt am Main: Peter Lang.

Abney, Steven. 1987. The English noun phrase. Cambridge, MA: Massachusetts Institute of Technology dissertation.

Aljović, Nadira. 2002. Long adjectival inflection and specificity in Serbo-Croatian. *Recherches linguistiques de Vincennes* 31. 27–42.

Bobaljik, Jonathan & Susi Wurmbrand. 2005. The domain of agreement. *Natural Language and Linguistic Theory* 23. 809–865.

Bobaljik, Jonathan & Susi Wurmbrand. 2013. Suspension across domains. In Ora Matushansky & Alec Marantz (eds.), *Distributed Morphology Today: Morphemes for Morris Halle*, 185–197. Cambridge, MA: MIT Press.

Bošković, Željko. 2001. *On the Nature of the Syntax-Phonology Interface: Cliticization and Related Phenomena*. Amsterdam: Elsevier.

Bošković, Željko. 2005. On the locality of left branch extraction and the structure of NP. *Studia Linguistica* 59(1). 1–45.

Bošković, Željko. 2013. Phases beyond clauses. In Lilla Schürcks, Anastasia Giannakidou & Urtzi Exteberria (eds.), *Nominal Constructions in Slavic and Beyond*, 75–128. Berlin: De Gruyter.

Cheng, Lisa Lai-Shen, and Laura J. Downing. 2016. Phasal syntax = cyclic phonology? *Syntax* 19(2). 156–191.

Chomsky, Noam. 1986. *Barriers*. Cambridge, MA: MIT Press.

Chomsky, Noam. 2000. Minimalist inquiries: The framework. In Roger Martin, David Michaels & Juan Uriagereka (eds.), *Step-by-Step: Essays on Minimalist Syntax in Honor of Howard Lasnnik*, 89–156. Cambridge, MA: MIT Press.

Chomsky, Noam. 2001. Derivation by phase. In Michael Kenstowicz (ed.), *Ken Hale: A Life in Language*, 1–52. Cambridge, MA: MIT Press. [Chomsky, Noam. 1999. Derivation by phase. MIT Occasional Papers in Linguistics 18].

Dobashi, Yoshihito. 2003. *Phonological phrasing and syntactic derivation*. Ithaca, NY: Cornell University dissertation.

Elfner, Emily. 2012. *Syntax-prosody interactions in Irish*. Amherst, MA: University of Massachusetts dissertation.

Embick, David & Rolf Noyer. 2001. Movement operations after syntax. *Linguistic Inquiry* 32(4). 555–595.

Franks, Steven. 2017. *Syntax and Spell-Out in Slavic*. Bloomington, IN: Slavica Publishers.

Grimshaw, Jane. 1991. Extended projections. Ms. Brandeis University.

Grimshaw, Jane. 2005. Extended projection. In *Words and Structure*, 1–74. Stanford: CSLI.

Harley, Haidi & Mercedes Tubino Blanco. 2013. Cycles, vocabulary items, and stem forms in Hiaki. In Ora Matushansky & Alec Marantz (eds.), *Distributed Morphology Today: Morphemes for Morris Halle*, 118–134, Cambridge, MA: MIT Press.

Inkelas, Sharon & Draga Zec. 1988. Serbo-Croatian pitch accent: The interaction of tone, stress, and intonation. *Language* 64(2). 227–248.

Ito, Junko & Armin Mester. 1992. Weak layering and word binarity. In Takeru Honma, Masao Okazaki, Toshiyuki Tabata & Shin-ichi Tanaka (eds.), *A New Century of Phonology and Phonological Theory: A Festschrift for Professor Shosuke Haraguchi on the Occasion of His Sixtieth Birthday*, 26–65. Tokyo: Kaitakusha.

Jackendoff, Ray. 1973. The base rules for prepositional phrases. In Stephen Anderson & Paul Kiparsky (eds.), *Festschrift for Morris Halle*, 345–356. New York: Holt, Rinehart, and Winston.

Kahnemuyipour, Arsalan. 2004. *The syntax of sentential stress*. Toronto: University of Toronto dissertation.

Kratzer, Angelika & Elisabeth Selkirk. 2007. Phase theory and prosodic spellout: The case of verbs. *The Linguistic Review* 24. 93–135.

Marantz, Alec. 2001. Words and things. Handout, MIT.

Marvin, Tatjana. 2002. *Topics in the stress and syntax of words*. Cambridge, MA: Massachusetts Institute of Technology dissertation.

Matsubara, Fuminori. 2000. p*P Phases. *Linguistic Analysis* 30. 127–161.

McCarthy, John J. & Alan Prince. 1993. Generalized alignment. In Geert Booij & Jaap van Marle (eds.), *Yearbook of Morphology 1993*, 79–153. Dordrecht: Kluwer.

Nespor, Marina & Irene Vogel. 1986. *Prosodic Phonology*. Dordrecht: Foris Publications.

Riđanović, Midhat & Nadira Aljović. 2009. On the shift of Bosnian accent from host to proclitic: New insights. In Steven Franks, Vrinda Chidambaram & Brian Joseph (eds.), *A Linguist's*

Linguist: Studies in South Slavic Linguistics in Honor of E. Wayles Browne, 387–402. Bloomington, IN: Slavica Publishers.

Ross, John. 1967. *Constraints on variables in syntax*. Cambridge, MA. Massachusetts Institute of Technology dissertation.

Schenker, Alexander M. 1993. Proto-Slavonic. In Greville Corbett & Bernard Comrie (eds.), *The Slavonic Languages*, 60–121. London/New York: Routledge.

Selkirk, Elisabeth. 1996. The prosodic structure of function words. In James Morgan & Katherine Demuth (eds.), *Signal to Syntax: Bootstrapping from Speech to Grammar in Early Acquisition*, 187–213. Oxford: Taylor & Francis.

Stjepanović, Sandra. 1998. On the placement of Serbo-Croatian clitics: Evidence from VP ellipsis. *Linguistic Inquiry* 29. 527–537.

Talić, Aida. 2015. Adverb extraction, specificity, and structural parallelism. *The Canadian Journal of Linguistics/La revue canadienne de linguistique* 60(3). 417–454.

Talić, Aida. 2018. Spelling out enclitics and giving their tone a voice: Cyclic clitic incorporation in BCS and breaking the cycle. *The Linguistic Review* 35(2). 307–370.

Talić, Aida. 2019. Upward P-cliticization, accent shift, and extraction out of PP. *Natural Language and Linguistic Theory* 37(3). 1103–1143.

Talić, Aida. 2020. Syntactic complexity Bosnian/Croatian/Serbian (BCS) long form adjectives and their tone. LSA Handout.

Yu, Kristine. 2021. Tonal marking of absolutive case in Samoan. *Natural Language & Linguistic Theory* 39. 291–365.

Zec, Draga. 1993. Rule domains and phonological change. In Sharon Hargus & Ellen M. Kaisse (eds.), *Studies in Lexical Phonology*, 365–405. San Diego: Academic Press.

Zec, Draga. 2005. Prosodic differences among function words. *Phonology* 22. 77–112.

Zec, Draga & Sharon Inkelas. 1991. The place of clitics in the prosodic hierarchy. *West Coast Conference on Formal Linguistics* (WCCFL) 10. 505–519.

Marcel den Dikken
A Phonosyntactic Representation of Hungarian 'Lowering'

Abstract: This paper presents a phonosyntactic analysis of Hungarian 'lowering' exploiting categorising heads in the syntactic representation of the major parts of speech, and deriving the difference between 'lowering' and non-'lowering' triggers from properties of these categorisers and the syntax of agreement and movement. Being or not being a 'lowering' trigger is a function of syntactic head movement of the acategorial root to the categoriser. Hungarian categorisers are endowed with the element |A| 'open'. Not having a timing slot of its own, the categoriser remains silent unless the categorised head combines with a functional suffix containing a linking vowel upon which it can be exponed.

Keywords: lowering, Hungarian, phonosyntax, agreement, movement, categorization, |A|

1 Introduction

This paper presents a phonosyntactic analysis of Hungarian 'lowering' exploiting categorising heads in the syntactic representation of the major parts of speech, and deriving the difference between lowering and non-lowering triggers from properties of these categorisers and the syntax of agreement and movement. Being or not being a lowering trigger is a function of syntactic head movement of the acategorial root to the categoriser. Hungarian categorisers are inherently endowed with the element |A| 'open'. Not having a timing slot of its own, the categoriser remains silent unless the categorised head combines with a functional suffix containing a linking vowel upon which it can be exponed. The exponence restrictions imposed on categorising heads also account for vowel~zero alternations differentiating between lowering and non-lowering stems.

Acknowledgements: I would like to thank Lena Borise, Éva Dékány, two anonymous reviewers, and the editors of this volume for their helpful and constructive comments and discussion.

Marcel den Dikken, Department of English Linguistics, SEAS, Eötvös Loránd University & Hungarian Research Centre for Linguistics, Budapest, Hungary

https://doi.org/10.1515/9783110730098-016

2 Hungarian Vowel Harmony and Lowering

As a rule, Hungarian roots and stems cause the vowels in their suffixes to harmonise for palatality (the front/back distinction) and, for ternary (three-way alternating) and quaternary (four-way alternating) suffixes, also for labiality (rounding). We see this in (1), for the plural, accusative and person/number suffixes of nouns,[1] and in (2), for the past-tense and person/number suffixes of verbs.[2]

(1)   Noun   N-PL   N-ACC   N-1SG
- a.   kürt   'horn'   kürt-ök   kürt-öt   kürt-öm   [−back,+high,+round]
- a'.   szirt   'cliff'   szirt-ek   szirt-et   szirt-em   [−back,+high,−round]
- b.   tök   'pumpkin'   tök-ök   tök-öt   tök-öm   [−back,−high,+round]
- b'.   kert   'garden'   kert-ek   kert-et   kert-em   [−back,−high,−round]
- c.   rum   'rum'   rum-ok   rum-ot   rum-om   [+back,+high,+round]
- d.   bolt   'shop'   bolt-ok   bolt-ot   bolt-om   [+back,−high,+round]
- e.   kard   'sword'   kard-ok   kard-ot   kard-om   [+back,+low]

(2)   Verb   V-PAST   V-1SG.DEF
- a.   süt   'to bake'   süt-ött   süt-öm   [−back,+high,+round]
- a'.   csíp   'to pinch, sting'   csíp-ett   csíp-em   [−back,+high,−round]
- b.   köt   'to knit'   köt-ött   köt-öm   [−back,−high,+round]
- b'.   kezd   'to begin'   kezd-ett   kezd-em   [−back,−high,−round]
- c.   fut   'to run'   fut-ott   fut-om[3]   [+back,+high,+round]
- d.   do   'to throw'   dob-ott   dob-om   [+back,−high,+round]
- e.   lát   'to see'   lát-ott   lát-om   [+back,+low]

---

[1] Person/number inflection appears on possessed nouns, cross-referencing the φ-features of the possessor.

[2] All Hungarian vowels alternate in length (with vowel length marked in the orthography with the aid of acute accents – double in the case of the front-rounded vowels ő [ø:] and ű [y:], and single elsewhere); long and short vowels behave alike in the harmony system. A twist is that a small subset of nouns and verbs with the phonetically [−back] vowels *i* [i], *í* [i:] and *é* [e:] pair up with back vowels in their suffixes: see (i) and (ii). The 'anti-harmonic' behaviour of these phonetically front vowels falls out from the text proposal if these are assigned no specification for the element |I| – i.e., they are not *phonologically* palatal. (See also van der Hulst 2018: §4.4.2.)

(i)   a.   zsír   'fat$_N$'   zsír-ok   'PL'   zsír-om   '1SG'
      b.   cél   'goal'   cél-ok   'PL'   cél-om   '1SG'

(ii)   hív   'call$_V$'   hív-ott   'PAST'   hív-om   '1SG.DEF'

[3] Though usually intransitive, *fut* can take a definite object, as in *futom a maratont* 'I am running the marathon'.

The forms in (1/2a,a′) and (1/2b,b′) illustrate the harmonic behaviour of quaternary suffixes attached to front-vowel hosts – rounded in the primeless cases and unrounded in the primed ones. The forms in (1/2c–e) exemplify backness harmony for the same set of suffixes.

Although we only see a three-way (ö/e/o) suffix-vowel alternation in the examples in (1) and (2), the suffixes illustrated there are called quaternary because they have a fourth form showing up under limited circumstances. While verb stems are always 'well-behaved', about 200 nouns and 'most adjectives' (Siptár and Törkenczy 2000: 226; Törkenczy 2011: 2980) behave in an out-of-the-ordinary way with regard to vowel harmony: they trigger what is generally referred to as 'lowering'.[4] For lowering triggers, there are only two options for the vowels in the suffixes: e [ɛ] for front-vowel hosts (see (3a,b)), and a [ɔ] (not seen in (1)) for nonpalatal hosts (as in (3c–e)).[5] For hosts that 'under normal circumstances' take e [ɛ] (i.e., for forms with front unrounded vowels: (1a′) and (1b′)), this special behaviour cannot be illustrated in standard (Budapest) Hungarian;[6] but for all other forms in (1), it can be.

---

[4] For nouns, lowering is idiosyncratic and unpredictable, though certain subregularities can be found: e.g., all long-vowel-final stems that add a [v] under attachment of a V-initial suffix are lowering triggers (ló 'horse'~lov-ak 'horse-PL'; Siptár and Törkenczy 2000: 230). Among the very few adjectives that do not trigger lowering is the high-frequency adjective nagy 'big'~nagy-ok 'big-PL' (Siptár and Törkenczy 2000: 230, fn. 35). For [v]-adding nominal roots, lowering can perhaps be explained from the perspective of the proposal advanced in this paper with an appeal to the idea that, for these roots, [v] is the exponent of the categorising 'little n': if the presence of [v] under n bars movement of the root to n, this in turn explains lowering. The fact that the adjective nagy is not a lowering trigger is not in any obvious way linkable to an independently established property of this root's categorising 'little a', however: it does not seem to me possible to morphosyntactically confirm the hypothesis that nagy must move up to the 'little a' whereas the vast majority of adjectives do not so move. (The diagnostic used in the text further below, viz., degree modification, yields the same result for nagy as it does for other gradable adjectives: elég nagy '(lit.) enough big'.) Thus, the few exceptions to lowering in the adjectival realm remain inexplicable for my phonosyntactic approach.

[5] Anti-harmonic í [iː] and é [eː] (recall fn. 2) also participate in this pattern: see (i).

(i) a. híd 'bridge'   híd-ak 'PL'   híd-am '1SG'
    b. héj 'crust, bark'   héj-ak 'PL'   héj-am '1SG'

[6] There are Hungarian dialects in which a distinction is made between mid [e] and low [ɛ]. In these dialects, even stems with front unrounded vowels overtly evince lowering: kép-et [keːpɛt] 'picture-ACC' versus gyep-et [ɟepet] 'lawn-ACC' (pronounced as [ɟɛpɛt] in the Budapest variety; see Siptár and Törkenczy 2000: 225). Apart from the anti-harmonic cases mentioned in fn. 5, in Budapest Hungarian lowering is only audible in the signal for stems with front rounded vowels or back vowels.

(3)

	N		N-PL	N-ACC	N-POSS:1SG
a.	sült	'roast'	sült-ek	sült-et	sült-em
b.	könyv	'book'	könyv-ek	könyv-et	könyv-em
c.	lyuk	'hole'	lyuk-ak	lyuk-at	lyuk-am
d.	hold	'moon'	hold-ak	hold-at	hold-am
e.	ház	'house'	ház-ak	ház-at	ház-am

The reduction of the inventory of harmonic forms to *e* [ɛ] and *a* [ɔ] is systematic in strings of inflectional suffixes. We see this in (4) (for the nouns in (1)) and (5) (for the verbs in (2)). In each set, there is a sequence of two inflectional suffixes. The first suffix behaves as previously illustrated; but the linking vowel of the second suffix only has a two-way choice: *e* [ɛ] for front-vowel hosts, and *a* [ɔ] for back-vowel ones.

(4)

	N		N-PL-ACC	
a.	kürt	'horn'	kürt-ök-et	*kürt-ök-öt
b.	tök	'pumpkin'	tök-ök-et	*tök-ök-öt
c.	rum	'rum'	rum-ok-at	*rum-ok-ot
d.	bolt	'shop'	bolt-ok-at	*bolt-ok-ot
e.	kard	'sword'	kard-ok-at	*kard-ok-ot

(5)

	V		V-PAST-SU:1SG	
a.	süt	'to bake'	süt-ött-em	*süt-ött-öm
b.	köt	'to knit'	köt-ött-em	*köt-ött-öm
c.	fut	'to run'	fut-ott-am	*fut-ott-om
d.	dob	'to throw'	dob-t-am	*dob-t-om
e.	lát	'to see'	lát-t-am	*lát-t-om

It is not the case, however, that anytime a suffix is added to a form that already has a harmonising inflectional suffix attached to it, the additional suffix will only have a choice of two harmonic vowels, *e* [ɛ] or *a* [ɔ]. This is clear from the behaviour of the spatial suffixes -*hVz* 'allative' and -*Vn* 'superessive'. With regular front-vowel roots, these ternary suffixes have two forms, -*hez*/-*en* and -*höz*/-*ön*, with the choice transparently determined by the labiality of the host vowel, in both the singular and the plural: see (6a,b). With front-vowel roots of the type in (3a,b), the suffix vowel is *ö* [œ] in the singular and *e* [ɛ] in the plural: (6c). And with back-vowel roots, the vowel *o* [o] (-*hoz*/-*on*) is the only option: whether the root is of type (1c–e) or of type (3c–e) has consequences for the form of the plural marker but not for that of the ternary spatial suffix. We see this in (6d,e).[7]

(6)
	N		N-PL	N-ALL	N-PL-ALL	N-SUP	N-PL-SUP
a.	kert	'garden'	kert-ek	kert-hez	kert-ek-hez	kert-en	kert-ek-en
b.	tök	'pumpkin'	tök-ök	tök-höz	tök-ök-höz	tök-ön	tök-ök-ön
c.	könyv	'book'	könyv-ek	könyv-höz	könyv-ek-hez	könyv-ön	könyv-ek-en
d.	bolt	'shop'	bolt-ok	bolt-hoz	bolt-ok-hoz	bolt-on	bolt-ok-on
e.	ház	'house'	ház-ak	ház-hoz	ház-ak-hoz	ház-on	ház-ak-on

Ever since Vago (1974), the bleaching of the colouration of the linking vowels of inflectional suffixes seen in (3)–(5) has been known as 'lowering'. For the back-vowel cases, this terminology is transparent: *a* [ɔ] is phonetically lower than *o* [o], and the two vowels form pairs with long vowels that likewise clearly differ in height (*á* [aː] and *ó* [oː], resp.). In the front realm, it is less obvious that lowering is involved: the vowel *e*, pronounced invariably as [ɛ] in Budapest Hungarian (recall fn. 6), patterns in the phonology of the language both with the long vowel *é* [eː], which is a mid vowel, and with the low vowel *a* [ɔ]; correspondingly, *e* [ɛ] is sometimes given a dual (mid/low) treatment in phonological analyses of Hungarian (e.g., van der Hulst 2018: 182). In this paper, I will not phonologise the phenomena illustrated in (3)–(5) in terms of actual lowering. But because the term 'lowering' is useful as a widely accepted descriptor, I will avail myself of it in what follows to refer to the phenomena in (3)–(5).

There are a plethora of purely phonological and morphophonological analyses on the market for Hungarian lowering (see, e.g., Vago 1974, 1980; Kornai 1991; Rebrus and Polgárdi 1997; Siptár and Törkenczy 2000; Rebrus 2000; van der Hulst 2018, and references cited there). The extreme brevity of this paper will not allow me to do justice to the extant literature. Rather, what I will endeavour to do in this short piece is to bring syntax into the picture, and provide a phonosyntactic analysis of 'lowering'. This analysis exploits categorising functional heads in the syntactic representation of the major parts of speech, deriving the difference in behaviour between lowering and non-lowering triggers from properties of the categorising heads that they combine with in their syntax and from the (non-) application of movement of the root up to the categoriser. This procures a simple account of the lowering facts without having to complicate the phonology, and

---

[7] Illustration here is confined to the forms with front-rounded vowels: front-unrounded vowels always trigger *-hez* and back vowels always combine with *-hoz*; the allative being a ternary suffix, there is no 'lowered' form *-haz*.

offers an outlook on vowel~zero alternations emerging in tandem with lowering that draws a parallel with '*do*-support'.

3 The Phonosyntax of Lowering

The first step in the development of an analysis of lowering that attributes a key role to morphosyntax is the important observation that lowering is not a property of roots as such. We see this, for instance, by considering the behaviour of the word *tűz*, which can be used both as a noun ('fire') and as a verb ('to blaze, glare').[8] As a noun, *tűz* triggers lowering;[9] but as a verb it does not:

(7) a. tüz-et/*-öt láttam
    fire-ACC see.PAST.1SG
    'I saw fire'

    b. tűz-ött/*-ett a nap
    blaze-PAST the sun
    'the sun was blazing'

In a similar vein, *vörös*, *komikus* and *szárnyas* can be adjectives (meaning 'red', 'comical', 'winged') or nouns ('communist', 'comedian', 'poultry'). Both in their adjectival use and in their nominal one, these forms can be marked with the plural suffix -*Vk*. But only only the adjectives trigger 'lowering':

(8) a. ezek vörös-ek/*-ök ezek komikus-ak/*-ok ezek szárnyas-ak/*-ok
    these red-PL these comical-PL these winged-PL
    'these are red' 'these are comical' 'these are winged'

    b. a vörös-ök/*-ek a komikus-ok/*-ak a szárnyas-ok/*-ak
    the red-PL the comedian-PL the poultry-PL
    'the reds/communists' 'the comedians' 'the poultry'

In current morphosyntactic theorising, lexical roots are assumed not to be endowed with categorial features: they have their categorial status determined

---

[8] The verb *tűz* can also mean 'to stitch', derived from the noun *tű* 'needle'. This sense of *tűz*$_V$ is irrelevant here.
[9] The root vowel of *tűz* shortens in (7a). This is entirely independent of lowering, however, and will be ignored.

in the syntactic context in which they appear, by dedicated categorising heads, labelled by the traditional part-of-speech categories and printed in lower-case italics (*a*, *n*, *v*, and possibly *p*).[10] When the root √TŰZ syntactically combines with 'little *n*', it is categorised as a noun, and when the same root finds itself in the complement of 'little *v*' in syntax, it is a verb. Similarly, when √VÖRÖS teams up with 'little *a*', it is an adjective; but 'little *n*' makes it a noun.

(9) a. [$_{nP}$ *n* [√TŰZ]] → *tűz*$_N$ 'fire'   [$_{aP}$ *a* [√VÖRÖS]] → *vörös*$_A$ 'red'
    b. [$_{vP}$ *v* [√TŰZ]] → *tűz*$_V$ 'blaze' [$_{nP}$ *n* [√VÖRÖS]] → *vörös*$_N$ 'red'

In light of this, the distribution of lowering with roots such as *tűz* and *vörös* can be recast as a function of the categorisers that these roots combine with in syntax. On this approach, lowering is not a property of the (acategorial) root but something determined by the categoriser ('little *x*'). In the remainder of this section, I will demonstrate how the categorising 'little *x*' can be exploited to maximum advantage in a syntactic account of the vocalic phonology of Hungarian suffixation.

There are two primary things that need to be explained about the behaviour of vowels in the Hungarian suffixation system, and 'little *x*' assists us with both. First, Hungarian suffixes never have a high linking vowel. (High-vowel suffixes do occur, but their vowel is never a linking vowel.) We could stipulate this for the linking vowels of each individual harmonising suffix. But it would be much more economical to pin the height restriction on something that they all have in common. In phonosyntax, the generalisation that the linking vowel of Hungarian suffixes is non-high can readily be translated into the statement that all catego-

---

10 The idea that roots are acategorial finds its origin (in the generative framework) in the theory of Distributed Morphology (DM; Halle and Marantz 1993). It is customary in the DM-inspired literature to assume that categorisation can only be performed by designated 'little *x*'s (although the acategoriality thesis as such is compatible with a more radical approach to categorisation according to which any functional head, not just 'little *x*', can carry this out).

DM takes the presyntactic lexicon to contain basic building blocks that are endowed with morphological features but not phonologically or semantically idiosyncratic content. In the proposal advanced in this paper, categorising 'little *x*'s in Hungarian are always equipped with the phonological element |A| 'open', which is part and parcel of their definition. For the analysis, it is essential that the phonosyntax has access to this phonological content. This is straightforward if phonological content is specified early. But a phonosyntactic analysis of the type presented in the text does not require early insertion of phonological features: the essence of the phonosyntactic approach is that phonology works with hierarchical structural representations and dependencies entirely analogous to those of syntax; there is syntax on the PF wing of the grammar. So long as the output of syntactic derivation is carried over into PF, phonosyntax will be able to couch its analyses in terms of these hierarchical structures even if phonological features are inserted late.

rising 'little *x*' heads of the language are endowed with the element |A| 'open'. Though the effects that *a*, *n* and *v* have on the category of their complement are different, their phonology, in Hungarian, is the same: *a*, *n* and *v* all have |A| associated with them.

The 'little *x*'s |A| element has no effect on the realisation of the vowel of the root: the root vowel's phonological content (|I,U| in the case of √TŰZ; |A,I,U| for √VÖRÖS) is specified directly on the root, and invariant. Phrased in terms of the minimalist syntactic theory of feature checking/valuation, the root has no unvalued features which the |A| of the 'little *x*' could value in an Agree relationship with the root: the root has an inherent phonological feature content that is fully valued. But though the |A| in 'little *x*' does not influence the form of the root vowel(s), it does cause the linking vowel(s) of all suffixes attached to the root to be non-high: the linking vowels of suffixes are not inherently valued for height (i.e., they are |uA|[11]), and harmonise with the |A| of the categorising 'little *x*' as a function of Agree. As a result, all √-external linking vowels are mid or low vowels.

The second thing that the inherent |A| element of 'little *x*' helps us with is the account of the distribution of lowering. For roots, being or not being a lowering trigger translates as a function of the absence or presence of syntactic head movement of the root to the categorising 'little *x*': lowering is correlated with *non*-raising of the root to 'little *x*'. Movement of √ to *x* causes the √+categoriser complex to acquire all of the lexical specifications of the vowel(s) of the root. As we will see in more detail below, this makes it possible for the vowel of the first inflectional suffix to exhibit both palatal and labial harmony with the root. In the absence of √-to-*x* movement, however, only *e* [ɛ] and *a* [ɔ] are possible as the linking vowels of inflectional suffixes attached to the stem. When there is no raising, the categorising 'little *x*' cannot acquire the full set of features of the root – it can only establish an Agree relation with the root, and the Agree relationship is limited in the amount of material it can see, which causes the bleaching of the linking vowels that characterises lowering.

The idea that the Agree relationship is limited in the amount of featural material that it can see is strongly supported by the morphosyntax of φ-feature agreement. In Den Dikken (2019) I argue that a feature represented on a left branch in the feature representation of a linguistic construct (i.e., an adjunct or specifier) cannot be targeted under Agree. For the morphosyntax of φ-feature agreement, this entails that person agreement (as opposed to number and gender agreement) is never possible under Agree (cf. also Baker 2011): the person feature (π) is struc-

---

11 The italicised lower-case *u* marks 'unvalued'; see Pesetsky & Torrego (2007) for the roots of this convention.

turally represented on a left branch in the feature structure of nominals (more specifically, πP is in the specifier position of the projection of number, #). Among other things (see Den Dikken 2019 for discussion), the hypothesis that (downward) Agree does not have access to φ-features in left-branch positions directly derives the fact that so-called long-distance agreement phenomena (in which agreeing verb and its Agree-goal are in different clauses) are confined to number and gender, and do not involve person.

For the phonosyntax of vowel harmony (also a case of agreement), the fact that Agree cannot see material represented on a left branch impacts labial harmony. |U| is a *secondary* articulation of the vowel of the root, a dependent element represented in an adjunct or specifier position to the primary articulation of the root (see Den Dikken and van der Hulst 2020: 109). On the upside, the fact that |U| is a left-branch element means that it can potentially scope over all the vowels in the root and trigger root-internal labial harmony. But |U|'s left-branch placement makes it inaccessible outside the root, as an Agree-goal to 'little *x*': 'little *x*' can Agree with √ for |A| and |I|, the root's primary articulations; but if √ lexically possesses a labial element |U|, this element is not a legitimate Agree-goal for the 'little *x*' because a head cannot Agree with an element on a left branch inside its complement. So whenever a root √ forgoes raising to the categoriser, the latter cannot be specified for |U|; it can only Agree with the root for |A| and |I|.

Concretely, for the root √TŰZ, whose vowel possesses both |I| and |U|, we get the product in (10a) for the noun (a lowering noun, as we have seen in (7a)), where there is no movement of the root to *n* and only an Agree relationship between *n* and |I|. For the verb (not a lowering trigger: (7b)), √-to-*v* takes place, yielding the structure in (10b). In (10a), the unvalued |*u*I| specification (freely assignable to 'little *x*' provided that a value can be assigned to it under Agree) gets valued by the matching |I| of the root, and after valuation the *n* is specified as |A,I|. In (10b), *v* also Agrees with |I|, but on top of that attracts √ and incorporates it. This creates an adjunction structure, with the feature set of the root ending up in the same position relative to *v* as secondary articulations to √.

(10) a.

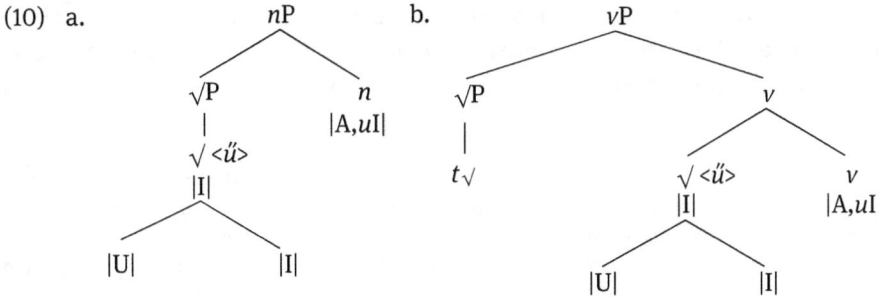

When the root adjoins to a categorising 'little x', the net result is x's inherent feature content plus a secondary articulation – labialisation if the material adjoined to x contains the element |U|. With the consolidated feature set of v in (10b) exponed on the linking vowel of the past-tense suffix, this yields (7b), *tűz-ött a nap*. But in (10a), where √ does not raise to n and n can only establish an Agree relation with the root for the features they share, the categoriser is necessarily devoid of |U|. The accusative of nominal *tűz* is thus *tűz-et*, not **tűz-öt* (7a).

In a similar vein, we get the derivations in (11) for the root √VÖRÖS. In (11a), this root combines with the adjectival categoriser a. Movement of the root up to a arguably does not take place in Hungarian: if they move at all, adjectival roots certainly do not move very far, as is indicated by the word-order facts of degree modification (*nagyon jó* 'very good', *elég jó* '(lit.) enough good', not **jó nagyon/ elég* 'good very/enough' – for *elég~enough*, note the word-order contrast between Hungarian and English). The fact that √VÖRÖS does not raise to a entails that a can only Agree with those features of the root that are directly represented on it, causing |U| to 'be overlooked'. Hence plural inflection of the adjective *vörös* gives rise to a linking vowel that is front but not round: *vörös-ek*, not **vörös-ök* (8a). The representation in (11a) makes the phonosyntax of adjectival *vörös* graphically explicit.

(11) a.   b.

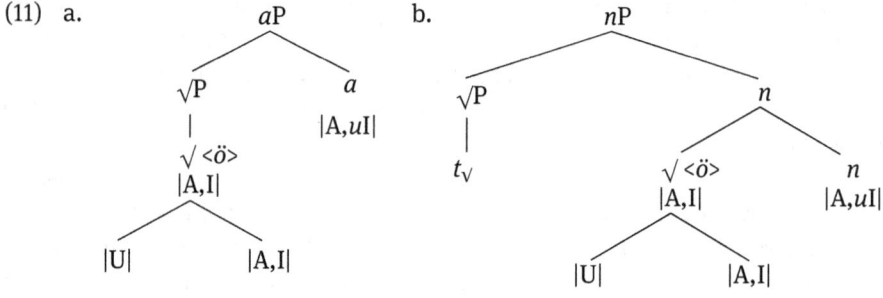

In (11b), we are dealing with nominal(ised) *vörös*. Here the root combines with 'little n'. In the case of nominal *tűz* 'fire' in (10a), raising of the root to n is blocked, by way of an idiosyncratic property.[12] To *vörös*, this idiosyncrasy does not apply: √VÖRÖS is not prevented from raising to n; the product of √VÖRÖS-to-n raising is

---

[12] This idiosyncratic property cannot be encoded on the root itself: after all, √TŰZ does raise to v (recall (10b)). Nor can n by itself be held responsible for the fact that √TŰZ cannot move up to it: n is not categorically resistant to serving as the host of a raised root; it is only for certain roots that such raising is ill-formed. So it must specifically be the *product* of adjunction of √TŰZ to n that is rejected: the output [$_n$ √TŰZ [$_n$ n]] is illicit.

depicted in (11b). Thanks to √-to-*n* raising, all of the root's vocalic information (including |U|), consolidated under √ at spell-out of *n*, becomes a secondary articulation to the inherent feature content of *n*: (8b).

For front-vowel roots, lowering (i.e., absence of √-to-*x* raising, on the phonosyntactic approach pursued here) results in the emergence of the element cluster |A,I| for the linking vowel of the first inflectional suffix attached to the stem, spelled out as *e* [ɛ]. With back-vowel roots of the lowering type (see (3c–e)), the element |I| is absent from the root, and as a consequence no |uI| can be postulated on the categorising 'little *x*': *x* is only endowed with |A|. As a consequence, for back-vowel roots the categorised product will be specified only as |A|. This in turn guarantees that the linking vowel of the first inflectional suffix attached to a back-vowel lowering stem will be spelled out as the realisation in Hungarian of 'plain' |A|, the open-most vowel of the language: *a* [ɔ]. The structure in (12a) illustrates, for the case of *ház* 'house' (3e).

(12)

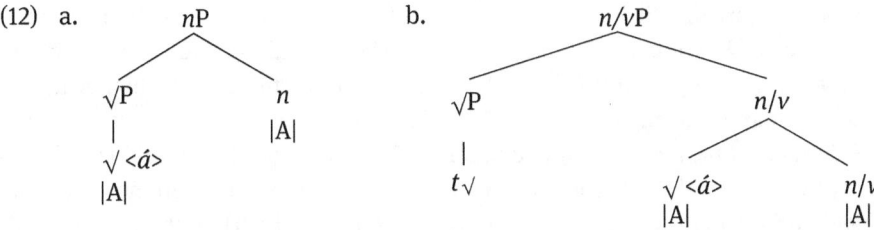

For back-vowel stems that are not lowering triggers, the linking vowel of the first inflectional suffix is the phonetically clearly rounded vowel *o* [o] – even if the root lacks |U|, as in the case of the verb *lát* (*lát-om* 'see-1SG.DEF', (2e)) or the non-lowering noun *kár* (*kár-ok* 'damage-PL'). In phonosyntactic terms, this means that the feature set of the entity formed by raising to *x* of a root √ that is not specified for |I| or |U| is spelled out as *o* [o] *qua* linking vowel, as in (12b). Recall that raising of √ to *x* involves the creation of an adjunction structure of the same type as one involving secondary articulation. The consolidated feature set of this adjunction structure is exponed as the linking vowel. With this set containing neither |I| nor |U|, the linking vowel cannot be *e* [ɛ] or *ö* [œ]: these are both palatal, but 'little *x*' is not specified for |I|. The high vowels are all off the table as well because |A| is an integral part of the √+*x* complex. We are not dealing with 'plain' |A| (spelled out as *a* [ɔ]) either because in the event of √-to-*x* movement 'little *x*' is not 'bare': it has the root's feature content attached to it. So the only candidate that remains is *o* [o], the default non-palatal mid vowel – phonetically rounded, but not phonologically equipped with |U| when serving as a linking vowel for suffixes to non-lowering back-vowel stems (just like *a* [ɔ] is never phonologically |U| in

Hungarian). This is a case of neutralisation (similar to the neutralisation of |I|=[i] and |∅|=[i]; see fn. 2): |A,U|=[o] *and* |A,√|=[o] (where '√' stands for the phonological features of a root incorporated into $x_{|A|}$ that does not have have a specification for |I| and may also not be specified for |U|).

We see throughout that the surface colouring of the linking vowel of the first inflectional suffix is the product of the way the phonosyntax specifies and affects the categorising 'little *x*' merged outside the projection of the root. The linking vowel of the first inflectional suffix is spelled out as an interpretation of the inherent feature content of *x* (always |A| and, in the case of front-vowel stems, |uI| as well) plus the feature content of the root – the latter only if √-to-*x* movement takes place in the course of the derivation.

The absence of √-to-*x* raising with lowering stems not only causes the linking vowel of the *first* inflectional suffix attached to the stem to have a colour palette limited to *e* [ɛ] and *a* [ɔ]: it limits the vocalisation of the linking element of all subsequent inflectional suffixes in the same way. Whenever the root fails to raise to the categorising 'little *x*', the element |U| found on the root is entirely inactive in the derivation outside *x*P: since even *x* (the head local to √) fails to establish an Agree relationship with √ for the element |U|, no functional head higher up the tree will manage to engage in a relationship for |U| either. Since the linking vowels of Hungarian harmonising inflectional suffixes are never inherently labial, it is only by virtue of the establishment of a syntactic relation between the functional head harbouring the higher inflectional marker with the |U| of the root that this marker's linking vowel could become labial. But no such relationship with the |U| of the root is establishable in the case of lowering stems. So for lowering stems, we correctly derive the generalisation that the entire string of inflectional suffixes attached to their right will show the effect of lowering. For the noun *tűz* 'fire' and the adjective *vörös* 'red', this is illustrated in (13):

(13) a. tüz-em-et/*-öt b. vörös-ek-et/*-öt
fire-1SG-ACC   red$_A$-PL-ACC
'my fire'   'red ones'

The verb *tűz* 'to blaze' in (10b) and the noun *vörös* 'red' in (11b) do feature √-to-*x* raising, causing the consolidated feature bundle of the root to become a secondary articulation for the categorising 'little *x*', which is exponed on the first available timing slot – the linking vowel of the first inflectional suffix following the categorised stem. This delivers *ö* [œ] as the linking vowel in (7b) and (8b), and also in (1a,b) and (2a,b). But beyond the first inflectional suffix, |U| can play no role in the inflectional phonosyntax even for non-lowering stems. The phonosyntax beyond *x*P only has access to the features that are represented on 'little *x*' and (by the Head Feature Convention) percolated up to xP. These features are exclusively those which the categoriser itself is specified for. In the particular case of Hungarian, this means that the √+x complex categoriser will always be specified for |A| (the inherently valued lexical content of all Hungarian 'little x's) and can in addition be specified for |I|, provided that 'little x' manages to value its |uI| against a matching |I| on the root (i.e., only with front-vowel roots). But the labial element |U| is never an ingredient of 'little x's inherent feature content – not even when x is exponed as a labialised vowel: |U| in (10b) and (11b) is part of the root *adjoined* to x; adjuncts (secondary articulations) do not project their features. This explains that when an inflectional suffix attaches to a non-lowering stem, all further inflectional suffixes attached to this host undergo lowering: the inventory of linking vowels for inflectional suffixes other than the first is always just {e [ɛ], a [ɔ]}. We see this in (4)–(5).

Note that we get lowering beyond the first inflectional suffix even if the first suffix itself is vowelless.[13] Consider the examples in (14):

(14) a. főz-ött b. főz-t-em/*-öm
cook-PAST(3SG.INDEF) cook-PAST-1SG
'(s)he cooked' 'I cooked'

The Hungarian past-tense suffix has two allomorphs: -*Vtt*, with a linking vowel, and purely consonantal -*t*. For a root such as *főz* 'cook', which is not itself a lowering trigger (see (14a)), we get lowering on the person/number markers in past-tense forms employing the vowelless suffix -*t*, as shown by (14b). This is as predicted: for the exponence of the linking vowel of the second inflectional suffix, it does not matter whether the set of vocalic elements on 'little x' is spelled out in the form of the linking vowel of the first inflectional suffix or not; what matters for that second suffix is that the 'little x' head (whether associated with a timing slot or not) is phonosyntactically specified for the elements |A| and, in the case of front-vowel stems, |I|, but never for |U|.

The linking vowel of the second inflectional suffix fails to acquire |U| regardless of whether this suffix triggers raising up to it or 'just' Agrees with the head of its complement. The categorising head 'little x' has the special property of being the head of a spell-out domain, which gives it the unique ability to consolidate the combined featural content of √ and to parse it as a secondary articulation for x's inherent feature content when an adjunction configuration is created in syntax. Any subsequent head movement will involve x, never √ – so beyond x,

---

[13] I will turn to vowel~zero alternations and their interaction with lowering in section 4.

the feature bundle of the root will never find itself in a position *directly* adjoined to (and interpretable as a secondary articulation of) a nucleus. Functional heads outside *x*P that cannot have their linking vowel spelled out by *x*'s feature content therefore cannot acquire a secondary articulation in phonosyntax. They are restricted to exponence of their own inherent feature content.

Now that the behaviour of inflectional suffixes in the realm of lowering has been covered,[14] let me address the fact that the spatial suffixes *-hVz* (allative) and *-Vn* (superessive) are not undergoers of lowering, not even if they are immediately preceded by an inflectional suffix that does lower (such as *ház-ak* 'house-PL' in (6e), repeated below, along with (6a–d)). These spatial suffixes are exponents of adpositions (Ps; see Dékány 2018; Den Dikken and Dékány 2018) merged outside the DP that the root, the categorising *n* and the DP-internal inflections are part of. DP (the maximal noun phrase) is a spell-out domain. Within DP, lowering stems and suffixes can wield their power, as a function of the application of DP-internal Agree and head-movement operations. But this power does not extend beyond DP: once DP has been spelled out, all we have is a string of DP-internal material, consolidating all the features present in DP and 'freezing' them into one large unit.

(6)
	N		N-PL	N-ALL	N-PL-ALL	N-SUP	N-PL-SUP
a.	kert	'garden'	kert-ek	kert-hez	kert-ek-hez	kert-en	kert-ek-en
b.	tök	'pumpkin'	tök-ök	tök-höz	tök-ök-höz	tök-ön	tök-ök-ön
c.	könyv	'book'	könyv-ek	könyv-höz	könyv-ek-hez	könyv-ön	könyv-ek-en
d.	bolt	'shop'	bolt-ok	bolt-hoz	bolt-ok-hoz	bolt-on	bolt-ok-on
e.	ház	'house'	ház-ak	ház-hoz	ház-ak-hoz	ház-on	ház-ak-on

The syntactic head of the Hungarian DP is the definite article, *a* 'the', which occurs to the left of the head. But it plainly is not this article that determines the external harmonic behaviour of the noun phrase. It is the phonological feature content of the string-*final* pronounced head in the DP that determines the realisation of the vowel of the postposition that selects the DP. In the plural examples

---

14 While it is true that all inflectional suffixes trigger lowering on suffixes following them (insofar as they are compatible with further suffixation, of course), it is not the case that the only suffixes that trigger lowering are inflectional in nature: as Siptár & Törkenczy (2000:229) point out, there are some derivational (category-changing) suffixes that are lowering triggers. Interestingly, 'all the derivational suffixes that lower are adjective-forming' (*loc. cit.*). From the perspective of the present proposal, this means that they involve 'little *a*', which in Hungarian resists movement up into it.

in (6), this head is Num (the head of 'Number Phrase'), spelled out as -Vk, whose linking vowel is the exponent of n. In the singular, where Num is either absent altogether or not pronounced, the string-final head of DP is the root itself. In the absence of any suffixes following the root, n remains silent (see Section 4). In the interesting case of (6c), this delivers a distinction between the singular and the plural in the selection of the vowel for the postposition: |A,I,U| (the entire feature set of the root) in the singular (könyv-höz/-ön), and just |A,I| (the features of n) in the plural (könyvek-hez/-en). In back-harmonic (6e), the vowel of the postposition is realised as o [o] in both the singular and the plural (despite the fact that there is no |U| anywhere in the DP). The absence of a [ɔ] from the list of harmonic variants for postpositions is once again the consequence of the creation of an adjunction structure in syntax: Hungarian suffixal postpositions incorporate their complement, creating a structure for their back-harmonic incarnation that is bigger than the structure of a [ɔ] ('plain' |A|), leading to the selection of o [o] as their vowel.

Thus, one of the benefits of a phonosyntactic approach to Hungarian vowel harmony and lowering is that the distinction between 'ternary' and 'quaternary' suffixes reduces entirely to the distinction between suffixes located outside and inside the spell-out domain of the lowering stem. The fact that quaternary suffixes exhibit lowering (i.e., have a [ɔ] as one of the exponents of their linking vowel) follows from the fact that they are inflectional suffixes added to a lowering stem within the confines of the stem's spell-out domain (or 'phase'). Ternary suffixes do not undergo lowering because they are added outside this spell-out domain, and are beyond the reach of the stem's phonosyntactic power.

4 Lowering and Vowel~Zero Alternation

Although the categorising 'little *x*' possesses vocalic feature content, it has no timing slot of its own on the timing (or CV-)tier. This means that in the absence of any suffix attached to the categorised product, 'little *x*' will remain entirely silent. However, when the categorised head combines in syntax with a functional head immediately outside *x*P whose exponent has a linking vowel, the feature content of 'little *x*' spells out as that linking vowel, which provides a position on the timing tier which 'little *x*'s vocalic feature content can dock onto.

A remarkable property of lowering stems is that a linking vowel is required even in the case of suffixation of a morpheme which would be phonotactically allowed to attach directly to the stem without the mediation of a vowel. We see this particularly clearly in the nominal domain, with the accusative case suffix, to be contrasted with the plural suffix:[15]

(15) a. a gáz-t   a gáz-ok
       the gas-ACC   the gas-PL

   b. a ház-at   a ház-ak
       the house-ACC the house-PL

The stem *gáz* is not a lowering trigger. We know this from plural *gáz-ok*, where a linking vowel is needed (because the string [zk] is phonotactically ill-formed in Hungarian), and this linking vowel surfaces as *o* [o] rather than *a* [ɔ]. For the accusative of *gáz*, no linking vowel is needed: direct suffixation of *-t* yields the string [zt], which is legitimate. Sailing on the compass of phonotactics alone, one would have expected *ház* (a lowering stem, in light of plural *ház-ak*) to have formed its accusative via direct *-t* suffixation as well. But what we find in (15b) is that a linking vowel is required here. The same is true for virtually all other lowering stems (see Siptár and Törkenczy 2000: 225, fn. 22 for a few exceptions which, like them, I will set aside, treating the generalisation as categorical). The question is what causes lowering stems to require a phonotactically redundant linking vowel.

Siptár and Törkenczy (2000: 238) propose that lowering stems have a morpheme-final defective vowel, and that this defective vowel (V_d) is incorporated into a following syllable and serves as the target for a floating 'open' feature associated with the stem.[16] This appears to kill two birds with one stone: the licensing of the stem-final V_d gives us the linking vowel, and the floating 'open' feature delivers the colour of that vowel. But the postulation of a morpheme-final vowel specifically for lowering stems is *ad hoc*, and the attribution of defectiveness to this vowel makes lowering stems look handicapped in a way that does not seem justified: lowering stems are different, not imperfect.

---

15 The linking vowel of plural *-Vk* is phonologically a part of the plural suffix (in the form of a timing slot; that this V is not an epenthetic vowel but an intrinsic part of the phonological representation of the plural marker is clear from pairs such as *hüvely-*(e)k* [hyvɛjɛk] 'sheath-PL' ~ *hüvelyk* [hyvɛjk] 'inch'), but syntactically a part of the noun (*n*). Relevant here is Den Dikken's (1999) discussion of syntactic 'migration' of plural *-k* separate from the linking vowel.

16 Siptár and Törkenczy's (2000: 238) proposal that lowering stems have a final floating 'open' feature bears a superficial resemblance to my attribution of the element |A| 'open' to categorising 'little *x*'. A reviewer is right to point out, however, that in my proposal, |A| is not a 'floating feature': it is the phonological definition of 'little *x*' in Hungarian.

For me, lowering stems differ from non-lowering stems in the application of √-to-x raising: the latter raise, the former do not. Thinking along the lines of this phonosyntactic characterisation of lowering, we are led to ask why absence of √-to-x movement should lead to an obligatory linking vowel. The answer suggests a partial parallel between the distribution of linking vowels and '*do*-support' in negated finite clauses. When the categorising 'little *x*' is in possession of locally unlicensed phonological content (unlicensed due to the absence of √-to-x raising), the phonological feature content of *x* can be licensed by being spelled out on a 'dummy' vowel in the *x*P-external suffix. Similarly, when the categorising 'little *x*' possesses locally unlicensed finite φ- and tense-feature content (unlicensed due to the intervention of sentential negation), the morphological feature content of *x* can be licensed by being spelled out on a 'dummy' auxiliary (*do*) in the *x*P-external T-head. In both cases, the absence of the factor that causes the feature content of 'little *x*' to remain locally unlicensed results in there being no need for a dummy. The parallel between the need for a linking vowel and the need for *do*-support is partial in two respects: *(i)* on standard assumptions, the latter does not implicate raising of the root to *x*; and *(ii)* in the former case, the problem can be circumvented by not performing any suffixation at all, as in nominative *a ház* 'the house', where $n_{|A|}$ survives without being exponed. With respect to *(i)*, it seems to me that Pollock's (1989) analysis of English verb placement and inflection may well be simplified and improved if √-to-*v* movement is mobilised as an active ingredient; but I do not currently have the opportunity to pursue this. In connection with *(ii)*, it should be pointed out that in the association of segmental feature content with the timing tier, it is not unusual to see underparsing of melodic material (see, e.g., Marantz's 1982 analysis of reduplication). So the non-exponence of the unlicensed |A| of *x* when all else fails is not entirely without precedent. But in any event, $x_{|A|}$ is not 'defective', nor is its distribution confined to lowering stems.

5 Concluding Remarks

The proposal advanced in this paper postulates for Hungarian that its categorising 'little *x*' is systematically endowed with the element |A| 'open', regardless of its categorial feature content. This explains the absence of high (i.e., non-|A|) linking vowels throughout the language. The |A|-endowed 'little *x*' also plays an instrumental role in the analysis of lowering. But $x_{|A|}$ is not confined to lowering contexts. Lowering is no defect inhering in 'little *x*' or the root; rather, lowering results from non-movement of the root to 'little *x*', which is a syntactic hypothesis. This opens up the possibility of symbiotic interaction between phonology and syntax in language acquisition.

Based on the fact that lowering stems are never verbs, I have postulated that syntactic movement of √ to the categoriser v takes place consistently. It is interesting to note that we know entirely independently of the phonology of lowering that √ always raises to v in Hungarian. Verbs in this language are well known for their ability to raise into the inflectional domain and beyond, into the left periphery of the clause. If the verbal root did not move to v, this would be difficult to understand. The prolific evidence in syntax for verb movement (entirely without regard for individual lexical idiosyncrasies) leads the child acquiring Hungarian to confidently conclude that √-to-v movement is categorical in the language – and that, concomitantly, verb stems never trigger lowering.

For adjectives, explicit evidence for movement of the root to the categoriser a is not forthcoming: indeed, as I mentioned in Section 3, the word-order facts of degree modification (in particular, the difference between Hungarian *elég jó* '(lit.) enough good' and English *good enough*) suggest that in the adjectival domain, roots do not move (much). Proceeding on the conservative presumption that in the absence of explicit evidence for movement, no ('vacuous') movement should be postulated, the language learner plausibly translates this into the hypothesis that roots do not raise to a. For their phonology, this entails that adjectives will consistently trigger lowering.

While verbs and adjectives are (almost) categorical in their raising or non-raising to 'little x', the category of nouns is not homogeneous. Though the majority of noun roots undergo √-to-n movement and, as a consequence, do not trigger lowering, a sizeable minority resist movement to n, and cause the linking vowels of their inflectional suffixes to be restricted to e [ɛ] and a [ɔ]. Unfortunately, the distribution of lowering with nouns does not seem to be tied in any direct or transparent way to (morpho)syntactic properties.[17] This means that the language learner cannot rely on independent (morpho)syntactic pointers to determine whether a noun root will raise to n or not: the distribution of this raising in syntax (and, concomitantly, the distribution of lowering in phonology) is truly idiosyncratic in the nominal realm.

But at least in the adjectival and verbal domains, the learner gets some useful help from syntax in figuring out whether there will be lowering or not. The fact that the distribution of √-to-x movement is linked to known syntactic asymmetries allows this paper's central hypothesis to make sense of the system-

---

[17] Etymology may occasionally provide a clue; but such a clue would not be of any help in language acquisition.

aticity of absence of lowering in the verbal realm (roots always raise to v) and the near-uniformity of lowering with adjectives (assuming that roots do not raise to a). And although it does not as yet give us a predictive purchase on the distribution of lowering in the nominal domain, the idiosyncratic behaviour of nouns regarding lowering can at least be linked to known cases of lexically based variation in head movement (see, e.g., the fact that θ-role assigning verbs do not move to T in English, whereas non-θ-role assigning verbs do).

References

Baker, Mark. 2011. When agreement is for number and gender but not person. *Natural Language & Linguistic Theory* 29. 875–915. doi: 10.1007/s11049-011-9147-z.

Dékány, Éva. 2018. The position of casemarkers relative to possessive agreement: Variation within Hungarian. *Natural Language & Linguistic Theory* 36. 365–400. https://doi.org/10.1007/s11049-017-9379-7.

Dikken, Marcel den. 1999. On the structural representation of possession and agreement: The case of (anti-)agreement in Hungarian possessed nominal phrases. In I. Kenesei (ed.), *Crossing Boundaries: Theoretical Advances in Central and Eastern European Languages*, 137–178. Amsterdam: John Benjamins.

Dikken, Marcel den. 2019. The attractions of agreement: Why person is different. *Frontiers in Psychology*. https://doi.org/10.3389/fpsyg.2019.00978.

Dikken, Marcel den & Éva Dékány. 2018. Adpositions and case: Alternative realisation and concord. *Finno-Ugric Languages & Linguistics* 7. 39–75.

Dikken, Marcel den & Harry van der Hulst. 2020. On some deep structural analogies between syntax and phonology. In Kunia Nasukawa (ed.), *Morpheme-Internal Recursion in Phonology*, 57–114. Berlin: De Gruyter Mouton.

Halle, Morris & Alec Marantz. 1993. Distributed morphology and the pieces of inflection. In K. Hale & S. J. Keyser (eds.), *The View from Building 20*, 111–176. Cambridge, MA: MIT Press.

Hulst, Harry van der. 2018. *Asymmetries in Vowel Harmony: A Representational Account*. Oxford: Oxford University Press.

Kornai, András. 1991. Hungarian vowel harmony. In I. Kenesei (ed.), *Approaches to Hungarian*, vol. 3, 183–240. Szeged: JATE.

Marantz, Alec. 1982. Re: Reduplication. *Linguistic Inquiry* 13. 435–483.

Pesetsky, David & Esther Torrego. 2007. The syntax of valuation and the interpretability of features. In S. Karimi, V. Samiian & W. Wilkins (eds.), *Phrasal and Clausal Architecture*, 262–294. Amsterdam: John Benjamins.

Pollock, Jean-Yves. 1989. Verb movement, universal grammar, and the structure of IP. *Linguistic Inquiry* 20. 365–424.

Rebrus, Péter. 2000. Morfofonologiai jelensegek [Morphophonological phenomena]. In F. Kiefer (ed.), *Strukturalis magyar nyelvtan III. Morfologia*, 763–947. Budapest: Akademiai Kiado.

Rebrus, Péter & Krisztina Polgárdi. 1997. Two default vowels in Hungarian? In G. Booij & J. van de Weijer (eds.), *Phonology in Progress – Progress in Phonology*, 257–275. (HILP Phonology Papers III). The Hague: Holland Academic Graphics.

Siptár, Péter & Miklós Törkenczy. 2000. *The Phonology of Hungarian*. Oxford: Oxford University Press.

Törkenczy, Miklós. 2011. Hungarian vowel harmony. In M. van Oostendorp, C. J. Ewen, E. V. Hume & K. Rice (eds.), *Blackwell Companion to Phonology*, vol. 5, 2963–2989. Oxford: Blackwell.

Vago, Robert M. 1974. Hungarian generative phonology. Cambridge, MA: Harvard University Doctoral dissertation; revised and condensed version published as Vago (1980).

Vago, Robert M. 1980. *The Sound Pattern of Hungarian*. Washington, DC: Georgetown University Press.

John A. Goldsmith
Zellig Harris, Phonological Boundaries, and Features

Abstract: We offer a close reading of a rarely discussed section in Zellig Harris's Methods in Structural Linguistics (1951), and show how Harris tried to develop a notion of phonological feature that was grounded in the distribution of neighboring segments, rather than in properties of the inventory of phonemes in a language. Along the way we illustrate the fact that Harris's conception of doing phonology was not in any way tied to a belief that analysis should be mechanical or automatic; what was important, instead, was that the analysis provided a compact description of the language, a view that would later be developed by Chomsky in the context of an evaluation metric.

Keywords: Zellig Harris, phonological features, phonology, syntagmatic relations, paradigmatic relations, Noam Chomsky, Swahili, phonological boundaries

1 Introduction

While Zellig Harris's book *Methods in Structural Linguistics* (1951) is cited from time to time, I suspect it is less often read, and when it is read, it is, I think, most often read with the aim of finding passages which confirm the reader's prior expectations of what will be found there.[1] Some readers expect to find Harris proposing methods that will automatically provide a phonemic analysis from a corpus or from an informant. Others expect to find a defense of Bloomfieldian or Sapirian phonemes. My impression is that it is the rare linguist who actually reads Harris's *Methods* with an open mind to what rules and barriers Harris was trying to break, and to the wildly imaginative twists he was willing to entertain when looking at interesting sets of data. *Methods* is not an exploration of how to come up with automatic or mechanical methods for phonological analysis. It is,

---

[1] I am pleased to offer this paper to a festschrift for Harry van der Hulst, who has been a great force in the development of phonological theory for as long as I can remember. I hope he'll find Harris's interest in phonological components as interesting and surprising as I did! My thanks to the editor of this collection and to a referee for helpful suggestions.

John A. Goldsmith, The University of Chicago

rather, a presentation and discussion of a large number of novel ways of rethinking phonology and morphophonology.[2]

There are for this reason all sorts of interesting analyses of phonology and morphology to be found in *Methods*, and I will describe two aspects of Swahili phonology that Harris explores there. The first involves the use of boundary symbols in phonology (boundaries in phonology ought to be impossible, if you were to believe what people tell you about what he said in the book, but there you are). The other is an approach to features that is completely different from the Trubetzkoy-Jakobson approach, and which is in some respects closer to the more recent post-generative approaches to segmental deconstruction associated with dependency phonology and related approaches. Harris uses the term "dependency" (e.g., 1951: 127) in explaining what he is doing, but calls the pieces that he pulls out "components." I think that Harris's work on "long components" maintains a small place in the collective memory of phonologists, but in the material that I will discuss here, Harris focuses on "unit-length components," and writes:

> As may be seen from the operations of setting them up, the unit-length component analysis of a whole language differs in purpose, procedure and result from the analysis into long components. Combinations of the two techniques may be possible in some languages, if it is desired to set up elements which can express both the distributional limitations of . . . the speech feature characteristics of this appendix.

At the end of the day, it is probably fair to say that Harris did not work out all of the ideas he had in this area: he was trying to account for phenomena that others would call "prosodic" or "suprasegmental," but at the same time he was also trying to offer his own kind of "phonological feature" (which could compete with the Trubetzkoy-Jakobson perspective), and he was doing it in a way that sounds, or looks, more like the decomposition of segments into government-style particles

---

[2] Noam Chomsky has noted on a number of occasions that his first deep dive into linguistics came from reading Harris's book carefully while it was in manuscript form, when he was an undergraduate at the University of Pennsylvania in the late 1940s. There's no doubt that Chomsky read it carefully, and thought about the ideas that Harris floated in the book. I have never heard Chomsky speak directly of the ideas in the book, though his colleague (and my teacher) Morris Halle was convinced that Harris's work was based on a desire to find a one-size-fits-all method of automatically analyzing linguistic data. I don't know if that idea derived from Halle's reading *Methods*, or if it came from discussions with his colleague; but Halle was quite certain of it. The present paper illustrates why this view of *Methods* is quite off the mark.

I might add that I read Harris's article on simultaneous components (1944) rather quickly in 1976, when Morris Halle, my dissertation advisor, told me that it would be necessary for me to explain the difference between Harris's work and that which I proposed in my dissertation (1976). I did not read Harris's *Methods* at that time, and I did not have the phonological breadth, or depth, to understand what Harris was trying to do in that book even if I had read it then.

than it does like Jakobson-Halle features.[3] Harris was also responding to Charles Hockett's ideas on the matter (Hockett 1947). The most important question that Harris did not answer – at least, this is my interpretation of what he wrote – is whether including components in our analysis ultimately leads us to eliminate phonemes. There is a section (1951: 135–136) devoted to this question, and no matter how often I read it, I cannot be sure what Harris's conclusion was. The best I can say is that Harris could see that things were better with components than without them, and that the analyses he came up with using components were unmistakably different than those using only phonemes. They were *better*, not just different, because using components allowed him to provide descriptions of morphemes which were identical in all environments (and when they seemed to vary in their realization in different environments, it was the result of work being done by the components themselves). But was Harris ready to jettison his phoneme? Probably not. Still, it is possible that if he had continued working on phonology after this book he would have gotten there. We cannot know.

The work on boundaries that I will describe would not surprise anyone who has studied generative phonology, though it is a bit surprising to find it in Harris (1951), I think (at least I was quite surprised to find it there). But the work on segment decomposition really *is* surprising, and to be best understood, it is helpful to put it side by side next to the Jakobsonian, or structuralist, point of view.[4] Here is the difference: for the European structuralists, the great insight was Trubetzkoy's (1939), that there are hidden structures within the vowel and consonant inventories of each language. The structures are different, like crystals may be different from one another (diamonds are not graphite, though both are made of carbon, and what makes a diamond a diamond is how the carbon atoms are organized with respect to each other), but because they are crystals, there is a regular pattern through our three-dimensional space governing the layout of the atoms. (These regular patterns are often referred to as spatial symmetries in physics.)

However, Trubetzkoy saw that there were patterns which were not *spatial* in the literal sense, but which could be used to understand the relationship between phonemes. Here is the crucial point: when we place our phonemes in a crystalline array, we are comparing two sounds in the abstract, or as Saussure (1916)

---

3 Readers of this volume will have no need for references to papers on government-style particles, knowing well such papers as Kaye, Lowenstamm, and Vergnaud (1985) and van der Hulst (1989). The Jakobson-Halle view of features was spelled out in Jakobson and Halle (1956).

4 I say "structuralist" advisedly; while the term is appropriate for the Jakobson-inspired work, I don't think the term "structuralist" is appropriate for talking about the American descriptivist community, from Bloomfield and Sapir through Harris and Hockett, as Blevins has argued (2013).

would say, *in absentia*: we say that there is a relationship between /i/ and /u/, and that relationship is a particular opposition which we might call [round]: /i/ is not round while /u/ is round. But an /i/ and an /u/ do not ever meet in space; they are alternative sounds, each of which will show up in this morpheme or that. It was out of these relations that Trubetzkoyan-Jakobsonian features emerged. For Trubetzkoy, what was fundamental was the oppositions, which is a relational notion that requires at least two objects to be in that relationship. It was out of *that*, in turn, that emerged the Jakobson (and later Jakobson-Halle) view that features were properties of the phonemes themselves. This is a big shift which as far as I know Jakobson never discussed explicitly.[5]

When Saussure used the term *in absentia*, he contrasted it with *in praesentia*: we can talk about relations between two segments which are both present, together in space and time, which is to say, when they are adjacent in an utterance, and that is what is meant by *in praesentia*. And this is the domain in which Zellig Harris proposed a feature-like system (Harris did not call it a feature system, though as we will see at the end of the paper, he did use the term once, in a non-Harrisian phonetic context).

Harris comes up with a decomposition of Swahili consonants into pieces that largely do not have any phonetic characteristics; they are motivated by the desire to account for distributional properties. He refers to these new elements as *components*. Certainly he found great fault in Trubetzkoy and Jakobson's reference to phonetics in their discussion of phonological features and oppositions. Harris would have wanted nothing to do with it, it seems to me. Footnote 4 on pages 125–126 refers to the Trubetzkoyan view of features, and to both his own alternative conception, and something similar that Charles Hockett (1947) had suggested around the same time. It is true that on occasion Harris does nod towards the phonetic view; on page 128, he writes, "in terms of articulation, we may say that the difference between /sp/ and /sv/ is one of the voicelessness or fortisness," when the difference, for Harris, is really just the presence or absence of a component. (Harris *does* say that he thinks the components "can be identified with articulatory movements or with features of sound waves" (1951: 142); I will return to this below.)

As an alternative to the structuralist's features, Harris came up with something else in a very language-particular way: a small set of symbols which could be laid out on a page in sequential order which seemed to provide an atomic sort of account of which consonants could occur in a given order in clusters in Swahili. I'll show some of the motivation that he provides for his approach.

---

5 See Goldsmith and Laks (2019), chapter 9. I have discussed much of the material in the present paper with Bernard Laks as well, and I owe some of the ideas here to those conversations.

In summary, then, Trubetzkoy and Jakobson's structuralist approach to segment decomposition was based on relations *in absentia*, that is, the relations between items in an inventory (of vowels, of consonants). For Harris, the decomposition was motivated by what sequences of consonants could be found in a given language *in praesentia*. (The terms *paradigmatic* and *syntagmatic* are also used to describe these two kinds of relations.)

2 Junctures and Boundaries

Harris's chapter on junctures is Chapter 8, and it comes just after a chapter about how to establish a set of phonemes for a language, and how to analyze utterances in terms of such phonemes. For Harris, the first question to ask after we have achieved a phonemic analysis is, Are we satisfied with what we have done? What does this analysis do well, and what does it fail to do? This might surprise someone who thought that Harris's goal in this book was to describe an automatic and universal method for arriving at a linguistic analysis – this is what he is often said to have done – but that is quite the opposite of what he was doing in the book. The method that he illustrates is a method no different from what generative phonologists adopt: he looks at the data, looks at his analysis, and tries to find places where his analysis is missing something and could therefore be made better. Reading Harris leads us to the natural question of what it might be that could strike Harris as less than perfect after he had developed a phonemic analysis of a language. Here are some of the answers that he gives.

First of all, we might find that there is a phoneme with very limited distributions, *especially* if there is another phoneme that is very similar. If we had kept the two distinct from each other in our phonemic analysis, it must have been because there was a *contrast* between them (two different utterances which are minimally different and contain these two sounds in the same context), but when all is said and done, some cases might just not feel right.

Harris felt exactly this way in the treatment of the two phonemes /ay/ and /ʌy/ in American English, which he finds in *minus* m[ay]nus and *slyness* sl[ʌy]ness, respectively (he sometimes notes a lengthening there: sl[ʌ·y]ness). The two diphthongs are not the same; the diphthong in *minus* is shorter, and begins from a more central position than the other vowel. Harris wrote that the difference involved "length, off-glide, and vocalic quality." (1951: 80)

And yet. The two vowels seem so similar, so willing to be allophones of the same phoneme. Couldn't we find a way to make the contexts in which they occur be *different*, so that they could become allophones? Yes, he wrote (1951: 80); we can set up a juncture, written now as a hyphen "-", then place it inside the word *slyness* and assign to *it* certain phonological features. It "occurs with the [vowel] that had the features that have now been assigned to the juncture." And "the tentative /ay/ phoneme is no longer a phoneme, and all previous occurrences are henceforth reanalyzed now as /ay-/."

Really?

To his colleagues at the time, this must have sounded like something halfway between lunacy and heresy, and it would have seemed like the suggestion of someone who had not really internalized what a phoneme was. What arguments could Harris give in his own defense?

The first argument that Harris offers is this: by adding an analysis with a boundary, we have decreased the inventory of phonemes by one, but of course this is not much of an argument, since we have at the very same moment increased the inventory of phonemes (or perhaps symbols) by one (we added the juncture, after all). Harris's argument actually is stronger, because he describes a dialect of English where there is *also* an apparent contrast between the vowels in *playful* and *trayful*; he describes the two words as pl[ey]ful/ and tr[ey]ful. For speakers with such a vowel system, two phonemes would be saved at the cost of introducing only the one juncture phoneme. (I myself do not show such a difference in these two words in my own speech, as far as I am aware.)

Second, Harris notes that the abstract element may account for other, quite separate phenomena. In the case at hand, Harris identifies this boundary element with one that would be posited in compound nouns, such as *night-rate* (whose pronunciation is quite different from that of *nitrate*); the allophones of the final sound of *night* in *night-rate* are quite different from the single phone possible in *nitrate*, and this difference can be described by positing a /-/ juncture in *night-rate*. Harris's third argument is that the /-/ juncture coincides with a position of possible pause. Harris also suggests (1951: 82) that this juncture element can be used to replace the notion of syllable; instead of saying that a segment is the first segment of a syllable, we can say that it is preceded by a /-/ juncture. I don't think that can be counted as an argument, if we are counting arguments, but it does shed light on Harris's opinion of the syllable and how it might play a role in a phonology.

One thing is for sure: Harris realizes he is on to a new method, with this postulation of boundaries. He writes, "by the setting up of the junctures, segments which had previously contrasted may now be associated together into one phoneme, since they are complementary in respect to the juncture." (1951: 86) Of course this flies in the face of phonemicist methodology; of course any contrast can now be accounted for without positing a new phoneme by positing a juncture that triggers a condition that the phoneme is realized in a special way when in the context of this boundary. So what does Harris do? Of course he tells his reader that he is doing nothing new!

> Although the explicit use of junctures is relatively recent, the fundamental technique is involved in such traditional linguistic considerations as 'word-final', 'syllabification', and the use of space between written words. (1951: 86)

Maybe so; but many phonologists were unhappy about allowing phoneme realization rules to be sensitive to contexts like "word-final" for precisely this reason. Now Harris does something curious, which is that he tells us what a linguist does:

> When a linguist sets up the phonemes of a language, he does not stop at the complementary elements of Chapter 7 [that is, traditional phonemic analysis, JG], but coalesces sets of these complementary elements by using considerations of juncture.

They do – if they are Zellig Harris. In fact, Harris goes on to point out that in order to get English right, we need to postulate two (abstract) boundary elements, one which he writes as "#" and the other as "-". The first appears between words, while the second appears inside certain words, like *slyness*, where the stem *sly* is longer than a syllable in a monomorphemic word like *minus* would be.[6]

What's going on here? It certainly looks like Harris is encouraging the phonologists to postulate boundary symbols in order to simplify the phonology – boundary symbols that are essentially the reflection of morphological structure. (What has happened to morphology-less phonology?) What does Harris say? That's exactly right, he says:

> The great importance of junctures lies in the fact that they can be so placed as to indicate various morphological boundaries. (1951: 87)

If a language has predictable penultimate stress, for example – like Swahili – then we can eliminate stress as an element of the phonemic representation just as long as we include word boundaries between the words (1951: 87). In fact, Harris goes on to point out that the phonologist would be wise to restrict his use of boundary symbols to cases where they really do mark morpheme boundaries. German presents an interesting case: the phonologist knows that word-final obstruents are devoiced in German, and so he might want to remove the voiceless obstruents from the phonemic inventory, replacing everywhere a /t/, for example, by /d#/, but this would have the unfortunate consequence of requiring us to place #'s in all sorts of places that are not at all morpheme boundaries, like right after a word-initial consonant: *Teil* 'part' would be /d#ayl/, and this would not correlate with morphological boundaries.

---

[6] Anyone familiar with the history of generative phonology will recognize here these two boundaries, and the origins of the controversies about the status of boundaries and rules associated with strata.

In the case of English phonology, Harris notes, every case where a /-/ boundary is needed, it corresponds to a morpheme boundary (as in *slyness*, for example). The converse however does not hold: not every morpheme boundary corresponds phonemically to a /-/. Harris says *playful* does not have a /-/ boundary, but *trayfull* (which he writes *tr[e·y]full*) does – purely on descriptive grounds.

Harris is quite clear (1951: 88) that phonemic analysis should certainly take morphemic analysis into account when the data of the language suggest that this be done, and phonological analysis can be simplified by positing phonological boundary elements which typically correspond to morphological boundaries:

> The agreement [between the needs of the phonemic analysis and the boundaries motivated by morphology] is, furthermore, due in part to the partial dependence between phonemes and morphemes.

This is the second moment when the reader may think that what Harris wrote is quite a bit different from what others say that he wrote. In fact, throughout this book Harris is at pains to show the legitimacy of using morphological information to inform the phonological analysis.

Back to the junctures. The phonologist just may have to guess where the morpheme boundaries are, by seeing how this simplifies the phonological analysis:

> In much linguistic practice, where phonemes are tentatively set up while preliminary guesses are being made as to morphemes, tentative junctures may be defined not on the basis of any knowledge that particular morphemes are worth uniting . . . but only on the basis of suspicions as to where morpheme boundaries lie in given utterances. (1951: 89)

To summarize, then, in contemporary terms: the phonologists may posit abstract boundary symbols – any number of them – in their phonology, if they suspect that a morphological analysis will find motivation for them. No one could read this carefully and interpret this method as one in which phonemic analysis precedes morphological analysis!

As I noted just above, Harris takes the boundary concept a step further, introducing a second boundary symbol, #, which in the first instance marks the end of an utterance. But the phonologist may find that there are two very similar phonemes that fail to both appear in utterance-final position (Harris's example is two versions of *k*, one released (let us say [k_1]) and one not ([k_2]). The one that appears in word final position [k_2] can be analyzed as /k/ plus # – *and* when we find that allophone in other positions inside the utterance, we can posit a # there as well! For example, if we find a contrast in the phrases "go to mar[k_2] it" and "go to mar[k_2]et", then we ought to analyze these with a single phoneme /k/ and with a junction # in the first case, that of "go to mark# it." Today we call this a word boundary, of course.

How does this differ from the Chomsky/Halle *SPE* analysis? The principal way in which it differs is that Harris does not take the presence of boundaries to be given ahead of time. They are to be included in the analysis if the phonologist finds that there is data that can be explained through the postulation of these boundaries, whereas in *SPE* the boundaries are the contribution of a small part of universal grammar. What might hang on this difference? The most natural way to answer this is to ask whether we will find languages with *no* reference to word boundaries in the kind of phonology we are looking at here. To my knowledge, the post-lexical rules (as we would use the term today) of Spanish apply as easily across word-boundary as within words (e.g., fortition of ð to /d/ after /n/ or utterance-initially).[7] In the *SPE* model, each phonological rule which applies across # must be specifically written to do so, and in this way, the *SPE* model does make some claims that differ from Harris's approach, though without a study of scores of languages, it would be difficult to make an argument which was solidly and empirically based.

3 Components and Consonant Clusters in Swahili

Chapter 10 of *Methods* deals with components, and Harris presented there a radically new way to decompose phonological segments in order to account for permitted sequences of segments. The chapter is called "phonemic long components," but by the end Harris observes that he actually has two kinds of components.

Table 1: Fundamental use of components.

General case	English example
XY occurs	*sp* occurs in English
XU does not occur	*sb* does not occur in English
WU occurs	*zb* occurs in English
we define XY as $\overline{WU}$	we define *sp* as $\overline{zb}$
Therefore:	Therefore:
X = $\overline{W}$	s = $\overline{z}$
Y = $\overline{U}$	p = $\overline{b}$
	bar = unvoicing

---

[7] There are *s*-aspirating dialects where, despite the fact that /s/ normally aspirates before consonant, a word-final /s/ aspirates even when followed by a vowel in the next word, and such a case would perhaps be inconsistent with what I have just written.

> It would be convenient [Harris wrote] for many purposes to replace the phonemes by a system of elements which would have no individual restrictions upon their distribution. Such extension of the freedom of occurrence of our elements is impossible with the phonemes which we have been using, since the operations [so far] have gone as far as the phonemic contrasts of the segments permitted. The phonemes were set up so as to be the least restricted successive (and in some cases simultaneous) elements representing speech. Therefore, the only possibilities for further analysis lie in the direction of changing our segments. (1951: 125)

What he has in mind is the treatment of the constraints on sequences of segments, and he takes as his first example the treatment of consonant clusters in English. Among possible clusters there is *sp*, which occurs, and *sb*, which does not. As Table 1 spells out, Harris will account for this by finding a component which exists over all of (we may think of that as non-voicing), and then this non-voicing is ripped out of the segment on the right (/p/), leaving it in *some* sense as a /b/, on Harris's view. That which is ripped out is what he calls a "component," and in his work, he represented components as horizontal lines that could spread over a domain of zero, one or more symbols. From the purely representational point of view, these horizontal lines could be simple, or jagged, or dotted, or anything else that would allow their identity to be evident. Having written this paper and used Harris's notation, with jagged and dotted lines, I can testify to how hard it is to read, write, and manipulate the representations in this analysis.

Here is his general strategy in words, expanding what I have written in Table 1, on the fundamental use of components; the reader may find that the table is clearer than the prose, but a difficult style always stood in the way of understanding Harris's writing, and in any event the idea will get clearer as we move into a real example:

> Suppose we have, say, four phonemes, X, Y, W, U, which are such that the sequence XY occurs, and the sequence WU occurs, but the sequence XU does not occur. Then we extract from the sequence XY (or from X and Y separately) a single long component α which is common to both X and Y. We now say that WU does not contain this component, and that the sequence XY consists of the sequence WU plus the component α. The component α is defined as spreading over the sequence XY, i.e., as having a length not of one unit segment but of two, and it is this definition that expresses the limitation of distribution of the phoneme. For it is now no longer necessary to say that XU does not occur: X contains α, and α extends over two unit lengths; there α extends over the phoneme following X, and if U follows X we obtain not a simple U, but U + α (which we define as Y).[8] (1951: 127–128]

---

8 This is preceded by: "if x occurs with y but not with z then x is to that extent limited in distribution (limited to occurring with y as against z). The componential indication of this is to say that x has a long component in common with y but not one in common with z (i.e. there is a long component one part of which occurs in x and another part of which occurs in y, but there is no long

Table 2: Swahili consonantal phonemes, for Harris.

p	t	k		
b	d	g		
f	s			
v	z			
l	r			
m	n	h		
ɣ	[θ	ð	ṭ	ʔ]

At this point, it looks like what Harris is doing is pulling out a (privative) feature, and that is correct, but he is also doing something else: there is a principle of spreading of that component, and that spreading is more like a generative rule (or for that matter a Firthian prosody) than a feature *per se*. In a footnote[9] Harris does raise the possibility that we might sometimes need it to be the case that "the bar stops when it gets to Z" – a locution that brings out the dynamic aspect of Harris's conception, something that I do not think he would say if he were not writing in a footnote, because on the whole he was loathe to offer dynamic sorts of analyses (but here, as in a few cases elsewhere, he acknowledges the necessity of a dynamic conception). Harris refers to the "unit segments" over which the component "spreads" as the component's "extension," or "domain," or "scope." To someone like this writer, looking at Harris's work today, it would appear that the "unit segments" resemble in some fashion units on a skeletal tier. It becomes clear why he used the ungainly notation of dotted and jagged lines: it was so that he could draw them on top of a sequence of other units.

The critical reader will not be ready to accept Harris's project without some further explanation, because Harris is clear that the decomposition he is engaged in produces neither phonemic nor morphophonemic representations, and as I mentioned earlier, he does not ultimately decide what they really *are*, not in a way comparable to what he does when explaining what phonemes and morphophonemes are. Perhaps if he had continued work on phonology after this book, this kind of componential analysis would have been developed and integrated into a larger picture, but in reality, that did not happened; Harris's interest moved to syntax over the decades that followed.

---

component shared by x and z). Stating the occurrence of long components is thus equivalent to stating limitations of phonemic distribution; but the long components can be dealt with much more conveniently than the statements about distribution."

9 Footnote 10 on pp. 128–129.

Harris's notation has bars of various sorts lying on top of units which form a sequence. The quotation above suggests that Harris considered expressing these with an α (and presumably β, γ etc., as needed), and we can imagine that these are functions with arguments, something along these lines: "spell" = /spɛl/ = /α (zb)ɛl/. But Harris shies away from this way of thinking about the components; he thinks of them more as particles. This becomes clearer in the context of an example.

Harris uses the phonemic or phonological system of Swahili as his case study. For everyone who works on Swahili, there are some uncertainties regarding the extent to which consonants that appear only in Arabic borrowings should be considered part of the Swahili inventory, and he appears to prefer leaving out the consonants that I have put in brackets, leaving us with an inventory of 16 consonants in Table 2.[10]

Table 3: Full componential analysis.

phoneme	components	phoneme	components with slash
m	(none)	v	slash
n	flat	z	flat slash
r	jagged	b	jagged slash
y	dotted	f	dotted slash
d	flat jagged	g	flat jagged slash
h	dotted jagged	p	dotted jagged slash
s	flat dotted	l	flat dotted slash
t	flat dotted jagged	k	flat dotted jagged slash

It might be best (for you, the reader) to reveal at least something of the system towards which the analysis is moving. (Harris does not do that, which makes for especially difficult reading.) Harris will propose four atomic units, three of which can in some sense spread over two units, and one which cannot. The ones that spread are "horizontal," from a purely graphical point of view; since they largely have no phonetic meaning, I will simply call them "flat," "jagged", and "dotted," and the one that does not spread is written by Harris as a "slash," i.e., "/".[11] If we imagine that each of these atoms (Harris's components) can independently

---

10 Harris gives a phonemic analysis of four palatalized sounds which treats them as sequences of consonant plus glide.
11 I have changed the symbols slightly to accomodate Latex: Harris's "jagged" component is more wavy than jagged, and his "dotted" is more dashed than dotted.

appear or not appear, this will provide us with 16 different combinations (since $2^4 = 16$). One of these combinations is the set with no atoms in it, and that is the phoneme /m/ (we will come back to this, but in essence the reason is that any consonant can follow /m/). Then there are three phonemes that are represented with one spreading component:

/n/	▬	flat
/r/	⌇	jagged
/γ/	....	dotted

There are three that are represented with two spreading components:

/d/ [⌇̄] flat and jagged

/s/ [⃛̄] flat and dotted

/h/ [⃛⌇] dotted and jagged

and one made of all three spreading components, flat, jagged, and dotted: /t/. Thus we have eight consonants.

Then eight more segments are built up out of *these* eight by adding another component, the slash "/"; if slash can appear or not appear, our first set of 8 expands to a set of 16. The analysis of consonants is given in Table 3. It seems to me that there is no natural phonetic interpretation for what the difference is between segments that are otherwise the same, as far as components are concerned, where one does not have the slash "/" and the other does (look at the pairs of sounds on each line: /m/ versus /v/, etc.), but we will come back to that. Now let us turn to how Harris argues for this kind of analysis.

Harris notes first that there are four sets of clusters, if we organize them by the first consonant of the cluster, which can be {m,n,r,s} but nothing else.[12] /m/ appears before all of the 16 consonants, and Harris's proposed analysis is remarkable: he proposes that /m/ is denoted with a typographically null symbol (i.e., a *space*, not the symbol ∅), and the component that is associated with it (which

---

[12] I believe the reason /m/ can be followed by any segment is that it is a noun class marker (the prefix Bantuists refer to as the Class 1 marker), and is therefore phonologically distant from what follows; we have already seen that Harris is no stranger to the use of boundary markers, which surely should have been employed here to account for why /m/ is followed by so many segment types. In pregenerative phonology it was normal to speak of open and close juncture, and /m/'s juncture to its right is open juncture. See, e.g., Lehiste (1960).

then spreads to the right onto any consonant there) is also a null symbol! Thus, /amba/ is to be represented as /a ba/.[13]

Table 4: Swahili clusters, for Harris.

$$
n \begin{bmatrix} t \\ k \\ d \\ g \\ s \\ z \\ l \\ n \\ r? \end{bmatrix} \text{but not } n \begin{bmatrix} p \\ b \\ f \\ v \\ m \\ h \\ y \end{bmatrix} \quad r \begin{bmatrix} t \\ k \\ d \\ g \end{bmatrix} \quad s \begin{bmatrix} t \\ k \\ l \end{bmatrix}
$$

(i) n + C clusters   (ii) r + C clusters   (iii) s + C clusters

The phoneme /n/ can be followed by nine phonemes, and Harris describes the sequence as a single -ish component, expressed symbolically as an "overbar," then followed by a limited number of symbols. When I refer to this component by name, therefore, I will call it "flat," because it is a flat overbar. Following the same logic as before, if we find (for example) a /k/ after an /n/, we call the /k/ a /p/ (remember, the phoneme /p/ does *not* appear after /n/), and we say that the component's effect on the /p/ is to form a /k/. Harris assumes that the phoneme /n/ should be componentially annotated with only the overbar component; it sits on top of a blank symbol, just like we saw in the way he treated an /m/ which was the first segment of a cluster: the difference between an /n/ and an /m/ is that the /n/ has an overbar, and the /m/ has absolutely nothing. In short, the phoneme sequence /VntV/ is written in terms of components as $\overline{V\ \ k}V$; it certainly *feels* like the representation *comes from* /V⁻kV/ in some dynamical, analytical sense whereby the component *spreads*; Harris does speak of a component "spreading" (e.g., 1951: 139, n. 28). I get the strong impression that Harris leans to the idea that all of these components should be pronounceable if they occur alone (see Table 4).

Harris also calls this "flat" component "α." If we were to make a chart of these effects of the component α, it would look like Table 5, where I have broken the phonemes up into components as well. If we compare this with Table 3, we see that the phonemes that follow /n/ are those that contain a "flat"; they get

---

[13] Harris does place right-leaning slashes around units that are components, and indeed components and phonemes are written within the same representation.

that "flat" by virtue of that flat-ness spreading onto them from the left. And that means, in addition, that for Harris these segments in the cluster are less specified, and are the segments in the first column of Table 3.

To repeat, both the phonemes /n/ and /m/ contain no "unit segment," or if you will the unit segment is an empty segment which – despite being empty – manages to take up space (or to force the presence of white space) on the written page (between two real unit segments). A sequence of /VnnV/ is thus written as /V‾V/. Harris does not say so explicitly, but clearly the sequence /VmmV/ is to be represented as /V   V/. (We could write these more explicitly as /V⁼V/ and /V__V/, but that would do violence to Harris's intention, I think.)[14] *All* of the phonemes in the left-hand column of Table 3 have a blank "unit segment," and all those in the right-hand column have a slash as their unit segment.

Table 5: Treatment of the *n*-component "α," aka "flat".

appears after /n/	its source	→	α(X) = X̄
k	P = [〰̂]		k = [〰̄̂]
g	b = [〰]		g = [〰̄]
t	h = [⋯̈]		t = [⋯̈̄]
d	r = [⋯]		d = [⋯̄]
s	y = [⋯]		s = [⋯̄]
n	m = [ ]		n = [‾‾]
z	v = [/]		z = [/̄]

We have been ignoring a problem: we see in Table 4 (i) that /n/ is followed by 9 consonants, but Harris *really* wants to divide the set of 16 consonants into two sets of 8. (This is an example of theoretical parsimony guiding Harris's scientific aesthetic; once again he works like any other modern phonologist, not like

---

14 I also think that there is real confusion here with regard to what tricks a formal system can be asked to perform, and that the system as described here is not self-consistent, but that is another matter. Harris writes (1951: 142, n. 39) that "it is noteworthy that zero (written as space), the absence of all components, indicates not juncture but /m/." This is an example of what I have in mind: what does Harris mean by "zero"? He probably does not mean the null set, because he would have used that term. He does not mean a null symbol in an alphabet, because he is talking about sets. I do not think it is worth the effort to consider every possible alternative possibility, because autosegmental representation solves these questions automatically, without them even rising to the level of a question. I think that Harris would ultimately have been comfortable with saying simply, That is how we notate these things in the componential approach, and this method has useful consequences.

someone groping towards mechanical learning procedures.) So he proposes that the combinations of components that we are looking at can be something slightly more abstract than a combination of phonemes, and that in particular /d/ and /r/ will in some cases have the same componential representation, and that whether the combination is the phoneme /d/ or /r/ can be determined if we observe where the boundary symbols are. Footnote 27 makes it a bit clearer and more convenient (*convenience* being something that Harris always prioritized) that the symbols he is creating here are not *phonemes*; he distinguishes phonemes and components when he writes:

> In phonemic writing it is convenient to distinguish them, since /d/ and /r/ contrast otherwise. However, the analysis into components is designed to show exactly what sequences occur, so that it is permissible to identify /nd/ and /nr/ in this analysis, and thereby reduce the number of phonemes after /n/ to the desired 8. (1951: 138)

Obviously this is an important step, in which a new set of objects (these *components*) encounters phonemes, and replaces them in part but not in whole, though bear in mind that these components have nothing at all to do with morphophonemes, which also plays an important role in these analyses.[15]

Table 6: Componential treatment of the phonemes following $r = \{t,k,d,g\}$.

Appears after /r/	X	→	$\bar{X}$
t	h = [〰]		t = [〰]
k	p = [〰]		k = [〰]
d	r = [〰]		d = [〰]
r	v = [/]		g = [〰]

Table 7: Componential treatment of the phoneme following $s = \{t,k,l\}$.

Appears after /s/	X	→	$\bar{\bar{X}}$
t	h = [〰]		t = [〰]
k	p = [〰]		k = [〰]
l	r = [〰]		l ?? = [〰]

---

[15] For the reader not accustomed to drawing a distinction between phonology and morphophonology in the Harrisian manner, it is convenient to think of morphophonology as lexical phonology, and Harris's phonemic analysis as post-lexical phonology.

In similar manner, the consonants that appear after /r/, which are {t,k,d,g}, are treated with a new component, which Harris indicates with a squiggly or *jagged* line (I have used a tilde or a jagged line for this); see Table 6. These are all phonemes that also appear after /n/, so there is also a "flat" component present here. Thus when the /r/ is followed by one of these four consonants, the /r/ is represented by two components: jagged and flat, and both spread to the second consonant in the cluster (and Harris says that a jagged component that is not aligned with a flat component does *not* spread, though I am not sure what case that corresponds to). Harris's account of *why* there are fewer phonemes possible after /r/ (compared to after /n/) is that the /r/ spreads more components to what follows (two of them), and so there are fewer phonemes that can appear there.

Now a new problem arises. While the components themselves do not have phonetic content (as far as I can see), nonetheless when they spread, there is a consistency condition in force. That is, Harris intends to account for why a particular set of segments occurs in the second column of a cluster, and to account for this by saying that what they all have in common is something that they are given by the segment on the left. It follows, then, that /r/ must have the two components "jagged" and "flat". But if /r/ has "flat", then it must be able to follow /n/ – but in fact it cannot. What is to be done?

Harris says (1951: 139, in the long footnote 29) that the solution is to say that the /r/ which is the first consonant in a cluster is not /r/, but is really /d/. This seemed impossible, because /d/ and /r/ contrast in certain environments. "All this is is only an apparent confusion, due to the fact that in this case the components require a different grouping of segments than did the phonemes." That is, nothing *forces* an analysis using components to be in a one-to-one relationship with a phonemic analysis: the componential analysis may be more "abstract," as we use the term today.

His solution is to stick to the analysis by which /r/ = "jagged" and /d/ = "flat" in three environments: after word-boundary, after /m/, and intervocalically. But now when considering "flat + jagged" which has spread over a cluster, Harris proposes that when it appears in the environment V—CV, it is an /r/, and in addition, when it after "flat" or "flat + jagged", it is a /d/ (Harris adds, "i.e., after /n/ or after itself"). In addition, there are two complex phones which I have not mentioned so far, but which Harris had treated as allophones of /d/ and /r/. He adds that "flat" + "jagged" will be realized as [d^r] in the environment #⁻—o, which of course means when it appears both after a word-initial /n/ and before /o/ (and it appears as [^{d}r] after word-initial /n/ plus other vowels).

There is one more thing to look at before we leave this particular problem, and it touches on one of the reasons why it is interesting to look at Harris's phonological analyses (which is to better understand just how committed he was to a phonemic analysis based on surface contrasts). In the same long footnote, Harris seems to suggest that his componential analysis saves the day for phonemics, in the sense that the alternation with /d/ and /r/ can be handled without a true morphophonemic rule. That is, a stem like "-refu" 'friend' has an /r/, but is /ndefu/ with the prefix "n-" (even though /n/ and /r/ do contrast elsewhere). However, on Harris's account, the prefix "n-" is treated as a "flat"-component, and the stem-initial consonant is a "flat-jagged" component, hence its "flat" component spreads, and its realization as [^{d}r] (the word is phonetically [n^{d}refu]).

The conclusion that I draw from this brief account is that Harris finds it interesting that his componential account allows for a purely mechanical analysis that avoids the concreteness restriction built into phonemics. Since he never explains what these componential analyses *are*–do they in any sense at all replace phonemic representations? apparently not – it is hard to draw a very strong conclusion. There is, I think, some reason to think he likes his components more than his phonemes, but little reason to think he would actually abandon his phonemes even if offered the opportunity to do so.

What he does write, however, strongly suggests that he takes the componential accounts to be phonological well-formedness conditions, because he points out several times that phoneme sequences such as /rn/ cannot appear in the language, and the *reason* they cannot is that there is no way to represent them componentially, with the appropriate spreading of the components. These are not morpheme structure conditions, because their impact is on word-level strings, looking across morphemes (or across morpheme boundaries, if you prefer).

Finally we consider the treatment of clusters in which the first consonant is /s/, which Harris analyzes as the combination of a "flat" and a "dotted" component V$\overline{\cdots}$V; see Table 7. The presence of the "flat" component was obvious, given what preceded, since these segments all follow /n/ as well. There is no way to proceed *except* to posit a new component, and so the "dotted" component is postulated. It then follows that the three consonants {k,t,l} must contain the "dotted" component. And a look at Table 3 shows that indeed that the assignment of components given there is exactly as needed.

I noted above that Harris suggests that the components have phonetic properties that are "features of sound waves." He takes "zero" to indicate labial nasal; "flat" (his a) "general retraction in mouth: with ["jagged"] it indicates palatal, otherwise dental position." With vowels it indicates far front or far back position, but I do not discuss the vowel system in this paper. The "dotted" component "indicates unvoicing, except when alone or with "flat" and "slash" or among the vowels. And so it goes. I do not see these descriptions as supporting the notion that the components have a consistent phonetic characterization.

4 Conclusion

There is more in Harris's discussion than I have presented, and it is no doubt of interest to look further into his presentation. What can we take away from the discussion so far?

First of all, it is clear that Harris's *components* were his way of reaching beyond phonemes and morphophonemes in order to understand language-dependent conditions on linear order in phonology. This approach was never picked up and developed by later phonologists. Halle and Chomsky adopted Jakobson's view of features, adding their own interpretations. In some respects the problems that he was trying to come to grips with were similar to those explored by feature geometry,[16] though feature geometry tended to focus on assimilatory phenomena.

Second, Harris focuses on properties of permitted clusters (which are properties *in praesentia*, or syntagmatic properties) to the exclusion of the inventory-based (*in absentia*) analysis which lay at the heart of the Trubetzkoy-Jakobson-Halle view of features.

Third, Harris engaged in a kind of numerological emphasis that is rarely seen in phonology: his analysis is heavily governed by the numbers of sets that can be defined by sets of components.

Finally, the analysis could hardly be further away from an analysis which would be the result of an automatic learning algorithm: that was not Harris's aim, as I have emphasized.

The private tour that I have offered in this paper of several pages in Zellig Harris's *Methods* illustrates a wider phenomenon which I have been discussing in print since Goldsmith (1990), the appearance in the work of Zellig Harris, Charles Hockett, and Kenneth Pike in the 1940s and 1950s of many ideas (often in embryonic form) that would be rediscovered by phonologists developing generative phonology, with these phonologists often traveling along intellectual byways that are covered by brush, to the point where it is not always easy to see how the ideas moved, mole-like, from one framework to another. (For further discussion of this, see Goldsmith and Laks 2019.)

---

16 See the review chapter by Clements and Hume (1995) for this work.

References

Blevins, James. 2013. American descriptivism ("structuralism"). In Keith Allen (ed.), *The Oxford Handbook of the History of Linguistics*, 419–438. Oxford: Oxford University Press.
Clements, G.N. & Elizabeth Hume. 1995. The internal organization of speech sounds. In John Goldsmith (ed.), *Handbook of Phonological Theory*, 245–306. Oxford: Basil Blackwell.
Goldsmith, John A. 1976. *Autosegmental phonology*. Cambridge, MA: MIT dissertation. Published in 1979 by Garland Press.
Goldsmith, John A. 1990. *Autosegmental and Metrical Phonology*. Oxford: Basil Blackwell.
Goldsmith, John A. & Bernard Laks. 2019. *Battle in the Mind Fields*. Chicago: University of Chicago Press.
Harris, Zellig S. 1944. Simultaneous components in phonology. *Language* 20. 181–205.
Harris, Zellig S. 1951. *Methods in Structural Linguistics*. Chicago: University of Chicago Press.
Hockett, Charles. 1947. Componential analysis of Sierra Popoluca. *International Journal of American Linguistics* 13. 258–267.
Hulst, Harry van der. 1989. Atoms of segmental structure: Components, gestures, and dependency. *Phonology* 6. 253–284.
Kaye, Jonathan, Jean Lowenstamm & Jean-Roger Vergnaud. 1985. The internal structure of phonological representations: A theory of charm and government. *Phonology Yearbook* 2. 305–328.
Jakobson, Roman & Morris Halle. 1956. *Fundamentals of Language*. 's-Gravenhage: Mouton.
Lehiste, Ilse. 1960. *An Acoustic Study of Internal Open Juncture*. Basel: Karger.
Saussure, Ferdinand de. 1916. *Cours de linguistique générale*. Charles Bally and Albert Sechehaye, eds. Paris: Payot.
Trubetzkoy, N. 1939. *Grundzüge der Phonologie*. (Travaux du Cercle linguistique de Prague 7). Prague: Cercle linguistique de Prague.

Ray Jackendoff and Jenny Audring
Blends and Overlaps in Relational Morphology

Abstract: The formalism of Relational Morphology (R. Jackendoff and J. Audring, *The Texture of the Lexicon*, Oxford University Press, 2020) offers a straightforward way to encode the lexical entry of a one-off blend such as *spork*, and to relate it to words it is built from, e.g. *spoon* and *fork*. The approach extends easily to cases of overlap, such as when *Spanish* and *English* are blended to form *Spanglish*.

Blending with overlap occurs not just with these one-off items, but also with certain affixes, for instance *-ery*. Nouns such as *mock-ery* and *nunn-ery* simply concatenate the base and the affix. But if the base ends in *-er*, for instance in *flatter*, the derived form is not **flatterery* but *flattery*. We argue that this haplology is not the result of a truncation process, but rather that the stretch *-er-* is an overlap of the base with the affix. We show that the formal principles that account for the form of one-off blends and overlaps are readily generalized to affixes such as *-ery* that can overlap with their bases. This generalization is expected in the Relational Morphology framework, but not in more traditional procedural approaches to these phenomena.

Keywords: morphological blends, morphological overlap, affixation, morphology, Relational Morphology, Parallel Architecture, haplology

1 Of *Pigs* and *Laughter*: Words, Relational Links, and Schemas

Relational Morphology (RM: Jackendoff and Audring 2020) is an approach to word structure based on the Parallel Architecture (Jackendoff 1997, 2002), with

---

Acknowledgment: This article is adapted from our book *The Texture of the Lexicon: Relational Morphology and the Parallel Architecture*, and appears here with the kind permission of Oxford University Press.

We are grateful to Harry van der Hulst for many enlightening and encouraging discussions, as we braved the (to us, new) terrors of the interfaces between morphology, phonology, and phonetics. *The Texture of the Lexicon* is far better thanks to his input. We also must thank Jay Keyser for his engagement with our treatment of overlaps, especially with the demonyms illustrated in (17).

Ray Jackendoff, Tufts University/MIT
Jenny Audring, Leiden University

https://doi.org/10.1515/9783110730098-018

strong affiliations to Construction Grammar (Goldberg 1995; Croft 2001; Hoffmann and Trousdale 2013) and especially Construction Morphology (Booij 2010, 2018). It advocates studying morphology – and linguistic structure in general – in terms of relations among lexical items rather than through traditional derivation by procedural rules. From this perspective, it develops an account of the complex interplay between regularity and quirkiness that is characteristic of morphological patterns, especially their phonological realization. The present article briefly lays out the theory's approach to one representative phenomenon: blending and overlap.

To lay the groundwork, we begin with a simple word such as *pig*. This consists of a piece of semantic structure (the meaning of the word), associated with a piece of phonological structure (/pɪg/) and the syntactic category Noun. We notate the association of these structures by co-subscripting them, as in (1). One can think of the subscripts as marking the ends of association lines; we call them **interface links**.

(1) Semantics: [PIG$_1$]
    Syntax: N$_1$
    Phonology: /pɪg$_1$/

Thus words (as well as other lexical items such as idioms and collocations) consist of a set of representations that are linked across levels.

Next consider a pair of words like *laugh* and *laughter*. The string *-ter* looks like a suffix, but it only occurs attached to the word *laugh*. It would be peculiar to posit a traditional rule along the lines of "to form a noun based on *laugh*, add *ter*": a rule that only applies to a single item is no rule at all. Yet we wish to capture the relation between the two words. RM relates *laugh* and *laughter* as in (2).

(2) Semantics: a. [LAUGH$_2$]   b. [ACT-OF/SOUND-OF$_4$ ([LAUGH$_2$])]$_3$
    Morphosyntax: V$_2$ [$_N$ V$_2$ aff$_4$]$_3$
    Phonology: /læf$_2$/   /læf$_2$ tər$_4$ /$_3$

Here, subscript 2 links the three levels of *laugh*, and similarly, subscript 3 links the three levels of *laughter*. However, subscript 2 also links *laugh* to the base of *laughter*, marking the two as the same. We call this connection a **relational link**. It is used, not to <u>derive</u> *laughter*, but rather to explicitly record the relation between the two lexical items. The presence of this relation "supports" or "motivates" *laughter*: it makes it less arbitrary than a word like *hurricane* that lacks internal structure and that is therefore formally unrelated to any other word. *Laughter* is easier to learn, then, because it has a previously known part; and it is easier to process, because of the extra activation that comes from *laugh*.[1]

This is not the only application of relational links. Consider the family of denominal adjectives with the suffix *-ish*, such as *piggish, childish, foolish,* and *thuggish*. (3a) shows the lexical entry for *piggish*; it is related to *pig* in the same way that *laughter* is related to *laugh*. However, the structure of *piggish* is further motivated by the general **schema** (3b), which expresses what *piggish* has in common with all the other relevant *-ish* words.[2]

(3) Semantics: a. $[LIKE_6 (PIG_1)]_5$ b. $[LIKE_6 (X_x)]_y$
     Morphosyntax: $[_A N_1 \text{aff}_6]_5$ $[_A N_x \text{aff}_6]_y$
     Phonology: $/\text{pig}_1 \text{ɪʃ}_6/_5$ $/\ldots_x \text{ɪʃ}_6/_y$

The affix in *piggish* is not just a piece of phonology tacked onto a word. Rather, the affix schema (3b) consists of a piece of semantics, a piece of morphosyntax, and a piece of phonology, associated by interface links. In this respect it is just like the previous examples (1), (2), and (3a). It differs only in that parts of its structure are variables: it says that the property of being 'like some X' can be expressed by a noun (N) that denotes X, plus an affix (aff), the combination being pronounced however that noun is pronounced, followed by the phonological string /ɪʃ/. (3a) is therefore to be regarded as relationally linked to (3b): it shares the parts of the adjectival suffix (coindex 6), and the rest of it instantiates the variables in (3b).

Note again that schema (3b) is not used to derive (3a), since *piggish* is an existing word. Rather, both the word and the schema are listed in the lexicon, and their relation is encoded in the relational links. Thus the base of *piggish* is motivated by (1), and, unlike *laughter*, its affix is also motivated, by schema (3b). In addition, this schema can be used productively to coin novel instances such as *Trumpish*. We understand productivity as the degree of openness of a schema's variable, i.e. its readiness to accept new lexical material (see Jackendoff and Audring 2020, chapter 2). In the case of *-ish*, the variable appears to be fairly open: recent formations include *beginnerish, dungeonish* and *gloomish* (Bauer, Lieber, and Plag 2013: 305).

---

[1] The notion of motivation goes back to de Saussure (1915), who, directly after his famous doctrine of the "arbitrariness of the sign," remarks that a sign need not be totally arbitrary: it can be "motivated" by the existence of other signs that share part of its structure.
[2] Note that there are other schemas involving adjectival *-ish*, as in *Irish* and *reddish*, which have different meanings; they are not discussed here.

This analysis illustrates an important tenet of RM, shared with Construction Grammar: so-called "rules of grammar" are encoded in the same form as words. As a consequence, the theory needs no metaphysical distinction between "lexicon" and "grammar." The difference between "words" and "rules" is simply that words are complete and free-standing entities, while rules, in the form of schemas, contain variables that must be instantiated in order to be used in a well-formed utterance.

2 One-Off Blends and Overlaps

With this much in place, we embark on our analysis of blends. Consider cases like (4).

(4) a. spork (= spoon + fork)
　　b. composium (= compose + symposium) (Boston Globe, 16 December 2014)
　　c. Spanglish (= Spanish + English)

Spork is obviously built from the onset of *spoon* and the rhyme of *fork*. Its meaning, 'object that serves both as a spoon and a fork', is built pragmatically from the meanings of the two words. However, *spork* has no internal morphosyntax: neither *sp* nor *ork* is a word, an affix, or an instance of a schema. This leads to a structure along the lines of (5), where the relevant phonological substrings in *spoon* and *fork* are coindexed with (i.e. marked the same as) the corresponding parts of *spork*. (For convenience, we restart numbering the coindices at 1.)

(5) Semantics:　　a. $SPOON_1$　　b. $FORK_2$　　c. $[SPOON_1 + FORK_2]_3$
　　Morphosyntax:　　　 N_1　　　　　　 N_2　　　　　　 N_3
　　Phonology:　　　 /$sp_4 uwn/_1$　　 /$f ɔrk_5/_2$　　 /$sp_4 ɔrk_5/_3$

Coindices 1, 2, and 3 are the interface links that tie together the three levels of *spoon*, *fork*, and *spork* respectively. In the semantics, coindices 1 and 2 also serve as relational links from the meanings of *spoon* and *fork* to the meaning of *spork*. The interest lies in the phonological level. Coindex 4 links the onsets of *spoon* and *spork*, and coindex 5 links the rhymes of *fork* and *spork*. Importantly, the phonological parses of *spoon* and *fork* in (5a) and (5b) are present only to support their relation to *spork*; they have no significance to semantics or morphosyntax. Hence there are no interface links between the phonological sequences /sp/ and /ork/ and the meanings SPOON and FORK, respectively, nor to the category N.

In other words, these coindexed segments simply show what is "borrowed" into the blend. The strings /uwn/ and /f/ have no index because they are not linked to any structure on other levels of the words they appear in, nor do they recur in the blend.

For clarity, (6) shows the relational links in phonology in terms of association lines.

(6) sp oon   f ork
       \\   /
      sp ork

This treatment needs a bit of refinement. As it stands, the same machinery could be used to license improbable blends such as *forsp and *orkoon, which also combine phonological substrings of the two base words. Such monsters can be prevented by adding the stipulation that blended fragments must retain their prosodic function: for instance, /sp/ must remain a syllabic onset, and /ork/ must remain a rhyme. We leave this constraint unformalized.[3]

In *compusium* and *Spanglish*, the composition of the two parts is more complex, because the constituents overlap. There is no reason to say that the string /mpoʊz/ comes exclusively from either *compose* or *symposium*, and there is no reason to say that /ɪʃ/ comes from either *Spanish* or *English*. Accordingly, we propose that these strings are related to both components equally. Such an analysis maximizes motivation: /-mpoʊz-/ is motivated by both *compose* and *symposium*, and /-ɪʃ/ is motivated by both *English* and *Spanish*. Given that overlap is common in blends, one might conclude that multiply motivated substrings make a blend more robust.

To notate overlap, we explicitly mark the beginning of a coindexed string as well as its end. (7) illustrates. Coindex 1 in (7c) links the phonology of *compose* to the corresponding stretch in *compusium*, and coindex 4 connects part of *symposium* to the parallel part of *compusium*. These coindices mark shared substrings that matter only in relation to the blended phonology; they are of no significance to morphosyntax or semantics. The brackets below informally pick out the extent of the overlap.

---

[3] *?Foon* does satisfy the prosodic constraint, but its onset is perhaps not distinctive enough to identify it as related to *fork*. Indeed, the word is used very occasionally (e.g. here: https://the-gadgeteer.com/2011/01/22/bored-with-your-spork-get-a-foon-instead/); but *spork* is clearly more successful. See Arndt-Lappe and Plag (2013) for discussion of further constraints on blending.

(7) Semantics: a. COMPOSE$_1$ b. SYMPOSIUM$_2$
    Morphosyntax: V$_1$ N$_2$
    Phonology: /$_1$kəmpoʊz$_1$/   sɪ $_4$mpoʊziəm$_4$ /$_2$

    Semantics: c. [SYMPOSIUM$_2$ ABOUT COMPOSING$_1$]$_3$
    Morphosyntax: N$_3$
    Phonology: $_3$/ $_1$kə $_4$mpoʊz$_1$ iəm$_4$ /$_3$

Spanglish is still a bit more complex, as it contains two disjoint parts of *Spanish*. This is shown in (8). The two fragments of *Spanish*, /spæ/ and /ɪʃ/, have coindices 5 and 6; the latter of these overlaps with the fragment /ŋglɪʃ/ from *English* (coindex 7).

(8) Semantics   a. SPANISH$_1$ b. ENGLISH$_2$
    Morphosyntax: N$_1$ N$_2$
    Phonology: $_1$/ $_5$spæ$_5$ n $_6$ʃ$_6$ /$_1$ $_2$/ ɪ $_7$ŋlɪʃ$_7$ /$_2$

    Semantics: c. [MIXTURE OF SPANISH$_1$ + ENGLISH$_2$]$_3$
    Morphosyntax: N$_3$
    Phonology: $_3$/ $_5$spæ$_5$ $_7$ŋgl $_6$ʃ$_{6,7}$ /$_3$

There is actually more overlap than is shown in (7) and (8). As with *spork*, *composium* maintains the prosody of its constituents; and *Spanglish* maintains not only prosody but also the nasality in the /n/-/ŋ/ segment. In the interest of readability, these factors have not been notated.

3 Blending and Overlap with Affixes

Blending with overlap is not confined to these sorts of one-off situations. Consider the suffix *-ery*. It attaches to noun, verb, and adjective bases, forming nouns of three semantic classes: state or action nominals such as *mockery*, place or institution nominals such as *nunnery*, and mass nominals such as *shrubbery* that denote collectives. (9) offers examples.

(9) a. *State/action nominals*
     Noun base: buffoonery, burglary, drudgery, knavery, slavery, snobbery, thievery
     Verb base: cajolery, debauchery, mockery
     Adjective base: bravery, drollery

   b. *Places/institutions*
     Noun base: deanery, nunnery, owlery (cf. *Harry Potter*)
     Verb base: distillery, eatery, hatchery, refinery, *Sandwich Meltery* (name of establishment in Boston's South Station)

   c. *Collectives*
     Noun base: drapery, imagery, jewelry, machinery, scenery, shrubbery
     Adjective base: greenery

Other examples fall into the same three semantic classes, but their bases end in *-er*. In these cases, instead of the expected two *-er*'s, there is only one, hence a haplology. For instance, the derived form with the base *delivery* is not **deliverery* but *delivery*. (10) gives some examples.

(10) a. *State/action nominals*
      Noun base: mummery, victory
      Verb base: delivery, discovery, flattery, pilfery, recovery

    b. *Places/institutions*
      Noun base: grocery, haberdashery

Further, some examples can be analyzed either as a verb plus *-ery* or as an agentive noun plus *-y*. For instance, *bakery* could be either *bake-ery* or *baker-y*. More examples appear in (11).[4]

---

[4] Some more complex cases: On the semantic side, *butchery* can denote either the act of butchering or a place where butchering (by butchers) takes place. *Trickery* can denote either the act of tricking someone or the performance of a trick. On the phonological side, *bigotry*, *entry*, and *poetry* condense *-ery* to *-ry*; this may be a consequence of independent principles that govern when /r/ is realized as syllabic or not. *Sorcery* truncates the final agentive *-or* of *sorceror* and is suffixed with the *-y* variant; this falls under the analysis of overlap below. Similarly, *misery* is related to *miserable* in sharing *miser-*; hence it too might be considered a case of truncation plus overlap.

(11) a. *State/action nominals*
      Noun or verb base: fakery, forgery, robbery
   b. *Places/institutions*
      Noun or verb base: bindery, brewery, cannery, tannery
   c. *Collectives*
      Noun or verb base: pottery

The overall generalization is that if the base ends in -*er*, the suffix is realized as -*y*, and otherwise both -*ery* and -*y* are possible (the latter in e.g. *assembly, blasphemy, honesty, jealousy, orthodoxy*). How is this distribution to be accounted for?

An initial impulse might be to consider the distribution as a phonological phenomenon along the lines of the Obligatory Contour Principle (OCP, Yip 1988): a prohibition of (or aversion to) adjacent identical syllables. However, in fact the alternation depends specifically on the affix -*ery*. Agentive -*er* does not trigger the alternation: someone who discovers something is a *discoverer*, not a *discover. Similarly, the comparative of the adjective *clever* is *cleverer*, not *clever*. The OCP, as least on its own, could not distinguish the acceptable configuration / . . . er-er/ from the unacceptable */ . . . er-ery/.

In addition, the grammar needs to say how the prohibition is operationalized. One possible solution would invoke deletion: -*ery* attaches to *flatter* to form *flatter-ery*, and one copy of -*er* deletes (this is the analysis favored by Bauer, Lieber, and Plag 2013: 251). However, there is no evidence to determine which of the -*er*'s deletes; it is an arbitrary choice. Alternatively, one could propose that -*ery* has an allomorph -*y* that is conditioned to appear after bases ending in -*er*. This analysis too is asymmetric: it claims that the -*er* that surfaces belongs to the base, and the missing -*er* belongs to the suffix. But there is no independent justification for this.

We propose a different hypothesis, based on the analysis of *composium* and *Spanglish*: -*ery* blends or overlaps with *flatter*. As a consequence of the overlap, the -*er*- stretch of *flattery* belongs to *both* the base *and* the affix. (12) illustrates the analysis (with the semantics of an action nominal).

(12) Semantics: a. FLATTER$_1$ b. [ACT-OF$_2$ (FLATTER$_1$)]$_3$
     Morphosyntax: V$_1$ [$_N$ V$_1$ aff$_2$]$_3$
     Phonology: /flærər$_1$/ $_3$/ $_1$flær $_2$ər$_1$ i$_2$ /$_3$

This analysis preserves the intuition that such forms involve haplology, but it has the advantage of being symmetrical. It is unnecessary to decide whether -*er* belongs to the base or to the suffix: it belongs to both. This analysis also explains why the alternation is conditioned specifically by identity: this follows automatically from the nature of overlap in general.

Given this structure, we can generalize to (13), a schema for the *-ery* suffix. It is related to (12b) in exactly the same way as the schema for *-ish* (3b) is related to *piggish* (3a). The difference is in the treatment of the phonology. We retain the idea that there are two allomorphs; however, they are both pronounced /əri/. One is the normal allomorph without overlap, as in *mockery* (13a); the other overlaps with the base, as in *flattery* (13b).

(13) Semantics: $[ACT\text{-}OF_2 (X_x)]_y$
      Morphosyntax: $[_N \ V/N/A_x \ aff_2 \ ]_y$
      Phonology: a. $_y/\ x \ldots x\ _2 əri_2 \ /_y$
                      b. $_y/\ x \ldots\ _2 ər_x\ i_2\ /_y$

The difference between (13a) and (13b) is where the base ends. In (13a), it ends in the usual place, before the suffix; but in (13b) the base ends with *-er*, which overlaps with the suffix. The two allomorphs are themselves connected by relational links, capturing their similarity (not shown here; details in Jackendoff and Audring 2020).

The general principle behind the choice between these forms is that if the base *can* overlap with this affix, it *must* do so (again, this only holds for this particular schema, as forms such as *discoverer* and *cleverer* do not trigger overlap). On the other hand, if the base can*not* overlap with the suffix, they are simply concatenated. The result is that *flattery* overlaps but *mockery* does not. This might be construed as a case of the Elsewhere Condition (Kiparsky 1982; Anderson 1992), in that the overlapped allomorph is more specific and therefore must be chosen whenever possible. In addition, the overlapped portion is motivated by both the base and the affix. If such multiple motivation is favored in cases like *Spanglish*, it ought to be favored in this case as well.

The same sort of situation is found in *-ion* nominals. This suffix has a collection of allomorphs, including most prominently *-tion* and *-ation*. Some *-ion* nominals, such as (14a), appear to be the affixation of *-ion* or *-tion* to the related verb (with palatalization of the base-final /t/). Other examples, such as (14b), are clearly the affixation of the allomorph *-ation* to the related verb.

(14) a. desert+ion, extort+ion, digest+ion
      b. alter+ation, condens+ation, improvis+ation

A third group, such as *alternation, rotation,* and *termination,* are related to verbs that end in *-ate.* Are they parsed as (15a), with the shorter allomorph, or as (15b), with truncation of *-ate*?

(15) a. alternat+(t)ion   [*alternate* + *-(t)ion* allomorph]
     b. altern+ation   [*alternate* + *-ation* allomorph]

(15a) might make more sense, in terms of transparency of the parse. But in fact there is really no fact of the matter as to whether *-ate-* belongs to the base or the affix. An alternative is that, like *flattery*, these words are blends, and *-ate-* is motivated simultaneously by the base and the affix. Two further cases of affixes that can overlap with their bases are shown in (16)-(17) (the latter from Keyser 2020). Again, the variants are introduced first (16–17a,b), followed by examples with overlap (16–17c).

(16) a. *-al* allomorph: dialectal (dialect), parental (parent), suicidal (suicide), infinitival (infinitive)
     b. *-ial* allomorph: adverbial (adverb), baronial (baron), gerundial (gerund), professorial (professor)
     c. *-ial* blended with base: bacterial (bacteria), malarial (malaria), inertial (inertia)

(17) a. *-an* allomorph: Roman (Rome), Cretan (Crete), Chicagoan (Chicago)
     b. *-ian* allomorph: Brazilian (Brazil), Ecuadorian (Ecuador), Washingtonian (Washington)
     c. *-ian* blended with base: Virginian (Virginia), Austrian (Austria), Bosnian (Bosnia)

4 The Consequences for Word Formation

These cases present a challenge to traditional word formation rules, which assume a unique source for each piece of a word. For example, in *flattery*, the *-er-* has to trace its derivational ancestry back either to *flatter* or to *-ery*, and the other *-er-* has to be deleted. An analysis of this sort appears in Aronoff (1976), for instance: he derives *alternation* from underlying *alternate+ation*, from which the first *-ate* truncates, as in (15b). However, an *-ate*-deletion rule misses the same facts as an *-er-* deletion. First, the deletion is in the context of an adjacent identical stretch of phonology, not only in the case of *alternation* but also with *flattery*, *bacterial*, and *Virginian*. Second, the choice of deleting the first or second *-ate-* is arbitrary; the same goes with *-ery-*, *-ial-*, and *-ian*.

The approach to blending and overlap in Relational Morphology explains these cases of affixal haplology: it allows for pieces of structure that are multiply (and therefore redundantly) motivated. Hence it is possible for the overlapping stretch of phonology to belong to its neighbors on both sides; it is not necessary to choose which neighbor it belongs to.

Multiple motivation is in fact not unprecedented: various other cases have been pointed out in Audring, Booij, and Jackendoff (2017) and (for compounds) Jackendoff (2010). Moreover, this treatment of overlapping affixes grows directly out of the treatment of one-off blends such as *composium* and *Spanglish*, about which derivational theories have nothing of interest to say. We therefore take the treatment of blends to be one of the ways in which a schema-theoretic grammar is superior to a rule-based grammar.

References

Anderson, Stephen. 1992. *A-Morphous Morphology*. Cambridge: Cambridge University Press.
Arndt-Lappe, Sabine & Ingo Plag. 2013. The role of prosodic structure in the formation of English blends. *English Language and Linguistics* 17. 537–563.
Aronoff, Mark. 1976. *Word Formation in Generative Grammar*. Cambridge, MA: MIT Press.
Audring, Jenny, Geert Booij & Ray Jackendoff. 2017. *Menscheln, kibbelen, sparkle*: Verbal diminutives between grammar and lexicon. *Linguistics in the Netherlands* 2017. 10–15.
Bauer, Laurie, Rochelle Lieber & Ingo Plag. 2013. *The Oxford Reference Guide to English Morphology*. Oxford: Oxford University Press.
Booij, Geert. 2010. *Construction Morphology*. Oxford: Oxford University Press.
Booij, Geert (ed.). 2018. *The Construction of Words: Advances in Construction Morphology*. Cham, Switzerland: Springer.
Croft, William. 2001. *Radical Construction Grammar*. Oxford: Oxford University Press.
De Saussure, Ferdinand. 1915. *Cours de linguistique générale*. English translation: *Course in General Linguistics*. New York: Philosophical Library, 1959.
Goldberg, Adele. 1995. *Constructions: A Construction Grammar Approach to Argument Structure*. Chicago: Chicago University Press.
Hoffmann, Thomas & Graeme Trousdale (eds.). 2013. *The Oxford Handbook of Construction Grammar*. Oxford: Oxford University Press.
Jackendoff, Ray. 1997. *The Architecture of the Language Faculty*. Cambridge, MA: MIT Press.
Jackendoff, Ray. 2002. *Foundations of Language*. Oxford: Oxford University Press.
Jackendoff, Ray. 2010. The ecology of English noun-noun compounds. In Ray Jackendoff, *Meaning and the Lexicon*, 413–451. Oxford: Oxford University Press.
Jackendoff, Ray & Jenny Audring. 2020. *The Texture of the Lexicon: Relational Morphology and the Parallel Architecture*. Oxford: Oxford University Press.
Keyser, S. Jay. 2020. Morphological overlap and repetition blindness. Ms., MIT.

Kiparsky, Paul. 1982. Word-formation and the lexicon. In Frances Ingemann (ed.), *Proceedings of the Mid-America Linguistics Conference*. Lawrence, KA.

Yip, Moira. 1988. The obligatory contour principle and phonological rules: A loss of identity. *Linguistic Inquiry* 19(1). 65–100.

Language Index

African languages 92–93
Akan 93
Albanian 47
Arabic 20, 23, 139–140, 147, 338
– Classical Arabic 278
Arawak 215–216
Arawakan 215
Austronesian 249, 251

Bangla (Tripura) 274
Bantu 97, 290
Berbice Dutch 214–215
Bosnian 289–290, 304, 356
Bulgarian 303

Carian 201–203, 217, 222–223
Carib 215–217, 223
Catalan (Eastern) 71, 86
Chinook 25
Chumburung 91ff.
Church Slavonic 302
Croatian 289–290, 304
Cushitic 17
Czech 274

Diola-Fogny 99
Dutch 1ff., 74, 108–109, 113, 138, 201, 214–215, 228, 235
– Amsterdam Dutch 12
– Eastern Dutch 5, 7
– Kempen dialect 5, 8–10
– Old Dutch 2
  – Old East Dutch 4
– Standard Dutch 1, 5–9, 137, 139–140, 146

Eastern Nilotic 93
English 1, 6, 12–14, 68, 71–77, 79, 81, 83, 86, 133, 135–143, 145–146, 166, 181, 187ff., 213, 220, 232, 278–279, 295–297, 307, 316, 323–325, 331–336, 347, 350–352
– American English 76, 232, 331
– British English 81

– Middle English 145–147
– Old English 1, 3, 6, 133ff.
  – Anglian 133, 143–144, 146
  – West Saxon 144
– Received Pronunciation (RP) 72, 76
Estonian 75

Finnish 71
Fon 213
French 9, 146, 192
Frisian 12–14

Gaelic 29
German 1–2, 4, 6, 9–10, 134, 139, 145, 333
– Old High German 1, 4, 9–10, 134
– Standard German 1
– Swiss German 9–10
Germanic 1–2, 134
– Common Germanic (CG) 1ff.
– Old Germanic 2–3
– Proto-Germanic 1, 4
– West-Germanic 5, 10
  – Ingwaeonic 5, 13
  – Old West-Germanic 1–4, 7, 13
Gitksan 27
Gothic 1, 10, 134
Greek
– Ancient Greek 201ff.
– Classical Greek 205
Guang 91, 96
Gunu 93

Hebrew 262
Hittite 202–203, 207, 221
Hungarian 33ff., 107ff., 307ff.
– Old Hungarian 68

Ịjọ (Eastern) 214–215
Indo-European 202, 204, 219
– Proto-Indo-European (PIE) 1, 3–4, 204, 209
Iraqw 17ff., 139
Irish 349
Italian 278

Japanese 71, 108

K'ekchi 140
Kinande 93
Korean 151–163
– Early Modern Seoul Korean 158
– Middle Korean 151ff.
– Modern Korean 151ff.
– Modern Seoul Korean 151, 157–158, 160–162

Latin 1, 208
Luwian 202–203, 207–208
Lycian 201–203, 217, 222
Lydian 203

Mangap-Mbula 249, 251–256, 259–260
Maybrat 249, 252, 256–257, 259–261

Nawuri 96, 99
Nivkh 140, 257–259
Nootka 140

Pirahã 275
Polish 165–168, 170–171, 173–177, 180–182

Portuguese 213
– Brazilian Portuguese 71, 86

Samoan 301
Saramaccan 213–214
Saxon
– Old Saxon 1–2, 4–5, 7, 11, 134
Semitic 40
Serbian 42, 289–290, 304
Sorbian 140–141, 143
Spanish 335, 347, 350–352
Swahili 23, 327–328, 330, 333, 335, 337–338, 340
Swedish 166, 169, 262
Syrian 56

Turkish 55
Twentish 1, 5, 8–9
– Old Twentish 8

Ukrainian 176

Yawelmani 27
Yiddish 39
Yupik 275

Subject Index

accent 1, 3, 11–13, 49, 58, 71, 78, 203, 262, 289ff.
– pitch accent 14, 289
acquisition 165, 167, 173, 175, 182-183, 227ff., 324
allomorph(s), allomorphy 33ff., 117, 155, 159, 201, 207, 209, 219, 255, 319, 354–356
allophone(s) 2, 4, 7, 91–92, 100, 138, 146, 168, 170–171, 173, 175, 182–183, 331–332, 334, 343
aperture 6, 12–13, 71–72, 85, 154
Articulatory Phonology 133, 135, 141, 143
assimilation 2, 11–12, 17–18, 23, 37–38, 52, 97, 137, 139, 165–166, 168, 171–172, 175–176, 178; see also spreading
Autosegmental Phonology 17–18, 72, 341

blends 347ff.
breaking 133–139, 141, 143, 145–147

categorization 307
child language 228, 230–231, 245
clitics 252, 274, 279, 289, 291–294, 296, 298–299
coalescence 91–93, 101–103, 333
compounds, compounding 4, 11, 23, 26, 39, 58, 63, 91, 93, 95–97, 99, 191–192, 206, 332, 357
constraints 36, 40–42, 51–52, 65, 114–115, 151, 154, 156–157, 161–162, 168, 228, 231, 243–244, 259, 261, 269, 279, 336, 351
contrast 19, 74–75, 81, 96, 109–110, 114–115, 166–170, 173–174, 182, 257, 267, 271, 301, 303, 316, 331–332, 334, 336, 342–344
corpus 35, 99, 235, 280, 327
creoles 213–214

Dependency Phonology (DP) 26, 72, 192, 198, 328
derivation 17ff., 46, 52, 56–58, 60–61, 91, 95, 97, 154, 157–158, 195, 207, 218, 249–253, 258, 260–261, 296–297, 300, 312–313, 316, 318, 320, 328, 347–348, 353, 356–357
dialects 1, 3–10, 13, 112, 133, 137, 143–144, 146, 153, 165–166, 168, 171, 174, 176–182, 211, 275, 297–299, 309, 332, 335, 356
diphthongs 1, 4–5, 9–10, 12–13, 19, 84, 134–136, 140, 146, 154, 158, 160, 210, 331
dissimilation 209, 212, 217

Element Theory 26, 187–188, 191–192

feature [ATR] 91ff., 153, 155–156, 160–161
feature [back] 2–3, 12, 29, 34, 107, 308
feature [high] 2, 29, 72, 92, 98, 100, 101, 103
feet (metrical) 46, 49, 77, 195–196, 198, 251, 253, 255, 260, 265, 270, 272–278, 280–281

gemination 2–4, 38, 41, 68, 134, 189, 222
Government Phonology (GP) 33, 39, 49–51, 71–78, 81, 83–86, 167, 175–176, 183, 187ff., 261, 268, 277, 283
grammar 1, 41, 53, 141, 205, 213, 215, 227–228, 231, 259, 267, 280, 282, 284, 289, 298, 313, 335, 348, 350, 354, 357
gutturals 17–18, 20–21, 25–27, 30

inflection 11, 108, 110, 112–113, 116–117, 119–122, 160, 172, 214, 222, 253, 302, 308, 310–311, 314, 316–321, 323–324

laryngeals 17–18, 20, 27, 165ff., 191–192, 194, 202, 209, 212, 217, 270
lexicon 33–35, 37, 39, 41, 43, 45, 47, 49, 51, 53, 55, 57, 59, 61, 63–65, 67–68, 74–75, 109, 181, 187–188, 194–195, 197–199, 215, 229–230, 243, 282, 313, 347, 349–350

morphology 1–2, 8, 11, 13, 23, 25–26, 34, 35, 39, 52–53, 57, 60, 67, 80, 107–108, 114, 122, 201, 211, 213–215, 218, 223,

230, 249, 252, 255, 259, 270, 289, 304, 313, 328, 333–334, 347–349, 351, 353, 355, 357
morphophonology 53, 108, 110, 115, 159, 202, 311, 328, 342

neutral (in vowel harmony) 94–95, 107ff., 152–154, 157

opacity (of consonants or morpheme boundaries) 17–18, 30, 52, 168
Optimality Theory (OT) 42, 59, 114, 195, 269, 308, 310
overlaps (morphology) 347ff.

paradigms 2, 6, 11, 38–39, 51, 68, 107ff., 252, 327, 331
perception 145–146, 168–169, 173, 194, 230–234, 239, 243–245, 282
phase (syntax) 249ff., 289ff., 321
phonetics 6–7, 10–12, 20, 24–25, 30, 34, 36, 40, 51–53, 75, 80, 103, 107ff., 134ff., 153–155, 160–163, 165–183, 190–192, 194, 202–204, 209, 228–232, 236, 243, 245, 249, 252, 256, 271, 308, 311, 317, 330, 338–339, 343–344, 347
pidgins 215
production 107, 116, 121, 140, 142, 144, 171, 194, 227–234, 236–245, 280, 282
prominence 11, 146, 192, 272, 291
prosody 49, 52, 71, 74, 76–77, 194, 229, 254, 269–270, 274–275, 279–281, 283, 289–293, 295–300, 303–304, 328, 337, 351–352

Radical CV Phonology (RCVP) 151ff., 181
recursion 265ff.
reduplication 20, 22, 24, 211, 323
rhythm 41, 78, 271, 274

sonority 42
spreading 18, 26, 28, 51, 91ff., 165–167, 175–176, 178, 181–182, 190, 193–196,

198, 290–294, 296–298, 300–301, 303–304, 336–341, 343–344; *see also* assimilation
stress 10, 14, 41, 71–72, 76–78, 80–81, 86, 188, 195, 197, 199, 249, 251, 253–256, 259–262, 274, 277, 290, 296–297, 333
– secondary stress 71, 77, 80, 296–297
suprasegmental 328
syllables 1–5, 9, 11–12, 17, 41, 49, 73, 77, 80, 83, 96, 98, 111, 134, 137–139, 159, 189, 194–196, 198, 204, 209, 211–212, 218–219, 228, 230–231, 241, 243, 251–254, 260–261, 265–266, 269–273, 275–278, 281, 283, 291, 296–301, 322, 332–333, 351, 353–354
syntax 33, 57, 60–63, 65–66, 249–252, 254, 257, 259–260, 265–271, 273–284, 289–293, 298, 302–303, 307, 311–314, 318–324, 337, 348

tone 72, 93, 96–97, 192, 289–294, 296–304
transparency 17–19, 22, 25, 30, 49, 56, 58, 152, 168, 311, 324, 356

umlaut 1–14, 154, 195
universal 154, 168, 230, 278, 335

visibility 56, 249ff.
voicing 38–40, 71, 108–109, 113–115, 165–183, 188, 192–196, 204, 234, 236, 238, 278, 330, 333, 336
vowel coalescence 91–92, 101, 103
vowel copy 17–30
vowel excrescence 133ff.
vowel harmony 10, 19, 27–29, 41, 68, 91, 107ff., 151ff., 308–309, 315, 321
vowel height 71

weight 76, 115, 212, 218, 253–254
word boundaries 91, 93, 95, 97–98, 100, 168, 172, 178, 291, 333–335
word structure 249ff., 347

Contents of Part II

Preface —— IX

Marika Butskhrikidze
The Status of /m/ in #/m/C Sequences in Georgian —— 1

Andrea Calabrese
Gemination in Middle Indic —— 19

John Harris
A Fake Diphthong in English —— 55

Ksenia Bogomolets
Deconstructing Secondary Stress —— 69

Irene Vogel
Is There Foot Structure in Isolating Languages? —— 99

Bing Li
Word Stress Placement in Wakhi —— 115

Rob Goedemans and Jelena Prokic
Mining Metrical Data —— 133

Ana Lívia Agostinho and Larry M. Hyman
Interpreting Non-Canonical Word Prosody in Afro-European Contact —— 151

Matthew Gordon
The Phonetic Basis for Tone-Stress Interactions: A Cross-Linguistic Study —— 171

B. Elan Dresher and Aditi Lahiri
Some Applications of the Primary Accent First Parameter —— 191

Anthi Revithiadou
Accent as Autosegment: A Unified Account of Lexical Accent and Lexical Stress Systems —— 209

Vincent J. van Heuven
Stress Deaf and Color Blind: Native Language Background and Perceptual Categories —— 233

Alexandre Vaxman
The Representation and Computation of Weight in Hybrid Accent Systems: The Case of Standard Eastern Mari —— 253

Wendy Sandler
From Latent to Blatant: Uncovering Phonological Iconicity in Sign Language Theatre —— 271

Rachel Channon
A New Feature Type: Functional Features in Sign Languages —— 291

Onno Crasborn and Els van der Kooij
The Emergence of the Second Hand in Sign Language Phonology: From Underlying to Surface Representations —— 319

Shengyun Gu
Phonological Processes in Shanghai Sign Language: Contexts, Constraints, and Structure —— 345

Language Index —— 363

Subject Index —— 367

www.ingramcontent.com/pod-product-compliance
Lightning Source LLC
Chambersburg PA
CBHW061930220426
43662CB00012B/1852